Hölderlin's Philosophy of Nature

New Perspectives in Ontology
Series Editors: Peter Gratton, Southeastern Louisiana University, and Sean J. McGrath, Memorial University of Newfoundland, Canada

Publishes the best new work on the question of being and the history of metaphysics

After the linguistic and structuralist turn of the twentieth century, a renaissance in metaphysics and ontology is occurring. Following in the wake of speculative realism and new materialism, this series aims to build on this renewed interest in perennial metaphysical questions, while opening up avenues of investigation long assumed to be closed. Working within the Continental tradition without being confined by it, the books in this series will move beyond the linguistic turn and rethink the oldest questions in a contemporary context. They will challenge old prejudices while drawing upon the speculative turn in post-Heideggerian ontology, the philosophy of nature and the philosophy of religion.

Editorial Advisory Board
Thomas J. J. Altizer, Maurizio Farraris, Paul Franks, Iain Hamilton Grant, Garth Green, Adrian Johnston, Catherine Malabou, Jeff Malpas, Marie-Eve Morin, Jeffrey Reid, Susan Ruddick, Michael Schulz, Hasana Sharp, Alison Stone, Peter Trawny, Uwe Voigt, Jason Wirth, Günter Zöller

Books available
The Political Theology of Schelling, Saitya Brata Das
Continental Realism and its Discontents, edited by Marie-Eve Morin
The Contingency of Necessity: Reason and God as Matters of Fact, Tyler Tritten
The Problem of Nature in Hegel's Final System, Wes Furlotte
Schelling's Naturalism: Motion, Space and the Volition of Thought, Ben Woodard
Thinking Nature: An Essay in Negative Ecology, Sean J. McGrath
Heidegger's Ontology of Events, James Bahoh
The Political Theology of Kierkegaard, Saitya Brata Das
The Schelling–Eschenmayer Controversy, 1801: Nature and Identity, Benjamin Berger and Daniel Whistler
Hölderlin's Philosophy of Nature, edited by Rochelle Tobias

Books forthcoming
The Late Schelling and the End of Christianity, Sean J. McGrath
Schelling's Ontology of Powers, Charlotte Alderwick
Affect and Attention After Deleuze and Whitehead: Ecological Attunement, Russell J. Duvernoy

www.edinburghuniversitypress.com/series/epnpio

Hölderlin's Philosophy of Nature

EDITED BY ROCHELLE TOBIAS

EDINBURGH
University Press

Edinburgh University Press is one of the leading university presses in the UK. We publish academic books and journals in our selected subject areas across the humanities and social sciences, combining cutting-edge scholarship with high editorial and production values to produce academic works of lasting importance. For more information visit our website: edinburghuniversitypress.com

© editorial matter and organisation Rochelle Tobias, 2020, 2022
© the chapters their several authors, 2020, 2022

Edinburgh University Press Ltd
The Tun – Holyrood Road
12(2f) Jackson's Entry
Edinburgh EH8 8PJ

First published in hardback by Edinburgh University Press 2020

Typeset in 11/13 Adobe Garamond by
Servis Filmsetting Ltd, Stockport, Cheshire

A CIP record for this book is available from the British Library

ISBN 978 1 4744 5415 5 (hardback)
ISBN 978 1 4744 5416 2 (paperback)
ISBN 978 1 4744 5418 6 (webready PDF)
ISBN 978 1 4744 5417 9 (epub)

The right of Rochelle Tobias to be identified as the Editor of this work has been asserted in accordance with the Copyright, Designs and Patents Act 1988, and the Copyright and Related Rights Regulations 2003 (SI No. 2498).

Contents

Acknowledgements vii
List of Abbreviations ix

1 Introduction 1

I Tragic Nature

2 Nature and Poetic Consciousness from Hölderlin to Rilke 23
   Jennifer Anna Gosetti-Ferencei

3 Raging with Care: The Poet's Liquid Fire 44
   Katrin Pahl

4 The Order of the Unbound: Time and History in Hölderlin's 'The Titans' 58
   Achim Geisenhanslüke

II Hölderlin's Rivers

5 The Untamed Earth: The Labour of Rivers in Hölderlin's 'The Ister' 75
   Rochelle Tobias

6 Hölderlin's Local Abstraction: The Natural-Historical Sublime in 'Voice of the People' 94
   Márton Dornbach

7 Translating Centaurs: Notes on Hölderlin's 'The Life-Giving' 123
   Bruno C. Duarte

III Natural Beauty and the Absolute

8 Hölderlin's Mythopoetics: From 'Aesthetic Letters' to the New Mythology   143
Luke Fischer

9 The Transition Between the Possible and the Real: Nature as Contingency in Hölderlin's 'The declining fatherland . . .'   164
Anja Lemke

10 'My whole being fell silent, and read': Peter Handke's Hölderlin and Heidegger Reception   178
Jacob Haubenreich

IV The Place of Poetry

11 Nature, Nurse, *Khôra*: Notes on the Poetics of Hölderlin's Ode 'Man'   199
Csaba Szabó

12 Not Rhythm   219
Jan Mieszkowski

13 allowed, disallowed   235
Thomas Schestag

Notes on Contributors   252
Index   256

Acknowledgements

The impetus for this volume was a conference held at the Johns Hopkins University in April 2017 under the title '*harmonisch entgegengesetzt*: Hölderlin's Philosophy of Nature'. I would like to thank all the speakers for their participation in the event and for their willingness to revise and expand on their reflections on Hölderlin's concept of nature for this volume. I would also like to extend my thanks to the Department of German and Romance Languages and Literatures at Johns Hopkins and the Max Kade Foundation for their generous support of the conference.

Preparation of a volume for publication requires numerous hands, and nowhere is this more true than in the case of a volume with contributions from multiple authors on three continents on a poet whose syntax is notoriously difficult and whose work does not lend itself easily to translation. I owe a debt of gratitude to the three doctoral students who carefully read through the essays to ensure that they were consistent in substance and style. They are Anita Martin, Almut Slizyk and Tegan White-Nesbitt. I would also like to thank Peter Williams, the copyeditor chosen by the press, for his scrupulous attention to detail when preparing the manuscript for publication.

Grateful acknowledgement is given to Jeremy Adler and Charlie Louth for permission to reprint the translation of 'The Life-Giver' as well as excerpts from other translations of Hölderlin's prose work, originally published in Friedrich Hölderlin, *Essays and Letters*, edited and translated with an Introduction by Adler and Louth, © Jeremy Adler and Charlie Louth, London: Penguin Classics, 2009.

Grateful acknowledgement is also given to the estate of Michael Hamburger for permission to reprint Hamburger's translations of 'Man', 'The Ister', 'The Titans' and 'Voice of the People', which appeared in

Friedrich Hölderlin, *Poems and Fragments*, trans. M. Hamburger, © Michael Hamburger, 3rd edn, London: Anvil Press Poetry, 1994.

An earlier version of the essay 'The Untamed Earth: The Labour of Rivers in Hölderlin's "The Ister"' by Rochelle Tobias appeared in *Literatur für Leser*, 39: 1 (2016), pp. 61–73. Grateful acknowledgement is given to *Literatur für Leser* for permission to reproduce a revised version of the essay in this volume.

R. T.

List of Abbreviations

All references to Hölderlin's work will be cited parenthetically in the notes and the text using the following abbreviations:

StA Hölderlin, Friedrich, *Sämtliche Werke: Große Stuttgarter Ausgabe*, ed. Friedrich Beißner, 8 vols (Stuttgart: Kohlhammer, 1943–85).

FHA Hölderlin, Friedrich, *Sämtliche Werke: Frankfurter Ausgabe*, ed. D. E. Sattler, 20 vols (Frankfurt am Main: Roter Stern & Stroemfeld, 1975–2008).

Empedocles Hölderlin, Friedrich, *The Death of Empedocles. A Mourning Play*, trans. and ed. David Farrell Krell (Albany, NY: SUNY Press, 2008).

Essays and Letters Hölderlin, Friedrich, *Essays and Letters*, edited and translated with an Introduction by Jeremy Adler and Charlie Louth (London: Penguin, 2009).

Hyperion Hölderlin, Friedrich, *Hyperion and Selected Poems*, ed. Eric L. Santner (New York: Continuum, 1990).

Poems and Fragments Hölderlin, Friedrich, *Poems and Fragments*, translated, with a Preface, Introduction and Notes, by Michael Hamburger, 3rd edn (London: Anvil Press Poetry, 1994).

Chapter 1

Introduction

Rochelle Tobias

The essays in this volume chart the relation between Hölderlin's poetic theory and his concept of nature as developed in his poetry, prose and dramatic works. At the heart of his *oeuvre* lies an understanding of nature and the role that consciousness plays in it which responds to but also revises the concerns of eighteenth- and nineteenth-century philosophy of nature. The latter has seen a revival of interest in recent years given its implications for contemporary environmental thought and materialist approaches to culture and history. F. W. J. Schelling's suggestion that nature produces consciousness as part of its own process of self-realisation has served as a catalyst for claims that the material world has an agency all its own and is not merely an instrument of the subject's will. Echoes of this position can be heard in Hölderlin's writing, as in a fragment written between 1802 and 1803 where he asserts that in its original state nature appears weak since all powers are 'justly and equally' distributed in it and nothing takes precedence over anything else (*FHA* XIV, 303, my translation). Nothing, in other words, assumes the role of subject in this state in which nature has yet to be divided into discrete entities. In contrast to contemporary theorists, however, Hölderlin also declares that nature can reveal itself in its strength only when mediated by a sign that is itself empty. Poetry is necessary for nature not only to appear but also to be thought. This represents Hölderlin's contribution to the tradition of natural philosophy and to the theory and practice of the lyric.

As we approach the 250th anniversary of the poet's birth – Hölderlin was born in 1770 and died in 1843 – his work speaks with renewed vigour in its emphasis on the cycle of appearing and disappearing that would seem to be tailor made for an age of ecological crisis. Long before the concept of the Anthropocene was introduced, Hölderlin was well aware that human history could not be extricated from natural history for complicated reasons including the impulse toward formlessness inherent in nature. One could say that he anticipated the idea of the human being as what Dipesh Chakrabarty has called a 'geological agent' in underscoring the droughts, floods and other disasters that humans at once trigger and endure – trigger as participants in a cosmic natural scheme, of which they are unaware, and endure as finite beings who must weather the elements.[1] A recurrent theme in the essays in this volume is consequently nature as an 'unconditioned condition', an absolute force in its relation to history, which Hölderlin understood in the broadest sense of the term as a cosmogony and theogony.[2] The essays in this volume are devoted to his vision of nature as that which generates and disrupts every individual form of life, every constellation of elements, and every world in which humans and gods face each other.

Hölderlin and natural philosophy

In a letter to Fichte from November 1800, a still relatively young Schelling – he was twenty-five at the time – had the boldness to declare that nature realises its highest power (*Potenz*) in the ego which, looked at from this perspective, serves nature's ends.[3] With this statement Schelling was not so much articulating a new position as elaborating on a claim he made in the *First Outline of a System of the Philosophy of Nature* (1799) and then summarised in the *System of Transcendental Idealism* (1800). In the latter work, he notes that for natural philosophy the highest goal of nature is to become an object to itself and that it achieves this aim through the human being, who reflects on the ecosystem or whole in which she herself is embedded.[4] The paradoxical nature of this process was not lost on Schelling. On the one hand, he had to find a foundation that was not determined by anything else, not even the 'not-I' which for Fichte was a necessary correlate of the 'I' and a condition for self-consciousness. On the other hand, he had to devise a method for representing this ground that itself precedes all thought, and this proved to be an all but insurmountable obstacle for philosophy, devoted as it is to the rational exposition of ideas and concepts. In the *System of Transcendental Idealism*, Schelling therefore proposes that it is only in art that we gain access to the absolute, which otherwise exceeds our cognitive capacities.[5] With this insight he abandoned natural philosophy, yet the project was to continue elsewhere: in the poetry and poetic theory of Hölderlin who throughout his career asked why nature needs thought and what role consciousness plays in it.

In studies of German Idealism and Romanticism, much has been made of the fact that Schelling, Hegel and Hölderlin were students together at the Lutheran seminary in Tubingen and that the three collaborated extensively in their early years. Hegel dedicated the only poem he wrote 'Eleusis' to Hölderlin in 1796, and while the authorship of the short manifesto 'The Oldest Programme for a System of German Idealism', dated around 1797, is debated, no one would contest that the call in it for a new mythology in the service of ideas and the transformation of ideas themselves into something aesthetic owes as much to Schelling as to Hölderlin.[6] The manuscript itself is written in Hegel's hand. Manfred Frank suggests that Schelling was the principal author given his argument in the *System of Transcendental Idealism* for a 'new mythology', whereas Eckart Förster contends that the text could only come from Hölderlin given his interest in and reception of Goethe's work.[7] Otto Pöggeler for his part attributes the sketch to Hegel.[8] Regardless of who conceived 'The Oldest Programme for a System of German Idealism', it is not difficult to hear strains of it in Hölderlin's one and only novel *Hyperion*, published in two instalments in 1797 and 1799.

Most notable among these is the idea that only in beauty do we glimpse the whole of which we are a part, only in beauty do we experience the oneness of nature before we have yet to divide it:

> To be one with all [*Eines zu seyn mit Allem*] – this is the life divine, this is man's heaven.
>
> To be one with all that lives, to return in blessed self-forgetfulness into the All of Nature – this is the pinnacle of thoughts and joys, this the sacred mountain peak, the place of eternal rest, where the noonday loses its oppressive heat and the thunder its voice, and the boiling sea is like the waving field of grain [*und das kochende Meer der Wooge des Kornfelds gleicht*].
>
> To be one with all that lives! At those words, Virtue puts off her wrathful armour, the mind of man lays its sceptre down, and all thoughts vanish before the image of the world in its eternal oneness [*vor der ewigeinigen Welt*]. (*Hyperion* 41–2, translation modified; *FHA* 11, 585)

What Hyperion describes as a moment of exuberance is simultaneously a moment of negation. One has to lose oneself in order to find oneself in the midst of nature and 'to be one with all', which recalls the Greek motto *hen kai pan* (one and all) that became a catchphrase for Spinozist thought in the eighteenth century. While Lessing may have introduced the slogan into German discourse, it was Friedrich Heinrich Jacobi who popularised it as a summary of Spinoza's idea of substance and his presumed pantheist tendencies. Goethe paid homage to this tradition in the poem 'One and All' [*Eins und Alles*] (1821) that ends with a celebration of death as a passage to eternal life in nature: 'For everything must dissolve into nothing / If it is to persist in being' [*Denn alles muß in Nichts zerfallen / Wenn es im Sein beharren will*].⁹

What can be gleaned from the passage in *Hyperion* is that to be one with everything is to banish all distinction between opposing entities. It is to inhabit a space in which there is no difference between figurative and literal heights (i.e. 'the *pinnacle* of thoughts and joys' and 'the sacred *mountain peak*'); water and land (i.e. 'the boiling *sea*' and 'the *waving* field of grain'); and finally earth and heaven (i.e. 'life divine' and 'man's heaven'). Yet to represent this state requires difference – a difference that must be posited to be overcome. The effort to resolve this paradox will drive much of Hölderlin's poetic theory and philosophical writing, not to speak of his poetic *oeuvre* from the early odes to the late hymns.

Already in the short text 'Being Judgement Possibility', which Hölderlin wrote in the flyleaf of his copy of Fichte's *Science of Knowledge* around 1795, he acknowledges the impossibility of representing the ground that both subject and object share: 'Being – expresses the connection between subject and object' (*Essays and Letters*, 231). The ontological foundation of the two resists all representation since representation would divide it into parts, which contradicts the very meaning of unity as in-difference or undividedness. One could say that it de-natures nature in its oneness. Hölderlin's interest, however, is not in demonstrating the whole of Being from which all individual entities emerge. By his own admission he cannot. It is to demonstrate that, contrary to Fichte, the 'I' is not its own foundation and consequently cannot serve as the foundation for anything else. Dieter Henrich claims that the text also contains an implicit critique of Schelling, who at the time sought to locate the unconditioned condition for thinking in consciousness.¹⁰

As Hölderlin would have it, the 'I' is not originary but the product of a judgement [*Urtheil*], which he understands literally as an 'Ur-Theilung', a division of Being into a subject and an object (*FHA* XVII, 156). In keeping with Fichte, he indicates that the 'I' comes to be in positing itself since it is only in and through this act that it establishes itself as an ego, which is to say a being whose very definition is that it is capable of positing itself. Rolf-Peter Horstmann thus observes that for Fichte the existence of the ego is simultaneously its essence.¹¹ Where Hölderlin differs from the Idealist philosopher is in his insistence that an 'I' so conceived can never be one with itself. As a self-positing being it can relate to itself only as an identical but opposing object. Karin Schutjer notes the paradox of an 'I' that is limited by its own nature as consciousness: 'Consciousness . . . always involves a reflexive structure, a subject-object opposition. Thus there can be no access within consciousness to the pure unity of an absolute ego, for such a unity would require suspending the conditions of consciousness.'[12] Hölderlin himself attempts to express this idea with the economy and precision of a mathematical formulation: 'Identity therefore is not = to absolute Being' (*FHA* XVII, 156, my translation).

In a letter to Hegel from January 1795 he enlarges on this claim and calls into question whether the 'I' can relate to itself at all. Indeed the case he makes to Hegel is a classic example of an *argumentum ad absurdum*:

> [Fichte's] absolute *I* (= Spinoza's substance) contains all reality; it is everything & outside it there is nothing; therefore for this absolute *I* there is no object, for otherwise all reality would not be in it; but a consciousness without an object is not conceivable, and if I myself am this object then as such I am necessarily limited, even if only in time, and therefore not absolute. (*Essays and Letters*, 48)

The paradox that Hölderlin traces in the letter can be summarised as follows: On the one hand, if the 'I' is, as Fichte argues, the foundation for everything, then there can be nothing outside it; on the other hand, if the 'I' is defined as consciousness, then it needs an object outside it to be itself. Hölderlin draws two mutually exclusive conclusions from this state of affairs. Either the 'I' does not exist as consciousness and has no priority over anything else, or conversely it exists but merely as a conditioned being that cannot account for its own foundation. In his later work, Hölderlin will increasingly opt for the latter position and in so doing align himself with a natural philosophical tradition that conceives nature as the condition of possibility for consciousness or, in Hegelian terms, as the identity of identity and difference.

Nature and history

As the unity of subject and object or the identity of identity and difference, nature is first and foremost what sustains a series of relations between opposing terms, such as mortals and immortals, heaven and earth, physical nature and culture, love and strife, and fire and water, to cite a few examples. In his theory of poetic tonality Hölderlin refers to the balance achieved between rival forces as 'harmonious opposition' (*Essays and Letters*, 283), but the concept also applies to the laws governing history, as intimated by the poet in several unfinished prose texts. What defines an epoch is the great accord or harmony achieved between elements that would otherwise vanquish each other. In 'The Rhine', this accord is described as the wedding of heaven and earth:

> Dann feiern das Brautfest Menschen und Götter,
> Es feiern die Lebenden all,
> Und ausgeglichen
> Ist eine Weile das Schicksaal.
>
> (FHA VIII, 632)

> Then gods and mortals celebrate their nuptials
> All the living celebrate,
> And Fate for a while
> Is levelled out, suspended.
>
> (Poems and Fragments, 441)

As significant as the idea of a marriage between mortals and immortals is, it is important to observe that the poem does not end with this celebration of the order established by the Rhine in which everything finds its proper place. Instead the poem closes with a reference to the confusion that returns at night when the sun sets and nothing is visible on the horizon. The poet writes regarding his friend Isaak von Sinclair:

> ... und nimmer ist dir
> Verborgen das Lächeln des Herrschers
> Bei Tage, wenn
> Es fieberhaft und angekettet das
> Lebendige scheinet oder auch
> Bei Nacht, wenn alles gemischt
> Ist ordnungslos und wiederkehrt
> Uralte Verwirrung.
> (*FHA* VIII, 633)

> ... and never from you
> The smile of the Ruler is hidden
> By day, when all
> That lives seems febrile
> And fettered, or also
> By night, when all is mingled
> Chaotically and back again comes
> Primaeval confusion.
>
> (Poems and Fragments, 443)

What sets the friend apart from all other human beings and earns him the poet's praise is that he alone is able to intuit the divine not only 'by day' but also 'by night'. His heightened sensitivity draws attention to what makes intuition possible in all other circumstances. According to these verses, it is the light of the sun that renders Creation visible, which is hardly a surprise. What is surprising is that the light makes the world appear 'febrile / And fettered' [*fieberhaft und angekettet*]. The sun, like the light of reason, is a divisive force. It splits nature into individual phenomena, as judgement splits Being into subject and object. The poet's friend is unique in recognising in the darkness the benevolent smile of God. Not even the poet would seem to share his gift. For him nature freed of all human condition amounts to 'Primaeval confusion' [*Uralte Verwirrung*], which is his turn of phrase for the biblical *tohu va-vohu* or chaos in Hesiod's *Theogony*.

Heidegger enshrined a reading of Hölderlin that underscores the retreat of the gods and the long night into which western culture has fallen with the end of metaphysics, which for him, like Hegel, begins with the rising of the sun in the east and its setting in the west, albeit with the distinction that this is not a movement toward absolute knowledge but instead toward the forgetting of being. The following passage from 'Hölderlin and the Essence of Poetry' typifies Heidegger's approach to a poet whom he considered the last great German voice:

> [B]y providing anew the essence of poetry, Hölderlin first determines a new time. It is the time of the gods who have fled *and* of the God who is coming. It is the *time of need* because it stands in a double lack and a double not: in the no-longer of the gods who have fled and the not yet of the God who is coming.[13]

The drama of this statement notwithstanding, it would be hard to argue that Hölderlin was not preoccupied with the night as an interlude in which all previous relations dissolve and the accomplishments of culture are laid to waste. In 'Bread and Wine' he laments, 'But where are they [the temples and cities]? Where do the famed ones flourish, the festival's crown? / Thebes wilts, as does Athens' [*Aber wo sind sie? wo blühn die Bekannten, die Kronen des Festes? / Thebe welkt und Athen*] (*FHA* VI, 260). In the unfinished essay 'The declining fatherland . . .' [*Das untergehende Vaterland . . .*], also known as 'Becoming in Dissolution' [*Das Werden im Vergehen*], he refers to these ruins of ancient civilisations as the *real* principle to distinguish them from the *ideal* nature of a culture that has subsided and exists now only in memory. Even ruins, however, possess a particular power, as he is quick to note in his account of how one epoch declines and another emerges.

What defines an age as an age and separates it from other historical moments is the constellation of elements in it with emphasis on the idea of a constellation as that which enables elements to appear while at the same time confining them to this one arrangement. In other words, every age is characterised by a set of relations that provide phenomena with a place, while also limiting the scope of their activity to this one place. For Hölderlin this condition becomes apparent as soon as an age declines and the constraints that had previously governed its members dissolve:

> In living existence, one kind of relation and *kind of substance* predominates; although all others can be discerned in it, in the transition the possibility of

all relations predominates, but the particular one is to be extracted, to be drawn from it, so that through it as infinity the finite effect emerges [*so daß durch sie Unendlichkeit, die endliche Wirkung hervorgeht*]. (*Essays and Letters*, 271; *FHA* XIV, 174)

The statement contains *in nuce* Hölderlin's theory of historical progress. As an age or world subsides, what had previously been unimaginable suddenly becomes possible. Indeed 'the possibility of *all* relations predominates' or comes to the fore, which is what makes the transition between ages at once terrifying and intoxicating – terrifying because it leaves the subject without a ground, intoxicating because it presents the subject with an opportunity to fashion a world out of an infinite array of possibilities.

To do so, however, the subject must be able to lift itself from a state in which nothing is real or actual (*wirklich*) for a variety of reasons. Hölderlin quips, 'Nothing comes out of nothingness' (*Essays and Letters*, 272), in an obvious retort to the doctrine of *creatio ex nihilo* that had shaped the notion of genesis from the Bible onwards. Yet the quip belies a more serious concern – namely, that the disappearance of a world will not be followed by the appearance of another world or, in the words of 'The Rhine', that 'primaeval confusion' will return. The experience attributed to the poet's friend Sinclair in the poem is instructive in this regard. Unlike his compatriots, he is able to discern in the darkness of the night 'the smile of the Ruler' and for this reason is not threatened by the chaos that ensues when the sun of his historical age sets.

A similar process is hinted at in 'The declining fatherland . . .'. Hölderlin speaks in passing of the pain that the subject experiences as its world dissolves:

> [In this first, raw pain], the newly emergent, the ideal, is undefined, more an object of fear, whereas by contrast the dissolution itself *seems* existent [*ein Bestehendes*], more real, even if nothing, [*reales Nichts*], and the real or that which is dissolving is contained in necessity in the state between being and not-being. (*Essays and Letters*, 272, translation modified; *FHA* XIV, 175)

The elliptical nature of this passage notwithstanding, a few points can be discerned. The initial terror that the subject feels at the dissolution of the world is caused in part by the absence of any alternative to this dissolution. Whatever form of life could replace the elapsed world is still undefined, and without any alternative on the horizon nothing is left to fill the void but nothing itself. Hölderlin indicates that the dissolution '*seems* existent, more real, even if nothing', which would seem to be a shorthand way of saying that it constitutes a reality that is not yet anything in particular, i.e. 'no one thing', to recall the etymology of the word 'nothing'; the German word *nichts* likewise derives from *nicht etwas*.[14] In the still raw pain that accompanies a decline, nothingness in the sense of 'no one thing' appears as a perpetual state, leaving the subject without a foothold, perhaps even without consciousness of itself. For this same reason, however, nothingness can also appear as anything. It can present itself as something existent [*Bestehendes*] that is of potentially endless duration.

On more than one occasion, Hölderlin suggests that the dissolution of a world can be experienced as a transition only after the fact, which is to say only once the experiencing subject has gained a position outside it. Early in the essay he notes that '*the decline or transition of the fatherland*' (*Essays and Letters*, 271) can be felt only to the degree that 'something newly emergent, youthful and possible is also felt' (*Essays and Letters*, 271, translation modified). And later in the text he underscores that 'the comprehension, the animation, not of that which has become incomprehensible and fatal, but of the incomprehensibleness . . . of the dissolution itself' (*Essays and Letters*, 272, translation modified) would not happen, were it not for that which is 'harmonious, comprehensible and alive' (*Essays and Letters*, 272). Yet the most explicit statement on the belated construction or perception of a transition comes as Hölderlin explores how a continuum can be built out of a disruptive experience:

> The dissolution, therefore, as necessary, from the viewpoint of ideal memory, as such becomes an ideal object of the newly developed life, a look back along the path, which had to be travelled, from the beginning of the dissolution up to the point where out of the new life, a memory of the dissolved, and, out of that, as explanation and union of the gap and the contrast which sets in between the new and the past, the memory of the dissolution can follow. (*Essays and Letters*, 272, translation modified)

The dissolution first reveals itself to be a transition after the fact, as it is remembered from the vantage point of a future in which a new life has formed or is in the process of being constructed. According to this passage, the memory of the transition is necessary to fill the gap between the world that has dissolved and the one that takes its place.

Yet elsewhere in the essay Hölderlin suggests that the memory of the transition arises not in the future but in the present and that it is precisely the formation of this memory in a period of upheaval that ensures that a new world emerges from what would otherwise be sheer nothingness or, in the previously quoted passage from 'The Rhine', 'Primaeval confusion'. Central to this process is the release of forces previously bound up in a particular world or age. Unleashed they gain the potential that they lacked when they stood merely as components of a web of relations. What is critical for Hölderlin, however, is not so much the unlimited possibilities that these forces gain, as the role that experience plays in converting possibility into actuality: '[T]he possible which steps into reality

[*Wirklichkeit*], as reality dissolves, this has a real effect [*dies wirkt*], and it effects [*es bewirkt*] both the sensation of the dissolution and the memory of that which is dissolved' (*Essays and Letters*, 272; *FHA* XIV, 174). The possible becomes real as it takes effect. The passage is premised on the pun that reality (*Wirklichkeit*) comes to be in effecting something or bringing it about (*bewirken*) and in having an effect (*wirken*). The medium for this transformation is consciousness itself which, out of a multitude of possibilities, remembers one variant and in so doing starts the process of formation of a new world or form of life. The future grows out of a memory of the past that is still, as it were, being formed, and this memory shapes the future by realising one of the infinite possibilities in what Hölderlin called the 'world of all worlds' (*Essays and Letters*, 271) and what we might call nature unconstrained. To see God's smile in the night sky, as the poet's friend in 'The Rhine' does, is to recognise boundless possibility in what is otherwise nothing, or 'no one thing'. Whether this effort succeeds, whether a future can be forged from the past is the issue Hölderlin takes up in the notes he wrote to accompany his translations of *Oedipus* and *Antigone*.

Nature and tragedy

For all its rigour, Hölderlin's account of the transition between historical eras leaves an important matter unresolved. Nowhere in the text does he address what motivates the process in which a culture dissolves – a culture, moreover, in which all forces would seem to exist in a relation of mutual dependence. Hölderlin will not arrive at a solution to this problem until he embarks on his translations of Sophocles' tragedies in 1802, a project that will likewise inform his late hymns. In some respects, his explanation of the impetus for the tragic *muthos* follows long-established tradition. What unleashes the tragic action in, for example, *Oedipus Rex* is a violation of divine law. Oedipus oversteps his bounds in interpreting the oracle regarding the plague devastating Thebes as if he were a priest with access to divine knowledge: '[The oracle] could mean: judge strictly, in a general way, hold a pure court, maintain good civil order in the state. But thereupon Oedipus immediately speaks like a priest' (*Essays and Letters*, 319). In so doing Oedipus invites the gods to intervene in human affairs. He recasts the suffering of his city as retribution for a crime that requires not just punishment but ritual purification, a clearing of the ground in which such a crime could fester.

Where Hölderlin's account of tragedy differs from conventional interpretations is in his emphasis on the formal principles of the genre, as if what were at stake in any tragedy was the possibility of dramatic representation at all:

> The representation of the tragic depends primarily in this: that the fearful enormity [*das Ungeheure*] of God and man uniting, and the power of nature becoming boundlessly one with man's innermost being in rage, thereby comprehends itself, that the infinite unification purifies itself through infinite separation. (*Essays and Letters*, 323; *FHA* XVI, 257)

More so than any other genre, tragedy has to contend with how to portray the pairing or uniting of God and man, and this proves to be an all but insurmountable challenge since the pairing of the two obliterates all distinctions, like those between mortal and immortal, heaven and earth, sacred and profane. Without such distinctions, thought has no object to represent to itself, which recalls Hölderlin's argument in the previously cited letter from 1795 to Hegel in which he claimed that consciousness without an object is inconceivable. It is indeed striking how consistent Hölderlin's account of tragedy is with his earlier thought on the relation of being to judgement. In both cases the limit of what can be known turns out to be the One, that is the unity of the most rudimentary opposition between a subject that is identical to itself (the I) and an object that constitutes its other (the not-I). If in history the whole of Being erupts in periods of transition as the 'world of all worlds', in tragedy it comes to the fore in the caesura that interrupts the tragic sequence to re-inscribe the boundary separating humans and gods that had been challenged by the tragic hero.

Hölderlin oscillates in his comments on the caesura between thematic and metrical considerations. Thematically the caesura is tied to the moment in Sophocles' dramas when Tiresias appears and restrains the powers of nature long enough to enable the destiny of the hero to become evident. In *Antigone* the seer's speech fatally strikes the body, whereas in *Oedipus* it strikes the intellect or spirit, but in both cases it ushers in a period of 'infinite separation' between humans and gods, whose distinction must be maintained for the sake of *finite* nature. Hölderlin expands on this dimension of the caesura in his discussion of tragic prosody. As he reminds us, the laws governing the genre are few with the consequence that the tragic work always runs the risk of devouring itself. The succession of ideas introduced in it could accelerate to the point where the succession itself would collapse were it not for the caesura which checks this flow and allows a single representation to come to the foreground.

This explanation of the force that underlies tragedy finds an uncanny echo in Schelling's account of nature as pure productivity. In his *First Outline*, he takes the Fichtean definition of the subject as pure 'activity' (*Tathandlung*) and transfers it to nature, which henceforth acquires the status of a cause that is never apparent in itself. Indeed a nature so conceived could never become apparent in itself as it is not a thing, but the ground from which all things arise and to which all things attest in their existence. If nature is to appear at all, then, it must check itself, and here is where Schelling's ontology converges with Hölderlin's poetics. Indeed the philosopher describes the drives to expand and retract in nature in a manner that resonates uncannily with the poet's notion of 'harmonious opposition': 'The inhibition of the universal activity of Nature (without which 'apparent products' would never once come to be) may be represented . . . as the *work of opposed tendencies* in nature'.[15] Just as the caesura interrupts tragedy's flow enabling a single representation to appear, so too nature inhibits its activity or flow, enabling discrete phenomena to appear. In both cases, the source that gives rise to phenomena in a moment of expansion checks itself and in so doing ensures that whatever is produced bears witness to its origin. Hölderlin pays tribute to this dynamic when he writes, 'What dwells near the origin / hesitates to leave the place' [*Schwer verläßt / Was nahe dem Ursprung wohnet, den Ort*] (*FHA* VIII, 614). At the same time, the force that animates phenomena also threatens them, as it is never exhausted in any one representation. Hölderlin's contribution to the philosophy of nature was to see that the force that organises the living world could also become a destructive or aorgic force, turning meadows into wastelands and returning gardens to wilderness.

In the fragment 'As on a holiday . . .' [*Wie wenn am Feiertage . . .*] a farmer goes out to survey his fields the morning after a storm, and although we are assured that the tumult of the night has passed, there is still danger in the air:

> In sein Gestade wieder tritt der Strom,
> Und frisch der Boden grünt
> Und von des Himmels erquickendem Reegen
> Der Weinstock trauft und glänzend
> In stiller Sonne stehn die Bäume des Haines.
>
> (*FHA* VIII, 555)

> The river enters its banks once more,
> New verdure sprouts from the soil,
> And with the gladdening rain of heaven
> The grapevine drips, and gleaming
> In tranquil sunlight stand the trees of the grove.
>
> (*Poems and Fragments*, 395)

The danger implicit in these lines is that of a disaster averted. What this time amounted to a baptism by fire and water could the next time be a conflagration or flood. The poem is one of many in which Hölderlin grapples with cosmic forces that cannot be contained in a representation, which is why so many of his works remain unfinished and so many of his manuscripts resemble palimpsests. In one fragmentary text he writes, 'They are still / Untethered' [*Noch sind sie / Unangebunden*] (*StA* II, 217), regarding the Titans who dwell in the deep, but the same could be said of the Olympian gods, who rule from the heights and on occasion rain fire on the earth. The fate of the speaker in 'As on a holiday . . .' stands as a cautionary tale. He is literally thrown from his position after having ventured too close to the gods, robbed of the power of speech that had made him a poet before he was branded a false prophet.

Hölderlin's work is filled with examples of tragic sacrifice, especially as it pertains to the poet, who inevitably discovers that there is no mediation between heaven and earth, not because the two are opposed but because they are the same – 'the one differentiated in itself [*das Eine in sich selber Unterschiedne*]. Hölderlin first invokes this Heraclitean concept in *Hyperion*: 'The great saying, the *hen diapheron heautôi* (the one differentiated in itself) of Heraclitus, could be found only by a Greek, for it is the very being of Beauty' (*Hyperion*, 67). One of the challenges of reading Hölderlin's poetry is his thought of nature as an absolute unity or oneness, since what is not yet distinct from anything else does not permit its articulation in concepts. The absence of differentiation from without, however, necessitates differentiation from within. This is the source of Schelling's preoccupation with the powers of expansion and contraction that enable nature to turn its infinite productivity into an infinite series of finite products. Yet the philosopher's explanation of this dynamic leaves something unsettled. Why does nature need thought? Why does it depend on consciousness? This is where Hölderlin's work becomes the 'new mythology' envisioned in 'The Oldest Programme for a System of German Idealism' (*Essays and Letters*, 342).

On numerous occasions Hölderlin reminds us that the gods need us. In 'Mnemosyne' he tells us, 'The gods are not capable / Of everything. Mortals sooner reach / The abyss' [*Nicht vermögen / Die Himmlischen alles. Nemlich es reichen / Die Sterblichen eh' an den Abgrund*] (*FHA* VIII, 732, my translation), in lines often overshadowed by Heidegger's interpretation but which bear reconsidering in light of the insight they provide regarding the god's faculties or *Vermögen*.[16] The theme comes up again in the crucial middle stanza of 'The Rhine':

> Es haben aber an eigner
> Unsterblichkeit die Götter genug, und bedürfen
> Die Himmlischen eines Dings,
> So sind's Heroën und Menschen
> Und Sterbliche sonst. Denn weil
> Die Seeligsten nichts fühlen von selbst,
> Muß wohl, wenn solches zu sagen

> Erlaubt ist, in der Götter Nahmen
> Theilnehmend fühlen ein Andrer,
> Den brauchen sie.
>
> (*FHA* VIII, 631)

> But their own immortality
> Suffices the gods, and if
> The Heavenly have need of one thing,
> It is of heroes and human beings
> And other mortals. For since
> The most Blessed in themselves feel nothing
> Another, if to say such a thing is
> Permitted, must, I suppose,
> Vicariously feel in the name of the gods,
> And him they need.
>
> (*Poems and Fragments*, 437)

What stands out in this stanza is the emphasis on the gods' feelings, or rather their lack thereof without the contribution of mortals who feel 'in their names' or 'on their behalf', as a standard reading of the locution 'in der Götter Nahmen' would suggest. The lines, however, permit another, more literal interpretation. Mortals not only 'take part' in the names of the gods but also 'take' their names 'apart' – 'in der Götter Nahmen / *Theilnehmend*'. In doing so they create a division in the One, which enables the gods to 'feel themselves'. The split or *Ur-Teilung* that humans initiate derives from their capacity to judge (*urteilen*), which may at first seem like a check on the gods' power. Hölderlin, however, turns this dynamic on its head. Thanks to the rift that mortals introduce into the One, the gods can draw and sculpt the earth. In feeling themselves, they create the habitat in which they preside and mortals dwell. Nowhere is the artistic capacity of the gods expressed more forcefully than in the unfinished poem 'Wenn aber die Himmlischen', where the speaker praises the accomplishments of the gods as builders, sculptors and draftsmen:

> Wenn aber die Himmlischen haben
> *Gebaut*, still ist es
> Auf Erden, und *wohlgestalt* stehn
> Die betroffenen Bergen. *Gezeichnet*
> Sind ihre Stirnen.
>
> (*FHA* VIII, 755, emphasis added)

> But when the gods have finished
> *Building*, silence reigns
> On earth and the mountains stand
> *Carefully wrought*, the peaks
> Finely *etched*.
>
> (My translation, emphasis added)

Curious as it may seem, then, it is the rift in being that humans generate that creates the gods as the other of human beings in all significant respects. They are immortal, where humans are mortal; they are ubiquitous, where humans are confined to one place; and finally they craft the world that humans inhabit but never produce as their own invention. Yet Hölderlin's unique insight was to comprehend that both humans and gods are subordinate to nature insofar as they constitute two sides of the same, i.e. a unity that cannot be expressed except in opposing terms. Stefan Büttner remarks that the aorgic and organic impulses that compete in nature are relative terms, and the same observation applies to all the rival forces alluded to in Hölderlin's work – the Olympians and the Titans, the Orient and the Occident, the living and the dead, the depths and the heights, to name a few examples.[17] To capture these opposing pairs in a single, comprehensive image was Hölderlin's consistent ambition and represents his contribution to the natural philosophy of his day and to contemporary environmental thought in an age of ecological crisis.

The essays collected in this volume are organised around four themes. The first section 'Tragic Nature' considers nature as the stage for the conflict between human and inhuman forces characteristic of tragedy. In 'Nature and Poetic Consciousness from Hölderlin to Rilke', Jennifer Gosetti-Ferencei examines the tragic excess of inwardness in Hölderlin's landscapes and ties this excess to the inability of consciousness to grasp nature. As a counterpoint to Hölderlin she looks at the natural world in Rilke's *Sonnets to Orpheus* where she shows that the lyric subject retreats to make space for other perspectives associated with the *Dingwelt*. She interprets the difference between Hölderlin and Rilke as one between egological and ecological subjectivity. Katrin Pahl builds on the idea of ecological subjectivity to develop a notion of care that reaches beyond the typical opposition between humans and gods to include other living organisms. Her primary example for this is Hölderlin's unfinished tragedy *The Death of Empedocles*. In 'Raging with Care: The Poet's Liquid Fire', Pahl draws on the pre-Socratic thinker's cosmology and natural philosophy with emphasis on his theory of the elements or roots and the forces of love and strife to interpret the relationship between Achilles and Empedocles and its implications for the creative process. Finally, Achim Geisenhanslüke in 'The Order of the Unbound: Time and History in Hölderlin's "The Titans"' argues that what generates history for Hölderlin is the constant struggle between the Olympian gods that establish order and harmony and the Titans that disrupt this order and represent a more originary force, although this force can only be represented in negative terms. Titanic power constitutes the freedom from all domination, including the determinations of the Olympian gods and the claims of reason. Geisenhanslüke explains that the opposition between these two forces matches the famed quarrel of the ancients and moderns in eighteenth-century thought. The harmony and balance that the ancients achieved in art expresses the victory of the Olympian gods. Modern art, by contrast, longs for freedom from these constraints through a merger with the absolute or aorgic nature. Hölderlin's poetry fits squarely in the latter tradition.

The next section 'Hölderlin's Rivers' is devoted to the so-called river poems in which the poet reflects on the relationship between Germany and Greece, modernity and antiquity, and finally Hesperian pathos and Junonian sobriety. Yet the river poems need not be interpreted solely within this historical-philosophical scheme. As the contributions suggest, rivers also provide Hölderlin with an occasion to consider the relation of part and whole, humans and gods, and change and constancy. Speculative physics is central to Rochelle Tobias's contribution 'The Untamed Earth: The Labour of Rivers in Hölderlin's "The Ister"'. Tobias considers the relation of rivers to history in Hölderlin's late poetry and in his translations of Pindar's fragments. She contends that Hölderlin develops his theory of history through a broader reflection on the four elements, in which each element is said to need its opposite in order to restrain its potentially infinite expansiveness. She shows that this is particularly true of the earth, which would turn into an ever-expanding desert, were it not for the paths that rivers etch in it. Such etchings at the same time submit the earth to a peculiar temporality in which the past returns as the future and antiquity reappears as modernity. Hölderlin's cosmology is intertwined with his idea of historical reversals outlined in his letters to Böhlendorff and in his notes on Sophocles' tragedies. In 'Hölderlin's Local Abstraction: The Natural-Historical Sublime in "Voice of the People"', Márton Dornbach enlarges on the discussion of rivers and history with an eye toward historical catastrophes. He notes the dialectical tension implicit in the treatment of rivers in Hölderlin's work, which on the one hand represent the sublime and on the other serve as specific geographical and historical phenomena. He argues with an eye toward Schelling that this tension is an example of identity-in-difference and explores this dynamic by tracing the desire for union with the absolute in 'Voice of the People'. As he demonstrates, this desire is held in check only by the recognition of the need for constraint. He concludes his analysis by developing the parallels between Hölderlin's treatment of the historical example of the people of Xanthus in the ode and the poet's comments elsewhere on Greek antiquity, European modernity and the French Revolution. Bruno C. Duarte's essay 'Translating Centaurs: Notes on Hölderlin's "The Life-Giving"' closes this section with a meditation on Hölderlin's translation of the Pindar fragment 'The Life-

Giving' [*Das Belebende*], which is devoted to centaurs as the spirit of rivers. Duarte traces how the translation presents concepts through images and images through concepts, thereby putting into question the conventional distinction between literal and figurative language.

The third section 'Natural Beauty and the Absolute' returns to Hölderlin's one and only novel, where he first sketches his notion of All-Unifying Nature, which will persist throughout his work, albeit with some significant modifications. In 'Hölderlin's Mythopoetics: From "Aesthetic Letters" to the New Mythology', Luke Fischer analyses Hölderlin's early theoretical writings and the novel *Hyperion* in the context of German Idealist efforts to overcome the subject-object divide and to grasp the Absolute. Fischer argues that the Absolute cannot be grasped conceptually. It can only be experienced in a vision of the beautiful, which offers a glimpse into All-Unifying Nature. In reflections on Hölderlin's poetry and prose, Fischer makes the case that 'aesthetic intuition' offers a resource for philosophy, which otherwise would not be able to approach the absolute through intellectual means. Anja Lemke charts how this notion fares in Hölderlin's later work. In her contribution 'The Transition Between the Possible and the Real: Nature as Contingency in "The declining fatherland . . ."', she contends that in 'The declining fatherland . . .' Hölderlin abandons the idea of all-unifying nature that had fuelled his earlier writing and especially *Hyperion* and turns instead to the notion of infinite possibility that erupts in the present as a contingency that cannot otherwise be contained. Hölderlin's idea of the 'world of all worlds' will come to define his understanding of nature and tragedy in his late period. It will also push his work in the direction of modernity, in which the present is experienced as a moment of radical rupture and upheaval. Jacob Haubenreich extends this approach by looking at the after-life of Hölderlin's *Hyperion* in Peter Handke's notebooks and especially his narrative *Die Lehre der Sainte-Victoire* (1980). In ' "My whole being fell silent, and read": Peter Handke's Hölderlin and Heidegger Reception' on the 'New Mythology', Haubenreich uses the lens of Handke's notebooks to revisit the meaning of natural beauty in *Hyperion* and to reflect on the materiality of writing, as expressed in Handke's journals and Hölderlin's manuscripts.

The final section 'The Place of Poetry' elaborates on Haubenreich's meditations on the material dimensions of Hölderlin's writing to explore poetry as the place where nature appears in its autonomy and peculiar productive power as a language we have yet to understand. In 'Nature, Nurse, *Khôra*: Notes on the Poetics of Hölderlin's Ode "Man" ', Szabó analyses the emergence of language in the early ode 'Man' as a place that bears an astonishing resemblance to the *khôra* in Plato's *Timaeus*. Like the *khôra*, it receives or encloses in itself what Benjamin called 'non-sensuous similarities', and this becomes apparent when in a paradigmatic instance of naming language imitates the productive power of nature, giving birth to itself as it gives birth to nature. In addition to Benjamin's 'On the Mimetic Faculty', Szabó refers to Kant's *Conjectural Beginning of Human History* to distinguish the philosopher's idea of freedom from nature from the poet's idea of freedom in the natural world. Jan Mieszkowski continues this reflection in 'Not Rhythm' by analysing the apocryphal statement attributed to Hölderlin, 'Everything is rhythm'. He claims that rhythm is as much the suspension of contingency as its continuation and looks at the ode 'Voice of the People' to reflect on the analogy between voice and rivers that the poem simultaneously raises and undermines. The precariousness of this analogy calls into question the distinction between sense and nonsense, patterns and randomness and melody and noise. Thomas Schestag closes this collection with a probing meditation. In 'allowed, disallowed', Schestag turns to Kant to explore a deed that is neither commanded nor prohibited but permitted. Licence forms a third but also ill-defined term next to a command and a prohibition in Kant's *Metaphysics of Morals*. The issue of licence appears in Hölderlin's poetry as well – specifically in 'The Rhine', where the speaker raises the question of whether he has the licence to say something. The motif of foliage embedded in the German term for licence (*Erlaubnis*) appears again in the poem 'Andenken' in the "leafless mast" (*der entlaubte Mast*) that accompanies sailors at sea. Schestag suggests that the mast stands in for what remains – namely, the leaf of a poem – that is neither compelled nor enjoined but permitted based on nothing but the chance or even the gift of nature and of poetry.

Notes

1. Chakrabarty, 'Climate of History', pp. 206–7. In this landmark essay on the consequences of global warming for historiography and, more broadly, humanist inquiry Chakrabarty advances the claim that the understanding that the human being has a carbon footprint and is to this degree a geological agent has led to the entangling of human history and natural history, which from the Enlightenment to the late twentieth century were considered separate categories. Human history has been expanded in space to have planetary dimensions, as, conversely, natural history has been accelerated to an almost human time scale, as witnessed in the time-lapse photographs of glaciers melting.
2. Kant, *Critique of Pure Reason*, B561/A533, p. 543. Kant identified the freedom of the will as the 'unconditioned condition of every voluntary act'. Natural philosophy seeks to locate this cause in nature itself, rather than in the subject.
3. Fichte and Schelling, *The Philosophical Rupture*, p. 44.
4. Schelling, *System of Transcendental Idealism*, p. 6.
5. Ibid. pp. 219–33.
6. See *Essays and Letters*, p. 342. Schelling expresses a similar view in the exuberant closing lines of his Introduction to *Ideas Toward a Philosophy of Nature*, 'Nature should be Mind made visible, Mind the invisible Nature'. To the extent that nature carries its

organising principle or spirit in itself, it is at one and the same time something physical and intellectual. Conversely, the mind that is otherwise hidden finds expression in nature, which not only demonstrates the operations of the mind but also embodies them. See Schelling, *Ideas*, pp. 41–2.
7. Regarding the question of the authorship of 'The Oldest Programme,' see Frank, *Der kommende Gott*, pp. 153–87 and Förster, 'To Lend Wings to Physics', pp. 190–3.
8. Pöggeler, 'Hegel', pp. 17–32.
9. Goethe, 'Eins und Alles', *Werke*, vol. 1, p. 369.
10. Henrich, 'Hölderlin in Jena', pp. 114–17.
11. See Horstmann, 'The Early Philosophy of Fichte and Schelling', p. 123.
12. Schutjer, *Narrating Community*, p. 168.
13. Heidegger, 'Hölderlin and the Essence of Poetry', p. 64.
14. See the entry for 'nothing' in the *Oxford English Dictionary*: http://www.oed.com/view/Entry/128579?rskey=qwTrAy&result=1#eid (last accessed 9 April 2019). The *OED* says 'nothing' as a noun derives from 'none' and 'thing', and 'none' itself is a contraction for 'no one'. For the etymology of the German noun *nichts*, see the entry in the *Grimm's Dictionary of the German Language*: http://woerterbuchnetz.de/cgi-bin/WBNetz/wbgui_py?sigle=DWB (last accessed 9 April 2019). The Grimm's Dictionary says that *nichts* derives from the negation of *ichtes* or *ichts*, which is the Middle High German word for 'something' (in modern German: *etwas*).
15. Schelling, *First Outline*, p. 17 (emphasis added).
16. See Heidegger, 'What Are Poets For?', pp. 90–3.
17. Büttner, 'Natur', p. 238.

Bibliography

Büttner, Stefan, 'Natur – Ein Grundwort Hölderlins', *Hölderlin-Jahrbuch* 26 (1988–89), pp. 224–47.
Chakrabarty, Dipesh, 'The Climate of History: Four Theses', *Critical Inquiry*, 35 (Winter 2009), pp. 197–222.
Deutsches Wörterbuch von Jacob Grimm und Wilhelm Grimm, http://woerterbuchnetz.de/cgi-bin/WBNetz/wbgui_py?sigle=DWB (last accessed 9 April 2019).
Fichte, J. G. and F. W. J. Schelling, *The Philosophical Rupture Between Fichte and Schelling: Selected Texts and Correspondence (1800–1802)*, ed. and trans. Michael G. Vater and David W. Wood (Albany: SUNY Press, 2012).
Förster, Eckart, '"To Lend Wings to Physics Once Again": Hölderlin and the "Oldest System-Programme of German Idealism"', *European Journal of Philosophy*, 3: 2 (1995), pp. 174–98.
Frank, Manfred, *Der kommende Gott: Vorlesungen über die neue Mythologie* (Frankfurt am Main: Suhrkamp, 1982).
Goethe, J. W. von, *Werke: Hamburger Ausgabe in 14 Bänden*, ed. Erich Trunz, 14 vols (Munich: Deutscher Taschenbuchverlag, 2014).
Heidegger, Martin, 'What Are Poets For', in M. Heidegger, *Poetry, Language, Thought*, trans. Albert Hofstadter (New York: Harper & Row, 1971), pp. 89–139.
Heidegger, Martin, *Elucidations of Hölderlin's Poetry*, trans. Keith Hoeller (Amherst, NY: Humanity Books, 2000).
Henrich, Dieter, 'Hölderlin in Jena', trans. Taylor Carman, in D. Henrich, *The Course of Remembrance and Other Essays on Hölderlin*, ed. with a foreword by Eckart Förster (Stanford: Stanford University Press, 1997), pp. 90–118.
Horstmann, Rolf-Peter, 'The Early Philosophy of Fichte and Schelling', in Karl Ameriks (ed.), *The Cambridge Companion to German Idealism* (Cambridge: Cambridge University Press, 2000), pp. 117–40.

Kant, Immanuel, *Critique of Pure Reason*, trans. Paul Guyer and Allen W. Wood (Cambridge: Cambridge University Press, 1998).
Oxford English Dictionary, http://www.oed.com (last accessed 9 April 2019).
Pöggeler, Otto, 'Hegel, der Verfasser des ältesten Systemprogramms des deutschen Idealismus: Ein handschriftlicher Fund', in Hans-Georg Gadamer (ed.), *Hegel-Tage-Urbino 1965* (Bonn: Bouvier, 1969), pp. 17–32.
Schelling, F. W. J., *First Outline of a System of the Philosophy of Nature*, trans. with an intro. and notes by Keith R. Peterson (Albany: SUNY Press, 2004).
Schelling, F. W. J., *Ideas for a Philosophy of Nature as Introduction for the Study of Science, 1797*, trans. Errol E. Harris and Peter Heath with an intro. by Robert Stern (Cambridge: Cambridge University Press, 1988).
Schelling, F. W. J., *System of Transcendental Idealism (1800)*, trans. Peter Heath with an intro. by Michael Vater (Charlottesville: University of Virginia Press, 1978).
Schutjer, Karin, *Narrating Community after Kant: Schiller, Goethe and Hölderlin* (Detroit: Wayne State University Press, 2001).

Part I
Tragic Nature

Chapter 2

Nature and Poetic Consciousness from Hölderlin to Rilke

Jennifer Anna Gosetti-Ferencei

Introduction

While the poets Hölderlin and Rilke each invite voluminous exegesis and are often evoked together in a common thematic context – not least because of the interest Heidegger took in both poets and, in his wake, that of Blanchot and Gadamer – they have invited little direct comparison in literary scholarship.[1] Rilke, coming upon Hölderlin's work via Norbert von Hellingrath around the beginning of a decade of relative poetic silence (ending in February 1922), may be thought to have drawn some sense of the importance of the poet's role, and some images and linguistic mannerisms, but little by way of philosophical or poetological influence from his romantic predecessor. In contrast to this view, it has been argued that Rilke's relation to Hölderlin can be considered his 'bid to situate himself in a distinctly German poetic lineage', yet Hölderlin's direct influence has been demonstrated in respect to but a few minor poems.[2] There has been little, if any, scholarly indication that Rilke's distinct poetic accomplishments, or even his central preoccupations, bear distinctly Hölderlinian features. Turning then to two undeniably singular bodies of work, we would conclude that they remain, after all, very different poets. While this is no doubt the case, I will here argue that the poetics of Hölderlin and Rilke are in fact deeply connected by a common notion – that of distinctly poetic consciousness – and by a common problem – the relation of poetic consciousness to nature. Reading these poets together may illuminate the possibilities for a poetic contribution to revising our relation to the natural world.

It is worth reviewing the differences between these poets before setting out to demonstrate their common problematic. Hölderlin's poetry, in the context of Romanticism, is steeped in Enlightenment philosophy and contends with idealism, Pietism, and revolution; Rilke aims to make sense of modernist visual art, in the cultural shadow of Baudelaire and Nietzsche, and largely avoids national themes. Both poets engage the novel form to express the bereftness of the modern age.[3] But the protagonist of Hölderlin's novel, *Hyperion*, for all his contemplation, is centrifugally directed, attempting to find wholeness in love, friendship and political action – recounting these entirely in letters to others. In contrast, the titular protagonist of Rilke's *Die Aufzeichnungen des Malte Laurids Brigge*, traumatised by the electroshock of urban Paris, retreats alone into the library and the art museum, drawing their resources toward the restoration of self by writing mostly in a private journal. Hölderlin describes, and indeed is poetically motivated by, the possibility of an intellectual intuition, a grasp of the whole of being in which sensation and cognition are equally infused. Rilke, himself, like Malte, 'learning to see', poetises a phenomenology of perception in imagery of almost tactile tenderness toward things of this world. Hölderlin's poetic thought traverses widely across space, time and history; the particular in his poetry is often complement to the universal – he once recognised that in poetry, 'I shy away too much from the common and the ordinary in real life' [*ich scheue das Gemeine und Gewöhnliche im wirklichen Leben zu sehr*] (StA VI, 289). Rilke's poetic vision, in contrast, is often focused on everyday things and parts of things, with no apparent need to connect these to principles of history, to the divine, or – but for his angels – to a cosmic order. Both poets evoke ancient Greek mythology. To Hölderlin, the relationship with the ancients is felt as an inescapable poetological destiny. But Rilke's Apollo is a fragment in a museum, his Orpheus conjured in response to a modern predicament. Angels and animals, as figures half-shadowing transcendence, mark Rilke's ontological boundaries for the human consciousness, yet it is Hölderlin's speaker who seems to suffer direct exposure, like his Empedocles figure, to the fire of heaven itself.

Despite these significant contrasts, I hope to show that a Hölderlinian current invigilates Rilke's most accomplished poetic thinking. A sensitive contextualisation of Rilke within the framework of Hölderlin's response to idealism can help to illuminate the possibilities for ecologically-oriented consciousness in Rilke, while demonstrating the sustained relevance of Hölderlin's writings for modernism. The ecological implications generated from a comparative consideration may be more substantial than either Rilke or Hölderlin's poetics alone, and traditional interpretations of either, might secure.

Hölderlinian nature and tragic subjectivity

The theme of nature in Hölderlin can be traced along a number of axes. Philosophically nature is thought in connection with the concepts of life, freedom and necessity, the sensuous and the sacred, and the primordial unity of being. In metaphysical terms, nature is the ground of being, the elusive origin of both subject and object, self and world, an origin from which we are separated by predicative judgement and intellection, and for which we may long for reunification. Mythically nature is the source and object of poetic inspiration, as it is for Hölderlin's tragic character Empedocles, based on the last ancient Greek philosopher to write in verse, who himself described nature as a sphere held together by the opposition of love and strife. It is poetry that allows human beings to relate to nature in connection with the divine.

All of these themes are prominent in Hölderlin's epistolary novel *Hyperion*. As Hyperion writes to Bellarmin:

> Eines zu sein mit Allem, das ist Leben der Gottheit, das ist der Himmel des Menschen.
> Eines zu sein mit Allem, was lebt, in seliger Selbstvergessenheit wiederzukehren ins All der Natur, das ist der Gipfel der Gedanken und Freuden, das ist die heilige Bergshöhe, der Ort der ewigen Ruhe, wo der Mittage seine Schwüle und der Donner seine Stimme verliert und das kochende Meer der Woge des Kornfelds gleicht.
> Eines zu sein mit Allem, was lebt! Mit diesem Worte legt . . . der Geist des Menschen den Zepter weg, und alle Gedanken schwinden vor dem Bilde der ewigen Welt. (*FHA* XI, 585)
>
> To be one with all, that is the life of the divinity, this is the heaven of humanity.
> To be one with all that lives, to return in blessed self-forgetfulness into the All of Nature – this is the pinnacle of thoughts and joys, this the sacred mountain peak, the place of eternal rest, where the midday loses its oppressive heat and the thunder its voice and the boiling sea is like a waving field of grain.
> To be one with all that lives! At those words . . . the mind of man lays down its sceptre, and all thoughts vanish before the image of the eternal world. (My translation)

This view of nature as primal unity that encompasses the human being will, as Hölderlin's novel progresses, become more nuanced and conflicted. For nature will be experienced in fleeting and repeated episodes of joy, Hyperion soon finds himself hurled down by the inevitable activity of reflection:

> Ich denke nach und finde mich, wie ich zuvor war, allein ... die ewig-einige Welt, ist hin; die Natur verschließt die Arme, und ich stehe, wie ein Fremdling, vor ihr, und verstehe sie nicht. (*FHA* XI, 585–6)
>
> I reflect and find myself, as I was before, alone ... the eternally united world is gone; nature closes its arms, and I stand like a stranger before her, and do not understand her. (My translation)

Alteration of the moods of blissful belonging and great yearning, joyful self-forgetting and desperate forlornness, express the problem of self-reflection for consciousness, and trace a path of potentially infinitised longing. While a number of experiences – concerning the perception of nature's beauty, love, friendship, revolution – energise Hyperion, they all occasion, if transiently, a feeling of union between human consciousness and the natural order. But moments of inevitable reflection collapse this sense of belonging. By the end of the novel – with Hyperion's promise 'Nächstens mehr' ('more soon'), unfulfilled in the text – the protagonist has reached a more accomplished, though more anguished, understanding of nature, the complexity of which has demanded an education of the soul (*FHA* XI, 782).[4] The 'eccentric path' [*die exzentrische Bahn*] of Hyperion follows a progressive alteration of tones which respects no single centre, but moves elliptically around the dual poles of joy and loss, unity and discord, nature and destiny (*FHA* X, 47). The model reflects Hölderlin's interest in the elliptical orbit of the planets as discovered by Kepler, who had studied at the same seminary in Tübingen.[5] Hyperion must learn that the infinite can be grasped, as Hölderlin writes in *Anmerkungen zur Antigonä* ('Notes on the *Antigone*'), only 'from an askew perspective' [*aus linkischem Gesichtspunkt*] (*FHA* XVI, 421; my translation).

Hölderlin's early poem 'Die Eichenbäume' ('The Oak Trees') renders in an ostensibly simpler tone the poet's connection to, and sense of division from, nature. Hölderlin wrote the hexameter poem in 1796, and it was published, like the first part of Hölderlin's novel, by Schiller in the following year. Here nature is manifest both as the local garden for human dwelling and as the oak trees which stand apart from and free of any commerce with the human:

> Aus den Gärten komm' ich zu euch, ihr Söhne des Berges!
> Aus den Gärten, da lebt die Natur geduldig und häuslich,
> Pflegend und wieder gepflegt mit dem fleißigen Menschen zusammen.
> Aber ihr, Ihr Herrlichen! steht, wie ein Volk von Titanen
> In der zahmeren Welt und gehört nur euch und dem Himmel,
> Der euch nährt' und erzog und der Erde, die euch geboren.
> Keiner von euch ist noch in die Schule der Menschen gegangen,
> Und ihr drängt euch fröhlich und frei, aus der kräftigen Wurzel,
> Unter einander herauf und ergreift, wie der Adler die Beute,

Mit gewaltigem Arme den Raum, und gegen die Wolken
Ist euch heiter und groß die sonnige Krone gerichtet.
Eine Welt ist jeder von euch, wie die Sterne des Himmels
Lebt ihr, jeder ein Gott, in freiem Bunde zusammen.
Könnt' ich die Knechtschaft nur erdulden, ich neidete nimmer
Diesen Wald und schmiegte mich gern ans gesellige Leben.
Fesselte nur nicht mehr ans gesellige Leben das Herz mich,
Das von Liebe nicht läßt, wie gern würd' ich unter euch wohnen!
(*FHA* III, 51)

Out of the gardens I come to you, you sons of the mountain!
Out of the gardens, where Nature lives patient and domestic,
Caring and cared for in return together with the diligent human.
But you, you regal ones, stand like a nation of Titans
In the tamer world, and belong only to yourselves and to the heaven
That nurtured and raised you, and to the earth that bore you.
None of you has yet gone to the school of human beings,
And happy and free you thrust yourselves up, from powerful roots,
Amongst yourselves, and grasp, like the eagle does its prey, the space
With powerful arms, and towards the clouds
Is your sunny crown, with joy, grandly directed.
Each of you is a world, like the stars of the heavens
You live, each a god, in free covenant together.
Could I only bear the servitude, I would never envy
This forest and I would gladly submit myself to communal life.
If only my heart no longer bound me to communal life,
Which out of love does not let go, how gladly I would live amongst you.
(My translation)

The apparent simplicity of this poem lies in its singular object of attention, the oak trees that live apart in the forest, away from human dwelling. Yet the poem achieves a complex rendering of nature with multiple metaphoric equivalences for the oak trees: while from a mechanistic view of nature they would be seen as immobile and insensate organisms, merely rooted in the soil underfoot, Hölderlin likens them to an eagle, to gods and to stars – all of these evocative of freedom and freedom from human influence. For this nature is not cultivated, the nature of fields and gardens, but sovereign and even divine.

Perhaps most intriguing is that Hölderlin's speaker acknowledges the trees as each 'a world' of its own: 'Eine Welt ist jeder von euch.' With this designation the speaker supports his admiration of the oaks' freedom. But on what basis can the speaker claim that each oak is a world? From their roots dug deep into the soil, the trees grow upwards, trunks and branches ever ascending, and with their 'arms' grasping toward the clouds, their crowns receive – literally absorb – the light of the sun. The oak tree, then, is a living structure that joins dimensions of nature: physically, visually and symbolically they connect the earth to the heavens. The poem also provides indications of the primal elements (or 'roots') such as named by Empedocles, whose fragment 'On Nature' Hölderlin had been reading.[6] The speaker mentions roots (earth), clouds (which may harbour water), the tree's branches grasping space (air) and filled with sunlight (fire). Joining these elements, the world-creating oaks are divine. They were initially (line 4) merely compared to the Titans – who legendarily attempted to reach heaven by piling up mountains – but now (line 13) they are identified directly as 'jeder ein Gott'. It has been argued that Hölderlin's early work 'obsesses over the intimacy between God and plant life' and yet the human being stands apart, for 'human knowledge and human action fall outside of this divine-natural economy.'[7]

In contrast to the oak trees, the human being is not free. The repetition of 'Aus den Gärten' at the poem's outset emphasises the liberation for which the poet yearns, as does his explicit contrast between the trees' joy and freedom and the 'Schule der Menschen'. The negative connotation of such schooling is expressed explicitly in Hyperion's lament:[8]

> Ach! wär' ich nie in eure Schulen gegangen. Die Wissenschaft, der ich in den Schacht hinunter folgte, von der ich, jugendlich thöricht, die Bestätigung meiner reinen Freude erwartete, die hat mir alles verdorben.
> Ich bin bei euch so recht vernünftig geworden, habe gründlich mich unterscheiden gelernt von dem, was mich umgibt, bin nun vereinzelt mit der schönen Welt, bin so ausgeworfern aus dem Garten der Natur. (FHA XI, 586)

> Oh! had I never attended your schools. Philosophy, which I followed down into the mineshaft, from which, in youthful folly, I awaited the confirmation of my pure joy-for me, it has spoiled everything.
> I have become so thoroughly rational among you, I have learned so fundamentally to differentiate myself from what surrounds me, I am now in a state of loneliness in the midst of the beautiful world, am very much outcast from the garden of nature. (My translation)

Despite the tone of ambivalence, the speaker of 'Die Eichenbäume' does not choose to abandon the human community for a Rousseauian solitude, admitting that, although it involves servitude, *das gesellige Leben* binds him through love. Nor does he make Empedocles' choice, rupturing boundaries to become one with nature in a tragic suicide. Neither solitary reverence nor self-sacrifice will satisfy the 'Dichterberuf' as Hölderlin will come to understand it: the poet must serve to bridge nature and human, gods and mortals, to wake the sleeping human culture to divine joy, as Hölderlin suggests in 'An unsre großen Dichter' (1798). The apparent simplicity of 'Die Eichenbäume' dissipates when the reader realises that the poem itself enacts the divination of our sense of nature through metaphor. In light of that, the anthropomorphisms of Hölderlin's description of the tree – their branches as 'arms', their emotion, 'fröhlich' – would appear neither contradictory nor sentimental, but purposive.

The conflict in 'Die Eichenbäume' has been interpreted primarily in social terms, reflecting Hölderlin's ambivalent need to emancipate himself from Schiller's influence, frustration over his social status and economic dependency, and even as politically 'mobilizing anti-French sentiment', with the Titans standing in for resistance against submission to cultivated society.[9] Yet there may be a more fundamental underlying problem, concerning human consciousness as such and its relation to nature. Human beings need society because we are no longer at home in nature; love binds humans together, but for human beings, with our means of reckoning, even this bond entails servitude and inherent division. Just as we have come to regard nature as mechanistic, we have failed to realise our own freedom in the natural world. In the preface to the penultimate version of *Hyperion*, Hölderlin complains that we have become estranged from nature, that unity has fallen to discord, and lordship and bondage alternate. Division among human beings may replicate the original division of consciousness from what Rilke will come to call 'das Offene' ('the open'). Hölderlin's view is that the subjugation of nature to human reckoning may underlie the subjugation of human beings to one another.

Indeed in *Hyperion*, and increasingly in the poetry from the turn of the century, the relationship to nature is more critically rendered than in 'Die Eichenbäume'. The poets are needed to restore a broken relation to nature and, recalling the departed gods, await a divine return. The loss of harmony with nature is reflected, for example, in the poem 'Die Kürze' ('Brevity'):

> . . . die Erd' ist kalt,
> Und der Vogel der Nacht schwirrt
> Unbequem vor das Auge dir.
>
> *(FHA* V, 480)

> . . . the earth is cold,
> and the bird of night whirls
> uneasily before your eyes.
>
> (My translation)

In 'Brod und Wein', the speaker addresses the role of poetry 'in dürftiger Zeit' and notes the distance of the divine:

> . . . Zwar leben die Götter
>   Aber über dem Haupt droben in anderer Welt.
> . . . und scheinens wenig zu achten,
>   Ob wir leben . . .
>
> *(FHA* VI, 251)

> . . . Though the gods are living,
>   Over our heads they live, up in a different world.
> . . . and, such is their kind wish to spare us,
>   Little they seem to care whether we live . . .
>
> (*Poems and Fragments*, 269)

In 'Dichterberuf' (1800–1), an expansion of the 1798 'An unsre großen Dichter', human culture is dominated by instrumental rationality, which views and counts the stars only through the lens of the telescope. In that context, the poet's vocation is no longer associated with the approach of the gods, but with their absence.

The crisis of nature emerging in the poetry here reflects a problem that had occupied Hölderlin's theoretical strivings for some years. Proposing to write 'New Letters on the Aesthetic Education of Man', he writes:

> In den philosophischen Briefen will ich das Prinzip finden, das mir die Trennungen, in denen wir denken und existieren, erklärt, das aber auch vermögend ist, den Widerstreit verschwinden zu machen, den Widerstreit zwischen dem Subjekt und dem Objekt, zwischen unserem Selbst und der Welt. (*FHA* XIX, 249)
>
> In the philosophical letters, I want to find the principle which explains to me the divisions in which we think and exist, and yet which is also capable of eliminating the conflict, the conflict between subject and object, between our self and the world. (My translation)

This opposition of self and world is characteristic of modern philosophy from Descartes through the eighteenth century, and it reflects for Hölderlin the state of modern human culture as such. Cartesianism had been surpassed by a dynamic model of rationality in Leibniz, determining its object through reason's 'progressive integration with the realm of the sensible and the particular'.[10] For Leibniz the contingent truths of experience can only approximate the necessary truths of a priori reason; subsumption of particulars under concepts was the task of rationality. Kant argued that we could never know the world or the particulars of reality directly, but only as the mediated synthesis of sense data legislated by concepts of the understanding or intellect. Kant's philosophy demands, too, the division between theoretical and practical reason, or human knowledge of nature and of freedom. However much that division is to be bridged by the aesthetic, an unassuaged anxiety in Kant's thought about this very division has been traced to the persistence of longing in Hölderlin.[11]

Yet it is in Kant's aesthetics that Hölderlin finds a potential solution, for the experience of beauty allows at least a momentary and symbolic unification of these realms. For Kant, beauty, though it evades conceptual determination – for it is experienced as purposive without any concept of purpose able to be assigned to it – is experienced as a symbol of the morally good. A phenomenal or sensuous experience offers, then, a glimpse of – an analogue for – noumenal freedom, thus bridging theoretical and practical reason, nature and freedom, for a subject otherwise rendered asunder. In a rejected preface to the penultimate version of *Hyperion*, written *c*.1795, Hölderlin suggests that the striving to unify ourselves with nature is inspired by the 'infinite unification' [*unendliche Vereinigung*] (*StA* III, 237) found in beauty.

It may be less the symbolism of this union through beauty than the more direct vitality provoked in the aesthetic subject that stimulates Hölderlin's poetology. Kant argues that in experiencing beauty in nature or art, imagination and understanding engage a free play that does not determine sense under concepts; this is quickening for the subject, who experiences an enhanced feeling of life. I have described elsewhere how Hölderlin aims to enable such vitality through poetry and to theorise the operations of the poetic mind in these vital terms.[12] In the wake of *Hyperion*, Hölderlin aims for a poetic method that would enable language not only to replicate but to intuit the vitality in nature, a concern extended to his own poetry which 'must turn toward life, liveliness, and reality'.[13] The feeling of life connects the human being with the primal organisation of nature as self-differentiating unity.

This motivates what I would be tempted to call Hölderlin's biopoetics, were it not for the recurrence of a more tragic element, an elegiac tone, that recurs in Hölderlin and reveals what has been called a 'fundamental preoccupation, even obsession, with separation and division, with borderlines'.[14] The persistence of longing in Hölderlin has been identified with multiple causes: Oedipal losses (his father having died at two and his stepfather at seven),[15] the estranging nature of language,[16] modern disenchantment, class division or the defeat of human aspiration to live the ideal.[17] Yet the cognitive roots of this division at least lie in the nature of human consciousness itself. This, I will suggest, will be echoed in Rilke's suggestion that human consciousness, by representing reality and fixing its presence conceptually, is turned against nature in the manner of one always departing.

We can see the philosophical basis for this motif in Hölderlin's reaction to the subjective idealism of Fichte's *Wissenschaftslehre*, his critique of Fichte's absolute first principle 'I = I', according to which the subject is said to generate the object of knowledge. In the spring of 1775 (when Hölderlin was in Jena where he attended Fichte's lectures), Hölderlin writes 'Seyn, Urtheil, Modalität' ('Being, Judgement, Modality/Possibility') on the endpaper of a book, arguing essentially that subjectivity can never ground knowledge of being, because it is preceded genetically and logically by that which subtends the division (in 'I = I') in the first place. For Hölderlin knowledge or predication (judgement) already implies a separation, the loss of a primordial unity. Subjective idealism, which seeks the truth of the object in rationality itself, is not only an impossible grounding for philosophy, but a philosophical expression of a tragic human condition. In the same 1795 preface mentioned earlier, Hölderlin writes:

> Die seelige Einigkeit, das Seyn, im einzigen Sinne des Worts, ist für uns verloren und wir mußten es verlieren, wenn wir es erstreben, erringen sollten. Wir reißen uns los vom friedlichen Hen Kai Pan der Welt, um es herzustellen, durch uns Selbst. (*StA*, III, 236)
>
> The blissful oneness, Being, in the singular sense of the word, is lost to us, and we had to lose it so that we should be able to strive for it and attain it. We tear ourselves loose from the peaceful Hen Kai Pan of the world in order to erect it as our own. (My translation)

This erection of the world as if it belongs to the subject will be expressed in the hubris of Empedocles, in having held nature in his sway, and Hölderlin considers tragedy the metaphor of an intellectual intuition. The goal of human striving is to reconcile this split, reconfigure to attunement between self and world. But any reconciliation will turn out to be realised only in an 'infinite approximation'. We never reach the point of unity, he writes, 'Where everything is One' [*wo Alles Eins ist*], rather 'the determinate line is united with the indeterminate one in infinite approximation' [*die bestimmte Linie vereinigt sich mit der unbestimmten nur in unendlicher Annäherung*] (*StA* III, 236). The achievement of what Hölderlin describes as 'Innigkeit' or inwardness would ever be only 'an accidental glimpse into a past that was never quite present' (*StA* III, 235).[18] Rilke's interest in interiority, including its articulation as 'Weltinnenraum', can now be examined in Hölderlinian poetological terms.

Rilkean Nature and Poetic Consciousness

Rilke's poetry, though often ecstatic, engages the tragic tone set by Hölderlin regarding the opposition between modern human consciousness and nature. While Hölderlin, in 'Die Eichenbäume', distinguishes the garden from the forest, or domesticated nature from a nature independent of human life, Rilke addresses nature primarily in human contexts. The *New Poems* (*Neue Gedichte*) treat domestic garden plants such as roses and hydrangeas, animals that may be encountered in city parks – the swan, the cat – or, in the case of the panther, an urban zoo, while in Rilke's novel, the sounds of a dog bellowing and a rooster crowing soothe

the nerves of a protagonist overwhelmed by the noise, traffic and urban crowds of Paris. It is not on the basis of the distance from human dwelling or activity, but by the way it has been contained, literally and epistemologically, within human frameworks, that Rilke distinguishes nature. Nature is often inseparable from art in Rilke, notwithstanding his concern, in an early essay, for the human construction of nature as aesthetic object, and of the resulting 'becoming landscape of the world' [*Landschaft-Werden der Welt*].[19] While individual natural beings may be intimately described, it is with awareness of loss that his speaker in the Elegies calls upon the more general animal life ('Kreatur'), or indeed the earth ('Erde') itself.[20] Rilke's awareness of the human threat to nature emerges somewhat belatedly in his reflections, in the *Sonette an Orpheus* (*Sonnets to Orpheus*) (1922), as his speaker despairs of the machine age. The poems of *Duineser Elegien* (*Duino Elegies*), completed in the same month as the *Sonnets*, criticise calculating representational consciousness that estranges humans from nature. These works bring Rilke into the orbit of the Hölderlinian concerns outlined in the first part of this essay, and it may be through Hölderlin that Rilke's poetic alternatives to modern alienation can be critically examined.

Rilke's understanding of nature is long in development. Interest in the natural world as the environmental surroundings of human life is first expressed in early prose works that discuss landscape painting.[21] Rilke ponders the depiction of landscape in the Renaissance, where nature appears as the background glowing behind human figures like 'a common soul' [*eine gemeinsame Seele*], suggesting harmony of the human with the surrounding natural world.[22] The background of the painting, Rilke suggests, expresses an encompassing reality 'wo Alle Einer sind'[23] – a phrase inevitably echoing Hyperion's rapturous praise of nature as *hen kai pan*. As human figures begin to disappear from landscape scenes in painting, Rilke suggests, nature itself seems to have absorbed human meaning, as if the world itself were transformed into landscape. While this may be a triumph for artistic representation, it comes at the cost of the anthropomorphisation of nature, of its distinctiveness from the human. It goes hand in hand with this that modern humanity, with its technological hegemony, has lost the feeling for the rhythms of natural time and the proximity and distances of natural space. In suggesting that the common ground between things and human beings has withdrawn, Rilke echoes Hyperion in his bereftness; for in such a situation, the human being is 'infinitely alone' [*unendlich allein*].[24] Rilke's reference in these writings to a common unity of human beings with other things of nature recalls Hölderlin's understanding of being as a unity that precedes division between subject and object, or self and world, and his poetological attempts to render, by way of an askew perspective, glimpses of that unity. Hölderlin, however, seems to come to the conclusion that we experience such unity only through recognition of its loss – and thus we can make sense of his emphasis on both tragedy and on the memorialising work, or *Andenken*, of the poet.

One of Rilke's more innovative strategies in registering this sense of loss is through a juxtaposition between the human being and the animal, contending that 'Mit allen Augen sieht die Kreatur / das Offene' ('with all its eyes the animal sees / the open').[25] In a passage of the *Elegies* vigorously criticised by Heidegger for its 'monstrous humanization' of the animal' and provoking much scholarly debate,[26] Rilke suggests that the human being is barred from the pure perception of nature, while the animal perceives 'ungrasped, and without regard to its own state, pure' [*ungefasst und ohne Blick / auf seinen Zustand, rein*].[27] We might here consider this motif as an adaptation of a Hölderlinian vision, with Rilke displacing the ecstatic side of Hyperion's still romantic, polarised consciousness onto the animal. Just as Hyperion, having tasted the bliss of felt belonging, laments the state of being excluded from nature, Rilke's speaker in the *Elegies* laments that human beings, set apart from nature, only see it with inverted eyes. While Hyperion describes being hurled down by a moment of reflection, Rilke's speaker diagnoses reflective consciousness as an obstacle to pure seeing:

> Die Schöpfung immer zugewendet, sehen
> wir nur auf ihr die Spiegelung des Frein,
> von uns verdunkelt.
>
> Always turned toward creation, in it
> we see only the reflection of the open
> Darkened by ourselves.[28]

Instead of an intuition of unity, of Hölderlin's *hen kai pan*, human consciousness is piecemeal, for we take, Rilke writes in the *Sonnets*, 'pieces and parts, as if they were the whole' [*Stückwerk und Teile, als sei es das Ganze*].[29] Modern consciousness, Rilke argues, pursues nature with maps and machines, wheels and boilers and hammers. We set down – in the earth as well as in our thoughts – only straight, calculated lines, rather than lovely meandering paths. Modern consciousness registers being only as positive presence, rather than including the full natural cycles of life and death.

Rilke follows Hölderlin, too, in associating modern alienation from nature with the loss of the gods, and in reckoning with the modern predicament through the poetic mediation of ancient Greece. Hölderlin writes repeatedly of Empedocles – in poetry, in a theoretical essay and in attempts at a tragic drama – while Rilke composes his sonnet cycles – arguably his most accomplished poetry – under the figuration of Orpheus, the legendary poet who was able to charm all natural beings with his song. Although differing from Hölderlin in his investment in a mythical past, Rilke may too be read as a poet of remembrance. The *Sonnets* are devoted both to a poet from a lost age and to a contemporary dancer who died in her youth, and the restoration of finitude to our grasp of reality seems to be one of their principal aims. In this the poetic consciousness remains in service to the world in its fullest rendering, including death as nature's other side.

But how can modern poetic language, lacking Orphic lyre and the ancient association of nature with the sacred, overcome the obstacles of calculative representation, the disenchantment of the machine age, to enable a communion with nature as more than positively reckoned presence? Hölderlin's solution to this problem, as we have seen, involves attempts to thematise the ever-askew perspective, vigilance about the tragic excesses of inwardness, and the indirect evocations of poetic remembrance that are not without risk for the poet so exposed. If for Hölderlin the tragic situation of human consciousness is overcome only indirectly, Rilke attempts to construct another orientation to nature through a modern Orphic poeticisation. In the *Sonnets* the earth is said to have learned poetry by heart, from poems, as it were, printed on its stems and roots.[30] The earth, it is suggested, responds to us differently when we poetise, and it is through a poetical attention that we can realise the full dimensionality of nature. Poetising serves then not only as a means to recover a lost nature, but to draw nature forth as present in the fullest sense. Yet for Rilke, this poetical attention will require both interiorisation and invention on the part of the poet.[31]

One example that bears comparison to Hölderlin is Rilke's opening sonnet, in which the Orphic motif – indeed the very idea of poetising nature – is introduced by the image of a tree, evoked in what seems to be a straightforward indicative description: 'Da stieg ein Baum' ('There rose a tree'). The tree is recognised in the upward momentum that might evoke its growth, and immediately associated, in the next sentence of the first line, with transcendence. While Hölderlin's rendering of oaks in 'Die Eichenbäume' generates multiple metaphors for the trees suggesting their divinity, and implicitly includes all of the Empedoclean roots or elements in his description, the trees are nevertheless also described in their own right, in distinction from human society and its forms of cultivation. The tree of Rilke's first Orphic sonnet, in contrast, serves as a metaphor for poetic listening, and is interiorised in the second line: 'O Orpheus singing! O tall tree in the ear' [*O Orpheus singt! O hoher Baum im Ohr!*].[32] Reading the full force of this metaphor, it would seem that the tree appears in and through the song; the tree rises in the ear because it is no more (and no less) than what can be conjured by the poetic voice. While Hölderlin's speaker, by the end of 'Die Eichenbäume', chooses to leave the trees to rejoin human society, in Rilke's sonnet there is no recognition of the tree, or the forest which is conjured along with it, as separate from poetic consciousness. The recognition of a natural world outside poetic song arises later in the *Sonnets*, but only as surveyed and carved up by human technology.

The problem as to the status of the natural world outside human consciousness becomes more intriguing when we recall what may be Rilke's most celebrated poetic idea, the notion of 'world's inner space' [*Weltinnenraum*], which he had begun to formulate nearly a decade before writing the sonnets. With *Weltinnenraum*, it seems, Rilke attempts to overcome the division, as Hölderlin called it, 'between subject and object, our self and the world'. The idea behind Rilke's notion emerges in the essay 'Erlebnis' (1913), in which Rilke narrates an ecstatic experience wherein the vibrations from a tree and a bird in flight are felt so intimately by a human consciousness, it is as if subject and object had merged. This fusion is not complete, however, for in the effort to describe a space 'where everything is One' [*wo Alle Einer sind*], to repeat Rilke's earlier formulation cited above, Rilke contends with the difficulty of unifying different forms of extension. The tree can be felt as it were entering the subject through its physically proximal vibrations, but the bird is at an aerial distance. To capture this, Rilke briefly renders what might be phenomenologically identified as two distinctive experiences, such that the object that physically touches the subject (the tree and its vibrations) can be felt inside, as if wholly intimate with the subject, while in the case of the bird, consciousness must imaginatively merge outwardly, so that it feels at one with its flight.[33] The term 'Weltinnenraum' itself appears in an untitled poem from the following year, in which the speaker longs – again recalling the longings of Hyperion – for an unlimited unification with nature. Here the duality remaining in the 'Erlebnis' incident is resolved by reference to an encompassing space, a world-interior, extending through all beings: 'Durch alle Wesen reicht der eine Raum: Weltinnenraum' [*Through all beings extends the one space: world's inner space*].[34] The bird in flight and the tree are both evoked again here, but in ways that are compatibly interior to the subject: 'the birds fly silently / through us . . . and in me grows the tree' [*die Vögel fliegen still / durch uns hindurch . . . und in mir wächst der Baum*].[35] While in the essay Rilke needed the narrative form to describe the movement, reversal and communion of subject and object, in the poem we find a condensation or reduction of this theme into a single spatial concept that is to encompass all of the natural world and consciousness itself.

Weltinnenraum (world's inner space) could then be described as (and it is usually taken to mean) the imaginative envelopment of world within the interior of consciousness. On the conventional reading – and even on a carefully phenomenological explication[36] – the world is taken, we might say, into the shelter of the poetic 'I' or 'me'. If the tree and the bird are poetised as interior to consciousness, the division between self and world has been overcome. Through such poetry we may encounter the world apart from such divisions; we can recover an intimacy and communion with things; the common environment or background that we share with the world will be manifest along with consciousness itself. Nature, in such rendering, is no longer estranged, no longer mechanistic, but re-enchanted with the feeling of life. 'Nowhere . . . will there be world, as inside' [*Nirgends . . . wird Welt sein, als innen*], Rilke writes in the seventh of the *Elegies*.[37] Consciousness, for its part, will have to be, or will have been, transformed.

The problematic nature of this solution may be most aptly described in the Hölderlinian framework set out in the first part of this essay. For Hölderlin's critique of subjective idealism rested on the imbalance between subject and object, and an insistence on that which preceded their division as inaccessible to subjectivity in all but an analeptic mode. The absorption of world into the self on this rendering of *Weltinnenraum* would repeat, albeit in poetical terms, Fichte's error of conceiving the relation between subject and object from the side of subjectivity. With the notion of *Weltinnenraum* Rilke seems to take up, as Rochelle Tobias has argued, an egological rather than an ecological point of view.[38] The speaker's declaration that 'in mir wächst der Baum' – an internalisation ('in mir') repeated twice in the poem's final stanza – seems to come dangerously close to an Empedoclean hubris, which Hölderlin described as an excess of inwardness, an imbalance restored only on pain of self-sacrifice on the part of the poet. The concept of *Weltinnenraum* so understood would also confirm Heidegger's assessment that Rilke, after all, remains too 'metaphysical' – by which he means tethered to an anthropocentric understanding of consciousness such as epitomised in the philosophy of Descartes – to serve as essential poetry in a destitute time.[39]

In responding to this as a Hölderlinian problematic in Rilke, we may first of all ask whether an egological orientation to nature – however much Heidegger insists upon the absence of the human perspective from poetry and primordial language – may be unavoidable not just for Rilke and the modern poet but for poetic consciousness as such. Hölderlin himself seems to appreciate the persistence of the possibility of poetic hubris, not only through the characterisation of Empedocles, but through repeated suggestions in his poems of being cast down and left behind by nature and language itself, as when the earth lies 'speechless and cold' [*sprachlos und kalt*] (*Poems and Fragments*, 393). In this light we might interpret the poem 'Hälfte des Lebens' – which presents, in two stanzas, sharply contrasting images of summer vitality and the cold lifelessness of winter – as reflecting dual possibilities for poetic consciousness. The metaphor of the two seasons would not primarily convey the polarisation of ancient and modern culture, or the human chronology of youth and age, or as biographically reflecting the halves of Hölderlin's life in respective sanity and mental breakdown, nor the poetical resistance to synthesis, as in Adorno's account of the poem as paratactic.[40] Rather, the poem would present two possibilities for poetic consciousness itself: warm intimacy with nature, or a mind left alone with its own dead images. In Rilkean terms, the summer of that poem renders the vitality of the 'Open', while winter images evoke the human consciousness turned away from it, in the manner of having departed.

If *Weltinnenraum* raises a Hölderlinian problematic, we may consider another possible rendering of the notion, by attending to other moments in Rilke's writings where innerness or interiority and world are together evoked, and where the relation of subject and object is more ambiguous than interiorisation within the subject. For evocations of innerness or interiority as related to world may elsewhere suggest a reciprocal demand for the externalisation of consciousness in the midst of things. Rilke's repeated use of the imperative form of the verb 'werfen' in combination with interiority suggests an effort of projection on the part of the poetic consciousness toward a world or nature which remains other to it. In an untitled poem of 1924, for example, Rilke evokes the concept of inner space ('Innenraum'). Here we find, as in both the 1914 poem and in 'Erlebnis', images of a bird in flight and, in the following stanza, of a tree.

> Raum greift aus uns und übersetzt die Dinge:
> daß dir das Dasein eines Baums gelinge,
> wirf Innenraum um ihn, aus jenem Raum,
> der in dir west. Umgieb ihn mit Verhaltung.
> Er grenzt sich nicht. Erst in der Eingestaltung
> in dein Verzichten wird er wirklich Baum.[41]

> Space reaches from us and translates things:
> That you succeed with existence of a tree
> Throw inner space around it, from that space
> That is present in you. Surround it with restraint.
> It does not border itself. Not until it is formed
> In your renouncing does it truly become tree.

Here the thought of *Innenraum* does not evoke containment but, first of all, a form of translation. Poetic consciousness – or that of the reader – is instructed, not to take in world into the shelter of consciousness, but rather to project interiority outward ('wirf Innenraum um ihn'). While

Rilke's speaker identifies this (inner) space as reaching from the human subject – not unlike Kant's contention that space, along with time, are forms of intuition generated by the productive imagination[42] – the projection is, at the same time, a kind of renouncing. The formulation is admittedly ambiguous: the phrase 'Surround it with restraint' [*Umgieb ihn mit Verhaltung*] is undoubtedly an instruction, indicating the mode of translation that is to be enacted by consciousness, which (in Kantian fashion) would provide the perceptual coherence, the *Eingestaltung*, of the object by giving it spatial limits. The tree is, after all, said not to provide its own borders ('Er grenzt sich nicht'), and then presumably needs human consciousness to recognise, indeed to supply them. Yet the restraint may also be read as on the side of consciousness. Only in restraining itself, in *Verhaltung*, does consciousness realise, or respect, the boundaries that make the tree really ('wirklich') what it is. Only through consciousness holding back, in renouncing or *Verzichten*, can the tree be fully realised in the shelter of poetic recognition. In a stance of at once giving or projecting and in holding back or renouncing, may consciousness bring them to realisation.

We can thus consider a poetic mode, an attunement or attitude to the natural world, that allows for both unity with the world and individuation, both of consciousness and of things. *Weltinnenraum* would be accordingly achieved as a projected interiority that renders intimacy within things, but maintains their boundaries, their distance. This may be a matter less of providing to, than of recognising in, the things of the world, of nature, an inwardness – a depth irreducible to calculable materiality. Such inwardness would be in modern, Cartesian thought denied to the material world, to nature, and reserved for consciousness alone.

Conclusion

Like Hölderlin, Rilke explores poetic alternatives to the human objectification of nature through the idea of a distinctly poetic consciousness. Both can be read as contributions not only to a 'contemplative ecology',[43] but to a poetic critique of the possibilities for our reckoning with nature. The recognition of a more ambiguous form of *Weltinnenraum* and the possibility of conceiving a world-oriented interiority undermine the philosophical segregation of Rilke from Hölderlin established by Heidegger's interpretations. Rilke's rendering of nature and poetic consciousness has been criticised by Heidegger as metaphysically Cartesian and as anthropocentric, in contrast with a more essential relation to nature, and all but abandonment of subjectivity in Hölderlin.[44] At the same time, however, Hölderlin has been tied by Heidegger to a nationalist attachment to the local earth, to nature as geopolitical *Heimat*, which overlooks the critique of hubris and the tragic nature of Hölderlin's thought.[45] We have seen, however, that Hölderlin's consideration of nature, like that of Rilke, turns on the understanding and form of human consciousness.

Rilke's own address to Hölderlin seems to affirm an ecological orientation to the poetic task. His poem 'An Hölderlin' urges that the inheritance of the poet, indeed his poetic immortality, should draw us back to the earth. But the earth Rilke renders is not merely a local *Heimat*, anchored in the soil of ancestors. While other poets rest content in their cosy poems, content with their narrow similes, merely taking part, Rilke writes, Hölderlin is a wandering spirit. He migrates like the moon across the sky, illuminating and darkening the world below with his passage:

> . . . Du nur
> ziehst wie der Mond. Und unten hellt und verdunkelt
> deine Nächtliche sich, die heilig erschrockene Landschaft,
> die du in Abschieden fühlst.
>
> . . . only you
> move like the moon. And the nocturnal landscape below you,
> Your holy terrified landscape, brightens and darkens
> And in farewells you feel it.[46]

The poetic consciousness he attributes to Hölderlin is, like his late formulation of 'Innenraum', a matter of renunciation and giving:

> . . . Keiner
> gab sie erhabener hin, gab sie ans Ganze
> heiler zurück, unbedürftiger.
>
> . . . No other
> ever gave it away more sublimely, gave it back to the Whole
> more fully, more ungraspingly.[47]

Notes

1. One exception is Rudolf Schier, 'Trees and Transcendence', pp. 331–41. More recently, Hannah Vandegrift Eldridge takes up the two poets in a common study of the notion of poetic community, but her attention is 'to show how each, in historically and individually specific ways, takes up the problem of orienting finite, mortal subjects within an uncertain and sometimes hostile world', and 'not to argue comparatively about the two poets', as she explains in *Lyric Orientations*, pp. 2, 122.
2. Hölderlin's influence on 'Fünf Gesänge' and 'Seele im Raum' are discussed by Ryan, *Rilke, Modernism, and the Poetic Tradition*, pp. 98–155.
3. Their common sense of and response to modern alienation is discussed by Ryan, *Rilke, Modernism*, p. 152, and in Eldridge, *Lyric Orientations*.

4. See Gosetti-Ferencei, *Heidegger, Hölderlin, and the Subject of Poetic Language*, p. 115.
 5. See *Empedocles*, p. xvi, and Charles Bambach, *Thinking the Poetic Measure of Justice*, pp. 29–30.
 6. See 'General Introduction', in *Empedocles*, p. 14.
 7. Spencer, 'Divine Difference', p. 454.
 8. See Schier, 'Trees and Transcendence', pp. 331–41.
 9. The quote is from Pahl, *Tropes of Transport: Hegel and Emotion*, p. 252, fn. 34. See also Rudolph Schier, 'Trees and Transcendence', who associates Hölderlin's poem with a diagnosis of 'the spiritual predicament of man', p. 332. Adrian del Caro reads the poem in terms of Hölderlin's ambivalence about sociality, *Hölderlin: The Poetics of Being* (Detroit: Wayne State University Press, 1991), pp. 25–6. Hölderlin's striving for freedom and independence, particularly from the philosophical influence of Schiller, is emphasised by Nick Hoff, 'Introduction', p. xiv, Emery George, 'Miklós Radnóti and Friedrich Hölderlin', p. 102, and Momme Mommsen, 'Hölderlins Lösung von Schiller', pp. 203–44, especially 221–3.
10. Pfau, 'Critical Introduction', p. 3.
11. Richard Eldridge, *The Persistence of Romanticism*, p. 37.
12. See Gosetti-Ferencei, *Heidegger, Hölderlin, and the Subject of Poetic Language*, pp. 144–70.
13. Waibel, 'From the Metaphysis of the Beautiful to the Metaphysics of the True', p. 419.
14. Santner, *Friedrich Hölderlin*, p. 49.
15. Santner, 'Introduction', in *Hyperion*, p. xxiv.
16. De Man, 'Intentional Structure of the Romantic Image', pp. 65–77.
17. Eldridge, *The Persistence of Romanticism*, p. 32, pp. 44–8.
18. Pfau, 'Critical Introduction', p. 26.
19. Rilke, *Sämtliche Werke in sechs Bänden*, vol. V, p. 522.
20. Rilke, *Duino Elegies/Duineser Elegien*, pp. 46 and 56.
21. See Gosetti-Ferencei, 'Interstitial Space in Rilke's Short Prose Works', pp. 302–24.
22. Rilke, *Kommentierte Ausgabe*, vol. IV, pp. 103–4.
23. Ibid. vol. IV, p. 104.
24. Ibid. vol. IV, p. 213.
25. Rilke, *Duino Elegies*, pp. 46–7, translation modified.
26. Heidegger, *Parmenides*, p. 152. Giorgio Agamben responds by identifying the animal substrate of human beings exposed to what remains unrevealed, such as in captivation of our attention and in boredom, in *The Open: Man and Animal*, pp. 64–8. Eric L. Santner conceives Heidegger's critique of Rilke's notion in terms of strife of concealment and unconcealment, and thus in political terms, in *On Creaturely Life*, pp. 6–13. Derrida criticises Heidegger's subordination of the animal to Dasein and the related contention that animals are poor in world, in *The Animal That Therefore I Am*.
27. Rilke, *Duino Elegies*, pp. 48–9.
28. Ibid. pp. 46–8.
29. Rilke, *Sonnets to Orpheus*, pp. 46–7. Translations from this source are occasionally modified.
30. Ibid. pp. 56–7.
31. See Gosetti-Ferencei, 'Imaginative Ecologies'.
32. Rilke, *Sonnets to Orpheus*, p. 17.
33. Rilke, *Kommentierte Ausgabe*, vol. IV, p. 1027.
34. Ibid. vol. II, p. 113.
35. Ibid. vol. II, p. 113.
36. See Tobias, 'Ecology and Egology', pp. 218–22.
37. Rilke, *Kommentierte Ausgabe*, vol. II, p. 221.
38. Tobias, 'Ecology and Egology', pp. 218–22.
39. Heidegger, 'Wozu Dichter?', p. 300.
40. Theodor Adorno, 'Parataxis', pp. 109–52.

41. Rilke, *Kommentierte Ausgabe*, vol. II, p. 363, my translation.
42. Käte Hamburger first made this connection in 'Die Kategorie des Raumes in Rilkes Lyrik', pp. 35–42, esp. 40, 41.
43. Douglas E. Christie defines contemplative ecology as the effort 'to identify our deepest feeling for the natural world as part of a spiritual longing', in *The Blue Sapphire of the Mind*, p. 3.
44. Heidegger, 'Wozu Dichter?', pp. 269–320.
45. See Gosetti-Ferencei, *Heidegger, Hölderlin, and the Subject of Poetic Language*.
46. Rilke, 'To Hölderlin', p. 448.
47. Ibid. p. 449.

Bibliography

Adorno, Theodor, 'Parataxis: On Hölderlin's Late Poetry' in Adorno, *Notes to Literature*, ed. Rolf Tiedemann, trans. Shierry Weber Nicholsen (New York: Columbia University Press, 1992), vol. 2, pp. 109–52.

Agamben, Giorgio, *The Open: Man and Animal*, trans. Kevin Attell (Stanford: Stanford University Press, 2004).

Bambach, Charles, *Thinking the Poetic Measure of Justice: Hölderlin, Heidegger, Celan* (Albany: SUNY Press, 2013).

Christie, Douglas E., *The Blue Sapphire of the Mind: Notes Toward a Contemplative Ecology* (New York: Oxford University Press, 2012).

De Man, Paul, 'Intentional Structure of the Romantic Image', in Harold Bloom (ed.), *Romanticism and Consciousness: Essays in Criticism* (New York: W. W. Norton, 1970), pp. 65–77.

Del Caro, Adrian, *Hölderlin: The Poetics of Being* (Detroit: Wayne State University Press, 1991).

Derrida, Jacques, *The Animal That Therefore I Am*, ed. Marie-Louise Mallet, trans. David Wills (New York: Fordham University Press, 2008).

Eldridge, Hannah Vandegrift, *Lyric Orientations: Hölderlin, Rilke, and the Poetics of Community* (Ithaca, NY: Cornell University Press, 2015).

Eldridge, Richard, *The Persistence of Romanticism: Essays in Philosophy and Literature* (Cambridge: Cambridge University Press, 2001).

George, Emery, 'Miklós Radnóti and Friedrich Hölderlin as Readers of the Book of Nahum', *Hungarian Studies*, 5: 1 (1989), pp. 91–118.

Gosetti-Ferencei, Jennifer Anna, 'Interstitial Space in Rilke's Short Prose Works', *German Quarterly*, 80: 3 (2007), pp. 302–24.

Gosetti-Ferencei, Jennifer Anna, *Heidegger, Hölderlin, and the Subject of Poetic Language: Toward a New Poetics of Dasein* (New York: Fordham University Press, 2004).

Gosetti-Ferencei, Jennifer, 'Imaginative Ecologies in Rilke's Sonnets to Orpheus', in *Rilke's Sonnets to Orpheus: Philosophical and Critical Perspectives*, ed. Hannah Eldridge and Luke Fischer (Oxford: Oxford University Press, 2019).

Hamburger, Käte, 'Die Kategorie des Raumes in Rilkes Lyrik', *Blätter der Rilke-Gesellschaft*, 15 (1988), pp. 35–42.

Heidegger, Martin, 'Wozu Dichter?' in Heidegger, *Holzwege*, ed. F. W. von Hermann (Frankfurt am Main: Vittorio Klostermann, 1977), pp. 269–320.

Heidegger, Martin, *Parmenides*, trans. André Schuwer and Richar Rojcewicz (Bloomington, IN: Indiana University Press, 1998).

Heidegger, Martin, 'Hölderlin and the Essence of Poetry', in *Elucidations of Hölderlin's Poetry*, trans. Keith Hoeller (Amherst, NY: Humanity Books, 2000), pp. 51–65.

Hoff, Nick, 'Introduction', *Friedrich Hölderlin, Odes and Elegies*, ed. and trans. Nick Hoff (Middletown, CT: Wesleyan University Press, 2008), pp. xi–xxvi.

Mommsen, Momme, 'Hölderlins Lösung von Schiller: Zu Hölderlins Gedichten "An Herkules" und "Die Eichenbäume" und den Übersetzungen aus Ovid, Vergil und Euripides', *Jahrbuch der Deutschen Schillergesellschaft*, 9 (1965), pp. 203–44.
Pahl, Katrin, *Tropes of Transport: Hegel and Emotion* (Evanston, IL: Northwestern University Press, 2012).
Pfau, Thomas, 'Critical Introduction', *Friedrich Hölderlin, Essays and Letters on Theory*, ed. and trans. Thomas Pfau (Albany: SUNY Press, 1988), pp. 1–32.
Rilke, Rainer Maria, 'To Hölderlin / An Hölderlin', trans. David Luke, in Angel Flores (ed.), *An Anthology of German Poetry from Hölderlin to Rilke* (New York: Doubleday, 1960), pp. 48–9.
Rilke, Rainer Maria, *Duino Elegies/Duineser Elegien Bilingual Edition*, trans. Edward Snow (New York: North Point Press, 2000).
Rilke, Rainer Maria, *Kommentierte Ausgabe in vier Bänden*, ed. Manfred Engel and Ulrich Fülleborn, 4 vols (Frankfurt am Main: Insel Verlag, 1996).
Rilke, Rainer Maria, *Sämtliche Werke in sechs Bänden*, ed. Ruth Sieber-Rilke and Ernst Zinn, 6 vols (Frankfurt am Main: Insel, 1955–66).
Rilke, Rainer Maria, *Sonnets to Orpheus, Bilingual Edition*, trans. M. D. Herder Norton (New York: W. W. Norton, 1942).
Ryan, Judith, *Rilke, Modernism, and the Poetic Tradition* (Cambridge: Cambridge University Press, 2004).
Santner, Eric L., *Friedrich Hölderlin: Narrative Vigilance and the Poetic Imagination* (New Brunswick, NJ: Rutgers University Press, 1986).
Santner, Eric L., *On Creaturely Life: Rilke, Benjamin, Sebald* (Chicago: University of Chicago Press, 2006).
Schier, Rudolf, 'Trees and Transcendence: Hölderlin's "Die Eichenbäume and Rilke's "Herbst"', *German Life and Letters*, 20: 4 (1967), pp. 331–41.
Spencer, Tom, 'Divine Difference: On the Theological Divide between Hölderlin and Hegel', *German Quarterly*, 84: 4 (2011), pp. 437–56.
Tobias, Rochelle, 'Ecology and Egology: Husserl and Rilke on the Natural World', *The Yearbook of Comparative Literature*, vol. 58 (2012), pp. 218–22.
Waibel, Violetta L., 'From the Metaphysis of the Beautiful to the Metaphysics of the True: Hölderlin's Philosophy in the Horizon of Poetry', trans. Christina M. Geschwandter, in Matthew C. Altman (ed.), *The Palgrave Handbook of German Idealism* (New York: Palgrave, 2014), pp. 409–33.

Chapter 3

Raging with Care: The Poet's Liquid Fire

Katrin Pahl

This essay considers Hölderlin's transformative engagement with the cosmology or natural philosophy of the Presocratic thinker Empedocles in his tragic play *Empedocles*. Tracing a round dance between the natural elements (in particular the motifs of liquid and fire), the poetic tones (specifically the convergence of rage and care, and their relation to strife and love) and two models for the poet (Achilles and Empedocles), it explores the possibly queer logic of 'harmonious opposition' in Hölderlin's poetics and philosophy of nature.

The ancient Empedocles wrote philosophical poetry, of which only fragments are preserved. He was the first to suggest that there are four elements that combine to form the cosmos. Besides these, he recognises two forces as agents of cosmic change – love (the power of attraction) and strife (the force of repulsion). So goes the usual summary, at least, which takes the Empedoclean elements for independent and changeless essences. However, the textual evidence looks quite different and presents a much less mechanistic picture. Hölderlin was alive to the vibrancy of the Empedoclean cosmos and plays it up in his tragedy *Empedocles* and other writings engaging the poet-philosopher.

Fragment B6 provides the most explicit evidence of four primary elements in Empedoclean cosmology:

> The four roots of all things hear first:
> Shining Zeus, life-giving Hera, Aidoneus,
> and Nestis, who by her tears moistens the mortal spring.[1]

While the number four appears here, Empedocles does not actually speak of elements, but of roots (*rhízōmata*).[2] This suggests a more dynamic, organic and self-actuating process than the Aristotelian language of 'elements'. Aristotle's profound influence on the history of philosophy at times distorts our understanding of the Presocratics. By way of his disciple Theophrastus, Aristotle's interpretation of Empedocles as the philosopher of earth, water, air and fire has become the dominant one, even though Aristotle, who finds in Empedocles the historical prefiguration of his own conception of the material principles of bodies, to a certain extent projects his own philosophy onto Empedocles.[3]

Granted, Empedocles does at times paint a rather mechanical picture of the various unions of the different 'roots' that produce the world or cosmos – or what Hölderlin calls 'nature'. Here is, for example, the Empedoclean description of the formation of the animal skeleton:

> Pleasant earth in well-wrought crucibles
> got two parts of glittering Nestis, out of its eight parts,
> and four from Hephaestus; and white bones were produced,
> joined by the marvelous glue of Harmony.[4]

The element earth is mentioned here and with this piece of the puzzle in hand one can decode Nestis as the personification of water and Hephaestus as fire. What follows from this is a description of the production of bone from two parts earth, two parts water and four parts fire. The passage, then, paints a picture not so much of roots growing together out of mutual affection but of elements mixed in a crucible with a pinch of Harmony for better cohesion. Nevertheless, the reader's impulse to decipher and de-personify Empedocles' insight in verse might be misguided, even more so since he originally introduces the roots as deities. Hence, these deities are not personifications or figures for literal, profane and inert material, but instead the roots are conceived as dynamic, self-actuating powers, that is deities. And perhaps it is only the absence of the fourth root in this example, namely 'life-giving Hera', as the first quotation had it, that renders this particular combination so mechanical and devoid of life, producing only dead bone.

The juxtaposition of both fragments shows that Empedocles does not exactly produce a straightforward taxonomy of nature. Fragment B6 gives the names of four deities: Zeus, Hera, Aidoneus and Nestis. Fragment B96 provides three names but only two of them designate elements or roots: Nestis and Hephaestus. This fragment thus adds a fifth root deity, so we have Zeus, Hera, Aidoneus, Nestis and Hephaestus. Hephaestus is the god of fire and the forge. Shining Zeus might be the luminous sky; he also wields the lightning bolt, that is to say he hurls fire from the sky. Nestis is a Sicilian water goddess. Aidoneus is a version of Aides or Hades – the god of the underworld, the earth. And Hera?

If we assume (with Aristotle) that the four elements are earth, water, air and fire, then air is still missing from the picture (unless the sky god Zeus figures air). Across the history of his reception, Empedocles' four (or five) root deities have been interpreted in vastly different and at times opposing ways (for example, Hades has been read as earth and then as air and Hera was considered air and then earth).[5] Michael Shaw argues – and references Hölderlin as someone who understood Empedocles better than Aristotle[6] – that the fourth Empedoclean root is actually ether. He reads the four roots as earth (Aidoneus), water (Nestis), fire (Zeus) and ether ('live-giving Hera').[7]

In Presocratic philosophy and cosmology, *aether* or *aither* names the upper air, the outer layer of the cosmos – a stratum of bright, dry and fiery air, distinct from the lower, earthly air that is comparatively moist or misty. Even though extremely fine, ether is material; the sun and the superlunary stars are made of the fiery substance. Presocratic ether thus differs from the metaphysical or spiritual fifth element, or quintessence, that Aristotle introduces under the same name. Ether or 'life-giving Hera' generates life on earth. While the ideas of so-called Orphism have not been dated with any certainty,[8] the fifth Orphic hymn, 'To Ether', describes ether as 'life-spark for every creature'.[9] Shaw sees ether as that Empedoclean root that adds life to a body, 'playing the role soon to be fulfilled by an immaterial Platonic or Aristotelian soul'.[10]

It strikes me as a sign of a pre- or non-patriarchal world view that Empedocles – who establishes no hierarchy between his four roots (two of them male, two female) – might consider Hera the goddess of ether. As the dominant cosmology establishes a hierarchy between gods and goddesses, the element tends to be personified male (as the god Aether). The fifth Orphic hymn draws an explicit hierarchy by describing ether as the 'best cosmic element' and conveys patriarchal values by correlating it with 'Zeus's lofty dwelling, endless power', while Plato and Aristotle buttress unequal power relations by deeming ether immaterial and valuing form over matter and the metaphysical over the physical.[11]

Hölderlin not only chooses Empedocles as protagonist for his single drama and unwittingly reproduces the fragmentary character of Empedocles' literary remains with his three unfinished versions of *Empedocles*; he also shows a profound understanding of the vibrancy of matter and the non-mechanistic interplay of the non-numerable roots in the Empedoclean cosmos. Hölderlin's character Empedocles deeply feels the inner intimacy of nature and articulates this in the expositional first monologue of the tragic play. Here is the only slightly revised second version (1799):

Und fernher, wirkend über der Erde vernahm
Ich wohl dein Wiederkehren,

Schöner Tag und meine Vertrauten euch,
Ihr schnellgeschäftgen Kräfte
Der Höh – und nahe seid auch ihr
Mir wieder, seid wie sonst ihr Glüklichen
Ihr irrelosen Bäume meines Hains!
Ihr ruhetet und wuchs't und täglich tränkte
Des Himmels Quelle die Bescheidenen
Mit Licht und Lebensfunken säte
Befruchtend auf die Blühenden der Aether. –
O innige Natur!

(*FHA* XIII, 825)

And from afar, transforming all above the earth
I sensed your imminent recurrence, lovely day
And my familiar friends, you energetic forces of
The heights – and you are close to me
Again, as once before you blessed ones
You never-erring trees within my grove!
You grew in sweet repose and daily drank
From heaven's source you humble ones
With light and sparks of life replete
The ether pollinating all your blossoms. –
O intimate nature!

(*Empedocles*, 123)

Empedocles mentions earth, water or liquid (*Quelle*), light and ether. The 'forces of / The heights' include liquid, light and ether. They nourish – 'and daily drank / From heaven's source' – and stimulate – 'With light and sparks of life replete' – the trees that flourish on earth. Life-giving ether here tends toward the male (*Aether* and *Tag* are grammatically masculine, the feminine *Quelle* is further determined with a masculine qualifier as *des Himmels Quelle*, and seeding [*säte / Befruchtend*] is often – though not necessarily – connoted male).[12] The elements are not easily disentangled – light is liquid, sparks are earthbound – and it is probably misguided to want to disentangle them since this address to nature acknowledges and savours nature's interconnectedness – what the ancient Empedocles called love and Hölderlin here terms intimacy (*Innigkeit*).

Hölderlin generally connotes ether as male and as nourishing, caring and life-giving. His earlier elegy 'To Aether' (1797/8) apostrophises 'Father Ether! [*Vater Aether!*]' as the primary life source and the primary source of affection:

> noch ehe die Mutter
> In die Arme mich nahm, und ihre Brüste mich tränkten,
> Faßtest du zärtlich mich an und gossest himmlischen Trank mir,
> Mir den heiligen Othem zuerst in den keimenden Busen.

(*FHA* III, 80)

> even before the mother
> took me in her arms, and gave me to drink from the breasts
> you touched me tenderly and poured me heavenly drink,
> the holy breath first into my budding bosom.
>
> (My translation)

Here again, ether is both airy and liquid: breath and drink at the same time. Ether's tenderness has an airy quality that still reverberates in the delightful echo: 'Father Aether! . . . Father! Cheerful bright! [*Vater Aether! . . . Vater! Heiter!*]' of the poem 'Bread and Wine' (*FHA* VI, 249; *Poems and Fragments*, 267, translation modified).

Hölderlin's mourning-play *Empedocles* is set on the island of Sicily. The first monologue of its third version (1799/1800), which begins after the protagonist's expulsion from the city of Agrigent, has Empedocles, who lives now on Mount Etna, basking in the clear light of the new day:

> als wüchsen
> Mir Schwingen an, so ist mir wohl und leicht
> Hier oben, hier, und reich genug und froh
> Und herrlich wohn' ich, wo den Feuerkelch
> Mit Geist gefüllt bis an den Rand, bekränzt
> Mit Blumen, die er selber sich erzog,
> Gastfreundlich mir der Vater Aetna beut.
>
> (*FHA* XIII, 931)

> as though
> I'd grown strong pinions, with me all is well and airy
> Up here above it all, and rich enough and glad enough
> And splendidly I dwell here where the fiery chalice,
> Filled with spirit to the brim and wreathed
> With flowers he himself has cultivated
> My father Etna offers me with hospitality.
>
> (*Empedocles*, 172, translation modified)

Note the near homophony of *Vater Aetna* and *Vater Aether*. With its crater of lava, here described as 'fiery chalice, / filled with spirit to the brim', Mount Etna offers Empedocles relatively easy access to the divine root that is otherwise beyond reach because it fills the upper regions of the sky. The expression 'as though I'd grown strong pinions', recalls Plato's *Phaidros*, where Socrates, in his second speech, gives an account of the immortal soul as winged and able to fly outside the sky (beyond the material world altogether) to behold the ideas.[13] Empedocles will join this source of life by jumping to his death, since ether here blends with fire.

According to Plato's Socrates, some remember the radiant beauty of the ideas when they see beauty on earth. On the wings of love for a male beauty, the philosopher ascends to the immaterial ether. Hölderlin's Empedocles is on his way up the mountain toward the life-and-death-giving fire likewise assisted by a beautiful male youth: Pausanias. Is Hölderlin's *Geist* material like the historical Empedocles' ether or immaterial like Plato's ideas? Can we read the beginning of Hölderlin's most important essay in poetics (written shortly after he abandoned the *Empedocles* project), 'When the poet is once in command of the spirit [*des Geistes mächtig*]', as 'When the poet once controls the fire' (*FHA* XIV, 303; *Essays and Letters*, 277)? Or does it mean 'When the poet has once comprehended'? The first sentence of the essay recaps its extremely long dependent clause as 'when he has understood this [*dieses eingesehen hat*]', suggesting perhaps a purely intellectual or metaphysical intuition in the tradition of Plato and Aristotle. But Hölderlin's attention to the simultaneous pulls of 'conflict' (*Widerstreit*) and 'community' (*Gemeinschaft*) in the same sentence and throughout the essay certainly echo the Empedoclean forces of strife and love that affect the four, or rather four+, roots. What is more, the fact that Hölderlin requires spirit to be felt, rather than cognised, suggests that he considers spirit material.[14]

Hölderlin's philosophy of nature is deeply intertwined with his poetic practice and his poetological reflections. Shortly after abandoning the *Empedocles* project, he articulates his ideas about the triad of tones – naive, heroic (or energetic) and idealic [*idealisch*] – that had already for some time emerged in his poems.[15] While the Empedoclean roots and Hölderlin's poetic tones cannot be mapped onto one another, because one set includes at least four entities or qualities and the other three, Empedocles' cosmology and Hölderlin's poetics converge in that both offer pseudo- or quasi-taxonomies. Empedocles' roots are not stable and passive elements that separate neatly and can be combined at will but deities that engage in relations of affection and aggression. Because they are not pure forms but have always already formed alliances and smudged the line that one might attempt to draw between them, the supposedly four roots of the Empedoclean cosmos are not neatly separable and thus not exactly numerable. The same holds true for Hölderlin's poetic tones. Even though his poetological tables suggest neatness, his poetological texts demand that each poem not only alternate tones but also that the alternative tones resonate in or behind each tone foregrounded. I am interested in this queer logic, which creates relations between elements or qualities that might seem different in number or not but are effectively not numerable. This logic relies on shifts and slides, initiating a kind of round dance – from Zeus and the idealic to light to Apollo and the heroic to fire to Hephaestus, for example, or from air to ether to Hera, the *Vater*.

The twenty-page poetological fragment that begins with 'When the poet is once in command of the spirit . . .' offers the poetological notion of the harmonious opposition or discordant accord (*das Harmonischentgegengesetzte*) (*FHA* XIV, 307; *Essays and Letters*, 281). With this notion, Hölderlin holds together in one '*judgement* [that] is original division [*Ur-teil*]' (*FHA* XVII, 156; *Essays and Letters*, 231) – or cuts together-apart, as Karen Barad would say – two normally opposing qualities, namely harmony and opposition, discord and accord, repulsion and affection, or mixture and separation.[16] The notion of the harmoniously opposed, in its simplest form, suggests a binary – it combines two forces: harmony and opposition, which correspond to the Empedoclean forces of love and strife. Then we have three poetic genres – the epic, the dramatic and the lyric, which sing in three different tones – the naive, the energetic and the idealic. Or rather, each genre puts the stress on one of these tones while also sounding the others. Hölderlin choreographs them all as harmoniously opposed, but since three genres cannot fit into a binary, the round dance begins. At first, it forms a three-step. Union on the first beat and then differentiation into two: a sort of waltz with a dactylic rhythm (one in two). Or else the anapaestic meter of the dialectic with the antithesis moving toward a stronger synthesis (two in one). When Hölderlin revives the four roots of the ancient cosmologist Empedocles, the logic of the binary, which for us moderns is most powerfully and pervasively articulated in the gender binary, is queered even further. Now *Vater Aether* exhibits a nourishing tenderness and evokes a situation of primordial non-differentiatedness, which moderns usually associate with the maternal, and in or behind him, we can hear Hera and the echo of the ancient Empedocles casting ether as female and earth as male (Aidoneus).

When Hölderlin's Empedocles walks up Mount Etna, the four elements come to the fore. The earth was always there, already in the city, where Empedocles tended his garden. With the imposing mountain, it takes on a more sublime character. Fire appears both in the form of the sun, to which Empedocles is now exposed without shelter, and in the form of the volcanic lava. The air breezes from the sea and conveys the relative freedom and airiness outside the city. The elevation opens the view onto the sea, and the element of water recurs in the mountain springs that quench the thirst and cool the heated climbers. Thus far a rather prosaic and clumsy version of the interplay of the four elements. In Hölderlin's words, they are more fluidly blended than separately identified and adopt an astonishing, sonorous dynamism:

> Es öffnen groß
> Sich hier vor uns die heilgen Elemente.
> . . .
> An seinen vesten Ufern wallt und ruht
> Das alte Meer, und das Gebirge steigt

> Mit seiner Ströme Klang, es woogt und rauscht
> Sein grüner Wald von Thal zu Thal hinunter.
> Und oben weilt das Licht, der Aether stillt
> Den Geist und das geheimere Verlangen.
>
> (FHA XIII, 933)

>   They open mightily
> Before us here, the holy elements
> . . .
> On firm shores surging then reposing
> The ancient sea, and mountains all ascending
> To heed the roaring of their streams; their green woods
> Waving and rushing down from vale to vale.
> While the light lingers above, as ether stills
> The spirit and the more mysterious yearnings.
>
> (Empedocles, 174, translation modified)

There is the 'firm' and solid earth, against which the 'ancient' and, hence, steady sea both seethes and rests. The earth climbs and the forest runs down. Both echo the voice and roar of streams that might as well be lava flows and of the surging sea. The soundscape is tumultuous and complex enough to host the reverberations of spraying lava and flames that lick up to the sky, even if these are only hinted at. Solely light and ether remain calm and aloof, yet satisfying in their own way. The passage presents a potent scenario of love and strife or rage and care among the 'elements'.

While we have already seen that Hölderlin's Empedocles is attuned to the complex dynamics of love and strife, I would now like to introduce another character, namely Achilles. Both stand in for the poet and both have a complex and ambiguous – though differently weighted – relation to the ancient Empedoclean forces of love and strife or care and rage. Empedocles as the poet-philosopher and Achilles as the poet-athlete, both have a special connection to liquid fire. Achilles was 'dipped in fire [*in Feuer getaucht*]', as the first line of the third version of Hölderlin's poem *Mnemosyne* has it (*FHA* VIII, 739; *Poems and Fragments*, 519) – submerged in the river Styx at the beginning of his life. Empedocles ends his life bathing in a chalice of fire, the *Feuerkelch* of Mount Etna.

Hölderlin's Empedocles, the student of nature, engages in a labour of love. For him, thinking means loving or caring for all of nature, and tending his garden is tantamount to thinking. However, with this labour of love he also cuts himself off from the *polis*. He excludes or excepts himself from the community and takes exception to the careless attitude of others. He is the exceptional lover: 'compelled . . . / Immortally to love [*Unsterblichliebend*]' (*FHA* XIII, 829; *Empedocles*, 126). He undyingly loves immortals and refuses to mix and mingle with the narrow-minded mortals and their limited capacities.

Empedocles not only (ambiguously) gives love but also receives care – from nature as well as from his disciple Pausanias. Nature gives him pleasure and she does so with tenderness and love, as Empedocles appreciates: 'The mountain springs were gurgling tenderly, all / Your joys, O earth! As true as she is true / And warm and fully ripening in labor and in love, / You gave all this to me' [*Und zärtlich tönten ihrer Berge Quellen – / All' deine Freuden, Erde! Wahr, wie sie, / Und warm und voll, aus Müh' und Liebe reifen, / Sie alle gabst du mir*] (*FHA* XIII, 829; *Empedocles*, 123). Meanwhile Pausanias takes care of Empedocles in exile; he finds him shelter, food and drink from the mountain springs. The disciple also gives his beauty to the poet. Hölderlin dedicates the second act of the first version of *Empedocles* to Charis, quoting seven lines in praise of Charis from Pindar's first Olympian hymn as a kind of epigraph.[17] Charis figures dazzling beauty, radiance, grace, charm but also kindness, beneficence and generosity. She gives the gift of creativity and the gift of beauty. Empedocles acknowledges that Pausanias sacrifices his own beauty for the teacher: 'O all-sacrificing heart! And this one / For my sake flings away his golden youth!' [*O allesopfernd Herz! Und dieser giebt / Schon mir zu lieb die goldne Jugend weg!*] (*FHA* XIII, 938; *Empedocles*, 179) He thanks him by vanishing during one of the moments when Pausanias must leave to find provisions. Empedocles conceives of his disappearance as a self-sacrifice on the altar of nature: a leap into the life-giving fire: 'O nature! . . . O life! . . . O father ether!' (*FHA* XIII, 709; *Empedocles*, 51) For the poet-philosopher love is mutual and mixed with abandonment.[18]

On the other side, we have the poet-athlete: Achilles, the supreme warrior. In a note written in the same notebook as later *Empedocles*, Hölderlin calls him his 'favourite among the heroes, so strong and gentle, the most perfectly achieved and the most transient blossom of the heroic world' (*Essays and Letters*, 249). In Hölderlin's notes for a project of letters on Homer, Achilles appears as if he were himself a poem. He is characterised as 'idealic' [*idealisch*] and changing in tone, 'on the other hand lamenting and avenging, inexpressibly touching and then terrible again' (*Essays and Letters*, 250–1, translation modified). His character harmoniously opposes – or accords with the discords of – tenderness and violence (Hölderlin describes him as 'melancholically tender' [*melancholischzärtlich*] and in the same phrase apostrophises him 'omnipotent' [*allgewaltig*] (*Essays and Letters*, 250). Aggression and love commingle inextricably in this character, this fruit of a rape condoned by the Olympian gods.[19] A mother, raging with care, killed one child from the violent union after the other, until Achilles survived the baptism in the fiery waters of Styx.

Hölderlin considers Achilles a kind of poet. He calls him a 'genius' [*genialisch*] (*Essays and Letters*, 250). Achilles serves as the figure of the poet-warrior, the poet-hero, or, if one prefers Rainer Nägele's foregrounding of the athletic quality of Hölderlin's tragic bodies, the poet-athlete.[20] Achilles has proven that he can take the fire, the lightning, the sun or 'fire of the sky' from Apollo, the sun god of knowledge and poetry (*Essays and Letters*, 213). Because he is '[d]ipped in fire', as Hölderlin puts it in 'Mnemosyne', he is 'tried [*geprüfet*]' (*FHA* VIII, 739; *Poems and Fragments*, 519) – 'in command of the spirit', perhaps. Achilles is strong enough to expose himself to heavenly fire – a 'fellow poet', whom as Hölderlin notes in 'As on a holiday' [*Wie wenn am Feiertage*]

> it behoves to stand
> Bareheaded beneath God's thunder-storms,
> To grasp the Father's ray, no less, with our own hand [*mit eigner Hand*]
> And, wrapping in song the heavenly gift,
> To offer it to the people
>   (*FHA* VIII, 558; *Poems and Fragments*, 397–9, translation modified)

It takes a warrior's body, an athlete's body, to grasp the father's ray (*Stral*), which, given the German signifier, shapeshifts from fire to water, like Achilles' mother Thetis when she is pursued by a mortal.[21] It takes a hero's body to produce songs that can qualify as 'striking and creating [*treffend und schaffend*]' (*FHA* VI, 249; *Poems and Fragments*, 267, translation modified), as Hölderlin tells us in 'Bread and Wine'. To find words that hit the mark (*treffende Worte*), words like arrows, as Pindar says of his poetry, it takes a body forged in fire, not only because it is an athletic feat to reach the aim but also because, as Nägele puts it, 'the moment of an impact erases the difference between active and passive'.[22] It is dangerous to attempt to create something striking, because hitting involves being hit. It takes 'the heroic Greek body shaped by an economy of protection against the violence of an excessive transport' to be able to withstand being hit by Apollo Hekatèbolos (the one who does not miss).[23]

Hölderlin writes in his second letter to Böhlendorff from November 1802, 'As one says of heroes I can probably say of myself: that Apollo has struck me' (*FHA* XIX, 499; *Essays and Letters*, 213). The *Iliad* describes Apollo approaching Patroclus from behind and hitting him with his flat hand between the shoulders, knocking off his helmet first and eventually all of his armour (which Patroclus had borrowed from Achilles).[24] Suddenly unprotected and naked, Patroclus stands there in the middle of the battlefield, frozen, shocked and stunned by Apollo, who is known for his athletic beauty and his love for Hyacinth, whom he accidentally killed in a discus game. If Apollo's signature beardlessness was not enough of a signifier for male–male love,[25] the god definitely became one after Johann Winckelmann's much respected and widely circulated celebration of the

Apollo Belvedere.²⁶ So we can assume that Hölderlin knows what he is doing when he describes himself as struck by Apollo. Even the supreme warrior and poet-athlete Achilles is not ultimately able to withstand Apollo's aim: he is slain in battle by Priam's son Paris, whose arrow Apollo guides to the precise target of his heel.

I might have begun by classifying Empedocles as a lover and Achilles as an aggressor, but they both embody the competing impulses of love and strife or care and rage, accentuating each differently at times. 'The Nymph', a first draft of the poem that Hölderlin later titles 'Mnemosyne', creates a binary when it commemorates the tragic deaths of ancient heroes:

> . . . und es starben
> Noch andere viel. Mit eigener Hand
> Viel traurige, wilden Muths, doch göttlich
> Gezwungen, zuletzt, die anderen aber
> Im Geschike stehend, im Feld . . .
>
> (*FHA* VIII, 733)

> And many others died. With their own hand
> Many sad ones, of fierce audacity, yet divinely
> Forced, in the end, the others however
> Destined, standing in the field . . .
>
> (My translation)

According to the taxonomy established here, Empedocles and Achilles belong to different camps. Empedocles kills himself 'with [his] own hand'. Achilles dies on the battlefield. However, their opposition is not clearcut. Achilles dies in battle as a poet. And Empedocles races to the top of Mount Etna like an athlete: 'pain . . . speeds his flight, and like the driver of a chariot, / When on the course the chariot's wheels begin / To smoke, the man in danger hurtles all / The faster toward his victor's wreath!' [. . . *es / Beschleunigen ihm / Die Schmerzen den Flug und wie der Wagenlenker, / Wenn ihm das Rad in der Bahn / Zu rauchen beginnt, eilt / Der Gefährdete nur schneller zum Kranze!*] (*FHA* XIII, 836; *Empedocles*, 135).²⁷

In the first version, Empedocles, speaking to the Agrigentians who have come to apologise and invite him to return to the city, adopts an even more solemn tone than usual as he adumbrates his self-sacrifice: 'And well I know my lot [*Und wohlbewußt ist mir mein Loos*]' (*FHA* XIII, 750, *Empedocles*, 97). The scene carries strong, albeit inverted, allusions to the story of Jesus on the evening of his betrayal and arrest. While Jesus removes himself from his company in the garden of Gethsemane to pray and ask to let this cup pass him by, Empedocles is visited by his people who offer reconciliation and a way out, but Empedocles insists on drinking the cup: 'and you extend / To me the terrifying chalice, the fermenting cup, / Nature! That he who sings you drink a draft of it, / His spirit's ultimate enthusiasms! / I am at peace with it' [*und reichest du / Den Schrekensbecher, mir, den gährenden / Natur! damit dein Sänger noch aus ihm / Die lezte der Begeisterungen trinke! / Zufrieden bin ichs*] (*FHA* XIII, 755; *Empedocles*, 103). Actually, he insists on jumping into the cup: rather than swallowing the poison, he wants to be swallowed by liquid fire. It is positively undecidable, in this context, which gesture would be more aggressive and which more receptive – drinking or leaping. To oppose action and suffering is of no use here.

In the third version, Pausanias offers not exactly a way out (he painfully learned that Empedocles will not accept it) but company. Pausanias proposes to throw himself into the volcano with his beloved teacher. While, in the end, he will decline the offer and insist on his solitary sacrifice, Empedocles is for a moment taken by the idea:

> Ja! herrlich wärs, wenn in die Grabesflamme
> So Arm in Arm statt Eines Einsamen
> Ein festlich Paar am Tagesende gieng',
> Und gerne nähm' ich, was ich hier geliebt,
> Wie seine Quellen all ein edler Strom,
> der heilgen Nacht zum Opfertrank, hinunter.
>
> (*FHA* XIII, 938)

> Yes! It would be splendid if into the pyre's flames
> Thus arm in arm instead of one left all alone
> A festive pair at end of day went off companionably
> And gladly I would take the one that here I loved,
> The way a noble stream sweeps all its tributaries
> Into the depths below, libations to the holy night.
>
> (*Empedocles*, 180)

Who is drinking whom here? Empedocles compares himself to a river swallowing its tributaries and being swallowed in the end by (in this case not the ocean but) the underworld, 'the holy night'. The fact that the original says *Quellen* (sources) rather than tributaries makes the passage particularly interesting. A stream source springs from the earth; so we have here a rather direct juxtaposition of springing from and jumping into the earth. The master–disciple love couple jump together festively, arm in arm, 'companionably' and equally into the funeral pyre. It is the younger one, the one who is usually thought of as the spiritual offspring of the teacher, the one who might otherwise be asked to disseminate the master's teachings, who is here figured as the source of the noble stream, that is as its originator. A queer kind of filiation, indeed.

Notes

1. Graham, *The Texts of Early Greek Philosophy*, p. 344.
2. Element derives from the Latin *elementum*. The equivalent Greek term would be *stoikheion*.
3. See Shaw, 'Aither and the Four Roots in Empedocles', pp. 171–3.
4. Graham, *The Texts of Early Greek Philosophy*, p. 380.
5. For a historical overview of the interpretations of fragment B6, see Shaw, 'Aither and the Four Roots in Empedocles', pp. 177–82.
6. Ibid. p. 192.
7. Ibid. p. 190.
8. See Athanassakis and Wolkow, *The Orphic Hymns*, x–xii.
9. Ibid. p. 8.
10. Shaw, 'Aither and the Four Roots in Empedocles', p. 186.
11. Athanassakis and Wolkow, *The Orphic Hymns*, p. 8.
12. Krell renders the sense of abundance and the sense of fertilisation in the original *säte befruchtend* with the words 'replete' and 'pollinating', thereby disambiguating the gender connotation. See Hölderlin, *Empedocles*, trans. Krell, p. 123, hereafter cited parenthetically in the text.
13. Plato, *Phaedrus*, pp. 51–8.
14. For example, *FHA* XIV, 310, *Essays and Letters*, 285: 'In this point the spirit is feelable in its infinity [*in seiner Unendlichkeit fühlbar*]'. The extended beginning of the first sentence reads, 'When the poet is once in command of the spirit, when he has felt [*gefühlt*] . . . the common soul' (*FHA* XIV, 303, *Essays and Letters*, 277).
15. See *FHA* XIV, 325–6, 340–1, 369–72; *Essays and Letters*, pp. 299–300, 302–6, 307–8, 309.
16. Barad, 'Diffracting Diffraction: Cutting Together-Apart'.
17. 'Charis, who brings all / That's mild to mortals, / Also brings honor, / And makes us believe the unbelievable, / Which often does come to the fore. / Yet the days that are still to come / Are wisest witnesses' (*Empedocles*, 233). Hölderlin quotes these verses in Greek. His translations of Pindar (around 1800–3) do not include the First Olympian Hymn. See Benjamin Hederich's entry to Charis in Hederich, *Gründliches mythologisches Lexikon*, p. 695. He describes her as the spouse of Vulcanus, another god of fire and double of Hephaestus, who forged Jupiter's thunderbolts. Charis is one of the three Graces who are frequently depicted as dancing in the round, because generosity and beneficence spread joy as they go round. See Hederich, *Gründliches mythologisches Lexikon*, p. 1180.
18. One can construe Empedocles' abandonment of Pausanias and of the city as an act of care.
19. Thetis, the water goddess and mother of Achilles, was so beautiful that Zeus and Poseidon wanted to marry her. But since the oracle predicted that her son would become greater than his father, the gods abandoned their desire and tried to couple her with a mortal. Thetis did not want a mortal and whenever one approached her she changed shape (turned into a ferocious animal or, incidentally, into fire or water). Finally, the centaur Chiron taught the mortal Peleus how to keep a hold of her even as she changed shape. The so-called wedding, which I read as rape, was celebrated in the company of the gods (whose presence I read as the need to confirm that their own temptation was successfully averted). She bears seven children, all of whom (except for the last one, Achilles) she kills in the attempt to burn the mortal part off them.
20. Nägele, 'Ancient Sports and Modern Transports: Hölderlin's Tragic Bodies'.
21. *Stral* or *Strahl* can refer to a ray of light or a jet of liquid. Regarding shapeshifting Thetis, see note 19.

22. Nägele, 'Ancient Sports and Modern Transports: Hölderlin's Tragic Bodies', p. 259. For the reference to Pindar, see p. 258 and footnote 35.
23. Ibid. p. 266.
24. Homer, *Iliad*, pp. 313–14.
25. For a notion of 'Greek love' beyond pederasty, involving two equally (or interchangeably) beautiful, youthful and thus beardless men, see Butler, 'Homer's Deep'. Butler also emphasises the simultaneous presence of anger and love in Achilles and reads him as a lover of words in 'Homer's Deep', p. 38 and p. 43 respectively.
26. See the chapter on Winckelmann in Derks, *Die Schande der heiligen Päderastie*, Richter, 'Winckelmann's Progeny' and Richter and McGrath, 'Representing Homosexuality', p. 51.
27. This is Panthea's imagery in the second version. Rhea once saw Empedocles (in the first version) as an athlete in the Olympic games (*FHA* XIII, 697).

Bibliography

Athanassakis, Apostolos N. and Wolkow, Benjamin M., *The Orphic Hymns* (Baltimore: Johns Hopkins University Press, 2013).
Barad, Karen, 'Diffracting Diffraction: Cutting Together-Apart', *Parallax*, 3 (2014), pp. 168–87.
Butler, Shane, 'Homer's Deep', in Shane Butler (ed.), *Deep Classics: Rethinking Classical Reception* (London: Bloomsbury, 2016), pp. 21–48.
Derks, Paul, *Die Schande der Heiligen Päderastie. Homosexualität und Öffentlichkeit in der deutschen Literatur 1750–1850* (Berlin: Rosa Winkel, 1990).
Graham, Daniel (ed.), *The Texts of Early Greek Philosophy: The Complete Fragments and Selected Testimonies of the Major Presocratics*, 2 vols (Cambridge: Cambridge University Press, 2011).
Hederich, Benjamin, *Gründliches mythologisches Lexikon* (Darmstadt: Wissenschaftliche Buchgesellschaft, 1996).
Homer, *Iliad*, trans. E. V. Rieu (Harmondsworth: Penguin, 1978).
Nägele, Rainer, 'Ancient Sports and Modern Transports: Hölderlin's Tragic Bodies', in Aris Fioretos (ed.), *The Solid Letter: Readings of Friedrich Hölderlin* (Stanford: Stanford University Press, 2000), pp. 247–67.
Plato, *Phaedrus and the Seventh and Eighth Letters,* trans. Walter Hamilton (London: Penguin, 1973).
Richter, Simon, 'Winckelmann's Progeny: Homosocial Networking in the Eighteenth Century', in Alice A. Kuzniar (ed.), *Outing Goethe and His Age* (Stanford: Stanford University Press, 1996), pp. 33–46.
Richter, Simon and McGrath, Patrick, 'Representing Homosexuality: Winckelmann and the Aesthetics of Friendship', *Monatshefte für deutschen Unterricht, deutsche Sprache und Literatur*, 86: 1 (Spring 1994), pp. 45–58.
Shaw, Michael M., 'Aither and the Four Roots in Empedocles', *Research in Phenomenology*, 44: 2 (Spring 2014), pp. 170–93.

Chapter 4

The Order of the Unbound: Time and History in Hölderlin's 'The Titans'

Achim Geisenhanslüke

Time and history

The first stanza of Friedrich Hölderlin's poem 'Mnemosyne' contains the following lines that have elicited much scholarly commentary: 'And always / There is a yearning that seeks the unbound' [*Und immer / Ins Ungebundene gehet eine Sehnsucht*](*Poems and Fragments*, 519; StA II, 197). They seem to fit seamlessly into Hölderlin's distinction between Greek and Hesperian poetry: whereas the art of the Greeks, according to Hölderlin, consisted in a progression from limitless nature to palpable depiction in the finite and limited forms of art, Hesperian art moves in the opposite direction, proceeding from an artistic skill of representation [*Darstellungsgabe*] and culminating in the aorgic flux of nature.[1] The modern poet, in this schema, therefore faces the task of reversing the tendency towards limitation that dominates Greek art, and thus of releasing its bound elements in order to pave the way for a new and autonomous form of art.

A striking feature of Hölderin's late poems in this context is how they set these unbound elements into relation with the older order of the Titans. This occurs in 'Mnemosyne', for instance, when Hölderlin links the unbound – as the object of yearning – to an image of the Titans: 'For crookedly / Like horses go the imprisoned / Elements and ancient laws / Of the earth' [*Nämlich unrecht, / Wie Rosse, gehen die gefangenen / Element' und alten / Gesetze der Erd*] (*Poems and Fragments*, 519; StA II, 197). In speaking of the 'imprisoned elements' and the ancient laws of the earth, Hölderlin alludes to the reign of the Titans. In contrast to the Olympians, the Titans – as Hesiod's *Theogony* had demonstrated – embodied a prior order that the Olympians would overcome and replace. Hölderlin leaves no doubt here that the Titans represent a hostile and destructive force: He refers to their path as 'crooked'. Nevertheless, a paradox persists: Hölderlin's structural opposition of Greek and Hesperian poetry would seem to demand that one turns towards this unbound force – or, more precisely, this force of the unbound – in order to achieve a form of freedom unknown to antiquity. At stake therefore is a scenario which Hesiod's *Theogony* summoned only in order to ward it off as something terrifying, namely the notion that, more than simply marking a beginning, the reign of the Olympians might signal an ending in time, one that coincides with the Titans' liberation. According to the view of the ancient Greeks, the age of the Olympian gods, and by extension the age of human civilisation, would therefore be embedded in an encompassing temporality that is marked by the release of the natural powers associated with the Titans and for this reason is legible as a form of natural history [*Naturgeschichte*] within which the history of humanity is inscribed. In evoking the reign of the Titans and the possibility of their return, Hölderlin thus thinks time not according to human history but according to nature, much as Spinoza does.[2] Regardless of how Hölderlin's account of the Titans differs from Hesiod's in this context, one thing is clear: with its allusions to the ancient laws of the earth, Hölderlin's late poems paint an image of the Titans that is inscribed in a philosophy of history and which therefore entails a certain thinking of time. At stake is thus, in a historico-philosophical sense, the perpetual *querelle des Anciens et des Modernes* and, by extension, the liberation of modern poetry from the ancient law of imitation, a point Peter Szondi demonstrates in linking genre with philosophy of history in Hölderlin.[3] Far more difficult to determine, however, is the question: what sort of thinking of time does Hölderlin's philosophy of history invite? As 'Mnemosyne' suggests, the central problem in this regard is a temporal one. The ending of the first stanza demonstrates this: 'Forward, however, and back we will / Not look. Be lulled and rocked as / On a swaying skiff of the sea' [*Vorwärts und rückwärts wollen wir / Nicht sehn. Uns wiegen lassen, wie / Auf schwankem Kahne der See*] (*Poems and Fragments*, 519; StA II, 197). The refusal to look forwards and backwards serves as a clear reference to the temporal dimensions of future and past, as well as to the relation between hope and memory. Moreover, the movement of rocking on water, which Hölderlin borrows from Rousseau's *Reveries of a Solitary Walker* – an aspect which Jürgen Link, in his interpretation of the relation between Hölderlin and Rousseau, traces back to Hölderlin's novel *Hyperion* and calls an 'inventive return'[4] – suggests itself that Hölderlin is concerned with an experience of the temporal moment, with a form of presence tied to the present moment that may, in a historico-philosophical sense, be grasped as the *kairos* of a sudden transformation from the old to the new. Hölderlin's late writings track this transformation both poetically and politically.

Time that tears: 'The Titans'

Hölderlin's late poem fragment 'The Titans' begins with the lines: 'Not yet, however, / The time has come' [*Nicht ist es aber / Die Zeit*] (*Poems and Fragments*, 555; *StA* II, 217). Interpretations of the poem have to some degree and with good reason cast doubt on the meaning of the poem's title. Brigitte Duvillard argues, from the perspective of textual criticism, that 'the ancient myth of the Titans contributes nothing to an understanding of the poem's vast internal relations and the title offers a misleading key to interpretation'.[5] Still, Duvillard acknowledges that the poem contains the components of a specific philosophy of time, evident in its opposition of fulfilled and unfulfilled forms of time: 'Not only does a godless time contrast with a time of fulfilment in the fragment "The Titans" but two opposing types of day stand against each other as well; one that is measured and another in the extreme form of the encounter'.[6] In this way, the poem begins in fact with a gesture of privation, typical for Hölderlin: its opening 'Not' announces an absence or lack which – the poem holds open this possibility – may be assuaged at a future moment but which nevertheless marks the present as unfulfilled. As Anke Bennholdt-Thomsen writes:

> At the point in time to which the beginning of the poem refers, a time defined by the absence of the kairological, to borrow an expression of Jürgen Link, the Titans are unbound, unfree, and self-enclosed to such a degree that any participation in the cosmic events that the hymns announce is foreclosed.[7]

In this sense the Titans could be seen as standing for a time that is not yet defined by the laws of the gods, a time as originary as it is indeterminate. The lines 'Not yet, however, / The time has come' [*Nicht ist es aber / Die Zeit*] (*Poems and Fragments*, 555; *StA* II, 217) must then, in this context, be read in two separate yet interrelated ways. On the one hand, they state that it is not yet time to tether and bind the Titans by banning them to Tartarus; time is, in this sense, prehistorical time and its beginning is first marked by the Titans' battle with the Olympians. On the other hand, they suggest more radically that time is not, that temporal determinations are not yet valid, and that this prehistoric time marks in fact a pretemporal order. That would mean that the time of the Titans – the time of Kronos – is fundamentally distinct from the time of the Olympian gods, indeed to such a degree that from the perspective of the gods and mortals, the time of the Titans can be perceived only as outside of or anterior to time. This is the sense in which Hölderlin, in his reference to the myth of Niobe in his 'Notes on the *Antigone*', refers to Zeus as the 'Father of Time' (*Essays and Letters*, 328, translation modified). Both time and history first commence with the battle of the Titans, with the 'gigantomachia peri tēs ousias' [a Battle of Giants concerning Being], which as Heidegger suggests in the first pages of *Being and Time* must always be rekindled and which proves in this context to be a battle for time.[8] Accordingly, Hölderlin's subsequent lines, 'They still are / Untethered' [*Noch sind sie / Unangebunden*] (*Poems and Fragments*, 555; StA II, 217), precisely by virtue of the temporal markers they contain (here 'still' and later in the poem 'then'), indicate that time is emphatically – that is, as a time beyond familiar chronology – not time, or rather that time is not. In this sense, the following line, 'What's divine does not strike the / unconcerned' [*Göttliches trifft unteilnehmende nicht*] (*Poems and Fragments*, 555; StA II, 217), suggests that the gods have not yet found an adversary in the Titans and therefore cannot begin to unfurl their own temporality; the subsequent line, 'Then let them reckon / With Delphi' [*Dann mögen sie rechnen mit Delphi*] (*Poems and Fragments*, 555; StA II, 217), likewise implies that the divine order of the Olympians, in the figure of Delphi, can only be instituted in its full temporal and historical significance after the triumph over the Titans.

Insofar as the temporal indeterminacy of the Titans is expressed as the privation of what is yet to come, it brings into view the temporal determinacy of the speaker in the present, who is situated in an interstitial time: 'Meanwhile in festive hours, / And so that I may rest, allow me / To think of the dead' [*Indessen, gib in Feierstunden / Und daß ich ruhen möge, der Toten / Zu denken*] (*Poems and Fragments*, 555; StA II, 217). At the centre of the poetic experience that shapes the lyrical voice lies an experience of the present moment of festivity and thus, by extension, memory in the form of a requiem similar to the one presented in 'Mnemosyne', in which Achilles, Ajax and Patroclus are named as objects of mourning. Memory is thus directed towards the underworld, to the ancient heroes that reside there, from whom the mourning speaker is separated through the experience of isolation in the present: 'But I am on my own' [*Ich aber bin allein*] (*Poems and Fragments*, 555; StA II, 217). In a manner familiar from *Hyperion*, which, as described above, is inspired by Rousseau, the speaker lays claim to a melancholic experience of isolation that entails a particular dynamic of time. In the retroverted act of mourning the speaker experiences the fact that time does not move, that it has come to a standstill and that the possibility of historical novelty is foreclosed. The speaker endures in this threshold of time in order to set in motion a new dynamic, one whose retroversion implies not only a concern with the divine order of the Olympians but also a turn towards the Titan's temporal order of a radically alternate time.

Hölderlin and the Titans

Against this backdrop scholars have long suggested that Hölderlin's appraisal of the Titans is unequivocally critical, as is the case in Hesiod. In his analysis of the myth of the Titans in Hölderlin, Arthur Häny has foregrounded the positive weight they receive in *Hyperion* and, by extension, the connection drawn between the Titans and the poet: 'The Titans and the poet live in a tense relation of interconnection.'[9] In particular, Anke Bennholdt-Thomsen has warned against the tendency to cast the Titans in Hölderlin's late work as distinctly adversarial. To be sure, for Bennholdt-Thomsen the Titans figure undoubtedly as representatives of the aorgic and are thus aligned with a boundary-defying and destructive force of nature: 'The Titans appear in Hölderlin's poetry as representatives of the abyss, of aorgic nature, of the night of the gods.'[10] But as proxies of the aorgic, the Titans likewise embody an autonomous principle beyond dialectical synthesis, as Bennholdt-Thomsen suggests:

> My thesis is not simply that the Titans, as seemingly autonomous counterparts to the heavenly gods, serve in the process of history as necessary opponents of peaceful progression, who must appear as such so that they may be overcome, negated and sublated in the consummation of a natural process. Such a view would be dialectically synthesizing. Rather I adopt the position that, if indeed the Titans' function as antipodes lies in divine nature itself, then they signify a fundamental opposition, a hostility of divine spirit itself, which can never nor shall ever be fully overcome, which can only temporarily appear harmonious precisely because it is progressive.[11]

In this view, the Titans figure as a counterforce to the divine order of the Olympians. Overcoming this order can never be accomplished once and for all but is rather, insofar as the possibility of historical progress may be questioned, called into question itself. The prospect of the Titans' triumph over the gods therefore appears in this context to be less fateful than the possible persistence of a ruling order that would bind the ancient elements for eternity and in doing so foreclose the possibility of historical progress. The efforts of the modern poet, who must reverse the ancient course of nature from the aorgic to the organic, thus coincide with the call for liberating the Titans from their bondage. This liberation would constitute less a purpose in its own right, aimed at securing victory over the Olympians, than a perilous yet necessary means to setting time and history back in motion.

In this way, the philosophy of history upon which Hölderlin bases his opposition of the ancients and the moderns is itself premised on a conception of various distinct forms of time, one that was already definitive for ancient poetry. Pindar, in particular, provided the model for a mode of thinking of time which Hölderlin would then historically inflect, as Michael Theunissen has argued: 'Hölderlin sees time as historical. To do so he divides time into three forms: leisurely time, time that cuts or tears and a more humane time.'[12] In the context of antiquity, leisurely time [*die müßige Zeit*] can be seen as precisely the 'unconcerned' [*unteilnehmende*] time prior to the clash between the Titans and the gods; the time that tears ahead or away [*die reißende Zeit*] would, by contrast, be the time of the Titans whose destructive order threatens to encroach upon the lives of both the gods and mortals; and humane time [*die humane Zeit*], finally, would be that of Olympian reign in union with mortals. Yet when placed in the context of Hölderlin's distinction between Greek and Hesperian poetry, this tripartite schema of time extends beyond antiquity and applies to modernity as well. For modernity, leisurely time would constitute the time of the present, which can no longer recall the overcoming of the Titans as the necessary precondition for the reign of the Olympians. The task of recollection would then fall to the isolated poet working against the course of time. For modernity, time that tears would be the time of the renewed liberation of the Titans' power, which Hölderlin consciously associated with the experience of the French Revolution. And humane time, finally, a time of human reign, in which humanity would no longer be subordinated to the gods but would, in giving forth its own laws, find autonomy over the reign of the Olympian gods. Seen against the backdrop of Hölderlin's opposition between ancient and modern poetry, his tripartite temporal schema likewise serves as a poetological reflection on genre that is primarily concerned with the place of tragedy. Theunissen has in this regard characterised leisurely time as pre-tragic, humane time as post-tragic and time that tears, by extension, as tragic proper:

> Hölderlin seeks to ground his tripartite division of time into a leisurely time, a time that tears and a humane time in the Greek tragic texts themselves by locating the time that tears, which occupies a midpoint between leisurely and humane time, at the very centre of the tragedies. With this centre or midpoint he announces a turn in time.[13]

Hölderlin thus finds at the very centre of ancient tragedy a time that is torn, embodied by the late lyric poetry of the Titans. Bennholdt-Thomsen draws attention to this point as well:

> In the mythology of his [Hölderlin's] late work the Titans are figures of time that tears, a time recognized by the poet to be tragic and which tragedy can

transform from and 'eyeless confusion' into a time that is seen as necessary and consciously made.[14]

It is in this sense that, in his notes to his translations of Sophocles, Hölderlin presents the time that tears as a movement of decentring, as a time that 'tears away into the eccentric sphere of the dead', as he writes in his 'Notes on the *Oedipus*' (*Essays and Letters*, 318, translation modified). In one reading of this quote, Werner Hamacher has described such a temporality in Hölderlin as the time 'of a pure form which, moving beyond itself, tears itself away'.[15]

With the historico-philosophical transition from antiquity to modernity, however, tragedy is displaced by the lyric – like in the form of the late hymns such as 'Mnemosyne' or 'The Titans' – as the midpoint or centre of poetic literature. This is a lyric that is fragmented and which positions itself in a 'time of need' [*dürftige Zeit*], confronting a present that is oblivious to history with the force of *memoria*: 'For we lack / Song that loosens the mind' [*Denn es fehlet / An Gesang, der löset den Geist*] (*Poems and Fragments*, 555; StA II, 217). Once again, the image here is one of privation, marked by the absence of the song whose power of recollection is now imagined with regard to the mind and spirit; this is the very force that in antiquity was embodied by the gods as a counterforce to the sons of the earth, the Titans. The poet comes to occupy an intermediary position between the earth and the heavens, between nature and art, though not one that implies outright harmony. Rather, it is a position defined by the strife between the polarising forces of the organic and the aorgic, on the one hand, and which, on the other hand, is itself subject to historical change, such that the relation between the Titans and the gods must be redefined for modernity.

The poet and the bee

The poetological reflection that Hölderlin develops in his conception of time and history in *The Titans* applies therefore to the poet's own relationship to the Titans and the gods. Hölderlin figures this relation in 'The Titans' through recourse to an image, one he employs in *Hyperion* as well, that he likewise borrows from the Greeks, namely that of the bee:

Mich aber umsummet
Die Bien und wo der Ackersmann
Die Furchen macht singen gegen
Dem Lichte die Vögel.

(*StA* II, 218)

> But around me hums
> The bee, and where the ploughman draws
> His furrows, birds are singing
> Against the light.
>
> *(Poems and Fragments,* 557)[16]

As he does in the opening passage of his novel, Hölderlin employs the metaphor of the bees here to portray the intermediary spirit of the poet. Such a close alliance between the poet and the bees can already be found in Plato, who in the early dialogue *Ion* summons the art of poetic speech as a divine force that moves poet, rhapsode and audience alike. Plato compares this power of poetic speech first with Euripides' magnetic stone and then with the flight of the bee:

> For the poets tell us, I believe, that the songs they bring us are the sweets they cull from honey-dropping founts in certain gardens and glades of the Muses – like the bees, and winging the air as these do. And what they tell is true. For a poet is a light and winged and sacred thing, and is unable ever to compose until he has been inspired and put out of his senses, and his mind is no longer in him.[17]

Plato likens the poet to the bee as a muse that inspires and exalts humans with its serenade. Both Homer and Hesiod had already compared the poet's song with the taste of sweet honey, a comparison supported by the lexical similarity between *melos* (song) and *meli* (honey) that Pindar's poetry frequently made use of. Like the poet's song, honey figures as a product of the heavens and of the air. According to the ancient Greeks, the bees did not themselves produce honey but simply collected the honeydew that fell from the heavens. Similarly, the poet could be seen as a collector of this sweet stuff, which, in turn, constitutes the stuff of the poet's poetry.[18] In this way, the principle of *poikilia* – the variegation and colourfulness of the bees and the flowers between which they fly – became an ideal for the diverse and varied speech that was, above all, specific to the poet. Indeed, poetry is, in this sense, sweet and honey-drenched speech, and the poet an intermediary between humans and the gods: 'Many give help / To Heaven. And them / The poet sees' [*Manche helfen / Dem Himmel. Diese siehet / Der Dichter*] (*Poems and Fragments*, 557; StA II, 218).

Into the depths

Against this backdrop, Hölderlin develops in 'The Titans' an idyllic image of contemporary life as rooted in antiquity, an image that itself rests on a certain link between the gods and mortals:

> Wenn aber ist entzündet
> Der geschäftige Tag
> Und an der Kette, die
> Den Blitz ableitet
> Von der Stunde des Aufgangs
> Himmlischer Tau glänzt,
> Muß unter Sterblichen auch
> Das Hohe sich fühlen.
>
> (*StA*, II, 218)

> But when the busy day
> Has been kindled
> And on the chain that
> Conducts the lightning
> From the hour of sunrise
> Glistens heavenly dew,
> Among mortals also
> What is high must feel at home.
>
> (*Poems and Fragments*, 557)

Drawing attention to the temporal organisation of the day, Hölderlin employs a concept that, as Hermann Fränkel has shown, harks back to the very beginning of the ancient Greek's conception of time: 'The day is a discrete and ascertainable unit of lived experience; a temporal element to which everyone necessarily and deliberately conforms. The Greeks' concept of time is developed and expanded from this starting point in the concept of the day.'[19] Hölderlin, too, conceives of the day as a unit of lived experience: it marks a busy and bustling world, enmeshed in bartering and trade, within which humans seem to have a definite and fixed place: 'pensive it is / On Earth, and not for nothing / Are eyes fixed on the ground' [*sinnig ist es / Auf Erden und es sind nicht umsonst / Die Augen an den Boden geheftet*] (*Poems and Fragments*, 559; *StA* II, 219). The historical temporality Hölderlin describes here is remarkably positively connoted, in contrast to many other verses of his late poems. As Bennholdt-Thomsen and Alfredo Guzzoni argue: 'It is noteworthy that the depiction of the present is free of the starkly negative tone in which Hölderlin otherwise makes reference to his contemporary time.'[20] Yet even this rather positive depiction is not free of ambiguity. Indeed, the text appears to sketch a downward movement, which, as in the case of Greek poetry, proceeds from a point above to one below: the day that has been kindled evokes the rays of sun that glisten from the heavens down to earth, the image of the lightning rod the Enlightenment's attempts to thwart nature's destructive force, that is the heavenly fire sent by Zeus.[21] And the chain upon which heavenly dew glistens – just as it does on the honey that falls to the earth – suggests that the pastoral idyll depicted here is subject to what is by no means a self-evident condition, namely the unfreedom of mortals whose 'eyes [are] fixed on the ground' [*Augen an den Boden geheftet (sind)*] (*Poems and Fragments*, 559; *StA* II, 219). Elsewhere Hölderlin develops a similar image, as in 'Blödigkeit' [Timidness] where the father of the gods, Zeus, 'At the turning of Time holds us, the sleepy ones, / Upright still with his golden / Leading-strings, as one holds a child' [*Zur Wende der Zeit, uns die Entschlafenden / Aufgerichtet an goldenen Gängelbanden, wie Kinder, hält*] (*Poems and Fragments*, 209; *StA* II, 66). As a poetic image of sunrays beaming down to earth – and at the same time a Rousseauian critique of the widespread eighteenth-century pedagogical practice of teaching children to walk with walking devices – the leading strings in 'Blödigkeit' find their way into 'Die Titanen' in the form of the chain linking gods with mortals. It is in the context of this Enlightenment order of commercial relations that the human gaze is fixed upon the ground rather than the heavens, and it is against this order that Hölderlin conjures a different, more radical form of Enlightenment.

Indicative of this poetically and politically radicalised Enlightenment is Hölderlin's valorisation of the crude and the coarse, itself an image of the Titans' lowly domain: 'For measure demands that / Crudity, coarseness exist, so that / What is pure shall know itself' [*Denn unter dem Maße / Des Rohen brauchet es auch / Damit das Reine sich kenne*] (*Poems and Fragments*, 559; *StA* II, 219). Similar to Hegel, Hölderlin conceives of what is elevated and pure in the form of a relation-to-self, as a relationship therefore whose terms are, accordingly, what is high and what is low, the spiritual and the natural-material, the divine and the human or, in this case, the Titanic: 'Among mortals also / What is high must feel at home' [*Muß unter Sterblichen auch / Das Hohe sich fühlen*] (*Poems and Fragments*, 557; *StA* II, 218). The mortals thus appear as a reflection of the divine, as the harmonious but unfree counterpart to the gods, in which the latter may find their own sensuous depiction. Yet in grappling with this relation between the pure and the crude, Hölderlin moves beyond what can be perceived by the senses; his concern is with the sphere of knowledge and cognition. In order to achieve cognition of itself, the pure requires the crude, just as the gods do the Titans, as their own inherent principle of opposition. Hölderlin's valorisation of the Titans in his late poems is premised then on the idea that this other of the gods must be given its own weight, that nature be grasped not simply as a principle of spirit or the mind but as a force in its own right, an assertion that the Titans themselves make and mobilise against Olympian reign. Decisive in this context is not each individual term of the relation but, like for Hegel, the relation between the variables itself. For the loss of one pole or term threatens to unravel the entire relation. And for this reason, then, the gods themselves display a substantial interest in the life of the Titans, and the father of the gods himself reaches into the abyss in which the Titans reside:

> Und in die Tiefe greifet
> Daß es lebendig werde
> Der Allerschütterer, meinen die
> Es komme der Himmlische
> Zu Toten herab und gewaltig dämmerts
> Im ungebundenen Abgrund
> Im allesmerkenden auf.
>
> (StA II 219)

> And down into the depth
> To make it come to life,
> Reaches he who shakes all things,
> They believe the Heavenly comes
> Down to the dead, and mightily
> In the unfettered abyss,
> The all-perceiving, light breaks.
>
> (*Poems and Fragments*, 559)

Hölderlin's image of the unfettered abyss is multivalent: it alludes to both Tartarus as the site of the Titan's imprisonment and to Hades as the place in which the dead reside. The gesture of poetic *memoria* invoked in the first stanza of the poem is now juxtaposed with the liberation of the Titans, as both are revealed to constitute one and the same plunge into the depths. Such a movement is required in order that 'it come to life'. In this way, the organic – the aim of Greek poetry as it derives from the aorgic – turns out to be itself dependent upon the anterior force of the unbound; Zeus, as the father of the gods and the father of time, is reliant upon the power of the Titans; spirit and mind do not rule over but are part of nature. Hölderlin's alternative enlightenment aims therefore at reconciliation that would not necessarily presume the triumph of spirt but would, in unleashing nature, bring time and history into motion. '[If] now it erupts' [*Wenn schon es aufgärt*] (*Poems and Fragments*, 559; StA II, 219), as the poem pronounces, it also seethes and bubbles in the abyss. Such festering, which Hölderlin conceives, as Jürgen Link suggests, in the scientific terms of a chemical process in which bound and unbound elements collide, constitutes a necessary part in a historical dynamic that is not linear but rather made up of moments of fulfilment. The task of the poet is not to actualise or bring about this historical *kairos* of fulfilled time, just as little as it is Pindar's goal to win the athletic games of which his odes sing. Rather, the task consists in announcing the possibility of the *kairos* of fulfilled time amid the threat of forgetting the Titanic elements and therefore the threat of spirit's unilateral reign over nature. The poet's position is therefore an ambiguous one: in reading the signs that 'the bird of heaven / Makes [. . .] known to him', the father melancholically immerses himself in the depths of nature; yet while the father elevates himself, 'Marvellous in anger', the modern poet commits to a poetics of the calculable law, one that Hölderlin, as his poetological engagement with Greek tragedy and his own translations of Greek tragedy demonstrate, seeks to translate for the present. In this way, the wrath of the gods which also fuelled the passion of the Greek heroes Achilles, Aias and Oedipus, and upon which Hölderlin's later works reflect,[22] is counterbalanced by the poet's own melancholy. Such melancholy doesn't constitute an end in itself. Rather, it marks an attempt, 'in festive hours', to rescue the memory of past time in the *kairos* of a fulfilled time yet to come – a memory not only of the past but also one 'of the future', as Bennholdt-Thomsen put its.[23] This is a time that, in a precarious synthesis of past, future and present, is marked by what Hölderlin translates from Pindar's eighth Pythian Ode: 'luminous light is on man and lovely life' [*leuchtend Licht ist bei den Männern und liebliches Leben*] (*StA* V, 101).

Translated by Nathan Taylor

Notes

1. Klaus Düsing summarises the chiastic relation between Greek and modern poetry in Hölderlin as follows:

   > The Greeks assume an aorgic, unbound infinity, which is natural to them, and achieve in their art a self-formation and self-limitation, such that they can recognize themselves as defined. Hesperians, one is inclined to interpret from Hölderlin's complex remarks, assume as their origin an inanimate limitedness and firm lawfulness that has become artificial; relying on nature or the course of nature, they strive to move beyond rigid limitedness towards the aorgic and infinite. (Düsing, 'Die Theorie der Tragödie bei Hölderlin und Hegel', p. 66)

2. On Hölderlin's concept of nature see Büttner, 'Natur – ein Grundwort Hölderlins', pp. 224–47. Büttner makes especially clear that the opposing forces of the organic and aorgic do not simply represent contradicting forces in Hölderlin but are dialectically related as two sides of the same medallion.
3. See Szondi, *Hölderlin-Studien*, pp. 119–69.
4. See Link, *Hölderlin-Rousseau. Inventive Rückkehr*, p. 15.
5. Duvillard, 'Das hymnische Fragment *Die Titanen*', p. 151.
6. Ibid. p. 157.
7. Bennholdt-Thomsen and Guzzoni, *Analecta Hölderliana II*, p. 35.
8. Heidegger, *Being and Time*, p. 1.
9. Häny, *Hölderlins Titanenmythos*, p. 45.
10. Bennholdt-Thomsen, 'Die Bedeutung der Titanen in Hölderlins Spätwerk', p. 227.
11. Ibid. p. 252.
12. Theunissen, *Pindar: Menschenlos und Wende der Zeit*, p. 961.
13. Ibid. p. 962.

14. Bennholdt-Thomsen, 'Die Bedeutung der Titanen im Hölderlins Spätwerk', pp. 239–40.
15. Hamacher, 'Parusie, Mauern', p. 123.
16. Similar language is used in 'Wenn nämlich der Rebe Saft' ['For when the grape vine's sap']:

> Und Bienen
> Wenn Sie vom Wohlgeruche
> Des Frühlings trunken, der Geist
> Der Sonne rühret, irren ihr nach
> Die Getriebenen, wenn aber
> Ein Strahl brennt, kehren sie
> Mit Gesumm, vielahnend,
> darob die Eiche rauschet
>
> And bees
> When, drunken with the fragrance
> Of Spring, they are stirred
> By the spirit of the sun,
> Driven on, they fumble for it,
> But when a ray burns,
> Buzzing, they turn back,
> Divining much / above it
> the oak-tree rustles
>
> (StA II, 216; Poems and Fragments, 535)

17. Plato, *Ion*, pp. 421–3, translation modified.
18. See Waszink, *Biene und Honig als Symbol des Dichters und der Dichtung in der griechisch-römischen Antike*, p. 6.
19. Fränkel, 'Die Zeitauffassung in der frühgriechischen Literatur', p. 5.
20. Bennholdt-Thomsen and Guzzoni, *Alaecta Hölderliana II*, p. 36.
21. On the lightning rod as an image of the Enlightenment and sign for contemporary mercantile age, see Link, 'Naturgeschichtliche Modellsymbolik und Hermetik', p. 155.
22. See Schmidt, 'Der Begriff des Zorns', p. 136: 'And just as in the late poems nature's great power is elevated to the mythic realm of divine wrath, so too is the realm of the "positive" mythologized as that of the Titans.'
23. Bennholdt-Thomsen, 'Zum zeitlichen Index von Andersheit', p. 28.

Bibliography

Bennholdt-Thomsen, Anke, 'Die Bedeutung der Titanen in Hölderlins Spätwerk', *Hölderlin Jahrbuch* 25 (1986–87), pp. 226–54.
Bennholdt-Thomsen, Anke, 'Zum zeitlichen Index von Andersheit beim späten Hölderlin: Eine quellenkundliche Untersuchung der Früchte-Strophe von Mnemosyne', in Emil Angehrn, Christian Iber, Georg Lohmann and Roman Pocai (eds), *Der Sinn der Zeit* (Weilerswist: Velbrueck, 2002), pp. 279–93.
Bennholdt-Thomsen, Anke and Guzzoni, Alfredo, *Analecta Hölderliana II: Die Aufgabe des Vaterlands* (Würzburg: Königshausen & Neymann, 2004).
Büttner, Stefan, 'Natur – ein Grundwort Hölderlins', *Hölderlin-Jahrbuch* 26 (1988–89), pp. 224–47.
Düsing, Klaus, 'Die Theorie der Tragödie bei Hölderlin und Hegel', in Christoph Jamme

and Otto Pöggeler (ed.), *Jenseits des Idealismus. Hölderlins letzte Homburger Jahre (1804–1806)* (Bonn: Bouvier, 1988), pp. 55–82.
Duvillard, Brigitte, 'Das hymnische Fragment *Die Titanen*: Von der Mythologie zur Meteorologie', in Christoph Jamme and Anja Lemke (eds), *'Es bleibet aber eine Spur / Doch eines Wortes': Zur späten Hymnik und Tragödientheorie Friedrich Hölderlins* (München: Fink, 2004), pp. 135–51.
Fränkel, Hermann, 'Die Zeitauffassung in der frühgriechischen Literatur', in Fränkel, *Wege und Formen frühgriechischen Denkens* (München: Beck, 1955), pp. 1–22.
Hamacher, Werner, 'Parusie, Mauern, Mittelbarkeit und Zeitlichkeit, später Hölderlin', *Hölderlin-Jahrbuch*, 34 (2004–5), pp. 93–142.
Häny, Arthur, *Hölderlins Titanenmythos* (Zurich: Atlantis Verlag, 1948).
Heidegger, Martin, *Being and Time*, trans. Joan Stambaugh (Albany: State University of New York Press, 1996).
Link, Jürgen, 'Naturgeschichtliche Modellsymbolik und Hermetik in Hölderlins Hymne nach 1802 (mit einem näheren Blick auf *Die Titanen*)', in Sandra Heinen and Harald Nehr (eds), *Krisen des Verstehens um 1800* (Würzburg: Königshausen & Neumann, 2004), pp. 153–67.
Link, Jürgen, *Hölderlin-Rousseau: Inventive Rückkehr* (Opladen: Springer, 1999).
Plato, *Statesman. Philebus. Ion*, trans. Harold North Fowler and W. R. M. Lamb, Loeb Classical Library 164 (Cambridge, MA: Harvard University Press, 1925).
Schmidt, Jochen, 'Der Begriff des Zorns in Hölderlins Spätwerk', in *Hölderlin-Jahrbuch*, 15 (1967), pp. 128–57.
Szondi, Peter, *Hölderlin-Studien: Mit einem Traktat über philologische Erkenntnis* (Frankfurt am Main: Suhrkamp, 1970).
Theunissen, Michael, *Pindar: Menschenlos und Wende der Zeit* (Munich: C. H. Beck, 2000).
Waszink, Jan Hendrik, *Biene und Honig als Symbol des Dichters und der Dichtung in der griechisch-römischen Antike* (Opladen: Springer, 1974).

Part II
Hölderlin's Rivers

Chapter 5

The Untamed Earth: The Labour of Rivers in Hölderlin's 'The Ister'

Rochelle Tobias

What would move a river to leave its hiding place? What could compel it to abandon its source? Why would it venture into a valley where it would be exposed to the heat of the sun, when it could still enjoy the protection of trees and rock? These are familiar questions in Hölderlin's late poetry, which returns again and again to the theme of the rivers that at once connect mortals and immortals, while at the same time holding them apart so that each may relate to the other as 'harmoniously opposing' terms, to borrow an expression from Hölderlin's poetic theory.[1] Rivers make music, or better yet they establish harmony. It is, however, a harmony that can be disrupted at any point owing to an excess of matter or spirit. Rivers can overflow, or alternatively they can dry up; they can resist the banks that surround them, or these same banks can resist and impede their progress. Either event exposes the uneasy relationship between spirit and matter that is the basis of life for Hölderlin.

Life emerges out of a conflict, a contest between organic and aorgic tendencies, which can be quelled but never overcome or resolved permanently.[2] Whenever these two tendencies are reconciled, a cosmic accord is achieved, which is expressed in art and poetry. For Hölderlin, poetry flows like the rivers that turn deserts into luxuriant fields, as he notes in more than one poem. In 'The Ister', for instance, he writes with uncharacteristic bluntness, 'For rivers make arable / The Land' (*Poems and Fragments*, 513) and in 'The Rhine' he likewise underscores that the river, which he identifies as a father, 'supports dear children / In cities which he has founded' [*liebe Kinder nährt / In Städten die er gegründet*] (*Poems and Fragments*, 435; *FHA* VIII, 830). Finally in 'As on a holiday . . .' he compares the rivers that irrigate fields to the grapevine, which combines heavenly fire (i.e. lightening) and telluric elements in its fruit and in so doing tames both impulses. Indeed the synthesis of these two harmoniously opposing forces produces wine, which is as much a symbol of culture as of agriculture, of poetry as of collective life: 'And hence it is that without danger now / The sons of Earth drink heavenly fire' [*Und daher trinken himmlischen Feuer jetzt / Die Erdensöhne ohne Gefahr*] (*Poems and Fragments* 397; *FHA* VIII, 558).

Yet the achievements of culture are short-lived and no poem demonstrates this more forcefully than 'As on a holiday . . .' which breaks off as soon as the poet attempts to assume the role of mediator between mortals and immortals and is rejected as a false prophet:

> Ich sei genaht, die Himmlischen zu schauen,
> Sie selbst, sie werfen mich tief unter die Lebenden,
> Den falschen Priester, ins Dunkel, daß ich
> Das warnende Lied den Gelehrigen singe.
> Dort
>
> (*FHA* VIII, 559)

> That I approached to see the Heavenly,
> And they themselves cast me down, deep down
> Below the living, into the dark cast down
> The false priest that I am, to sing,
> For those who have ears to hear, the warning song.
> There
>
> (*Poems and Fragments*, 399)

'There' is the last word of the poem and as much a beginning as an end: the beginning of a sentence that was never to be written and a caesura that indefinitely suspends the text, since the poet turns out to be the tragic sacrifice of his own work. That is, he dies as the figure he claimed to be – a heroic poet who could withstand God's presence and grasp '[t]he Father's ray, no less, with our own two hands' [*Des Vaters Stral, ihn selbst, mit eigner Hand*] (*Poems and Fragments*, 397; *FHA* VIII, 558) – and what remains in his absence is merely a place, 'There', which refers as much to the text as to the now vacant position of the poet. 'As on a holiday . . .' ends abruptly, or more precisely it stops *in medias res* because the consciousness that motivated it disappears, consumed by the divine fire it had struggled to grasp.

In his 'Notes on the *Antigone*' Hölderlin observes that in tragedy God comes to the foreground in the tragic hero's death, and this comment would seem particularly apt with respect to 'As on a holiday . . .' even if it is not a dramatic work. As Hölderlin indicates elsewhere, what distinguishes genres is not their external form – say, whether they are written in epic hexameters or elegiac distiches – but the relation of their underlying tone (i.e. *Grundton, Bedeutung*) to their mode of presentation (i.e. *Darstellung, Kunstcharakter, Ausdruck*), a relation that can vary from work to work and which allows for such hybrid genres as a lyric tragedy and a tragic lyric.[3] 'As on a holiday . . .' belongs to the latter category insofar as its underlying tone or meaning is ideal (pertaining to the *conception* of the poet as mediator) whereas its representation is heroic (pertaining to the *adventures* of an individual), which constitute the basic criteria for tragedy. (Tone and representation or artistic character are always opposing and their alternating relation is consequently dialectical.) That Hölderlin considers *Antigone* to be a lyric tragedy provides support for the claim that the two works are comparable in spite of their manifest differences.[4] Yet the ultimate basis for their comparison is not their genre. If anything, this is merely an expression of the form that death takes in each – a form that determines their underlying tone and artistic character or representation.

What constitutes the caesura in both texts is a spiritual death. In 'As on a holiday . . .' it occurs in the word 'There', which marks the point of the poet's retreat: the place where he disappears from his work, which functions henceforth as his epitaph. In *Antigone*, it occurs in the third act as the protagonist considers the fate of Niobe whose transformation into stone prefigures her own death in a sealed cave. Regarding this scene, Hölderlin writes:

> It is a great help to the secretly working soul that at the highest stage of consciousness it retreats from consciousness and, before the present God actually takes hold of it [*und ehe sie wirklich der gegenwärtige Gott ergreift*], the soul confronts him with bold and often even blasphemous words and so preserves the sacred, living possibility of spirit.
>
> In high consciousness [*hohem Bewußtsein*] the soul always compares itself to objects that have no consciousness but which take on the form of consciousness in the soul's fate. One such object is a land laid to waste, which in its original abundant fertility amplifies the effects of the sun too much and thus becomes a desert. This is the fate of the Phrygian Niobe, as it is the fate of innocent nature everywhere, which in its virtuosity becomes all-too-organic to the same degree that man draws closer to the aorgic [*in eben dem Grade ins Allzuorganische gehet, wie der Mensch sich dem Aorgischen nähert*]. (*FHA* XVI, 414–15, my translation)

Hölderlin expands here on the idea of 'infidelity' [*Untreue*] (*FHA* XVI, 258) introduced in his 'Notes on the Oedipus' where gods and humans are said to turn away from each other as part of a process of purification after having trodden too close to each other in an act that violated the separation of realms. In *Oedipus Rex*, the gods abandon humanity for humanity's sake, as the poet notes, when he comments that 'divine infidelity' is easier to bear than the attention of the gods. In *Antigone*, by contrast, the soul abandons God for God's sake. Or rather: it abandons consciousness at the precise moment when the latter reaches its summit ('das *höchste* Bewußtseyn') and is all but indistinguishable from God.[5] At such moments Spirit is tempted to assert itself, that is to take hold of everything it can incorporate into itself. What prevents it from appropriating everything and, by extension, from devouring itself is the soul that in blaspheming God maintains the distinctions between humans and gods, earth and heaven, the organic and aorgic. Put otherwise, in resisting its absorption into Spirit, the soul maintains the differences that are necessary for Spirit to continue to animate the material world.

To ensure this possibility, however, the soul must sacrifice itself. This is the significance of the story of Niobe in the above-cited passage. In the *Iliad* Niobe is forced to see her children slaughtered and is turned to stone herself after boasting of her incomparable beauty in an unbridled act of hubris. Hölderlin would say she invites the divine fire with these boasts, much like a bountiful land that attracts the rays of the sun and becomes a lifeless desert. Yet what links these two stories is not so much the transformation of a once fertile land or womb into a barren space. It is the power that the inorganic world acquires as the soul comes increasingly to identify with it and not with consciousness. The soul as the *locus classicus* of interiority is turned inside out; it is associated with a series of external objects that stand opposite Spirit not just as a vehicle for Spirit's impress but as a force in their own right. Exteriorised, the soul functions 'as the spirit of the eternally living, unwritten wilderness and the world of the dead' [*als der Geist der ewig lebenden ungeschriebenen Wildniß und der Todtenwelt*] (*FHA* XVI, 413; my translation), which is how Hölderlin refers to the 'aorgic' tendency elsewhere in the 'Notes on the *Antigone*'.

This is the terrain into which rivers wander. It is one in which the sun turns a living nature into an expanding desert, which allows for no distinction between elements. What would lead a river to enter this space is a genuine question for Hölderlin and not merely a metaphorical one. How the wet interacts with the dry, water with earth, and finally water with fire and air is central to his cosmology. The lines, 'Not for nothing do rivers flow / Through dry land' [*Umsonst nicht gehn / Im Trokenen die Ströme*] (*Poems and Fragments* 515; *FHA* VIII, 727) from 'The Ister' are consistent with this concern. What purpose the flowing of rivers serves in this poem and elsewhere in Hölderlin's writing is the subject of this essay.

Fire of heavens

The opening lines of 'The Ister' are among the most exultant Hölderlin wrote.[6] In them, the poet calls on the sun to appear after what has presumably been a prolonged period of darkness:

> Jetzt komme, Feuer!
> Begierig sind wir
> Zu schauen den Tag,
> Und wenn die Prüfung
> Ist durch die Knie gegangen,
> Mag einer spüren das Waldgeschrei.
>
> (*FHA* VIII, 727)

> Now come, fire!
> We are impatient
> To look upon Day,
> And when the trial
> Has passed through the knees,
> One may perceive the cries in the wood.
>
> (*Poems and Fragments*, 513)

However simple these lines may seem, they represent a self-fulfilling prophecy. As soon as the speaker utters the word 'Now', he signals that the moment has *now* come in which we can speak of the dawning of the day or the arrival of the sun. In other words he indicates that the hour of renewal and rebirth is here, even if he heralds it as yet to come in a reversal of night and day, before and after, which is central to the structure of the poem.

The title 'The Ister' derives from the Greek *Istros*, which in antiquity was the name for the lower portion of the Danube, where the latter feeds into the Black Sea. The Danube is unusual in that it runs not from east to west but west to east, as the poem notes on several occasions, including at the outset of the third stanza:

> Der scheinet aber fast
> Rükwärts zu gehen und
> Ich mein, er müsse kommen
> Von Osten.
>
> (*FHA* VIII, 727)

> Yet this river seems almost
> To travel backwards and
> I think it must come from
> The East.
>
> (*Poems and Fragments*, 515, translation modified)

This is the first of two occasions in which the speaker reflects on how the river appears to him. The second occurs at the end of the same stanza when he comments on the river's lacklustre pace at its beginning: 'But all too patient / He seems to me' [*Aber allzugedultig / Scheint der mir*] (*Poems and Fragments* 515; *FHA* VIII, 728). What is significant about these remarks, however, is not their personification of the river but the parallel they draw between the river Ister and the poem Ister, both of which are loath to leave their source. Both hesitate to move forward when the future that awaits them seems to lie in their past – specifically in the East where Indo-European culture is born, as Hegel, Novalis and Schopenhauer noted in what became a familiar trope of German romanticism.

The poem 'The Ister' like the river Ister turns back as soon as it starts. In fact, no sooner does it announce the coming of the day than it directs its attention toward the path the poet must have travelled to greet this day and make this pronouncement – in short, to write this poem:

> Wir singen aber vom Indus her
> Fernangekommen und
> Vom Alpheus.
>
> (*FHA* VIII, 727)

> But, as for us, we sing from the Indus,
> Arrived from afar, and
> From the Alpheus.
>
> (*Poems and Fragments*, 513)

In one of the most conspicuous instances of enjambment in the poem, the poet conflates what would seem to be the subject of his song – 'Wir singen aber vom Indus her' – with the story of his origins, as in the statement, 'Wir sind vom Indus her fernangekommen'. This is hardly a surprising gesture given that we have come to expect poets to recount their past and to reflect on their adventures. Yet the overlap in these lines is more complicated than this. It is not merely that the poet sings of the place from which he and his fellow poets come. It is that his history is simultaneously the history of song. In other words, his story is simultaneously the story of culture as it moves from east to west, from the Indus Valley to Northern Europe via ancient Greece. This is the third meaning of the lines that the enjambment brings to the fore. The poet sings not only *of* the Indus river but also *from* this very place ('vom Indus her'). His song has 'come from afar', it is '[f]ernangekommen' in that it carries its origins within it.

In the so-called Böhlendorff letter – the letter Hölderlin wrote to his friend Casimir Ulrich Böhlendorff in December 1801 on the eve of his departure to Bordeaux – he underscores the reversal of ancient and modern as well as eastern and western cultures outlined above.[7] The premise of the letter is that the most difficult skills to learn are those that are innate. He points to the ancient Greeks to argue that because the Hellenes were given to 'sacred pathos' (*FHA* XIX, 492–3), their art remains composed, sober and sedate; modern Europeans by contrast are given to measure and thus tend to be exuberant in their art to overcome the restrictions they impose on their surroundings.[8] The chiastic relation between innate character and artistic expression, however, is not limited to a single culture.

It operates across cultures as well, and this is where Hölderlin's anthropological theory of art becomes an aesthetic model of history. In what is perhaps the most revealing statement in the letter he recommends, 'But what is one's own needs to be learned like what is foreign. This is what makes the Greeks indispensible for us' [*Aber das Eigene muß so gut gelernt seyn, wie das Fremde. Deswegen sind uns die Griechen unentbehrlich*] (*FHA* XIX, 492). The matter-of-factness of this statement should not belie its audaciousness. If the Greeks are indispensable to modern Europeans, it is because they bring to the fore the essential character and innate gifts of the moderns, which otherwise lies hidden from them. For Hölderlin, classical Greek art is quintessentially modern in that it expresses the restraint typical of European culture, even if the moderns are unaware of it. Conversely modern art displays the passion that the ancient Greeks had to struggle to contain given their unique closeness to the gods or what Hölderlin calls 'the fire of the heavens' (*FHA* XIX, 492). This fire, which is native to the Greeks, can only safely manifest itself abroad in Hesperia, the western land, the Occident.

Read against this backdrop the speaker's appeal, 'Now come, fire', is an affirmation of the presence of fire in the Ister – that is, in both the poem and the river. Fire is the inspiration that gives rise to the work, even if the speaker claims it has yet to arrive. This is consistent with Hölderlin's reflections on his own unfinished tragedy in 'The Ground of Empedocles'. There he writes, 'The tragic ode begins in the highest fire, pure spirit, pure interiority has overstepped its bounds' (*FHA* XII, 413). Every ode and, as Hölderlin would have it, every river begins with a breach that it struggles to catch up with after the fact, making the projection of the future a diagnosis of the past. A similar reversal holds true for the river Ister, which runs geographically from west to east, but which is nourished by rivers running east to west, including the Alpheus. Indeed in the *Aeneid* the Alpheus is said to pass under the Ionian Sea only to resurface in the island of Ortygia, modern day Sicily, where it feeds into the Arethusa River:

> Alpheum fama est huc Elidis amnem
> occultas egisse vias subter mare, qui nunc
> ore, Arethusa, tuo Siculis confunditur undis.
>
> The tale runs that the Elean stream, Alpheus,
> Took hidden channels there under the sea,
> And through your fountain, Arethusa, now
> Infuses the salt waves.[9]

Of note is that in the *Aeneid* the island of Ortygia is located in Hesperia and as such provides a bridge between the rivers of the Orient and the Occident otherwise divided by the sea.

'The Ister' alludes to this geography when it describes the gulf separating the speaker from his projected home in the north:

> ... lange haben
> Das Schikliche wir gesucht,
> Nicht ohne Schwingen mag
> Zum Nächsten einer greifen
> Geradezu
> Und kommen auf die andere Seite.
>
> <div align="right">(<i>FHA</i> VIII, 727)</div>

> ... long we
> Have sought what is fitting,
> Not without wings may one
> Reach out for that which is nearest
> Directly
> And get to the other side.
>
> <div align="right">(<i>Poems and Fragments</i>, 513)</div>

Although the distance the speaker refers to may not be great, it requires extraordinary means to reach the 'other side' of what could be a mountain range or a sea. Given that the poem is devoted to a river and one moreover named in Greek, the latter hypothesis would seem more likely. Oceans are unbridgeable for human beings without the aid of wings; rivers by contrast can navigate large bodies of water subterraneously according to the ancient geological theory presented in the *Aeneid*. What, however, in this case is more significant is the pursuit that sends the speaker on his way, and here the letter to Böhlendorff proves to be particularly illuminating. To reach 'what is fitting' [*das Schickliche*], which is not only what is fitting for the poet but also what has been cut for him as his fate, he must venture overseas. Only in a foreign land does he discover what is 'nearest' to him [*das Nächste*], as only in Greek art does the modern subject discover what is native to him. '[L]ong we / Have sought what is fitting', the speaker tells us, as if he has been underway for centuries, if not since the time of the ancient Greeks. And to the degree that his history is simultaneously the history of culture, it is not improbable to say that he is an incarnation of Greek culture that finds its proper home abroad, in a foreign place.

Rivers and dwelling

In lines so simple they are almost gnomic, the poet declares:

> Hier aber wollen wir bauen.
> Denn Ströme machen urbar

> Das Land. Wenn nemlich Kräuter wachsen
> Und an denselben gehn
> Im Sommer zu trinken die Thiere,
> So gehn auch Menschen daran.
>
> (*FHA* VIII, 727)

> But here we wish to build.
> For rivers make arable
> The land. For when herbs are growing
> And to the same in summer
> The animals go to drink,
> There too will human kind go.
>
> (*Poems and Fragments*, 513)

According to these lines, the 'we' of the poem follows a river that has already made a place for it, which is in one sense a banal observation: civilisations tend to grow up around rivers where they find ample sustenance. On the other hand this place owes its being to a river that arguably comes from abroad insofar as it bears within itself the 'fire of heaven'. What the speaker calls 'here', then, arises by virtue of a 'there', which may account for the Ister's sluggishness at its ostensible beginning in the Black Forest. Indeed, the speaker emphasises that the river lingers at its source, which is simultaneously its mouth, insofar as it is a continuation of the Indus and the Alpheus.[10] Hence in the first explicit reference to the river, the poem underscores its stillness, as if it were a pool instead of a body of moving water:

> Man nennet aber diesen den Ister,
> Schön wohnt er. Es brennet der Säulen Laub,
> Und reget sich. Wild stehn
> Sie aufgerichtet, untereinander; darob
> Ein zweites Maas, springt vor
> Von Felsen das Dach.
>
> (*FHA* VIII, 727)

> This one, however, is called the Ister
> Beautifully he dwells. The pillars' foliage burns,
> And stirs. Wildly they stand
> Supporting one another; above,
> A second measure, juts out
> The roof of rocks.
>
> (*Poems and Fragments*, 513)

The unmistakable metaphor in these lines is that of a house. The river inhabits – 'Beautifully he dwells [*wohnt*]' – what would seem like an interior space with arboreal columns [*Säulen*] surrounding it and a stone roof that juts out over its head ('The roof [*Dach*] of rocks'). It is even conceivable that this setting is a temple given the columns and other architectural features the poem names, all of which serve to protect the Ister from the elements. As a result of this protection, it can rest while everything around it stirs. The foliage burns in the sun and quakes in the wind, and the trees press against each other as they compete for light to nourish their roots. The vertical axis formed by the trees and the horizontal axis formed by the roof satisfy the basic requirements for a temple.

The poem, however, establishes the sacred dimensions of this site in another way, which goes to the heart of the question regarding what distinguishes 'here' from 'there' and whether the river originates in the Orient or Occident. The tranquillity of the grove reminds the speaker of Hercules' trip to the source of the Ister where he finds respite from the heat:

> ... So wundert
> Mich nicht, daß er [der Ister]
> Den Herkules zu Gaste geladen,
> Fernglänzend, am Olympos drunten,
> Da der, sich Schatten zu suchen
> Vom heißen Isthmos kam.
>
> (*FHA* VIII, 727)

> No wonder, therefore,
> I say, this river
> Invited Hercules,
> Distantly gleaming, down by Olympus,
> When he, to look for shadows,
> Came up from the sultry isthmus.
>
> (*Poems and Fragments*, 513–15)

It is unclear whether the adjective 'distantly gleaming' [*fernglänzend*] refers to Hercules, whose fame would have spread far and wide in the mythological world, or to the Ister, whose reflection, even if filtered through trees, would have lured the hero to the north. The fact that this gleam issues equally plausibly from the two places attests to the difficulty of keeping them apart. The difficulty only increases, when one considers the classical intertext for these verses, which themselves represent an amalgam of ancient and modern culture. The allusion is to Pindar's Third Olympian Ode, for which Hölderlin produced a partial translation. The ode recounts in some detail how Hercules came to the north and discovered the olive tree on the banks of the Ister. He convinces the Hyperboreans to let him take the tree 'from the shaded source of the Ister' [*FHA* XV, 163] back to Olympia. Henceforth the olive branch is used to make garlands for victors at the Olympic games. Additionally it serves as an offering to Zeus at the temple dedicated to him in Olympia, which not incidentally lies on the banks of the Alpheus.

The story of the olive tree is at heart the story of transplanting culture, which explains in part why Hercules must return from the north with a plant rather than, say, a stone, which can flourish in foreign soil. In fact the tree comes to dominate the southern landscape, turning the parched valley alongside the Alpheus into an 'illustrious grove' [*erlauchten / Hain*] (*FHA* XV, 163) according to Pindar. The Peloponnesian Peninsula thus comes to resemble the thickly wooded hills surrounding the Ister in a remarkable instance of cultural reversal and exchange.

As Hölderlin was well aware, however, this dynamic works in the opposite direction as well, and the second strophe of 'The Ister' acknowledges this movement through another allusion, this time to Hölderlin's own work. In the hymn 'The Journey' [*Die Wanderung*] composed shortly before the Böhlendorff letter in 1801, the poet tells of another ancient people who travelled far to find relief from the piercing rays of the sun. But the people in this case are proto-Germans and their destination is not the Black Forest but the Black Sea:

> Es seien vor alter Zeit
> Die Eltern einst, das deutsche Geschlecht,
> Still fortgezogen von Wellen der Donau,
> Am Sommertage, da diese
> Sich Schatten suchten, zusammen
> Mit Kindern der Sonn'
> Am Schwarzen Meere gekommen;
> Und nicht umsonst sei dies
> Das gastfreundliche genennet.
>
> (*FHA* VIII, 618)

> The German people, had quietly
> Departed from the waves of the Danube
> One summer day, and when those
> Were looking for shade, had met
> With children of the Sun
> Not far from the Black Sea's beaches;
> And not for nothing that sea
> Was called the hospitable.
>
> (*Poems and Fragments*, 417)

The parallels between these verses and the second stanza of 'The Ister' are striking. Syntactically both rely on the formulation 'Not for nothing . . .': 'Nicht umsonst sei dies' and 'Nicht umsonst gehn / Im Trocknen'. Moreover just as Hercules travels north (and west) to look for shade ('sich Schatten zu suchen'), so too this supposed race of Ur-Germans travels south (and east) in search of shade, 'da diese / Sich Schatten suchten'. And just as Hercules is lured to the banks of the Ister and is received as a guest ('zu Gaste geladen'), so too this tribe is welcomed by the Black Sea, known as the Hospitable Sea ('Das Gastfreundliche') not only in this poem but in much of Greek and Roman antiquity. Whether in Hölderlin's mythical universe the Ur-German's trip to the south precedes Hercules' trip to the north is impossible to determine. A case could be made for either itinerary. What we do know is that they along with the 'children of the sun' sire a new race of men who disappear but would seem to be the forefathers of the poets in their ability to live in harmony with each other and with nature. Whether Hercules precedes or succeeds this race matters little. What matters more is that the two-fold movement north and south allows for a two-fold process of cultural appropriation. A northern people heads southeast for the shade of trees; perhaps it brings these trees back to the once parched north to form a grove around the Ister. In similar fashion a southern people leaves their now parched homeland for the northeast and discovers trees which they take home with them, possibly leaving the sun behind as a gift. As this brief sketch indicates, cool and hot, wet and dry, passion and restraint are reversible terms, as are beginning and end, southern and northern, past and future, and the Indus and the Ister. The Ister is a divided river in that it points in two directions at once, and this division, which seems to impede its flow, raises the question: what would prompt a river to move, a stream to flow?

The earth and signs

The sluggishness of the Danube at its beginning, which is simultaneously its terminus, is the source of some consternation for the poet. Throughout the third stanza he returns to this point again and again, each time acknowledging that this is merely his opinion, though he is unable or unwilling to dismiss it. In rapid succession he tells us, 'Yet this river seems almost / To run backwards' (lines 41–2), 'I think it must come / From the East' (lines 43–4), 'And why does / It cling to the mountains, straight' (lines 46–7) and finally '[B]ut all to patient / He seems to me, not / more free, and nearly derisive' (lines 58–60).[11] In its insolence and reluctance to move, the Danube stands in stark contrast to the Rhine, which according to the speaker is like a colt champing on the bit '[L]ike foals / He grinds the bit' [*Und Füllen gleich / In den Zaum knirscht er*] (*Poems and Fragments*, 517; *FHA* VIII, 728). The metaphor of a river as a foal is not unusual, but it has a special resonance for Hölderlin. For if the Rhine is like a foal, it is not because it refuses to accept constraints. The situation is, if anything, reversed. It refuses to accept constraints, because it is at heart a colt, a centaur, which is the god or spirit of rivers for Hölderlin. He develops this figure most explicitly in his translations of Pindar's fragments.[12]

In the note appended to his translation of the fragment 'The Life-Giver' [*Das Belebende*], he writes, 'The concept of centaurs is that of the spirit of a river insofar as it violently cuts a path and boundary on the originally pathless, upwards growing earth [*die ursprünglich pfadlose aufwärtswachsende Erde*]' (*FHA* XV, 363). The centaur, as presented here, tames an otherwise unruly earth – unruly not because it rebels against any authority but because in its continuous expansion and growth, it undoes all distinctions. If left to its own devices, the earth would become an undifferentiated mass. The same, however, could be said of rivers, which is why Hölderlin eventually suggests that the two mutually constrain each other and in so doing mutually protect themselves.

While Hölderlin begins with the violence of rivers, he quickly switches to the violence of dry land, and this shift calls into question what is more originary: the force exerted by water or earth, the power of the wet or the dry. According to Hölderlin's mythopoeic vision, at their origin rivers do not flow in any direction. When they surface, they spread in multiple directions at once, creating ponds, wetlands and grottos where wildlife can feed and drink.[13] Shades of this theory can be heard in the second stanza of 'The Ister' where the river is said to rest – 'Beautifully he dwells' – in the domestic setting it has created for itself. It is a place where 'herbs grow' (*Poems and Fragments*, 513) and 'in summer / The animals go to drink' (*Poems and Fragments*, 513), like the landscape Hölderlin describes in 'The Life-Giver' which is lush at the river's source in spite of the lack of any movement. Yet this state in which everything would seem to stand still cannot endure. What sets the water and possibly the process of history in motion is the dry land, which is Hölderlin's most stunning contribution to the theory of elements. It is the earth that compels water to move, long before water has an occasion to cut paths.[14] In other words, it is not spirit, but inert matter that moves water, even if water is usually considered the 'life-giving' force:

> Jemehr sich aber von seinen beiden Ufern das troknere fester bildete, und Richtung gewann durch festwurzelnde Bäume, und Gesträuche und den Weinstok, destomehr mußt' auch *der Strom, der seine Bewegung von der Gestalt des Ufers annahm*, Richtung gewinnen, bis er, von seinem Ursprung an gedrängt, an eine Stelle durchbrach, wo die Berge . . . am leichtesten zusammenhiengen. (*FHA* XV, 363–4, emphasis added)

> The more firmly the dry land constitutes itself from its two banks, and the more direction it gains from deeply rooting trees and bushes and grape vines, so much the more must the river, which acquires its momentum from the contours of the bank, gain direction until, propelled by its origin, it breaks through at the point where the mountain range . . . is at its weakest. (My translation)

Thanks to the contours (*Gestalt*) provided by the earth, the river can flow. Hölderlin elevates inert and immobile matter to the status of a prime mover in what would seem like a contradiction in terms. In a curious side-note, he singles out the grapevine as one of the plants that contributes to the solidity of the earth. The observation is motivated in part by the Pindar fragment in which the centaurs are said to learn 'the might of / honey-sweet wine' [*Die Gewalt / Des honigsüßen Weines*] (*FHA* XV, 363) before springing into action themselves. But the presence of this one plant on banks that constrain the centaurs would suggest that the potency of wine comes not from rivers but from the fire that rains upon it from above and feeds it from the caverns of the earth.

Thus in elaborating on the wine motif in the fragment, Hölderlin stresses again that the violence of rivers is merely a reflection of the violence that the solid earth brings to bear on it. To convert bodies of water into flowing streams, the earth must impress upon it a form that not only determines its direction but also gives it its tempo, energy, vitality:

> So *lernten* die Centauren *die Gewalt des honigsüßen Weins*, sie nahmen von dem festgebildeten, bäumereichen Ufer Bewegung und Richtung an ... [D]ie gestaltete Welle verdrängte die Ruhe des Teichs, auch die Lebensart am Ufer veränderte sich, der Überfall des Waldes, mit den Stürmen und den sicheren Fürsten des Forsts regte das müßige Leben der Haide auf, das stagnirende Gewässer ward so lange zurükgestoßen, vom jäheren Ufer, *bis es Arme gewann* und so mit eigener Richtung ... sich Bahn machte, eine Bestimmung annahm. (*FHA* XV, 364, emphasis in the original)

> Thus did the centaurs learn the might of honey-sweet wine. From the solid, tree-lined banks they acquired movement and direction ... Formed waves replaced the stillness of the pond, and even life on the banks changed. The swaying of the trees produced by storms and the confident sylvan princes disturbed the otherwise idle life on the moor. The stagnant waters were repeatedly repulsed by the steep banks, *till they grew arms* and so cut themselves a path, took on a destiny. (My translation)

No sooner does Hölderlin draw attention to the fact that the river's direction and pace are caused not by internal but external forces than he suddenly changes tack and enumerates the ways that rivers transform life on firm land. The paths that the water cuts and the arms or tributaries its gains in this fashion are all manifestations of the river as a sovereign force that carves the surface of the earth and in so doing dictates forms of life. However, it achieves this sovereignty only in a paradoxical manner, namely by submitting to the pressure of solid land and whatever power it displays is consequently nothing more than an orchestrated phenomenon. Hölderlin's commentary culminates in the paradox that rivers are determined to be a determining force; they are shaped to shape the earth.

Their form and tempo come from the land they are charged with engraving in a circular process. Thanks to this circle, however, they also make the earth legible for the first time as a living organism instead of a blank slate, 'the eternally living unwritten wilderness' [*die ewig lebende ungeschriebene Wildniß*] (*FHA* XVI, 413).

'The Ister' likewise addresses this dynamic in what is arguably its most contemplative moment:

> ... Umsonst nicht gehn
> Im Troknen die Ströme. Aber wie? Ein Zeichen braucht es
> Nichts anderes, schlecht und recht, daß es Sonn und Mond
> Trag' im Gemüth', untrennbar,
> Und fortgeh, Tag und Nacht auch, und
> Die Himmlischen warm sich fühlen aneinander.
> Darum sind jene auch
> Die Freude des Höchsten.
>
> (*FHA* VIII, 728)

> ... Not for nothing do rivers flow
> Through dry land. But how? A sign is needed,
> Nothing else, plain and honest, so that
> Sun and moon it may bear in mind, inseparable,
> And go away, day and night no less, and
> The Heavenly Powers feel warm one beside the other.
> That also is why these are
> The joy of the Highest.
>
> (*Poems and Fragments*, 515)

Few lines in Hölderlin have been treated as matter of factly as these. Critics all but agree that the poet speaks of rivers when he states, 'Ein Zeichen braucht es / Nichts anderes'.[15] But in the context of the poetry of Hölderlin, whose syntax is notoriously difficult and stretches the bounds of German grammar, the statement is relatively direct. The pronoun 'es' cannot refer to the river, and it is unlikely to be an impersonal 'es' given its recurrence two lines later as a personal pronoun in the statement 'so that / Sun and moon it may bear in mind' [*daß es Sonn' und Mond / Trag' im Gemüth*]. It also does not accord with the many impersonal statements in the poem such as 'Es brennet der Säulen Laub' [the pillar's foliage burns] (*FHA* VIII, 727; *Poems and Fragments*, 513), 'es treibet ein anderer da / Hoch schon die Pracht' [Another already there / Drives high the splendour] (*FHA* VIII, 728; *Poems and Fragments*, 513) or 'Es brauchet aber Stiche der Fels' [But the rock needs incisions] (*FHA* VIII, 728; *Poems and Fragments*, 517). Read in conjunction with the Pindar fragment, the pronoun 'es' would seem to refer to 'das Trokene', which requires a sign for reasons the poet then enumerates. 'The Ister' is consistent with the commentary on the Pindar fragment in that it is the dry land that compels the river to flow, to cut a path, to be a sign on an otherwise unmarked surface. Hence in 'The Life-Giver' he observes that the centaur brings its might to bear on 'the originally *pathless*, upwards growing earth'.

According to Grimm's Dictionary, the first signs were boundary markers on fields, and the association of agriculture with signs has a long history, as evidenced by the etymological link between the Latin *signum* and the German *sägen* and *sagen*, all of which derive from the Latin verb *secare*, to cut.[16] The poet acknowledges this tradition when in the closing lines of 'The Ister' he states, 'For the earth needs furrows / And the rock needs incisions' [*Denn Furchen brauchet die Erde / Und Stiche der Fels*][17] in a formulation reminiscent of the earlier meditation on why rivers venture from their origin. Yet the explanation does not clarify what makes rivers flow. If anything it avoids this question by focusing instead on what rivers do to make the earth inhabitable and traversable for us. Why the earth would need signs, however, is a question that has little to do with us. It concerns the earth's relation to itself, and any answer to this question is necessarily mythical, as it involves an intentionality or will that does not conform to human faculties.

Time is a river. Whether Heraclitus ever intended to propose this metaphor, it has become bound up with his name thanks to the position attributed to him in Plato's *Cratylus*: 'Heraclitus is supposed to say that all things are in motion and nothing at rest; he compares them to the stream of a river and says that you cannot go into the same river twice.'[18] 'The Ister' takes this quote, which has become a virtual truism, and converts it into something new and strange by treating the central figure as a literal phenomenon. According to this procedure, time is not only a river; rivers are also time and to make a river move is to set time in motion, to launch history, to establish day and night. If the 'dry land' [*das Trockne*] needs rivers, consequently, it is because it needs time, and to usher in the latter it must rely on a body that moves and reflects divine fire:

> Ein Zeichen braucht es
> Nichts anderes, schlecht und recht, daß es Sonn' und Mond
> Trag' im Gemüth, untrennbar,
> Und fortgeh, Tag und Nacht auch, und
> Die Himmlischen warm sich fühlen aneinander.
>
> (*FHA* VIII, 728)

Sun and moon, day and night gain a place on earth through rivers that mirror the stars. As a result of this reflection, the earth can have a history. It can move in time even if it is consigned to a single place, or rather even if it is nothing but place. For, as Hölderlin would have it, space would lack all distinctions, were it not for time, which separates what is from what is no longer and in so doing generates the first division. Without the labour of rivers, the earth would be what he calls in the 'Notes on the *Antigone*' 'the eternally living unwritten wilderness and world of the dead', that is an endlessly expanding but also spiritless mass. What the river gives the earth, then, is a medium of reflection in which the suns and moons it has witnessed can reside. Celestial bodies, which normally appear on different ends of the horizon and at different times, converge in the river that carries their reflection forward. But – and this is crucial – it also carries their reflection back ensuring that the past meets the future, the Orient the Occident, and antiquity modernity in a never-ending cycle. These are the lines that 'The Ister', the river and the poem, trace. As a tribute to the mystery of the Ister the poem ends with an oracular pronouncement: 'Yet what that one does, the river, / Nobody knows' [*Was aber jener thuet der Strom, / Weis niemand*] (*Poems and Fragments*, 517; *FHA* VIII, 729).

Notes

1. The term plays a central role in Hölderlin's theory of the alternation of tones in poetry. See Friedrich Hölderlin, 'Wenn der Dichter einmal des Geistes mächtig ist' (*FHA* XIV, 303–22).
2. Ernst Mörgel speculates that the term 'aorgic' is Hölderlin's own coinage. It resembles Schelling's term 'anorgic' but differs from this concept in important ways. For Schelling the organic and anorgic refer to opposing dimensions of nature. For Hölderlin the pair refers to the difference between humans equipped with the capacity for art and the forces of nature, which stand opposed to all human constructions. See Mörgel, *Natur als Revolution*, p. 15.
3. Hölderlin discusses the differences in poetic genres in the essay fragment 'Das lyrische dem Schein nach idealische Gedicht', which for many years was referred to as 'Über den Unterschied der Dichtarten', the title that Hölderlin editor Friedrich Beissner assigned to it. See *FHA* XIV, pp. 369–72.
4. Hölderlin states that the style of *Antigone* is lyrical in contrast to *Oedipus*, which is tragic, in the essay fragment 'Das lyrische dem Schein nach idealische Gedicht': 'Ist die intellectuale Anschauung subjectiver, und gehet die Trennung vorzüglich von den conzentrirenden Theilen aus, wie bei der Antigonä, so ist der Stil lyrisch, gehet sie mehr von den Nebentheilen aus und ist objective, so ist er episch, geht sie von dem höchsten Trennbaren, von Zeus aus wie bei Oedipus, so ist er tragisch' (*FHA* XIV, 372).
5. Françoise Dastur argues that as soon as consciousness opens itself up to the divine, it runs the risk of being eradicated. See Dastur, *Hölderlin: Le retournement natal*, pp. 91–3.
6. It should be noted that 'The Ister' is the title that Friedrich Beissner gave to the work. In the secondary literature, it is frequently referred to by its first line, 'Jetzt, komme Feuer'. While there are legitimate arguments for using the first line as a title, 'The Ister' strikes me as more fitting to the extent that it emphasises the river, which is the explicit theme of the poem, rather than fire, which is important but secondary.
7. Eric Santner points out that the letter is as much about reversal as it is about integration. Drawing on Peter Szondi's reading, he stresses that the challenge for the moderns

it to absorb antiquity, albeit in a peculiarly modern way. See Eric L. Santner, *Friedrich Hölderlin*, pp. 56–60. Peter Szondi's remarkably elegant meditation on the letter can be found in Peter Szondi, 'Überwindug des Klassizismus: Der Brief an Böhlendorff vom 4. Dezember 1801', in *Hölderlin-Studien*, pp. 95–118.

8. In *Arresting Language* Peter Fenves argues that in the eighteenth century Plato's notion of *enthousiazein* was often translated into German as *Schwärmerei*, which because of its etymological link to *Schwarm*, swarm, implies a blurring of boundaries. See Fenves, *Arresting Language*, pp. 98–102.

9. Virgil, *The Aeneid*, p. 90. The book and verse references are as follows: Book III, ll. 919–22 (Latin ll. 694–6).

10. A particularly notable example of the convergence of 'coming' and 'going' can be found at the outset of the third strophe: 'Der scheinet aber fast / Rükwärts zu *gehen* und / Ich mein, er müsse *kommen* / von Osten' (emphasis added, *FHA* VIII, 727). Other examples include: 'durch die Knie gegangen' (*FHA* VIII, 727), 'Fernangekommen' (*FHA* VIII, 727), 'Und kommen auf die andere Seite' (*FHA* VIII, 727), 'Und an denselben gehn' (*FHA* VIII, 727), 'Der Rhein ist seitwärts / Hinweggegangen. Umsonst nicht gehn / Im Troknen die Ströme' (*FHA* VIII, 729), 'Denn wie käm er / Herunter' (*FHA* VIII, 728), etc. Curiously the one strophe that does not play with variations of the verbs to go and to come is the second one concerning Hercules' visit to the Ister.

11. See *Poems and Fragments*, pp. 581–3. It should be noted that the line numbers differ in Sattler's Frankfurt edition of Hölderlin's work and Beissner's Stuttgart edition, which serves as the basis for Michael Hamburger's translations in *Poems and Fragments* in turn. The line numbers in the Frankfurt edition for the four passages quoted are: lines 42–3, lines 44–5, lines 46–7 and lines 61–4.

12. Heike Bartel explores the connection between Hölderlin's translation 'Das Belebende' and 'The Ister', though her interest is somewhat different than mine. She focuses on the function of rivers for the establishment of culture in both texts. In what follows I place more emphasis on a theory of elements as exemplified in the relation of rivers to terra firma. See Bartel, *Centaurengesänge*, pp. 166–72.

13. Maria Behre argues that rivers in Hölderlin's poetry are neither allegories nor metaphors but myths in that they represent the intersection of *poeisis* and *aesthesis*, artistic production and perception. See Behre, 'Hölderlins Stromdichtung', pp. 17–40, esp. 20–5

14. Martin Heidegger draws attention to the role of rivers in breaking paths but ignores the role that the land plays in this process in his brief reflection on 'Das Belebende'. See Heidegger, *Hölderlins Hymnen 'Germanien' und 'Der Rhein'*, p. 93.

15. See for instance Wolfgang Janke, *Archaischer Gesang*, p. 162 or Schwarz, *Vom Strom der Sprache*, p. 121.

16. Grimm's Dictionary says the following regarding signs: *'in bäume gehauenes oder an erdwällen angebrachtes grenzzeichen'*. See the entry for 'Zeichen' in http://woerterbuchnetz.de/cgi-bin/WBNetz/wbgui_py?sigle=DWB&mode=Vernetzung&lemid=GZ03102#XGZ03102 (last accessed 18 April 2019). For the link between saying [*sagen*], sawing [*sägen* and *secare*] and signs [*Signum, Zeichen*], see http://woerterbuchnetz.de/cgi-bin/WBNetz/wbgui_py?sigle=DWB&mode=Vernetzung&lemid=GS00614#XGS00614.

17. See *FHA* VIII, p. 728 and for the English *Poems and Fragments*, p. 583, translation modified. In the Stuttgart edition, the two lines appear in reverse order, 'Es brauchet aber Stiche der Fels / Und Furchen die Erd' (*StA* II, 191).

18. Plato, *Cratylus*, p. 439 (402a).

Bibliography

Bartel, Heike, *Centaurengesänge: Friedrich Hölderlins Pindarfragmente* (Würzburg: Königshausen & Neumann, 2000).
Behre, Maria, 'Hölderlins Stromdichtung: Zum Spannungsfeld von Naturwahrnehmung und Kunstauffassung', in Uwe Beyer (ed.), *Neue Wege zu Hölderlin* (Würzburg: Königshausen & Neumann, 1994), pp. 17–40.
Dastur, Françoise, *Hölderlin, le retournement natal: Tragédie et modernité, nature et poésie & autres essays* (Paris: encre marine, 1997).
Deutsches Wörterbuch von Jacob Grimm und Wilhelm Grimm, http://woerterbuchnetz.de/cgi-bin/WBNetz/wbgui_py?sigle=DWB (last accessed 9 April 2019).
Fenves, Peter, *Arresting Language: From Leibniz to Benjamin* (Stanford: Stanford University Press, 2001).
Heidegger, Martin, *Hölderlins Hymnen 'Germanien' und 'Der Rhein'*, ed. Susanne Ziegler, 3rd edn (Frankfurt am Main: Vittorio Klostermann, 1999).
Janke, Wolfgang, *Archaischer Gesang: Pindar – Hölderlin – Rilke: Werke und Wahrheit* (Würzburg: Königshausen & Neumann, 2005).
Mörgel, Ernst, *Natur als Revolution: Hölderlins Empedokles-Tragödie* (Stuttgart: Metzler, 1992).
Plato, *Cratylus*, trans. Benjamin Jowett, in Edith Hamilton and Huntington Cairns (eds), *The Collected Dialogues of Plato, Including the Letters* (Princeton: Princeton University Press, 1961).
Santner, Eric L, *Friedrich Hölderlin: Narrative Vigilance and the Poetic Imagination* (New Brunswick, NJ: Rutgers University Press, 1986).
Schwarz, Herta, *Vom Strom der Sprache: Schreibart und 'Tonart' in Hölderlins Donau-Hymnen* (Stuttgart: Metzler, 1994).
Szondi, Peter, 'Überwindug des Klassizismus: Der Brief an Böhlendorff vom 4. Dezember 1801', in *Hölderlin-Studien: Mit einem Traktat über philologische Erkenntnis* (Frankfurt am Main: Suhrkamp, 1970), pp. 95–118.
Virgil, *The Aeneid*, trans. Robert Fitzgerald (New York: Vintage, 1984).

Chapter 6

Hölderlin's Local Abstraction: The Natural-Historical Sublime in 'Voice of the People'

Márton Dornbach

> But he felt mainly indifference toward himself, and the same toward the abandoned city. He could not learn to love a place within himself where his last panic-stricken compatriot had been lost centuries before. Nor could he love the river's wild maelstroms and great floods, which swallowed and carried away any person just as they would a helpless object.[1]

1.

In one of his late poems Wallace Stevens imagines a paradoxical entity, clearly identified as such already in the title of the poem: 'The River of Rivers in Connecticut'.[2] Because the archetypal status of this 'unnamed flowing' seems inseparable from its sensible instantiations in a particular place, Stevens calls it a 'local abstraction'. The entity envisioned in the poem thus hovers between geographical particularity and a universality embracing the brotherhood of streams described by Goethe in 'Mahomet's Song' as rushing towards a common destination.[3] This feat of poetic conjuration may be viewed as Stevens's ironic solution to the difficulty posed by the 'atopic' character of the sublime, a difficulty that surfaces with exemplary clarity in Wordsworth's avowed inability to assign a proper name or a definite place to a torrent evoking the transcendent power of the imagination.[4] By relinquishing sublimity even as he flirts with it, Stevens succeeds in conjoining ideality with concreteness.

No such renunciation is required for the fusion of ideality and concreteness achieved in the famous line from Hölderlin's hymn 'The Rhine': 'A mystery are those of pure origin [*Reinentsprungenes*]' (*Poems and Fragments*, 433). The fusion is here epitomised by a proper name that has been said to derive from either the Greek verb *rein* (to flow) or the German adjective *rein* meaning 'pure'. Yet the exception afforded by this unique name only highlights the rule. For in Hölderlin's river hymns we typically find a tension between the geographical specificity of the landscape being described and the evocation of a sublime principle that transcends every particularity.

In what follows I approach this topographically elusive topic by examining a poem that Hölderlin completed during the gestation period of the Rhine hymn, and whose very structure and composition history foreground the relation between generic invocation and geographically concrete reference. 'Voice of the People' ('Stimme des Volks') is an alcaic ode that emerged in three stages, of which the last already displays qualities anticipating the late hymns. An epigrammatic two-strophe version from 1798 served as the basis for a thirteen-strophe draft composed in 1800; and that draft in its turn was incorporated with some modifications into the final text completed in 1801, which adds a feature characteristic of the Pindaric mode, namely a historical narrative consisting of eight strophes (*FHA* V, 580–96). Following minor changes made after Hölderlin's return from Bordeaux, the poem was published in the autumn of 1802 in the almanac *Flora*.

Already central to the two-strophe version, the kernel of the emergent poem is a generic analogy between the voice of the people and rivers. The eight-strophe narrative that concludes the final version opens, however, by referencing a particular river named Xanthos: 'By Xanthos once, in Grecian times, there stood / The town' [*Am Xanthos lag, in griechischer Zeit, die Stadt*] (*Poems and Fragments*, 185; *FHA* V, 594). The poem associates that river, not with the 'folk-lore of each of the senses' evoked in Stevens's river poem, but with folklore in the literal sense of a legend about a historical people. Critics have largely ignored the reference to the river that opens this historical account and the subsequent mention in the narrative of 'reeds from the river' [*des Stromes Rohr*]. Yet these reminiscences of a type of natural phenomenon foregrounded in the opening of the poem seem formally significant. Unless we are ready to view 'Voice of the People' as a mere aggregate of heterogeneous parts, we do well to attend to the arc that links the generality of the river analogy with the particular river Xanthos.[5] Not only does the progression from the former to the latter correspond to the process by which the poem emerged but it also determines the inner logic of the final text. To spell out this claim, I first consider the analogical invocation of rivers in the opening strophes, then proceed to examine the poetic logic that requires the turn to the Xanthos river, in order finally to clarify the implications of this excursion for Hölderlin's thinking about nature, history and politics.

The poem begins by rehearsing the proverb *vox populi, vox dei*, which has long served as an admonition about the inscrutability and unpredictability of the people. The lyrical subject rehearses this ambivalent glorification of the people with a certain hesitancy: 'The voice of God I called you and thought you once, / In holy youth; and still I do not recant!' [*Du seiest Gottes Stimme, so glaubt' ich sonst / In heil'ger Jugend; ja, und ich sag' es noch!*] (*Poems and Fragments*, 183; *FHA* V, 593). It is presumably to explain the impulse behind this assertion shadowed by doubt that the lyrical subject proceeds to invoke the rivers:

> Um unsre Weisheit unbekümmert
> Rauschen die Ströme doch auch, und dennoch,
>
> Wer liebt sie nicht? und immer bewegen sie
> Das Herz mir, hör' ich ferne die Schwindenden,
> Die Ahnungsvollen meine Bahn nicht,
> Aber gewisser ins Meer hin eilen.
>
> (*FHA* V, 593)

> No less indifferent to our wisdom
> Likewise the rivers rush on, but who does
>
> Not love them? Always too my own heart is moved
> When far away I hear those foreknowing ones,
> The fleeting, by a route not mine but
> Surer than mine, and more swift, roar seaward,
>
> (*Poems and Fragments*, 183)

Just as the lyrical subject cannot help being moved by the sound of rivers even as they ignore his wisdom and move away from him, likewise the voice of the people recedes from comprehension even as it stirs poetic imagination. The poem acknowledges this dual tendency through its restless movement through diverse registers. The active address of the poem's opening gives way in the second strophe to the passivity of being moved, and direct thematisation in the third strophe yields to an analogical characterisation in the fourth, which sets the stage for an extended argument whose momentum carries us to another analogy in the ninth strophe.

When the river analogy is introduced, it initially appears to be warranted by the purely formal consideration that the lyrical subject relates to the rivers and the voice of the people with the same apprehensive fascination. However, as the image of rivers undergoes further elaboration in strophes 3–4, the intrinsic character that the two phenomena have in common becomes the basis for a substantial analogy with the voice of the people:

> Denn selbstvergessen, allzubereit den Wunsch
> Der Götter zu erfüllen, ergreift zu gern

> Was sterblich ist, wenn offnen Aug's auf
>   Eigenen Pfaden es einmal wandelt,
>
> Ins All zurük die kürzeste Bahn; so stürzt
>   Der Strom hinab, er suchet die Ruh, es reißt,
>   Es ziehet wider Willen ihn, von
>   Klippe zu Klippe den Steuerlosen
>
> Das wunderbare Sehnen dem Abgrund zu.
>
> (FHA V, 593)

> For once they travel down their allotted paths
>   With open eyes, self-oblivious, too ready to
>   Comply with what the gods have wished them,
>   Only too gladly will mortal beings
>
> Speed back into the All by the shortest way;
>   So rivers plunge – not movement, but rest they seek –
>   Drawn on, pulled down against their will from
>   Boulder to boulder – abandoned, helmless –
>
> By that mysterious yearning toward the chasm.
>
> (Poems and Fragments, 183)

An intrinsic similarity was intimated already by the evocation of the lyrical subject's 'sacred youth' in the first strophe: if allegiance to a people is a way of maintaining fidelity to a temporal origin, similarly, to contemplate a river is to have a spatialised experience of origination. Since, however, as Wordsworth puts it, 'origin and tendency are notions inseparably co-relative', this analogy entails another one that is more decisive for the argument and whose temporal vector points into the future.[6] Strophes 5–7 accordingly construe the headlong rush of the rivers as an illustration of the people's yearning to overcome separation from the gods. In keeping with Hölderlin's critique of the Fichtean absolute 'I', the divine is here conceived as 'the unbound' [*das Ungebundne*], which is to say as something absolved from all relationality (*Essays and Letters*, 48, 231–2). The yearning for union with this absolute prompts an impulse to destroy those peculiarly human feats of imitation, artifice, and cultural accumulation that are necessitated by our separation from the divine and made possible by our affinity with it:

> Das Ungebundne reizet und Völker auch
>   Ergreift die Todeslust und kühne
>   Städte, nachdem sie versucht das Beste,
>
> Von Jahr zu Jahr forttreibend das Werk, sie hat
>   Ein heilig Ende troffen: die Erde grünt
>   Und stille vor den Sternen liegt, den
>   Betenden gleich, in den Sand geworfen

> Freiwillig überwunden die lange Kunst
>   Vor jenen Unnachahmbaren da; er selbst,
>   Der Mensch, mit eigner Hand zerbrach, die
>   Hohen zu ehren, sein Werk der Künstler.
>
>   (*FHA* V, 593–4)
>
> The unbound attracts, and whole peoples too
>   May come to long for death, and valiant
>   Towns that have striven to do the best thing,
>
> Year in, year out pursuing their task – these too
>   A holy end has stricken; the earth grows green,
>   And there beneath the stars, like mortals
>   Deep in their prayers, quite still, prostrated
>
> On sand, outgrown, and willingly, lies long art
>   Flung down before the inimitable ones; and he himself,
>   The man, the artist with his own two
>   Hands broke his work for their sake, in homage.
>
>   (*Poems and Fragments*, 183–5, translation modified)

In 'The Rhine', Hölderlin will offer a vast elaboration on the image of the river to evoke not only this destructive impulse but also the divine intervention ensuring that humans in their very separateness might continue to feel on behalf of the gods who are wanting in feeling (*FHA* VII, 188–91). By contrast, the argument of 'Voice of the People' switches to another analogy to describe the countervailing intervention. It is as if poetic imagination had to resist its attraction to elemental nature and move to a higher level of organisation – one that is essentially temporal – to find the right analogical register for the force that preserves the differentiation of earthly life. The relation between gods and humans is thus compared to the relation of succession between a father eagle and his fledglings:

> Doch minder nicht sind jene den Menschen hold,
>   Sie lieben wieder, so wie geliebt sie sind,
>   Und hemmen öfters, daß er lang im
>   Lichte sich freue, die Bahn des Menschen.
>
> Und, nicht des Adlers Jungen allein, sie wirft
>   Der Vater aus dem Neste, damit sie nicht
>   Zu lang' ihm bleiben, uns auch treibt mit
>   Richtigem Stachel hinaus der Herrscher.
>
>   (*FHA* V, 594)

> Yet they, the Heavenly, to men remain well-disposed,
>   As we love them so they will return our love
>   And lest too briefly he enjoy the
>   Light, will obstruct a man's course to ruin.

>   And not the eagle's fledglings alone their sire
>   Throws out of eyries, knowing that else too long
>   They'd idle – us the Ruler also
>   Goads into flight with a prong that's fitting.
>
>   (*Poems and Fragments*, 185)

By posing an obstacle to the human striving for union with him, the divinity rescues a precarious relationship of reciprocal dependence from collapsing into the void of indifferentiation. Previously figured as a polytheistic plurality ('Unnachahmbaren'), the divine absolute is now recast as a singular 'father' who intervenes to stabilise a relation to the 'unbound' along broadly Oedipal lines.[7]

Hölderlin's peculiar variation upon the Oedipal scenario comes into clear view if we attend to the ways in which the final text begins at this point to deviate from the first extended version. In the earlier version, the analogy of the fledgling eagles illustrated the stabilising act that forced a destructive urge to return to 'the birthplace' upon a roundabout path. A regressive impulse was thus sublimated into a qualified fidelity to 'the mother', requiring a measure of independence. In the final version, by contrast, the regressive urge responds to the lure of 'the unbound', rather than to nostalgia for an origin. As if to underline the force of the paternal intervention, the reference to the mother drops out. In the double bind that results, the divine is both the 'unbound' absolute whose lure destabilises mortals and the harsh father who condemns them to separateness. His intervention is no longer an act of benign pedagogy, as in the earlier version, but an expulsion whose violence is underscored by the image of the prong.

This modification helps explain the difference between the endings of the two versions. The earlier version reached a conclusion echoing Hölderlin's thought, proposed in the letter of 4 June 1799 to Karl Gok, that the 'more beautiful' path of advancing culture as well as 'the wilder' path of suicidal reabsorption into nature both respond to the same human calling to perfect nature (*Essays and Letters*, 135–6). In keeping with this thought, the conclusion of the earlier version assigned complementary 'parts' to the glory of tragic self-sacrifice and the roundabout path of restrained fidelity. Although the latter was praised as 'greater', an ambivalence persisted in the final strophe, which qualified the praise of calmness with a warning against excessive eagerness to rest. The dialectic of activity and rest developed in the antecedent strophes left this qualification open to contrary interpretations – either as a warning against complacency or as a warning against precipitous action to find rest.

In the final version, the revised analogy of the eagle fledglings intimates that the two perils are all but indistinguishable. This becomes clear if we consider the relation between the target of the analogy (the phenomenon it illuminates) and its source (the phenomenon it evokes to illuminate the target). Since the target is an intervention that blocks the impulse toward 'the unbound', one would expect the source domain to figure an act of tethering to a definite place or pursuit. Instead, by staging an act of expulsion the analogy suggests an excentric movement – one akin to the impulse countered by the intervention being illustrated. However, this incongruity is only apparent, for excessive susceptibility to the divine and lack of responsiveness to it are equally destructive to the position of exposure that allows humans to feel on behalf of gods who are unable to feel themselves. The indistinguishability of these two threats explains an otherwise puzzling inversion of temporality between the target and the source of the analogy. Whereas in the case of humans the divine intervention aims to avert a premature surrender of independent earthly life, the father eagle's act prevents overlong attachment. Again, a rigorous logic is at work in the juxtaposition of apparent opposites. Wanting to end life too early and not starting to live in the first place are equally injurious to the proper relation between humans and gods.

The extended ending of the final version reflects the acknowledgement that no formulaic prescription can do justice to the precariousness of this relation. As Kalliopi Nikolopoulou has pointed out, if the longer, earthly path is safer only because it lacks the certitude allegorised by the surer path of the rivers, then its espousal cannot – on pain of performative contradiction – take the form of theoretical certainty.[8] Instead of declaring the superiority of the longer path, therefore, the final version of the poem ends with a cautionary narrative that attests to the enduring fascination of the shorter path. Hölderlin's allegiances are, as Nikolopoulou puts it, 'genuinely divided between these two ontological orientations, which he finds necessary but mutually exclusive'.[9]

We may surmise that it was this unresolved ambivalence that prompted Hölderlin to make a startling new beginning at this point and embark on the complex narrative that concludes the final version of the poem:

> Am Xanthos lag, in griechischer Zeit, die Stadt,
>   Jezt aber, gleich den größeren, die dort ruhn,
>   Ist durch ein Schiksaal sie dem heilgen
>   Lichte des Tages hinweggekommen.
>
> Sie kamen aber, nicht in der offnen Schlacht,
>   Durch eigne Hand um. Fürchterlich ist davon,
>   Was dort geschehn, die wunderbare
>   Sage von Osten zu uns gelanget.
>
> Es reizte sie die Güte von Brutus. Denn
>   Als Feuer ausgegangen, so bot er sich,

Zu helfen ihnen, ob er gleich, als Feldherr,
    Stand in Belagerung vor den Toren.

Doch von den Mauern warfen die Diener sie,
Die er gesandt. Lebendiger ward darauf
    Das Feuer und sie freuten sich und ihnen
        Streket' entgegen die Hände Brutus

Und alle waren außer sich selbst. Geschrei
Entstand und Jauchzen. Drauf in die Flamme warf
    Sich Mann und Weib, von Knaben stürzt' auch
        Der von dem Dach, in der Väter Schwerdt der.

Nicht räthlich ist es, Helden zu trotzen. Längst
Wars aber vorbereitet. Die Väter auch,
    Da sie ergriffen waren, einst, und
        Heftig die persischen Feinde drängten,

Entzündeten, ergreiffend des Stromes Rohr,
Daß sie das Freie fänden, die Stadt. Und Haus
    Und Tempel nahm, zum heilgen Aether
        Fliegend, und Menschen hinweg die Flamme.

So hatten es die Kinder gehört, und wohl
Sind gut die Sagen, denn ein Gedächtnis sind
    Dem Höchsten sie, doch auch bedarf es
        Eines, die heiligen auszulegen.

                                                (*FHA* V, 594–6)

By Xanthos once, in Grecian times, there stood
    The town, but now, like greater ones resting there,
        Because a destiny ordained it
            Xanthos is lost to our holy daylight.

But not in open battle, by their own hands
    Her people perished. Dreadful and marvelous
        The legend of that town's destruction,
            Traveling on from the East, has reached us.

The kindliness of Brutus provoked them. For
    When fire broke out, most nobly he offered them
        His help, although he led those troops which
            Stood at their gates to besiege the township.

Yet from the walls they threw all the servants down
    Whom he had sent. Much livelier then at once
        The fire flared up, and they rejoiced, and
            Brutus extended his arms towards them,

All were beside themselves. And great crying there,
    Great jubilation sounded. Then into flames
        Leapt man and woman; of the boys one
            Plunged from the roof, into the fathers' sword another.

> It is not wise to fight against heroes. But
> Events long past prepared it. Their fathers
>   When they were quite encircled once and
>   Strongly the Persian forces pressed them,
>
> Took reeds from the river and, that they might
> Find that which is free, set ablaze their town;
>   And house and temple – breathed to holy
>   Aether – and men did the flame carry off there.
>
> So the children heard, and no doubt such lore
> Is good, because it serves to remind us of
>   The Highest, yet there's also need of
>   One to interpret these holy legends.
>   (*Poems and Fragments*, 185–7, translation modified)

In a first approach, this narrative appears to illustrate the antecedent praise of the 'shortest path'. Its first five strophes recall an episode related by Plutarch from the Roman Civil Wars, namely the self-destructive frenzy that overcame the Xanthians when their city was besieged by Brutus and the fire engulfing the city prompted the besieger to rush to the city's rescue.[10] However, the commentary given in the last three strophes presents a complication to the illustrative reading of the narrative. For here Hölderlin highlights a detail that Plutarch relegated to an afterthought: the collective suicide of the Xanthians was an act of imitation that repeated the self-immolation of their ancestors, who were under siege by the Persian general Harpagus, a disaster recorded by Herodotus. Viewed from the perspective of the preceding argument, this explanation for the later catastrophe would appear to introduce a new element, namely the determining force of historical precedents.

The argument preceding the narrative extension does not, to be sure, become irrelevant; the first destruction of Xanthos testifies powerfully to the lethal urge to escape the differentiation of earthly life. However, that older legend is evoked only to explain its later imitation. If the sixth strophe spoke of the impulse to abandon all artifice as a futile attempt at imitating the divine, the later catastrophe commemorated in the narrative shows that such excessive reverence for the inimitable may itself invite imitation. The heroes of the later catastrophe are accordingly no longer said to have 'won their part', as in the earlier version; rather, in the strophe that immediately precedes the narrative extension, they are said to have 'found a part', one that is a pre-given legacy rather than an independent achievement:

> Wohl jenen, die zur Ruhe gegangen sind,
>   Und vor der Zeit gefallen, auch die, auch die
>   Geopfert, gleich den Erstlingen der
>   Erndte, sie haben ein Theil gefunden.
>   (*FHA* V, 594)

> Those men I praise who early lay down to rest,
>   Who fell before their time, and those also, those
>   Like first-fruits of the harvest offered
>   Up – they too found a part, a portion.
>
> (Poems and Fragments, 185)

The foregrounding of this logic of imitative repetition marks a change in the perspective of the lyrical subject. Rainer Nägele focuses on this change in his reflection on the poem. In a reading informed by Habermas's account of the dialectic of the Enlightenment, Nägele argues that the poem shows Hölderlin intent on avoiding the reactionary recoil with which so many German intellectuals responded to the violence of the French Revolution. Instead of denouncing the irrational masses in the name of a rigoristic ideal of Enlightenment reason, Hölderlin elaborates a more genuinely rational discourse, one that does not simply exclude the passions agitating the people as sheer unreason but endures exposure to their otherness.[11] Through this 'tarrying with the negative', the lyrical subject of the poem becomes immersed in the vicissitudes of a voice whose source is not a self-centred subject but a discourse perpetuated through historical transmission.

However, to complicate Nägele's analysis, it must be noted that rigoristic denunciation of the irrational masses is not the only fallacy that the lyrical subject of Hölderlin's ode struggles to avoid. A danger lurks in the opposite direction as well. Recognition of the other is threatened not only by dogmatic rejection but also by projective assimilation. The enthusiasm felt by a poet witnessing revolutionary upheavals may lead to an empathetic identification that overrides whatever sober doubts he may otherwise harbour about the putative divinity of the people. A poet afflicted with experiential impoverishment will be especially prone to such fantasies. His urge to alleviate his suffering by communing with the divine may mislead him into looking for the latter in the wrong place, confirming Hölderlin's worry that a thinking born of need tends to create phantoms.[12] In the temptation to escape a personal crisis through communion with sublime forces lies an ironic warrant for the proverb *vox populi, vox dei*. Since neither the divine nor the people speaks in a voice that a human individual might readily understand, poetic attempts at investing them with an intelligible voice risk running together these two forms of alterity and reducing both to figments of a destitute self-consciousness. A passage from Hölderlin's novel *Hyperion* illustrates this very danger. Lacking a sufficiently stable sense of self in the face of the majesty of Greek antiquity, the excessive need engendered by Hyperion's titanic yearning leaves him unable to conceive of the past as a domain structured by distinct facts and individuals:

> [I]n my thought the high deeds of all the ages were mingled together, and as those gigantic forms, the clouds of heaven, united in one exultant storm, so the hundredfold victories of the Olympiads were united in me, so did they become one never-ending victory. (*Hyperion*, 12)

Thus history is assimilated to elemental nature.

The representational correlate of the fallacy just described can be discerned in the opening strophes of Hölderlin's ode. The people and the rivers are figured here in the abstract, stripped of all specificity. It is as if the lyrical subject claimed to enjoy direct intuitive access to a universal law binding all peoples and all rivers to the divine, which permitted him to abstract from the contingencies of experience. In this flight from particulars, the lyrical voice audible in the opening strophes of 'Voice of the People' shows itself prone to the very yearning for 'the unbound' of which it speaks. It thereby exemplifies the same striving to ascend to the divine purity of self-consciousness that Stanley Corngold identifies as the impulse that Hölderlin shared with his hero Empedocles.[13] Following that impulse requires an abandonment of mimetic representation, and hence, as the seventh strophe suggests, a surrendering of art. That a work of art cannot fully actualise this ideal is, as Corngold shows, the key insight that registers in the incompletion of 'The Death of Empedocles'. Reflecting on that turning point in Hölderlin's artistic development, Corngold quotes the vision of art relinquished from the seventh strophe of 'Voice of the People', thereby suggesting that the passage evokes *both* the aspiration that would rather transcend art than suffer its empirical entanglements *and* the subsequent insight into the need to renounce this self-defeating endeavour. The opening strophes of 'Voice of the People' attest to the impulse towards the 'unbound' that animates the former aspiration; yet the latter insight prevails when Hölderlin seals the manuscript of his ode with an impression of his left hand, thereby distancing himself from the artist, evoked in the sixth strophe, who 'with his own two / Hands broke his work.'[14]

The danger just outlined is arguably more directly relevant than the one highlighted by Nägele to the transformation of lyrical subjectivity in the course of the final text of 'Voice of the People'. From the outset, the ambivalence of the lyrical subject precludes dogmatic condemnation of the irrationality of the people. By contrast, projective appropriation becomes a danger for a lyrical subject precisely when he means to abandon himself without reserve to the objectivity of the people in that 'enthusiastic devotion' ('schwärmerische Ergebenheit') described in 'The Basis of Empedocles' (*FHA* XIII, 876–7). In the first half of the poem, retained from the earlier version, peoples and rivers are taken to be moved by the same overzealous yearning for the divine that Hölderlin also sees as the greatest danger for the poet – a conflation that actually exemplifies this danger. Paradoxically, it is precisely when the poem envisions the countervailing movement in strophes 8–9 that the pull of identification with the contemplated phenomena is at its strongest, so that the analogy of the fledgling eagles ends up being explicated, not in terms of the people standing over against the lyric subject, but with reference to a 'we' encompassing both: '. . . us the Ruler also / Goads into flight with a prong that's fitting' [. . . *uns auch treibt mit / Richtigem Stachel hinaus der Herrscher*] (*Poems and Fragments*, 185; *FHA* V, 594). This point of utmost tension between identification and resistance must, it seems, be reached if the lyric subject is to learn that he must refrain from presuming that his self-consciousness affords access to a putative universal form under which peoples and rivers partake of the divine.

Poetic tact thus requires that one resist the impulse toward symbolic appropriation of diverse phenomena. Instead, the lyric subject must acknowledge the otherness of peoples and rivers as well as their difference from one another, and accept that the history of each people and the course of each river manifests the workings of the divine in its own peculiar way. If the rushing of rivers toward unification symbolises an impulse to escape contingency by imagining universal symbols, then Hölderlin's ode progresses in the opposite direction as it turns from the rivers to the Xanthos river and the legend about the people associated with it. The sound to which the lyric subject now lends a sympathetic ear is no longer the natural one of rivers but the historical voice of a particular people, audible in a legend that both records and shapes the fate of that people. Exposure to this legend compels the lyric subject to discern a force at work in the history of the Xanthians that cannot be fully grasped in terms of his own plight. For whereas the earlier Xanthians acted on the same ecstatic, anti-mimetic aspiration that also animates lyric utterance, for the later Xanthians this very anti-mimetic impulse became an object of imitation.[15] As for the river Xanthos that gave the city its name, this particular river can no longer be elevated to a symbolic analogue for the people in general. Its significance for the fate of the Xanthians only emerges from the historical account that concludes the poem.

2.

To be sure, the narrative recounting the legend of Xanthos only heightens the ambivalence that surfaced already in the first extended version. Its conclusion praises legends for preserving a remembrance of 'the Highest', but not without cautioning that legends require interpretive mediation. Reflecting on this ambivalence, Eva Geulen suggests that the lyrical subject of the poem proves incapable of extricating himself from a 'self-destructive involvement with sayings and traditions'.[16] It is worth considering Geulen's argument in some detail, for it bears on the question of the relation between the opening invocation of rivers and the narrative extension of the final version.

Geulen's construal of this relation hinges on the lexical connection between utterance ('sagen') and legend ('Sage'). Indeed she suggests that the proverb invoked in the poem is a 'Sage' in both senses: its re-assertion in the opening strophe is 'nothing more than . . . the mere saying of a saying'. The subsequent invocation of rivers is, according to Geulen, a metaphorical auto-commentary on this iterative speech act rather than an assertion of similarity between the voice of the people and the rivers.[17] Having listened to his own words, the speaker becomes attentive to the uncontrollable flow of language, which leaves him unable to control the meaning and impact of the words, proverbs and legends that he inherits and rehearses. What the river analogy illustrates, in this view, is not the voice of the people but its uncontrollable influence upon the lyrical utterance. And since the lyrical subject cannot maintain the detachment asserted in the opening strophe, the poem's rehearsal of the legend of repeated self-destruction does not, according to Geulen, admit of a didactic construal. To be sure, the conclusion of the poem interprets this legend as illustrating, precisely, the need to interpret legends in order to avert the 'danger of being all too moved by the flow of language'. However, already the opening verses show the lyrical subject to be prone to this very danger. That he ends up succumbing to this danger can be seen from the reversal of chronological order in the narrative extension, which Geulen chalks up to an inability to maintain a clear distinction between the legend and its interpretation. Geulen concludes that the interpretation given in the poem is so thoroughly contaminated with the lethal energies at work in the legend as to leave 'no position, no safe site from whence a warning could be uttered'.

This argument rests on the questionable premise that only a literal quotation followed by commentary could defuse the legend, whereas interpretive paraphrase is bound to result in contamination with the lethal forces at work in the legend. Yet couldn't interpretive paraphrase just as well have the opposite effect, namely that of immunising mediation? An answer in the affirmative emerges from Hans-Jost Frey's reflections on 'Voice of the People'.[18] As Frey points out, the legend of Xanthos does the opposite of that which it recounts: preserving in artistic form the destruction of art, the legend effects 'a destruction of the destruction that it transmits.' If the later Xanthians felt compelled to imitate the heroes of the legend, it is because they failed to recognise the legend *as* legend, as an instance of art, and thus fell under its spell. What Hölderlin's poem achieves, by contrast, is an interpretation of the legend *as* legend. Frey's reading thus draws attention to that linkage between writing and interpretation that Hölderlin will enunciate at the end of 'Patmos'. The performance of the ancient proverb in the opening of 'Voice of the People' is not the 'mere saying of a saying' but a written simulation of the utterance of an ancient proverb preserved in written texts, whereas the narrative extension offers a written account of a legend recorded in texts by Plutarch and Herodotus. The lexical connection between 'sagen' and 'Sage' notwithstanding, the analogy between the opening performance of the ancient proverb and the recollection of the legend does not hold.

Although the formal consideration raised by Frey does not in itself suffice to explain how the poem succeeds in containing the destructive forces that it commemorates, Frey's emphasis on the artistic form of the narrative points in the right direction. For it suggests a perspective from which we can counter Geulen's claim that the concluding admonition about the need for interpretation is 'strangely abstract and curiously powerless in the face of the so vividly demonstrated seductiveness of legends'.[19] Attention to linguistic detail suggests that the quality noted by Geulen might be more fittingly described as a sobriety bordering on detachment that suffuses the entire narrative extension. This quality stands out all the more conspicuously against the foil of the ten preceding strophes, whose hypotactic constructions created a propulsive sweep that repeatedly overshot the divisions between strophes and even disturbed the alignment of larger units of meaning with clusters of strophes. By contrast, the syntactical oddities of the narrative extension are consistent with the gesture of spatio-temporal distancing with which the narration commences ('By Xanthos once, in Grecian times, there stood / The town'). Again and again, the flow of narration is halted by inversions, paratactic constructions and gnomic utterances. Although the images are violent and vivid, the effect of their embedding in a discontinuous narrative may be compared to that of a cinematic sequence in which fragments of a half-forgotten nightmare are recalled by a waking consciousness. Rather than signalling uncertainty on the lyric subject's part, the final strophe offers an understatement befitting a memory whose force has already been sufficiently tempered by poetic language to obviate a forceful declaration. The trajectory of Hölderlin's ode thus anticipates the course of such late hymns as 'The Rhine' and 'Patmos', which set out from a scene of sublime inspiration in order finally to come to an anti-climactic rest.[20]

In fact, the effect of interpretive immunisation is reinforced by an echo within the narrative extension of the argument developed in the first half of the poem. Just before the account of the later catastrophe gives way to a recollection of the earlier one, Hölderlin evokes a harrowing scene: 'of the boys one / Plunged from the roof, into the fathers' sword /another [*von Knaben stürzt' auch / Der von dem Dach, in der Väter Schwert der*] (*Poems and Fragments*, 187, translation modified; *FHA* V, 595). The syntactical inversion that results in the anastrophic placement of the pronoun 'der' corresponds to the fact that the paternal precedent here induces a catastrophic overturning of the relation between generations. A further oddity is highlighted by the homonymy between the genitive form of the definite article *die* and demonstrative pronoun *der*: a boy is said to be killed by a single sword belonging to a plurality of fathers. This incongruity suggests that the sword in question is perhaps not to be understood literally as a physical object. Indeed the image of the son dying by the sword of the fathers is separated by a mere line from a recurrence of the word 'fathers' in reference to the heroes of the earlier legend. And, in keeping with this genealogical construal of the relation of succession between the older and the later Xanthians, the heroes of the later legend are identified in the final strophe as 'children' who inherited the earlier legend. There is thus a sense in which the legend of the fathers' heroism becomes the sword upon which the children throw themselves.

Briefly flashing up in the narration, the scene of the son's suicide thus appears as an apocalyptic counterpart to the protective violence with which the father eagle of the ninth strophe expels his fledglings. Whereas the eagle analogy assigns the active pole to the father, its narrative counterpart figures the children as the agents of their own destruction at their fathers' hands, turning the 'fathers' sword' into a lethal alternative to the 'prong' with which the divine father counters the excessive love of humans. The scene of the dying son thus becomes a miniature allegory admonishing against imitative fidelity to a paternal model. We can now see that by foregrounding the problem of succession the narrative extension does not, after all, digress from the preceding argument, for that very problem was foreshadowed by the Oedipal nexus of the analogy of the fledgling eagles. The challenge of finding a proper relation to the divine father is recast in the narrative of Xanthos as the perilous task of inheriting a cultural past defined by direct exposure to the 'the unbound'. This construal of the relation between the analogy of the fledgling eagles and the narrative extension bears out Eric Santner's suggestion that 'Voice of the People' points ahead to Hölderlin's struggles in the so-called 'patriotic songs' [*vaterländische Gesänge*] to establish a viable mode of historical succession under the aegis of 'an oedipally structured, i.e., patriarchal, symbolic order'.[21]

The juncture of natural filiation and cultural succession provokes the question whether there is a line of biological descent corresponding to the chain of transmission linking the two catastrophes. This is, in the end, another way of asking what is meant by the term 'Volk' in the title of the poem. Although the suggested scale of the conflagration might alone suffice to rule out the possibility that the later Xanthians were biological descendants of the earlier heroes, in approaching this question we cannot treat the poem as a self-sufficient artifact. By invoking legends handed down to us, the poem acknowledges the precursor texts of Plutarch and Herodotus, and if nothing else, the concluding injunction to interpret legends should encourage us to take this intertextual dimension seriously. With respect to the genealogical question, Herodotus' account of the original catastrophe, which Hölderlin likely knew, appears particularly suggestive.[22] In short, it suggests that the protagonists of the later disaster cannot have been biological descendants of the heroes of the original legend. The key passage in Herodotus reads: 'Of the Xanthians who claim now to be Lycians the greater number – all saving eighty households, are of foreign descent; these eighty families as it chanced were at that time away from the city, and thus they survived.'[23] Hölderlin's reference to fathers and children must be understood, then, as a recourse to the conventional genealogical metaphor for cultural succession.

If, however, the anchoring of the Xanthians' ethnic identity in genealogical continuity involves a virtual element, so too does the experiential basis of the legend. In a structure familiar from reflections on the limits of historical testimony, those who underwent the full experience of destruction for that very reason did not live to tell the story, whereas those who could pass on the memory were able to do so only because they remained on the outside of that experience. Assuming that the narrative extension is responsive to Herodotus, we may take Hölderlin to suggest that the enduring identity of a people is constituted by an inherently problematic chain of transmission rather than genealogical filiation.

We may wonder, however, whether the history of the Xanthians is indeed paradigmatic in this respect of every people as such. There are, as I have suggested, poetological reasons, having to do with the hazards of lyrical subjectivity, that explain why the abstraction of Hölderlin's opening analogy between the people and rivers gives way to a meditation on a particular people associated with the river Xanthos. Still, we must ask why the fate of this particular people should command Hölderlin's attention so many centuries later. In taking up this question I will continue to assume that we do well to take the intertextual connection to Herodotus seriously. Accordingly, in what follows I will take my bearings from a single word that Herodotus uses in recounting the displacement of the eighty families that survived the conflagration. The verb *ekdemeo* is the standard ancient Greek expression for 'being away, travelling'. Yet a translator as attentive as Hölderlin to the root meaning of words might also have been sensitive to the ambiguous etymology of *ekdemeo*: the noun *demos* modified by the prefix *ek-* ('outside') can mean either 'people' or 'country, district, city'. The dual meaning of the verb thus epitomises the connection between the theme named in the title of the poem and the place determined by the river.

Let us first consider the geographical aspect. If we read the formulation used by Herodotus as meaning that the eighty families that survived were 'away from the city at that time', then we may recall the topographical determination of the city in the opening line 'By Xanthos once, in Grecian times, there stood / The town'. Although the city is not mentioned by name, we know from Plutarch that it too was named Xanthos after the river by which it was built. The name 'Xanthos' thus exemplifies a fact noted by Herder and Goethe, namely that rivers have the power to 'give names' to cities.[24] As in the case of the titular river of 'The Rhine', however, the name that the river imparts to the cities built on it is not an arbitrary one. Since the Xanthos river owes its name to the colour of its water (*xanthos* means 'yellow'), what we have here is a name that picks out a sensible property to designate a natural entity, which in its turn became the identifying marker of a human habitation. By virtue of this chain of signification, the toponym 'Xanthos' locates the city commemorated by Hölderlin at the point where the historical realm of culture emerges from the immediacy of nature.

This proximity to nature determines the fate of the city. Following the generic river image that opens the poem and the reference to the Xanthos river with which the narrative extension commences, the river theme resurfaces for a third time in Hölderlin's re-telling of the earlier legend, in which the Xanthians are said to have used 'reeds from the river' ('des Stromes Rohr') to immolate themselves. The odd specificity of the genitive construction, as well as the absence of any mention of the river in the corresponding passage in Herodotus, should prevent us from making light of this seemingly minor emendation of the story.[25] If the unnamed rivers of the opening verses were said to illustrate the lure of 'the unbound' to which peoples periodically succumb, here the river Xanthos actually grants lethal release to the Xanthians. In a transmutation of elements illustrating Heraclitus' pronouncement that the way up and the way down are the same, the water rushing towards the abyss becomes the source of a fire that pulls 'house and temple' up into the 'sacred ether'.

The poetological implications of this elemental scene can be brought into view if we attend to the faint echo of the myth of Pan in the reference to the 'reeds from the river'. That myth recounted how Syrinx, the daughter of the river god, was transformed into a reed so as to elude Pan's amorous advances and Pan, struck by the melody produced by the wind blowing through the reeds, fashioned a flute from a reed stalk. The echo of this story in Hölderlin's reference to the conflagration spread with the help of the river's reeds intimates the potential deadliness of that natural dimension – and of the pantheistic impulse to merge with it – in which art originates.

This mythic reminiscence calls for a qualification of my earlier claim that Hölderlin's turn to the legend of Xanthos is a matter of resisting the pull of abstraction and accepting contingency. For, by evoking the story of Xanthos, Hölderlin also broaches a problem of arguably universal importance, namely that of the ancient Greek legacy. In the 'Notes on the *Antigone*', Hölderlin refers to 'the natural process which is eternally hostile to man' to denote a striving in nature for re-absorption into the absolute, whose fervour threatens to consume the fragile human being (*Essays and Letters*, 330). The passage gives us a hint as to why the voice of the rivers moves the lyrical subject of Hölderlin's ode. With respect to this principle, however, Hölderlin posits a decisive difference between the ancient Greeks and Hesperian moderns. In terms recalling the restraining intervention of the gods in 'Voice of the People', Hölderlin writes of the 'more essential Zeus' of the moderns, who '*more decidedly forces down to earth* the natural process which is eternally hostile to man'. The comparative formulation suggests that in modernity the restraining of a natural impulse is not limited to art as was the case in antiquity; rather, the restraint dictated by the Greeks' artistic second nature has become first nature for the moderns.

The poetological conclusions that Hölderlin draws from this historical insight are spelled out in the letter of 4 December 1801 to Böhlendorff. Because the representational register in which an artist first achieves mastery is always going to be the obverse of his native temperament, and because the basic disposition of Hesperian modernity is sobriety, modern poets most easily excel in the creation of a passionate, fiery language. To appropriate his native sobriety, the modern poet needs the aesthetic detour of Greek art, which for that reason remains an 'indispensable' point of orientation (*Essays and Letters*, 208). Yet precisely because of the difference in basic disposition, this modern orientation towards antiquity remains prone to the danger of sterile imitation. In attempting to learn from the measured clarity of Greek art, the modern poet finds himself thrown back upon his own reflective nature, the very thing from which he must first distance himself if he is to develop artistic skill. Nor can he model his art after artistic renderings of Greek nature, since – to quote Philippe Lacoue-Labarthe's formulation – Greek nature 'never took place' in the form of art.[26]

Yet for all that it would be a mistake to conclude that the modern poet has no experiential access to the nature of the Greeks. As Lacoue-Labarthe notes in a parenthetical remark, the modern poet can still 'go to Bordeaux'. If Rousseau and Herder were right to claim that a people is shaped by the climate and the landscape it inhabits, then a visitor to a region associated with antiquity might still encounter people whose deeds and utterances retain an afterglow of that ancient fire. Such was the lesson recalled in Hölderlin's letter to Böhlendorff from November 1802 about his recent journey through revolutionary France, which gave him the sense of being 'better acquainted with the true essence of the Greeks' (*Essays and Letters*, 213).

Similarly, the lyrical subject who listens to the voice of the rivers in the opening stanza of 'Voice of the People' becomes attuned to 'the natural process which is eternally hostile to man' in a way that prepares the recollection of a legend testifying to the Greeks' fiery temper. In the opening passages, to be sure, the direction of this retrograde movement is at first merely hinted at in the lyrical subject's remembrance of his own 'sacred youth'.[27] In the narrative extension, however, the first destruction of the city built by the river renders the consequences of closeness to elemental nature fully clear. Conversely, the fortuitous departure of the eighty families mentioned by Herodotus and their subsequent return to Xanthos may be taken to illustrate the advantages of the longer, eccentric path described in the ninth strophe over the self-destructive ecstasy of those who remained there.

3.

This last point brings us to the second meaning of the word *ekdemeousi* used by Herodotus in relation to the survivors: they did not perish because they were 'away from the people' at the time of the catastrophe. If we now consider Hölderlin's recollection of the Xanthians in the context of his intense preoccupation with the ancient Greeks, then it must be noted that the river Xanthos was not the only stream that determined the fate of the Xanthians. Their city was also traversed by a metaphorical river, one of transmission and influence. It was Cicero who first wrote of an abundant stream that began to transport the treasures of Greek art and learning to Rome in the seventh century BC.[28] Whereas for Cicero the river metaphor registered the cultural affiliation between Greece and Rome, Horace, whose odes served as models for Hölderlin's, invoked the river analogy to acknowledge both the disruptive force of artistic inspiration and a disruption of its historical continuation. In comparing Pindar's poetry to a raging river and his own to the humble toils of a honeybee,

Horace identified Pindar as the founder of what Jochen Schmidt aptly calls a 'paradoxical tradition of break with the tradition' and at the same time gave expression to the successor's sense of inferiority.[29]

The legend of Xanthos illustrates the workings of this paradoxical tradition on a collective scale. The original destruction of the city shows what happens when a polity abandons the work of culture begun by its founders in order to return to the immediacy of nature. The moment of free spontaneity that this act of destruction in the political sphere has in common with artistic creation is underscored by the way in which the first syllable of the line 'Freiwillig überwunden die lange Kunst' ('long art is voluntarily overcome') threatens to violate alcaic meter, creating the most conspicuous point of metrical strain in the poem. Yet even though the break with tradition is free, it can in its turn become the substance of a binding tradition. The challenge facing moderns is precisely that of inheriting a culture animated by an impulse destructive of culture as such. In this way, the poem inflects a reflection begun in *Hyperion* upon the pitfalls of inheriting antiquity with an evocation of that 'hatred of culture' which prompts the hero's suicidal return to nature in Hölderlin's unfinished tragedy.[30]

If Herodotus' *Histories* are a key source of the river of Greco-Roman transmission, Plutarch's *Parallel Lives*, written to recall Greek counterparts of key figures in Roman history, belongs to the downstream stretch of the same river. To be sure, the fact that Plutarch's account of the demise of Xanthos in Roman times hearkens back to a precedent from Greek antiquity is merely a marginal instance of his interest in Greco-Roman parallels. For Hölderlin, however, that parallel is fraught with topical significance. For not only did Plutarch mediate the Greek legacy to his Roman contemporaries, his own work too would get carried along by a stream of transmission that extended all the way to Hölderlin's time. As Mario Praz writes, there was 'a moment in history when the Plutarchian ideal seemed to be embodied in actuality, and its spirit to live again in thinking, active man: and that was the moment of the French Revolution, dominated, if ever a historical period was, by the "moralized" conception of the ancient world as it was to be found in Plutarch'.[31]

Hölderlin's poem reflects upon the French revolutionary cult of Plutarch rather than merely emulating it, inasmuch as his use of Plutarchian material deviates from the one prevalent in contemporary France. Following Plutarch's interest in Greco-Roman parallels, French revolutionary invocations of Plutarch tended to elide differences between the two civilisations in order to glorify what Sándor Radnóti calls 'the constructed unity of an antiquity reborn'.[32] In Germany, however, that unity had already been undone in the 1750s by Winckelmann, under whose influence German writers revered ancient Greece in conscious opposition to the privileging of Roman models in French-influenced aristocratic courts. In keeping with this differentiation, Hölderlin in 'Voice of the People' singles out an episode from Plutarch in which the parallel between an event recalled from Greek times and its Roman-era imitation becomes the basis of a difference. For, to recall a point made by Frey, the repetition of the original catastrophe differs from that which it repeats precisely because it is an imitation mediated by historical memory.[33] Assuming, then, that the narrative extension of Hölderlin's ode offers an oblique commentary on the French Revolution, it might be taken to suggest that the derailment of the Revolution – and in particular the self-destructive fury of Jacobin terror – was due to a conflation between two distinct classes of ancient models. Such a reading would place 'Voice of the People' squarely in the lineage of compensatory reflections that were developed under the politically backward conditions of Germany by writers who rested their claim to superior insight upon a diagnosis of the intellectual blind spots responsible for the failure of the French Revolution.[34]

There is a sense in which the diagnosis just outlined is indeed apt. When a new translation of Winckelmann's history of ancient art was published in France in 1790, it was taken to lend support to the hope that the revolutionary revival of Roman republicanism would bring about an artistic flourishing comparable to that of Athens. Beside inverting the conviction harboured by Winckelmann and his German followers that aesthetic renewal had to pave the way for political emancipation, this expectation also conflated Greek with Roman models.[35] It is thus tempting to read Hölderlin's poem as an allegorical critique of French appropriations of Winckelmann.[36]

There is, moreover, a further respect in which the difference between Greece and Rome highlighted by Hölderlin's use of Plutarch played a decisive role in the French Revolution. Although a marked tendency to conflate Greek and Roman models was typical of the early stages of the Revolution, the antagonisms of the 1790s undid the previously unified legacy of antiquity.[37] Taking their guidance from Rousseau, Jacobin radicals such as Robespierre and Saint-Just espoused the Spartan model of republicanism, whose celebration of virtue and simplicity underwrote a preference for direct representation of the *volonté générale* by a unicameral legislature. By contrast, moderates such as Mounier and Mirabeau followed Montesquieu in favouring the Roman model of republicanism, which called for bicameral representation and a system of checks and balances. After a temporary triumph of the Spartan model in the Reign of Terror, the Roman model prevailed, only to prove equally untenable in the end. The transition first to a consular system and then to imperial rule repeated the course of Roman history – confirming Rousseau's and Montesquieu's worries that a republican constitution presupposed a small, homogeneous state and was therefore no more viable in France than it had been in Rome. Thus, by following ancient models 'too closely, too blindly, and too much', as Mortimer N. S. Sellers puts it, the French Revolution ended up 'discredit[ing] Roman and Greek antiquity as practical models for political reform'.[38] Against this backdrop, one might read the narrative extension of 'Voice of the People' as a diagnosis of Rome's failed imitation of Greek republicanism and a warning against contemporary French attempts at imitating that failed imitation. The difference between the original Xanthians' self-immolation under the influence of a lethal impulse born of nature and the later Xanthians' imitation of that act would then correspond to the difference (highlighted by Hegel) between the still relatively intimate, nature-bound order of Greek ethical life and the mediated, alienated world of the Roman empire.[39]

However, this reading of the narrative extension is not entirely satisfactory, for it remains one-sidedly focused on the formal structure of the historical record kept by Plutarch and does not take the particulars of Hölderlin's narrative into account. Suffice to mention here only a few details that bear on the difference between the two catastrophes. The Persians who besieged the city in the earlier instance are called 'enemies', and accordingly the self-destructive act of the Xanthians is said to be driven by a desire for freedom. Brutus, by contrast, is referred to as one of the 'heroes', and the Xanthians' self-immolation is a blind act of defiance provoked by his 'goodness', 'long prepared' by the memory of the original catastrophe. Erich Mayser has linked these nuances to the difference between the earlier Xanthians' revolt against a conquering tyrant and the successors' resistance to a proponent of the republican ideal.[40] On Mayser's interpretation, the misguided imitation of the earlier by the later Xanthians was due to the latter's application of an inherited model upon a fundamentally different situation.

Moreover, Mayser convincingly argues that this ancient case of false typology itself invites a typological interpretation in terms of modern-day upheavals. The allegorical referent of Hölderlin's meditation on the repeated catastrophe of Xanthos is, however, not revolutionary France but the German nationalist reaction to the French invasion. As Mayser notes, the political discourse of the period figured Brutus as an embodiment of liberal republicanism, whereas tyrannical invaders were routinely cast as latter-day Persians. The story of the Xanthians who confronted Brutus with the same suicidal defiance that their forefathers had once displayed in the face of the Persians thus suggests a diagnosis of the mistake made by those German patriots of the 1790s who reflexively saw the armies of revolutionary France as successors of the invasionary forces sent by Louis

XIV and Louis XV.[41] On this view, 'Voice of the People' dramatises the question facing Hölderlin: how to maintain allegiance to the revolutionary cause without condemning the stirrings of patriotic resistance among his own people as signs of reactionary backwardness? This quandary might explain the conjunction in the poem between a sympathetic susceptibility to the voice of the people and the admonition to interpret its legends, presumably with a view to averting disastrous conflations.

The lyrical subject's ambivalence in the opening strophe of the poem may be taken to encompass every people as such, rife with inchoate energies that can bring both liberation and devastation. Corresponding to the shift from the generic image of rivers to the concluding consideration of a historical destiny shaped by a particular river, the narrative extension gives the argument of the poem a sharper focus. However, the affective ambivalence between fascination and apprehension is now combined with an equivocity of allegorical reference. For even though we can agree with Mayser that the narrative extension allegorises a fallacy peculiar to the Germans of Hölderlin's time, we have also seen that the terms of the allegory are overdetermined in a way that renders it powerfully resonant for an understanding of revolutionary France as well. The allegory of Xanthos thus turns out to be applicable to both sides of the Franco-German conflict, inasmuch as it dramatises a fallacy in emulating ancient models to which both peoples were susceptible. To put it in the speculative terms that so exercised the imagination of Hölderlin and his contemporaries, the story of Xanthos brings to light a political identity-in-difference between France and Germany based on the historical difference-in-identity between ancient Greece and its Roman and modern successors.

It is important to be clear about the reason why the moment of difference must take precedence over that of continuity in the latter relation of succession. What warrants the cautionary tone of the poem's conclusion is not just the danger of relying upon the original legend in interpreting a situation to which it is not applicable. Even if applied to a similar situation, that model would still be ruinous by virtue of its very substance. Unlike earlier exponents of German Hellenophilia, Hölderlin is acutely aware of the perils of remembering a precursor civilisation exposed to elemental nature. Although the native temperament of the ancient Greeks remains concealed in their artworks, its destructive fire survives not only in historical accounts but also in landscapes that had shaped its characteristic dispositions.

This point takes us back to the opening sentence of the narrative, whose factual falsity thus far appears to have gone unnoticed: 'Am Xanthos lag, in griechischer Zeit, die Stadt.' Of course the events recounted in the immediately ensuing strophes took place in Roman, not Greek, times.

Yet the deeper truth of the anachronism that opens the poem emerges through the retrieval of the original legend. For a city to stand on the bank of the Xanthos river is indeed to be perpetually mired in Greek times. For German and Frenchman alike, to revisit such a city is to risk letting the recollected time engulf the present – a danger illustrated by the curious conjunction between the past tense and 'now' in the opening strophe of the narrative extension. The place name 'Xanthos' shared by the river and the city thus functions as a chronotopic anchor for what one might call the natural-historical sublime. That name stands, on the one hand, for the point of origination at which the 'natural process which is eternally hostile to men', exemplified by the river Xanthos and the reeds on its banks, first gave rise to a metaphorical river of transmission that perpetuates the lure of that natural element down to the present age; and it stands, on the other hand, for the people constituted by that metaphorical river, whose recurrent inundations have deposited layers and layers of wreckage and sedimented historical experience.

Yet 'Xanthos' also epitomises the way in which Hölderlin's conception of the Greeks conjoins the particularity of a contingent historical formation with the abstraction of his dichotomy between the ancient Greeks and their successors. Given the iterative logic of succession with which Hölderlin's poem is concerned, we do well not to take the innocuousness of that dichotomy for granted. Recently Kalliopi Nikolopoulou has ventured beyond the confines of literary interpretation narrowly understood and posed an ethical challenge to Hölderlin's assumption of an unbridgeable gulf separating modernity from the ancient Greeks.[42] German idealism was founded according to Nikolopoulou on a disavowal of that ancient legacy. By translating Greek tragedy into an interiorised idea of the tragic, Hölderlin and his contemporaries inaugurated a post-heroic modernity that insulates the reflective standpoint of theory from political conflicts. The price exacted by this sublation of tragedy is an inability to distinguish between outbursts of blind destructiveness and desperate acts of resistance in which passion is wedded to rational insight.

Earlier I suggested that the lyrical subject who speaks in 'Voice of the People' seeks to find a middle course between two pitfalls in confronting the natural-historical sublime: projective identification on the one hand and dogmatic repudiation on the other. Although Hölderlin arguably steers clear of the former danger through the excursion to Xanthos, the latter fallacy, initially avoided through the ambivalent self-positioning of the lyrical subject, eventually recurs when Hölderlin commemorates tragic agency only to pre-empt it, construing the ancients as radically foreign to our standpoint. In view of the typological considerations outlined in the above, we can now specify the cost of this sublation of tragic sacrifice. In considering the concluding admonition of the first longer version and the analogy of the fledgling eagles in the final text, I already noted a tendency on Hölderlin's part to intimate an equivalence between apocalyptic agency and complacent passivity. That conflation acquires a more concrete form in the narrative extension. For the story of Xanthos can be read as allegorising both sides of the great political conflict of the period. When construed in terms of the all-important dichotomy between Greek antiquity and Hesperian modernity, the conflict between post-revolutionary France and the German states becomes epiphenomenal to their shared modernity. This equivalence of the two sides is the upshot of the words attributed to the deranged poet – tentatively identified by E. M. Butler as Hölderlin – who was found worshipping statues of Greek gods in a park in France according to an anecdote related in 1852 by the writer Moritz Hartmann:

> 'Are *you* a Greek?' questioned the count, only half in earnest. 'No, on the contrary, I am a German', and again the stranger sighed. 'On the contrary? Is the German the opposite of the Greek?' 'Yes', said the German shortly, and he added after a pause: 'But then we all are; you, the Frenchman as well; and your enemy the Englishman too – all of us'.[43]

If all heroes of antiquity merge in the vehemence of Hyperion's projective identification, conversely an overly vigilant awareness of the gulf separating us from the ancients threatens to erase all-important political differences in the present, sanctioning withdrawal into a state of reflective ambivalence.

A passage from the letter to Böhlendorff from December 1801 describes this stance in terms that recall the theme of Empedoclean fire at the heart of Hölderlin's ode. Hölderlin's remarks there imply that ancient tragedy moved in a realm of 'the living' exposed to the flames of elemental nature. Compared to this lethal exposure, the modern poet must accept a fate that is less 'imposing' but 'deeper', and on which Hölderlin offers the following reflection: 'For that is the tragic with us, to go away from the kingdom of the living in total silence packed in some kind of container, not to pay for the flames we have been unable to control by being consumed in fire' (*Essays and Letters*, 208). Having to go away from the ardent realm of the living is the undramatic predicament – or what the 'Notes on the *Antigone*' will call 'fatelessness, *dusmoron*' (*Essays and Letters*, 330) – of the lyrical subject who speaks in the opening strophes of Hölderlin's ode, moved by the voice of the people even in his removal from it. His trajectory distantly repeats the longer path of those Xanthians who were able to preserve the memory of the disaster only because they happened to be away from the city on the river.

Notes

1. Nádas, *Parallel Stories*, p. 644, translation modified.
2. Stevens, *The Collected Poems of Wallace Stevens*, p. 533.
3. Goethe, *Sämtliche Werke*, vol. 1, pp. 193–5.
4. See Hartman, 'Blessing the Torrent: On Wordsworth's Later Style', p. 84.
5. Alone among critics Eva Geulen notes 'the complexity of the river image as it appears in the poem, which, like actual rivers, changes as the poem progresses, from plural into singular, from a mere image to a metaphor for the people, in order finally to achieve a geographically and historically concrete location in the city on the river Xanthos' (Geulen, 'That Mysterious Yearning', pp. 149–50).
6. Wordsworth, 'From *The Excursion* (1814)', p. 581.
7. The Oedipal logic of this scenario has been noted by Eric L. Santner, 'Introduction: Reading Hölderlin in the Age of Difference,' p. xxxiv. See also Laplanche, *Hölderlin and the Question of the Father*, pp. 40–1.
8. Nikolopoulou, *Tragically Speaking: On the Use and Abuse of Theory for Life*, pp. 216–17.
9. Ibid. p. 217.
10. Plutarch, *Lives: With an English Translation by Bernadotte Perrin*, vol. 6, p. 195.
11. Nägele, 'The Discourse of the Other: Hölderlin's Voice and the Voice of the People', pp. 56–60. See also Nägele, 'The Discourse of the Other: Hölderlin's Ode "Stimme des Volks" and the Dialectic of the Enlightenment', pp. 20–1.
12. See 'Seven Maxims', in *Essays and Letters*, pp. 242–3: '[T]he understanding which only arises out of need is always one-sided and crooked [. . .] when a man lacks great and pure subjects, he creates some phantom or other out of this and that, and closes his eyes so that he can interest himself in it, and live for it.' On the predicament of a lyric subject whose suffering prompts an impure approach to the divine, see Szondi, 'Der andere Pfeil', p. 51.
13. Corngold, 'Disowning Contingencies in Hölderlin's "Empedocles"', pp. 234–6.
14. The seal is mentioned by D. E. Sattler in Hölderlin, *Sämtliche Werke, Briefe und Dokumente in zeitlicher Folge. Band IX*, location 1427.
15. Nägele interprets the repeated destruction of Xanthos in terms of a repetition compulsion, which allows him to draw suggestive parallels to Freud. See Nägele, 'The Discourse of the Other', pp. 61–3. However, Freud's idea of repressed contents expressing themselves through a repetition compulsion does not seem applicable to a collective guided by a conscious memory. See the objections raised by Mayser, 'Hölderlins Stimme des Volks', pp. 253–4. In view of Hölderlin's reference to the gods as 'the inimitable ones', the repetition of the catastrophe is more plausibly construed as a manifestation of the peculiarly human capacity for imitation, a mark of the peculiarly human separateness from, as well as affinity with, the divine that necessitates and permits cultural transmission. The dynamics of imitation is highlighted in Herodotus's account of the earlier catastrophe: 'Thus Harpagus gained Xanthus, and Caunus too in somewhat like manner, the Caunians following for the most part the example of the Lycians' (Herodotus, *The Persian Wars*, vol. I, p. 221).
16. Geulen, 'That Mysterious Yearning', p. 147 and p. 151.
17. Geulen's rejection of any analogy between the rivers and the voice of the people may be questioned. Although we do well to heed Peter Szondi's argument against treating parallel passages as decisive evidence, it is hardly irrelevant in the present context that Hölderlin did posit the very analogy ruled out by Geulen in a passage echoing 'Voice of the People' in the third version of *The Death of Empedocles*, which prefaces an evocation of the people's divinely inspired impulse to destroy civilisation with the lines: 'More forcefully yet, / Like water, did the savage human wave / Beat on my breast, and the poor people's voice [*Des armen Volkes Stimme*], / Humming in blind confusion, reach my ear . . . It was the departure of my people's god! / Him I could hear', in *Poems*

and Fragments, p. 377. In the letter of 4 June 1799 to Karl Gok, Hölderlin writes: 'all the meandering *[irrenden]* rivers of human activity flow into the ocean of nature'. See *Essays and Letters*, p. 136. One might also question whether the lyric subject's hesitant rehearsal of the ancient proverb warrants Geulen's characterisation of it as 'the mere saying of a saying'.

18. Frey, 'Textrevision bei Hölderlin', pp. 109–10.
19. Geulen, 'That Mysterious Yearning', p. 147.
20. To appreciate the small distance that separates the note of precariously balanced dialectical tension on which Hölderlin's ode ends from the paratactic ending of such late hymns as 'Am Quell der Donau', 'Die Wanderung' and 'Der Ister', we might imagine an alternate version in which the final phrase 'yet there's also need of / One to interpret these holy legends' is preceded by a full stop instead of a comma.
21. Santner, 'Introduction', p. xxxv.
22. Hölderlin likely knew the *Histories*. See Anke Bennholdt-Thomsen and Alfredo Guzzoni, *Marginalien zu Hölderlins Werk*, pp. 9–114. Indeed, his comparison of the people to rivers may have been inspired by a passage about the people in the *Histories*: '[H]ow can they have knowledge, who have neither learnt nor for themselves seen what is best, but ever rush headlong and drive blindly onward, like a river in spate?' in Herodotus, *The Persian Wars*, vol. II, p. 107.
23. Herodotus, *The Persian Wars*, vol. I, p. 221.
24. See Jochen Schmidt's commentary in Hölderlin, *Sämtliche Gedichte*, p. 857.
25. A reference to reeds does occur in Plutarch's account of the later catastrophe, which mentions that the Xanthians who defied Brutus used 'reeds and wood and all manner of combustibles' to spread the fire, in Plutarch, *Lives*, vol. 6, p. 195. The explicit association of the reeds with the river is an accent added by Hölderlin. Hölderlin's insertion of an element taken from the account of the later catastrophe into his re-telling of the earlier one may be viewed as a textual sign of the collapse of chronological differentiation due to the contagious power of the original legend.
26. Lacoue-Labarthe, 'Hölderlin and the Greeks', p. 246.
27. Hartman coins the term 'temporal fugue' for the way in which Wordsworth's contemplation of a stream recalls both his youth and the 'dawn of human life itself', in 'Blessing the Torrent', p. 85. This conjunction of biographical and macrocosmic past in a 'double time scale' is characteristic of 'the new sense of the sublime' in Romantic landscape poetry, writes Charles Rosen in *The Romantic Generation*, p. 139.
28. Cicero, *The Republic and the Laws*, p. 184.
29. See Jochen Schmidt's remarks in the editorial apparatus to Hölderlin, *Sämtliche Gedichte*, p. 507.
30. Empedocles is said to be driven by a 'hatred of culture' *[Kulturhaß]* in the 'Frankfurter Plan'. See *FHA* XII, p. 28. Strophes 6–7 of the final version of 'Voice of the People' echo Empedocles' vision of rejuvenation through a destructive return to nature. Note the reference to 'the green of the earth' *[Der Erde Grün]* in *FHA* XII, p. 249. Although this rejuvenation requires a forgetting of inherited legends, the poet-philosopher who means to bring about this transformation must hope, lest the transformation should prove transient, that his own necessary perishing will in its turn be remembered in a legend. See *FHA* XII, p. 74, p. 246, pp. 257–8 and p. 281.
31. Praz, *On Neoclassicism*, pp. 97–8.
32. Radnóti, 'Why One Should Imitate the Greeks: On Winckelmann', p. 204.
33. Frey, 'Textrevision bei Hölderlin', p. 110.
34. On this lineage see Comay, *Mourning Sickness: Hegel and the French Revolution*, pp. 2–25.
35. Radnóti, 'Why One Should Imitate the Greeks', pp. 236–7.
36. This would be in keeping with the contrast, noted by Glenn Most, between the Greek Empedocles' orientation towards the essential and the 'Roman-like', 'hyperpolitical and calculating attitude' of the Agrigentians (quoted in Corngold, 'Disowning

Contingencies', p. 454n.) Although there is no evidence that Hölderlin was familiar with the French reception of Winckelmann, he may have sympathised with the misgivings about that line of reception which Schelling would express in 1807 in 'Über das Verhältnis der bildenden Künste zu der Natur', p. 325n.
37. In this paragraph I draw on Sellers, 'Revolution, French', pp. 822–6.
38. Ibid. p. 826.
39. Hegel, *Phänomenologie des Geistes*, pp. 289–305.
40. Mayser, 'Hölderlins Stimme des Volks', pp. 257–9.
41. Ibid. p. 260. Mayser argues that the story of Xanthos had a recent allegorical referent. In July 1796 Hölderlin fled Frankfurt with the Gontards to escape the siege by Kléber's army, which caused a fire that Kléber himself sought to extinguish, only to be rebuffed by the citizenry. Jürgen Link suggests that Hölderlin's aim in writing the poem was to persuade his German readers that Napoleon was not a tyrant but a benevolent, Republican Brutus. See Link, *Hölderlin-Rousseau: Inventive Rückkehr*, p. 148.
42. Nikolopoulou, *Tragically Speaking*, pp. xv–xxxii, pp. 209–45.
43. Quoted in E. M. Butler, *The Tyranny of Greece over Germany*, p. 203.

Bibliography

Bennholdt-Thomsen, Anke and Guzzoni, Alfredo, *Marginalien zu Hölderlins Werk* (Würzburg: Königshausen & Neumann, 2010).
Butler, E. M., *The Tyranny of Greece over Germany: A Study of the Influence Exercised by Greek Art and Poetry over the Great German Writers of the Eighteenth, Nineteenth and Twentieth Centuries* (Cambridge: Cambridge University Press, 1935).
Cicero, *The Republic and the Laws*, trans. Niall Rudd (Oxford: Oxford University Press, 1998).
Comay, Rebecca, *Mourning Sickness: Hegel and the French Revolution* (Stanford: Stanford University Press, 2011).
Corngold, Stanley, 'Disowning Contingencies in Hölderlin's "Empedocles"', in Aris Fioretos (ed.), *The Solid Letter: Readings of Friedrich Hölderlin* (Stanford: Stanford University Press, 1999), pp. 215–36.
Frey, Hans-Jost, 'Textrevision bei Hölderlin', in *Der unendliche Text* (Frankfurt: Suhrkamp, 1990), pp. 77–113.
Geulen, Eva, 'That Mysterious Yearning', in *The End of Art: Readings in a Rumor after Hegel*, trans. James McFarland (Stanford: Stanford, 2006), pp. 140–54.
Goethe, Johann Wolfgang, *Sämtliche Werke*, vol. 1, ed. Karl Eibl (Frankfurt: Deutscher Klassiker Verlag, 1987).
Hartman, Geoffrey, 'Blessing the Torrent: On Wordsworth's Later Style', in *The Unremarkable Wordsworth* (Minneapolis: University of Minnesota Press, 1987), pp. 75–89.
Hegel, G. W. F., *Phänomenologie des Geistes*, ed. Hans-Friedrich Wessels and Heinrich Clairmont (Hamburg: Meiner, 2006).
Herodotus, *The Persian Wars*, Vols I–IV, trans. A. D. Godley (Cambridge, MA: Harvard University Press, 1920–5).
Hölderlin, Friedrich, *Sämtliche Werke, Briefe und Dokument in zeitlicher Folge*, vol. 9 (*Oden; Elegien; Gesangentwürfe*), ed. D. E. Sattler. Kindle edition (Munich: Luchterhand, 2009).
Lacoue-Labarthe, Philippe, 'Hölderlin and the Greeks', in *Typography: Mimesis, Philosophy, Politics*, trans. Christopher Fynsk (Stanford: Stanford University Press, 1998), pp. 236–47.
Laplanche, Jean, *Hölderlin and the Question of the Father, with an Introduction by Rainer Nägele*, ed. and trans. Luke Carlson (Victoria: ELS Editions, 2007).

Link, Jürgen, *Hölderlin-Rousseau: Inventive Rückkehr* (Wiesbaden/Opladen: Westdeutscher Verlag, 1999).
Mayser, Erich, 'Hölderlins Stimme des Volks', *Hölderlin-Jahrbuch* (1984/5), pp. 252–63.
Nádas, Péter, *Parallel Stories*, trans. Imre Goldstein (London: Jonathan Cape, 2011).
Nägele, Rainer, 'The Discourse of the Other: Hölderlin's Ode "Stimme des Volks" and the Dialectic of the Enlightenment', in *Glyph: Johns Hopkins Textual Studies*, 5 (1979), pp. 1–33.
Nägele, Rainer, 'The Discourse of the Other: Hölderlin's Voice and the Voice of the People', in *Reading After Freud: Essays On Goethe, Hölderlin, Habermas, Nietzsche, Brecht, Celan, and Freud* (New York: Columbia University Press, 1987), pp. 47–65.
Nikolopoulou, Kalliopi, *Tragically Speaking: On the Use and Abuse of Theory for Life* (Lincoln and London: University of Nebraska Press, 2012).
Plutarch, *Lives: With an English Translation by Bernadotte Perrin*, vol. 6 (Cambridge, MA: Harvard University Press, 1993).
Praz, Mario, *On Neoclassicism*, trans. Angus Davidson (Evanston, IL: Northwestern University Press, 1969).
Radnóti, Sándor, 'Why One Should Imitate the Greeks: On Winckelmann', in Ferenc Hörcher and Endre Szécsényi (eds), *Aspects of the Enlightenment: Aesthetics, Politics, and Religion* (Budapest: Akadémiai Kiadó, 2004), pp. 202–37.
Rosen, Charles, *The Romantic Generation* (Cambridge, MA: Harvard University Press, 1995).
Santner, Eric L., 'Introduction: Reading Hölderlin in the Age of Difference', in *Selected Poems and Hyperion* (New York: Continuum, 1990), pp. xxiii–xli.
Schelling, F. W. J., 'Über das Verhältnis der bildenden Künste zu der Natur', in F. W. J. Schelling, *Sämmtliche Werke*, vol. 7, ed. K. F. A. Schelling (Stuttgart: J. C. Cotta, 1860), pp. 289–329.
Sellers, Mortimer N. S., 'Revolution, French', in Anthony Grafton, Glenn W. Most and Salvatore Settis (eds), *The Classical Tradition* (Cambridge, MA: Belknap Press, 2010), pp. 822–6.
Stevens, Wallace, *Collected Poems of Wallace Stevens* (New York: Vintage Books, 1990).
Szondi, Peter, 'Der andere Pfeil', in *Hölderlin-Studien: Mit einem Traktat über philologische Erkenntnis* (Frankfurt: Suhrkamp, 1967), pp. 37–61.
Wordsworth, William, 'From *The Excursion* (1814)', *William Wordsworth*, ed. Stephen Gill (Oxford: Oxford University Press, 2010).

Chapter 7

Translating Centaurs: Notes on Hölderlin's 'The Life-Giving'

Bruno C. Duarte

I

Between 1803 and 1805, Hölderlin translated and commented on nine fragments by Pindar that have come to be known in the critical literature as the Pindar Fragments. The last translated fragment concerns the fight between the Centaurs and the Lapiths at the wedding of Pirithous and Hippodame, after Eurytion, inebriated and driven by lust, attacks the bride. This mythological episode of strife and violence – the so-called centauromachy that ended with the defeat and expulsion of the centaurs – is translated, entitled and commented upon by Hölderlin as follows:

> The Life-Giving.
> The man-conquering: after
> The centaurs learnt
> The power
> Of the honey-sweet wine, suddenly they thrust
> The white milk with their hands, the table away, spontaneously,
> And drinking out of silver horns
> Intoxicated themselves.

The concept of the centaurs is surely that of the spirit of a river insofar as it forms a path and a boundary, with violence, on the originally pathless and upwards growing earth.

Its image is therefore at places in nature where the shore is rich in cliffs and grottoes, *especially at places where originally the river had to leave the mountain chain and had to cut across its direction.*

Hence centaurs are also originally teachers of the science of nature, because nature can best be examined from that viewpoint.

In regions such as this the river had originally to wander about aimlessly before it could tear out a course. By this means there formed, as beside ponds, damp meadows and caves in the earth for suckling creatures, and meanwhile the centaur was a wild herdsman, like the Odyssean Cyclops. The waters longingly sought their direction. But the more firmly the dry land took shape upon the banks and secured its direction by means of the firmly rooting trees, by bushes and grapevines, the more the river also, which took its motion from the shape of the bank, had to gain its direction until, forced on from its origin, it broke through at a point where the mountains that enclosed it were most loosely connected.

Thus the centaurs *learnt the power of the honey-sweet wine*, they took their motion and direction from the firmly formed banks, so rich in trees, and hurled *the white milk and the table away with their hands*, the fashioned wave drove away the calm of the pond, the way of life on the banks also changed, the attack of the wood with the storms and the secure princes of the forest aroused the leisurely life on the heath, the stagnating waters were so long repulsed from the steeper shore *until they grew arms*, and so with a direction of their own, drinking spontaneously *from silver horns*, made a path for themselves, took on a destiny.

The songs of Ossian especially are true centaur-songs, sung with the spirit of the river, and as if by the Greek Chiron, who also taught Achilles to play the lyre. (*FHA* XV, 363–4; *Essays and Letters*, 338–9, translation modified)

It would at first glance seem that Hölderlin puts forward a complete reinterpretation of the content of the myth, whose classical tradition was known to him in all likelihood from various sources, including Ovid and Homer.[1] Drawing on an imagined, partly attested kinship and identification of the mythical figure of the centaur with that of the river, he allegedly rewrites Pindar's account of the myth as the tale of a 'transition from the history of nature to the history of civilization arising from the geological signs and the words of language'.[2] As translator, Hölderlin 'turns the Pindar [text] on its head, forcing it into new meaning': that which appears in the original version as the 'eruption of the primitive side of the Centaurs', namely their ferocity and destructive power, is apparently viewed by Hölderlin as 'a process of civilization'.[3] Out of the interweaving of a 'geo-historical process of the formation of rivers' and a 'mythical-historical process of the centaur's becoming',[4] a 'cultural-historical parable' or even a 'cultural-historical etiology'[5] becomes apparent which is readily defined as a 'dialectic of origin and civilization'.[6]

As if made to measure, Hölderlin's terminology in his translation and commentary (*Richtung, Bestimmung, sich bilden, gestalten*) seems to be in line with the symbolism of other key concepts – namely law and right, wisdom, discipline, truth, fatherland, direction, tranquility, hope, discipline, sagacity or education – which are all pervasive in the Pindar

Fragments, allowing for their generalised psychological-metaphysical interpretation as an expression of the poet's longing for individual stability and continuity in the face of his own growing mental collapse after his return from France in 1802. As the story goes, in the midst of a 'period of instability' and 'at the end of his development towards an increasingly subjective view of Greek literature', Hölderlin would have 'turned to Pindar because his fragments dealt with those concepts which were now of greatest importance to him, above all those of *Gesetz* and *Ruhe*',[7] thus engaging in the 'reflectively redeeming' work of translation, with the aim of achieving a 'balance between the human and the divine sphere in the form of law'.[8] Similarly, from the moment the myth of the centaurs is 'transposed onto the image of the river landscape',[9] a simple story is found of how, out of chaos and violence, culture came into being. Suddenly, the hybrid figure of the centaur, half-man and half-horse, is presented as the 'mythical embodiment of a metaphor of transition', the latter being defined as a 'dialectical principle of opposition and unification'.[10]

In short, there appears to be a widespread consensus among scholars on how to read the commentary that Hölderlin wrote to accompany his translation of Pindar's fragment. Due to what appears to be a shared belief in evolutionary logic, they rarely, if ever, venture beyond the cohesion of meaning and context. In their pursuit of a comparative analysis of Pindar's 'true' rendering of the myth and its reinterpretation by Hölderlin, they seem convinced that the latter is little more than an allegory of organic development and fulfilment set in motion by either metaphors or dialectical logic. In insisting on the view that the fragment inverts and re-evaluates the myth as the story of the advance of culture, philological analysis apparently fails to notice the pictorial nature of the text itself, and for that same reason misses the extensive or expanded experience of the very word it keeps repeating in its many forms, often almost in passing: translation.

II

Hölderlin's commentary consists essentially of two parts. Whereas the first three paragraphs seemingly contain a partly figurative, partly speculative reading of the fragment, the three remaining segments function as a hollow form in which the actual inversion of the myth is carried out. Both parts relate to the two compound figures that are equated with each other – namely, the song of the Centaurs [*Kentaur-Gesang*] and the river-spirit [*Strom-Geist*] – but do so differently.

It would seem that the story that unfolds in the second part of the commentary (paragraphs 4 to 6) is there to provide an almost symmetrical narrative demonstration of the first part (paragraphs 1 to 3), acting as a variation on the same theme and thereby underscoring the analogy between the two parts. In the fourth paragraph, 'the concept of the centaurs' as 'the spirit of a river' is expressed through the parallel between the 'wild herdsman' and the aimless wandering of rivers. 'Its image' is then identified in the fifth paragraph in an expository manner with the formation of rivers. Hölderlin inserts isolated passages from his translation into his own commentary with the aim of securing the narrative flow of the preceding verses and concludes the commentary in the sixth and last paragraph with a subliminal definition of poetry that associates a phantom (namely, Ossian, later exposed as a literary forgery) with an archetypal notion of song and a mythological icon (namely, Chiron, the wise Centaur).

In contrast to these final digressions, the compact character of the three initial sentences of the commentary, followed by their development in the fourth paragraph, configure a fundamental conceptual and visual framework that brings to bear the vastness and depth of Hölderlin's remarks.

Two fundamentally heterogeneous, dissimilar figures come to coincide as they are placed on a single level of representation, that is on a unified temporal plane. The concept of the centaurs is made identical with *the concept* of the spirit of a river, after which it is assigned its own *image* within *nature*. Only then does the description of the movement of the water across the earth become equally determining of the centaurs (plural) and the spirit of a river (singular) as two intertwined conceptual forms that both rest upon their pictorial nature and seem to actually yearn for it in accordance with the inner logic and the placement of each utterance.

This can be seen most clearly in the use of the verbs and transitions which determine the cadence that links concept to image and image to nature: the river draws limits and boundaries upon the earth, cuts across (*durchreißen*) the mountain range and against its direction, and that would be the reason why the centaurs have learnt how to best view and perceive (*einsehn*) nature. While the first mention of the connective word 'deswegen' (hence, therefore) appears to be primarily an intensification of the first sentence, specifically locating the image of the centaur-river in nature ('Its image is *therefore* found at places in nature'), the second accomplishes the process of deduction by referring almost incidentally to its main assertion ('*Hence* Centaurs are also originally teachers of the science of nature'). It is as if the concept were lost in the course of the second paragraph, dissolved into an image, only to reappear implicitly in the third paragraph at the exact point where neither a concept nor an image is mentioned, although both are being pulled as one into an unheard of 'science' of nature.

Out of this uneven but firm scaffolding of thought, two different configurations emerge which are of great relevance for grasping the disruptive character of Hölderlin's gesture as a translator in *The Life-Giving* – the enlivening or the vivifying, *Das Belebende*. The first is the link between concept and image, the second draws on the conflation of the resulting concept-image, on the one hand, and nature, on the other.

III

The fact that Hölderlin's commentary 'paradoxically locates the "concept" of the Centaur in an image, "the spirit of a river"'[11] has not been overlooked by scholarship, but often that very paradox has been perceived only too readily as a self-justified attempt to arrive at what would appear to be a self-evident correlation of abstract concepts with sensory images.

Critical readings of the text have imagined this interweaving of 'concept' and 'image' either in the most candid or in the most convoluted of ways. Most are held captive by the narrative framework that pervades Hölderlin's line of reasoning. Just as they envisage the description of the process in nature as an anticipation of the generic determination of poetry and *Gesang* that comes at the end, so too they tend to consider the polarity of concept and image as an undemanding prologue to a more complex, but no less straightforward, dialectic of mediation, ultimately confusing both terms or simply losing sight of them in the midst of numerous theoretical intricacies.[12] In the end, it remains unclear what the shared image of the concept 'of the centaurs' [*von den Centauren*] and 'of the spirit of a river' [*vom Geist eines Stromes*] could be.

What is the 'image' [*Bild*] of the centaur? What is the 'image' of the concept if it is more than a literary formula or rhetorical trope? The paradox in Hölderlin's analogy of centaurs and rivers seems to lie not so much in the comparison itself, but rather in the way that the comparison immediately undermines the very metaphorical counterpoint on which it depends.

The history of poetry is full of centaurs that are at times even portrayed as rivers,[13] but rarely have the two been treated as one and the same. One could for instance turn to the visual arts and examine the typological changes in the centaur's iconography that symbolise its gradual humanisation as a mythological figure from a demonic, beastly creature to a harmonious or even bucolic figure.[14] Still – and similarly to what happens with most meta-narrative approaches to Hölderlin's text – no 'development of the centauric image'[15] seems sufficient to apprehend the implications of 'its image' *as a concept*.

In its most general sense, the interconnectedness of concept and image is as ancient and well-documented a problem as it is intractable at its root.

At some point, it inevitably becomes indistinguishable from the wider subject of time, turning on itself without end: does Hölderlin's commentary follow 'the use of the natural ("the spirit of a river") to arrive at something conceptual ("the Begriff of the Centaurs")', to use John Hamilton's phrasing,[16] or is it a comparison 'strictly between two abstracts: the concept "centaur" and the "spirit" of the river', as David Constantine puts it?[17] Is the 'abstract level' placed behind the 'descriptive level',[18] or is the opposite the case? To what extent is it evident that the 'mythical intuition' of the centaurs should take place only after the 'general definition' or the 'conceptual determination'[19] has been arrived at? In line with a traditional view of the entanglement of textual and visual elements in the context of literary criticism, the problem of the relation of the two becomes a matter of simple doubt: in which sequence do the verbal and visual elements unfold and interact? In this respect, it is only too revealing that the question of temporality should be resolved in a spatial perception of the centaur-river: '[I]ts image' is said to be found at certain 'places in nature'.

IV

The ubiquity of the concept of nature in Hölderlin's poetry has long been dissected in its many forms, normally by exploring the different kinds of structural oppositions that determine the various stages of his work, from direct borrowings such as the dualism of nature and art – or the aorgic and the organic – to thematic derivatives such as nature and history or nature and revolution. With such wide-ranging catchwords, anything is possible and, accordingly, it is tempting to read the opening lines of Hölderlin's commentary to Pindar's fragment – the positing of 'the concept of centaurs' as 'the spirit of a river' – by literally framing them against the notion of a reciprocal determination of nature and spirit that was all pervasive by the late eighteenth century.

Hölderlin's thinking is in no way impervious to such constructions. His lyric poetry is more than just abundant in images of rivers as signs of the gods,[20] charged with metaphysical and theological associations and pursued by scholarship as the quintessence of metaphor. In a periodisation of the history of the river as the metaphor of poetry and of genius, Hölderlin is said to represent a third generation, heir to the likes of Klopstock and Goethe.[21] Even if one circumvents Heidegger's and several other philosophical and philological readings of 'the streaming word' (*Der Rhein*, v. 34) as the consummated 'image' of poetry, the ensemble of Hölderlin's *Stromdichtung* seems almost fatally marked from the outside by the burden of metaphor. In principle, the same applies to the inescapable analysis of the similarities and differences between the movement of rivers described in those poems and the narrative contained in *The Life-Giving*. Again, anything is possible: one can just as easily claim to discern on etymological grounds 'a hidden comparison of the river with the centaurs' near the ending of *Der Ister*[22] as one can accept yet again the analogy between centaurs and rivers as a founding moment of civilisation only to see the analogy metaphorically duplicated or 'complemented' by yet another repetition of the affinities that link 'river and poetry'.[23] But what is one to make of the centaur-river as an image of nature, if such an identification were to resist or to reject its definition as a 'dialectical balancing movement'[24] or, alternately, as an 'explanatory metaphor for the emergence of the human spirit out of nature'[25]?

Assuming that the centaurs are to be conceived of as 'the naturally preexisting mythical expression of the natural forces of rivers at a certain moment of the historical development of the Earth'[26] and therefore attest to the identity of the formation process of both myth and nature, the question arises as to how such a formation comes into being, that is how it actually takes shape or falls into place both linguistically and physically, if it eschews metaphor entirely. For if Hölderlin's intention in transferring the 'myth of the centaurs onto the creative stage of the natural process of nature' is to seek the 'retrieval of a sensorium that the ancients possessed, according to which the mythical does not consist of bookish knowledge but rather depends on an experienced – past or present – reality of nature',[27] it is only fair to ask what lies at the root of that experience, and what does it entail for the translator writing 'The Life-Giving'?

V

In a widely discussed passage of the 'Notes on Antigone', in which Hölderlin elaborates on his philosophical-historical conception of the task of Hesperian or western art in its yearning to learn 'the free use of what is our own'[28] by confronting itself with the origin or the nature of Greek poetry, he mentions two verses (987–8) from Sophocles' *Antigone*, the tragedy that in his eyes signals the transition from Greek towards Hesperian culture. Quoting from his own translation, he justifies his handling of the original with the effort to 'bring it closer to our mode of representation', noting that 'in earnest' the name 'Zeus' should be rendered as 'Father of Time or: Father of the Earth, because it is his character, as opposed to the eternal tendency, to reverse *the striving out of this world into the other*, into a *striving out of another world into this one*'. And he concludes with an iconic turn of phrase: 'Namely, we must in all places depict the myth *in a more demonstrable way*' (*FHA* XVI, 415, my translation).

While it ostensibly exceeds previous determinations of the presentation or representation (*Darstellung*)[29] of mythical figures, this will to conceive of myth as something that must by force be verifiable or demonstrable to the extreme in the concreteness of language still relies heavily on the seductive and almost ready-made idea, according to which 'to interpret is to translate, and vice versa'.[30] As a result, in their willingness to correct or to illuminate his creative mistakes, critics of Hölderlin's poetics of tragedy tend to mimic the standpoint of the translator in the process of interpreting or explaining his translation a posteriori.

Such an approach can be said to be well-founded in the case of Hölderlin's remarks on his translations of *Oedipus* and *Antigone*, where he went so far as to provide all at once a thorough sketch of his poetics, a historical-metaphysical commentary on both tragedies and an exercise in immanent reading of his translation on the basis of several examples. Likewise, with Hölderlin's 1800 Pindar translation, a rigid formal exercise that foreshadowed the start of his so-called late poetry, the trained philologist still had the rudiments of a system at his disposal to imitate Hölderlins philological gesture with new philological methods.[31]

In the case of 'The Life-Giving', there is no such stable or safe ground to tread upon. That is why any positive identification of the translator as an exegete in his attempt to 'justify the assumption that the idea of the river, as it forms a path and a boundary, is presented in the form of the centaur',[32] often inevitably disintegrates into the counterfeit myth of subjectivity. The 'adaptation of the Pindaric myth to Hölderlin's mythology' then comes across as a 'subjectivization of the objects' which 'shows itself as objective' by tendentially projecting the 'inner world' of the poet onto a 'newly created world of hieroglyphic signs', thereby edifying a 'mythological system' of its own.[33] In other words, the exegesis would face the original text as an 'amplification of sorts, whereby the poet uses the condensed verses as a fruitful starting point for his own 'subjective' musings'.[34] Subjectivity, however, falls short of accounting for the roughness as well as the precision of 'The Life-Giving' in the way it not only presents, but also embodies myth 'in a more demonstrable way'.

VI

A set of notes entitled *On the Fable of the Ancients*, dating from 1803–4, which is the same period as the Pindar Fragments, enumerates the various elements that constitute ancient myth. After alluding in a sketch-like manner to the principles, the shape and the system of myth, Hölderlin writes in his table of contents, which, for all intents and purposes, functions as a diagram:

> Relation. Movability.
> Different forms which these undergo as principles, despite the necessity of their formation.
> Meaning and content of the same.
> (*FHA* XIV, 388, my translation)

Under 'mythological content', the text mentions the 'heroic', the 'purely human' and the 'sense of such fables in general', referring to its 'higher morals' and the 'infinity of wisdom', after which it states: 'Correlation of humans and spirits. / Nature, in its impact history' (*FHA* XIV, 388, my translation). This last remark is usually clarified by reference to a letter Hölderlin wrote Seckendorf in 1804, in which he offers a further definition of myth (or fable) as that which corresponds to 'the poetic view of history and the architectonics of the sky'.[35] In 'The Life-Giving', however, no direct connection is established between nature and history except metaphorically, and an architectonics of the sky seems not to exist. Instead, all action takes place on land at the exact same time, namely at a time of origin that predates recorded history and contradicts every sense of measured time as such. It is no coincidence that the word 'originally' [*ursprünglich*] is mentioned four times in Hölderlin's text, describing an isomorphic movement that alternates almost fortuitously between past and present. The river forms 'a path and a boundary' on the originally pathless earth, just as it had originally 'wandered about' at those 'places' and 'regions' of nature where it eventually abandoned the 'mountain chain', moving against its direction, and it is 'also originally' that the centaurs are said to be the 'teachers of natural science'.

While virtually everything in the narrative that follows would seem to point to a logic of progression, especially with the narrative's insistence on the image of the wandering or stagnating waters that seek their direction and determination – or their purpose or destiny [*Bestimmung*] – the text is never genuinely reliant on temporal linearity. In truth, it focuses on the indeterminacy of time by dislocating it without end. The original, simultaneous time that it addresses avoids succession – the precondition for every evolutionary understanding of the analogy – at all costs. There is strictly speaking no dialectical turn from nature to civilisation to speak of in terms of 'before' and 'after'. The very recurrence of the word 'direction' is not encased in one, but in several different movements within nature, and even though the reader is led to expect a denouement, an unequivocal solution to the storyline, what lies in waiting at the end is an abrupt inference that binds everything together by setting off an instant chain reaction. This sense of ruptured time is key to considering Hölderlin's text as more than a mere string of metaphors that one needs to make sense of within a teleological framework.

Each myth, Hölderlin's systematic overview of the ancient fable says, changes form according to the relation and movability of its parts, 'despite the necessity' of its 'formation' – it becomes ductile and malleable in spite of the firmness of its principles. This rule is taken to a new level with the attempt to bring centaurs into rivers and rivers into nature, which is not primarily determined by meaning and content, but rather fulfilled by the self-propelled and self-sustained act of inscribing – or translating – one form into another.

Admittedly, as a translator looking into the myth's internal plot, Hölderlin is all but indifferent to its content and clearly attempts to illuminate his own replica of it. But his focus is on the rotation and displacement of form, in an effort to bring into view the mythical space of nature as a blank space. It is from that hollow space – of relation and movability – that the translator re-emerges in a different light, no longer as a simple mediator, but as the one moving alongside concept and image, only distorting or rewriting the myth inasmuch as it is made to follow the inherently visual transfiguration of its own characters.

VII

Hölderlin's embedded narrative of centaurs as rivers, which openly revolves around the conflation of a mythical-conceptual with a natural-visual figure, is not merely filled with images. Rather, it wants to become an image itself intent on exceeding its own reflection as a strictly metaphorical or allegorical stance. In other words, it goes beyond the streaming spirit of a river, as the hidden prefiguration of the streaming word of poetry, or as a macroscopic parable of the origin of culture.

The search for the materiality and visuality of text, however, and of this text in particular, is fraught with many obstacles. There are fixed methods and categories at the intersection of classical and modern philology to approach Hölderlin's use of figurative language and define the limits of the actual or virtual imagery contained in his poetry. Often those limits are identified as the boundaries of his own mythopoetics, which is then catalogued and stored for further use. Where systems overlap due to the constraints imposed by a pre-existing tradition, as in the case of the Pindar Fragments, comparative analysis habitually plunges into broad contextualisation.

'The Life-Giving' has been widely exposed to such applied hermeneutics, perhaps to an even larger extent than the remaining fragments, since it appears to consist of a linear narrative depicting the birth of culture and civilisation. It is true that Hölderlin's concluding dictum seems to legitimise the methodical, restrained interpretation that most often has been placed upon it. With the appearance of the just and wise centaur, Chiron, previously named in the first of the fragments, *Unfaithfulness of Wisdom*, the story seemingly comes full-circle, even qualifying as 'the climax to the dialectic' presumably epitomised by the nine Pindar Fragments.[36] Moreover, the allusion to the 'centaur songs, sung with the spirit of the river, and as if by the Greek Chiron', apparently allows for the reconstruction of the whole fragment – or, in a more prosaic sense, of its 'whole picture' – as a peaceful tension, a dialectical balance of some kind between pure and purified savagery, at the end of which the wild centaurs would appear to be magically (metaphorically) transfigured into 'teachers of the science of nature', as stated near the beginning of the commentary. But not only is this far from being a mere humanistic platitude serving as the corollary to something akin to a natural history of civilisation, it is also blatantly indifferent to every forced demonstration of Hölderlin's potential attunement with the earth science of his time, particularly in the fields of geology and hydrology.

To be sure, as a complex essay in topography, 'The Life-Giving' can of course be contrasted to the much-discussed cartographic index of Hölderlin's poetry with its varying representations of space. Nonetheless, and despite the apparently redeeming or tranquilising twist that reduces an unruly plural (the centaurs as an archetypal image of transgression) to an evocative, well-proportioned individuality (Chiron as the source of lyric song or *Gesang*), there is still something in the process of transfiguration itself that remains concealed by virtue of being untamed, intimately tied as it is to the centaurs' original act of violence. Such inscrutability cannot be done away with simply by pushing Hölderlin's narrative into a simulacrum of *Bildung* that illustrates the passage from chaos to order, or, in even more plain terms, from *mythos* to *logos*. Rather, it needs to be addressed in terms of the inner structure and dynamics of transposition that it implies. Indeed, for all its supposed logical consistency, the deciphering of the commentary as an unruffled tale of mediation overlooks the most crucial of elements in Hölderlin's text, namely the radicality of his gesture as a translator.

VIII

There is an inherent violence to Hölderlin's attempt at translating centaurs as concepts that as rivers, in turn, become an image of nature only finally to cast their gaze over nature itself. In part, his gesture is coextensive with that of the centaurs as they appear in his own rendition of Pindar's text: 'by themselves', 'spontaneously' [*von selbst*], using their bare 'hands' [*mit Händen*], they thrust or push away [*treiben*] the table. So, too, the translator does violence to the text facing him, not once, but twice: in his attempt to reshape Pindar's verses, he devises a parallel prose narrative that destroys every 'source text' as much as every 'original translation' of the myth.

The reasons for this double-edged assault on the text on the part of the translator have been thoroughly explained either as intentional (biographically founded) or inadvertent (but etymologically explainable) decisions. But Hölderlin's transgressive position as a translator here eludes every merely contextual or linguistic analysis. Contrary to what has been suggested by nearly every reading of this text, translation is not a backdrop against which one can pursue a psychological, metaphysical or historical clarification of Hölderlin's thinking, and even less an excuse to dig deeper into the 'private mythology'[37] of his lyric poetry where similar themes appear, let alone the urge to collect one more piece of evidence that would further corroborate his alleged programme of 'demythologization'. The fact is that, long after completion of the philological inventory of its syntactic, semantic and structural errors, Hölderlin's text keeps reflecting insistently upon the act of translating beyond what is known to be its frame of reference.

As he begins to write his commentary, he has already clearly lost sight of the Greek text and has become almost oblivious to the idea of translation as a mere exercise in interlinguistic mediation. In fact, his text dismantles the foundations of that very idea altogether. What it strives to accomplish, by reflecting on the passage from concept to image and from image to nature, is a physical sense of transformation which can only be made visible through a literal movement of transposition that evades and cancels all strictly exegetical or historical categories as such. As if pulling the (spirit of a) river out of the (concept of) centaurs only to immediately perform the opposite movement by retranslating it into a unified concept-image of nature, the text's self-referential stance is pushed to the extreme: it draws the analogy in the most tangible of ways while at the same time serving as the demonstration of the very motion it aims at depicting.

In point of fact, the articulation of concept and image hinges on the formal similarity of the three parts that compose 'The Life-Giving': title, translation and commentary. Both triadic movements take place on a single surface (nature), at the same time (originally), on equal grounds. Because they exist simultaneously and stand side by side, as everything else within the text, there can be no separation whatsoever between them. As a consequence, Hölderlin's multi-layered prose text is not so much the commentary of a translation as a constitutive part of that same translation, if not its most essential trait. His commentary truly is the expanded form of the translated verse text, which has become entirely his own after the effacing of the original, though never in the sense of a poeticised exegesis or a subjective poetry of interpretation. As purely discursive as it may appear, the commentary is now a translating act in its own right.

There is no 'original' in 'The Life-Giving' that is not pervaded at its root by translation. From beginning to end, every part of the text is literally inhabited by translation or enacted by it. As it becomes all-inclusive, however, translation is everything, except a transparent structure of mediation.

IX

With the exception of his Notes on Sophocles' *King Oedipus* and *Antigone*, Hölderlin's lapidary formulations of what he saw as the laws and principles of translation appear for the most part scattered throughout his work as part of an ongoing reflection on the relation of the ancients and the moderns, Hellas and Hesperia. Highly dense and individualised, his schematic reflections on the paradoxical dynamics between the Greek and the German strongly resist appropriation and tend to be self-enclosing. Nonetheless, for all its fundamentally autonomous character and distinctive terminology, his obsession with the relation of the native to the foreign is hardly foreign itself to just about every discourse focusing on *the nature of translation* as an intrinsically oscillating movement, in method or style, between naturalisation and denaturalisation, naturalness and unnaturalness, and other similar categories. In one way or another, it presupposes a clear – primarily linguistic or cultural – distinction between original and translation.

By contrast, 'The Life-Giving' clearly goes beyond such antinomies and attempts something virtually impossible, both in essence and in execution, in that it summons an extensive and ultimately unfathomable experience of translation by replicating – in itself and by itself, *von selbst* – the time-space continuum of the scene it is pursuing.

Hölderlin's narration of centaurs and rivers simulates succession repeatedly, but never carries it into effect in a definite manner. It might well contain a latent wish for mediation and an eye for the unfolding of history, but it plays itself – as a process – on a different level. Namely, it constantly enunciates a sequence of events only to replace it immediately with raw simultaneity. All its 'stages' and 'moments' are in reality coexistent and thwart the sense of progression it seems to evoke: all take place 'originally', in immemorial time – and it is 'also originally', one could add, that translation finally reveals itself in all its density and breadth.

What is the origin of translation, outside of its recorded history within the history of language(s)? In many ways, Hölderlin's gesture as a translator is the attempt to answer this question not only by transforming but also by incorporating its object as a radically self-reflective experience that pulls against a limited, circumscribed understanding of translation.

Indeed, his text only tells 'a story' inasmuch as it continuously reflects upon its own composition as the immediate transposition of a textual plane onto a visual plane, and vice versa. As a (mythological) concept, the centaurs are shifted onto an (actual) image, i.e. the rivers as they move (as one spirit) in nature but, in order for this concept-image to become manifest, it has to be perceived as nature itself.

> The concept of the centaurs is surely that of the spirit of the river, insofar as it forms a path and a boundary, with violence, on the originally pathless and upwards growing earth. | Its image is therefore at places in nature where the shore is rich in cliffs and grottoes, *especially at places where originally the river had to leave the mountain chain and had to cut across its direction.* | Hence centaurs are also originally teachers of the science of nature, because nature can best examined from that viewpoint. (*FHA* XV, 363–4; *Essays and Letters*, 338–9, translation modified)

Written as it was in the early years of the nineteenth century, at a pivotal point in the history of the natural sciences, Hölderlin's mention here of the term 'Naturwissensschaft' can have all sorts of theoretical implications[38] – or none. Be that as it may, and despite the many, more or less arbitrary correlations of his thinking to the earliest or to a contemporary understanding of nature,[39] neither the chronology of science nor that of philosophy seem to loom large in 'The Life-Giving'. Factually devoid of historical references and literary precedents, the image of the centaurs as the 'teachers of the science of nature' remains highly perplexing both in motivation and in detail. Yet it is precisely such inscrutability that stands at the core of what it means to translate 'originally'.

After the centaurs become intertwined with nature by cutting their way through it [*durchreißen, Grenze machen*], they need to view it [*einsehn*] not only from without but also from within – again: originally. The same could be said of the translator as he surrounds and enters his object with the aim of reflecting upon it without ever leaving it. By staging a figurative analogy as if it were a literal analogy between the mythical and the natural, concept and image, he undoes and reinvents the 'movement and the phenomenalization of concepts and of every aspect of serious meaning'[40] that Hölderlin once believed to discern in Greek art. Ultimately, what the translator impersonates is not the centaur, nor the river, but the analogy itself.

Therein lies the sign of a fundamentally extensive – and largely unknown – pre-history of translation, which on a hyperbolic note could be said to be the *analogon* of the science of nature as depicted above: not the anticipation of scientific discourse as we know it, but the arcane knowledge of something that can only be experienced in a space that at once negates and fulfils time in order to become visible. It is within that space, at certain 'places in nature', that concept and image exist and manifest themselves as simultaneous, forming a still frame wherein the passage from one to the other – the physical act of translation as such – will come to be inscribed.

Notes

1. See Ovid, *Metamorphoses*, 210 sqq., Homer, *Iliad*, II, 742 sqq., Homer, *Odyssey* XXI, 295 sqq.
2. Franz, *Pindarfragmente*, pp. 267–8. All translations are my own except where otherwise noted.
3. Louth, 'Figures of Transition', pp. 57–8.
4. Koczisky, 'Warum ist der Kentaur', pp. 72–3.
5. Koczisky, *Mythenfiguren*, p. 28.
6. Böschenstein, 'Le renversement du texte', p. 60.
7. Harrison, *Hölderlin and Greek Literature*, p. 287, pp. 300–1.
8. Böschenstein, 'Göttliche Instanz', p. 48, p. 63. Even more general considerations of Hölderlin's overall reception of Pindar emphasise the 'relinquishment of utopia' or a 'loss of utopia' in the Pindar Fragments as a consequence of Hölderlin's 'mental disruption' (Theunissen, *Pindar*, pp. 972–80). See also: Fink, *Pindarfragmente*, pp. 36–7, 131–2.
9. Beißner, *Hölderlins Übersetzungen*, p. 44.
10. Ibid. p. 54.
11. Adler, 'Philosophical Archeology', p. 35.
12. See for instance Koczisky, *Mythenfiguren*, pp. 14–16 and Koczisky, 'Warum ist der Kentaur', p. 70.
13. Killy, 'Welt in der Welt', p. 39.
14. Morawietz, *Der gezähmte Kentaur*, pp. 22–3, 39–43, 46–7, 169–70.
15. Blanckenhagen, 'Easy Monsters', p. 88.
16. Hamilton, *Soliciting Darkness*, p. 303.
17. Constantine, *Hölderlin*, p. 291.
18. Bartel, *Centaurengesänge*, p.167.
19. Killy, 'Hölderlins Interpretation', pp. 217–18.
20. Büttner, *Natur*, pp. 242–5.
21. Müller, *Das Strommotiv*, pp. 1–5, 229–30.
22. Schmidt, *Hölderlins später Widerruf*, pp. 13–15; Killy, 'Welt in der Welt', p. 41.

23. Procopan, *Hölderlins Donauhymnen*, pp. 132–3, p. 153, p. 161.
24. Behre, 'Hölderlins Stromdichtung', p. 36.
25. Götz, *Über Sicherheit und Sprache*, p. 241.
26. Bennholdt-Tomsen and Guzzoni, 'Das Irren der Ströme', p. 341.
27. Ibid. pp. 342–3.
28. Hölderlin, *Essays and Letters*, p. 207.
29. See *FHA* XIV, pp. 11–49.
30. Constantine, 'Translation and Exegesis', p. 395.
31. Hölderlin's reception of Pindar is widely documented. See, for example: Bremer and Lehle, 'Pindar-Übersetzung'; Louth, *Hölderlin and the Dynamics of Translation*, pp. 103–49; Benn, *Hölderlin and Pindar*; Seifert, *Hölderlin und Pindar*; Seifert, *Untersuchungen*; Vöhler, *Pindarrezeptionen*.
32. Killy, 'Hölderlins Interpretation', p. 226.
33. Ibid. p. 232.
34. Hamilton, *Soliciting Darkness*, p. 297.
35. Hölderlin, *Essays and Letters*, p. 218.
36. Adler, *Philosophical Archaeology*, p. 38.
37. See Killy, 'Welt in der Welt', p. 53.
38. See Götz, *Über Sicherheit*, pp. 244–5; Jamme and Pöggeler, *Jenseits des Idealismus*, p. 143; Link, *Hölderlin-Rousseau*, pp. 90–1.
39. See, for example, Hölscher, 'Vom Ursprung'; Waibel, 'Wechselbestimmung'.
40. Hölderlin, *Essays and Letters*, p. 214.

Bibliography

Adler, Jeremy, 'Philosophical Archeology – Hölderlin's Pindar Fragments: A Translation with an Interpretation', *Comparative Criticism*, 6 (1984), pp. 23–46.
Bartel, Heike, *Centaurengesänge: Friedrich Hölderlins Pindarfragmente* (Würzburg: Königshausen & Neumann, 2000).
Behre, Maria, 'Hölderlins Stromdichtung – Zum Spannungsfeld von Naturwahrnehmung und Kunstauffassung', in Uwe Beyer (ed.), *Neue Wege zu Hölderlin* (Würzburg: Königshausen & Neumann, 1994), pp. 17–40.
Beißner, Friedrich, *Hölderlins Übersetzungen aus dem Griechischen* (Stuttgart: Metzler 1933).
Benn, Maurice B., *Hölderlin and Pindar* (The Hague: Mouton, 1962).
Bennholdt-Tomsen, Anke and Guzzoni, Alfredo, 'Das Irren der Ströme', *Hölderlin-Jahrbuch*, 34 (2004–5), pp. 330–52.
Blanckenhagen, Peter H. von, 'Easy Monsters', in Ann E. Farkas, Prudence O. Harper and Evelyn B. Harrison (eds), *Monsters and Demons in the Ancient and Medieval Worlds* (Mainz: Philipp von Zabern, 1987), pp. 85–94.
Böschenstein, Bernhard, 'Göttliche Instanz und irdische Antwort in Hölderlins drei Übersetzungsmodellen: Pindar: Hymnen – Sophokles – Pindar: Fragmente', *Hölderlin-Jahrbuch*, 29 (1994–5), pp. 47–63.
Böschenstein, Bernhard, 'Le renversement du texte: Hölderlin interprète de Pindare', *Littérature*, 99 (1995), pp. 53–61.
Bremer, Dieter and Lehle, Christiane, 'Zu Hölderlins Pindar-Übersetzung: Kritischer Rückblick und mögliche Perspektiven', in Uwe Beyer (ed.), *Neue Wege zu Hölderlin* (Würzburg: Königshausen & Neumann, 1994), pp. 71–111.
Büttner, Stefan, 'Natur – Ein Grundwort Hölderlins', *Hölderlin-Jahrbuch*, 26 (1988–9), pp. 224–47.
Constantine, David, 'Translation and Exegesis in Hölderlin', *Modern Language Review*, 81 (1986), pp. 388–97.

Constantine, David, *Hölderlin* (Oxford: Oxford University Press, 1988).
Fink, Markus, *Pindarfragmente: Neun Hölderlin-Deutungen* (Tübingen: Walter de Gruyter, 2011).
Franz, Michael, 'Pindarfragmente', in Johann Kreuzer (ed.), *Hölderlin-Handbuch* (Stuttgart: Springer, 2002), pp. 254–69.
Götz, Martin, *Über Sicherheit und Sprache angesichts 'Untreue der Weisheit' und 'Die Asyle' von Friedrich Hölderlin* (Tübingen: Walter de Gruyter, 2012).
Hamilton, John T., *Soliciting Darkness: Pindar, Obscurity and the Classical Tradition*. (Cambridge, MA and London: Harvard University Press, 2003).
Harrison, Robin B., *Hölderlin and Greek Literature* (Oxford: Clarendon Press, 1975).
Hölscher, Uvo, 'Vom Ursprung der Naturphilosophie', *Hölderlin-Jahrbuch* 30 (1996–97), pp. 1–14.
Homer, *The Iliad*, trans. Robert Fagles (London: Penguin Books, 1991).
Homer, *The Odyssey*, trans. Robert Fagles (London: Penguin Books, 1996).
Jamme, Christoph and Pöggeler, Otto (eds), *Jenseits des Idealismus* (Bonn: Bouvier, 1988).
Killy, Walther, 'Hölderlins Interpretation des Pindarfragments 166 (Schr.)', *Antike und Abendland*, 4 (1954), pp. 216–33.
Killy, Walther, 'Welt in der Welt', in *Wandlungen des lyrischen Bildes* (Göttingen: Vandenhoeck & Ruprecht, 1967), pp. 36–62.
Kocziskzy, Eva, 'Warum ist der Kentaur ein Stromgeist?', *Jahrbuch der ungarischen Germanistik* (1992), pp. 67–79.
Kocziskzy, Eva, *Mythenfiguren in Hölderlins Spätwerk* (Würzburg: Königshausen & Neumann, 1997).
Link, Jürgen, *Hölderlin-Rousseau: Inventive Rückkehr* (Wiesbaden: Westdeutscher Verlag, 1999).
Louth, Charlie, *Hölderlin and the Dynamics of Translation* (Oxford: David Brown Book Co., 1998).
Louth, Charlie, 'Figures of Transition: Centaurs in Goethe and Hölderlin', *New Comparison*, 27/28 (2001), pp. 50–8.
Morawietz, Georg, *Der gezähmte Kentaur: Bedeutungsveränderung der Kentaurenbilder in der Antike* (Munich: Biering & Brinkmann, 2000).
Müller, Richard M., *Das Strommotiv und die deutsche Klassik* (Bonn: Bouvier, 1957).
Ovid, *Metamorphoses*, trans. Arthur Golding (London: Penguin Books, 2002).
Procopan, Norina, *Hölderlins Donauhymnen: Zur Funktion der Strommetapher in den späthymnischen Gesängen 'Am Quell der Donau', 'Die Wanderung' und 'Der Ister'* (Eggingen: Edition Isele, 2004).
Schmidt, Jochen, *Hölderlins später Widerruf in den Oden 'Chiron', 'Blödigkeit' und 'Ganymed'* (Tübingen: Niemeyer, 1978).
Seifert, Albrecht, *Untersuchungen zu Hölderlins Pindar-Rezeption* (München: W. Fink, 1982).
Seifert, Albrecht, *Hölderlin und Pindar* (Eggingen: Edition Isele, 1998).
Theunissen, Michael, *Pindar. Menschenlos und Wende der Zeit* (München: C. H. Beck, 2000).
Vöhler, Martin, *Pindarrezeptionen. Sechs Studien zum Wandel des Pindarverständnisses von Erasmus bis Herder* (Heidelberg: Winter, 2005).
Waibel, Violetta, 'Wechselbestimmung: Zum Verhältnis von Hölderlin, Schiller und Fichte in Jena', in Wolfgang H. Schrader (ed.), *Fichte und die Romantik: Hölderlin, Schelling, Hegel und die späte Wissenschaftslehre* (Amsterdam: Rodopi, 1997), pp. 43–70.

Part III
Natural Beauty and the Absolute

Chapter 8

Hölderlin's Mythopoetics: From 'Aesthetic Letters' to the New Mythology

Luke Fischer

Introduction

Like his contemporaries, Friedrich Schiller and Friedrich von Hardenberg (Novalis), Friedrich Hölderlin's approach to poetry was deeply informed by his philosophical thought. While Hölderlin has long been regarded as a philosophical poet, his most influential philosophical interpreter, Martin Heidegger, severed his poetry from the context of German idealism. In recent decades, in contrast, Hölderlin has come to be identified not only as a philosophical poet but also as a crucial figure in the development of post-Kantian philosophy (in important respects anticipating and influencing Friedrich Schelling and G. W. F. Hegel).[1] However, there is still a need for further research on the precise and complex connections between Hölderlin's philosophical views and his poetry. The present essay gives particular attention to how Hölderlin's aesthetics informs the mythological dimensions of his poetry.

Hölderlin's philosophical aesthetics underpinned his poetry and also played a decisive role in the emergence of absolute idealism – in contradistinction to subjective idealism. While Hölderlin, Schelling and Hegel followed Kant and Fichte – and earlier, Descartes – in granting a pivotal place to the thinking subject, their deepest concern was to overcome the opposition and dualism between subject and object and to articulate the ultimate unity of mind and world, which they termed the 'Absolute'. With regard to the philosophical importance granted to poetry and, more specifically, mythology, as well as a shared interest in articulating a deeper unity between mind and nature, there is an especially close proximity between Hölderlin and Schelling. (Their shared views, as I later elaborate, are vitally relevant to our contemporary situation of ecological crisis.)[2] Hegel, relative to the Romantics and Hölderlin, is known for lowering the status of art in comparison to philosophy; art, according to Hegel, has twice been superseded – by the Christian religion and the philosophy of absolute idealism – as a form of Absolute Spirit. It is remarkable that Hegel nevertheless identifies the crucial role that aesthetics plays in the emergence of the philosophical standpoint of absolute idealism.

In his lectures on aesthetics Hegel explains that it is Schiller, especially in his *On the Aesthetic Education of Humankind in a Series of Letters* (1795), who makes a decisive breakthrough towards absolute idealism by demonstrating how the beautiful reconciles oppositions that are not yet fully reconciled in Kant's aesthetics.[3] Schelling then takes the crucial further step in showing how the unity that Schiller attributes to the subjective experience and creation of art reveals the unity of the Absolute and the unifying idea of philosophy.[4] Much of what Hegel attributes to Schelling's *System of Transcendental Idealism* of 1800 (without naming the text) was, in fact, first articulated by Hölderlin a few years prior. While Schelling was the first to publish these ideas in a systematic philosophical form, his thinking shows a clear debt to Hölderlin.

The primary aim of this essay is to reconstruct how Hölderlin builds on Schiller's aesthetics and poetics and how his mature poetry, especially his elegies and hymns (circa 1800), is the ultimate expression of his philosophical and aesthetic programme. More specifically, I argue that Schiller's ideas concerning the unity of the beautiful are expanded to the Absolute in Hölderlin (circa 1795), and show how Schiller's articulation of the importance of an aesthetic education, becomes in Hölderlin the programme for a 'new mythology'. In contrast to Hegel's mature system,[5] in which it is only philosophy that can resolve the oppositions of modernity, Hölderlin held the view, as did Schelling, that these oppositions could only be resolved in the form of a new, syncretic mythology, which, I argue, Hölderlin attempted to realise in his own poetry.

From 'Aesthetic Letters' to the New Mythology

In his *On the Aesthetic Education of Humankind in a Series of Letters* (1795), Schiller conceives human nature as polarised into a rational or formal drive and a sensuous or material drive.[6] Outside the realm of the aesthetic these two drives conflict with one another. Individuals given to the sensuous drive are ruled by their passions in a state that opposes their rational and moral nature. Individuals one-sidedly devoted to rationality are abstracted from particularity, feeling and the senses, and their duty to universal morals opposes their sensuous desires. In the realm of the aesthetic, a harmony between these otherwise opposed drives is achieved. This entails the emergence of a new, third drive, namely the *play* drive. Aesthetic harmony fulfils an anthropological ideal in that it enables the free, harmonious and full expression of human nature and reconciles the opposition between the sensuous and the rational. Building on this anthropological significance, Schiller envisages the political ideal of an aesthetic state in which aesthetically educated citizens freely collaborate and achieve a collective harmony where the individual is neither subordinated to the general will of the state nor driven by anarchic self-interest.

While Hölderlin was an admirer of Schiller's aesthetics (and also influenced Schiller[7]), during his stay in Jena (1795) – where he frequently met with Schiller (as well as Goethe) and attended Fichte's lectures at the university – he began to formulate ideas that he came to envisage as a project of 'New Letters on the Aesthetic Education of Humankind', which would build on yet go beyond Schiller's *Aesthetic Letters*. Although Hölderlin never realised this project, his key ideas can be reconstructed on the basis of various texts and letters. Immanuel Niethammer was keen to publish Hölderlin's planned work in his *Philosophical Journal* and in his letter to Niethammer from 24 February 1796, Hölderlin summarises his main aims:

> In the philosophical letters I want to find the principle that will explain to my satisfaction the divisions in which we think and exist, but which is also capable of making the conflict disappear, the conflict between the subject and the object, between ourselves and the world, and between reason and revelation, – theoretically, through intellectual intuition, without our practical reason having to intervene. To do this we need an aesthetic sense, and I shall call my philosophical letters *New Letters on the Aesthetic Education of Man*. And in them I will go on from philosophy to poetry and religion. (*Essays and Letters*, 68)

Hölderlin plans not only to show how the opposition between human faculties – reason and sensibility – can be resolved through the aesthetic as Schiller had done, but also to resolve the metaphysical opposition between subject and object, self and world. In other words, he plans to articulate the ultimate unity of being or the Absolute. The epistemic key to articulating this unity is the aesthetic. He also plans to discuss the relation between poetry and religion, which is not a central concern for Schiller.

In the widely discussed philosophical fragment, 'Being Judgement Possibility' (1795), Hölderlin describes the Absolute or being as the unity of subject and object (*Essays and Letters*, 231). However, contrary to Fichte, he argues that it cannot be grasped in the form of self-consciousness, in the identity of subject and object that is linguistically captured in the proposition 'I am I'. According to Hölderlin the unity of being must precede self-consciousness and escapes this form of self-consciousness, which for Hölderlin implies a division from an original unity. For something to appear to me (the subject) as an object, even if this object is myself (a subject), there must be some difference and division between subject and object, a division that cannot hold for what is truly Absolute (*Essays and Letters*, 231).

In that Hölderlin does not think that the Absolute can be grasped from a philosophical standpoint such as Fichte's, the question arises as to whether the Absolute can be known by some other means or must remain unknowable? Dieter Henrich basically maintains the view that it is unknowable. While Hölderlin describes 'intellectual intuition' as grasping the ultimate unity of subject and object, Henrich regards 'intellectual intuition' as a hypothetical notion in a Kantian sense (we can imagine it as the possession of a divine intellect but it is beyond the capacities of a finite human mind).[8] In contrast, Frederick Beiser argues that while Hölderlin's 'Absolute' is inaccessible to rational judgement it is directly revealed in aesthetic contemplation.[9] As will become clear, I share Beiser's view on this matter. Moreover, it is precisely in this connection between the aesthetic and the Absolute that Hölderlin identifies the philosophical significance of poetry.

In his letter to Niethammer, Hölderlin writes that to resolve the opposition between subject and object 'we need an aesthetic sense'. And, in a letter to Schiller from 4 September 1795, Hölderlin draws an even closer link between intellectual intuition and the aesthetic:

> I am attempting to work out for myself the idea of an infinite progress in philosophy by showing that the unremitting demand that must be made of any system, the union of subject and object in an absolute . . . *I* or whatever one wants to call it, though possible aesthetically, in an act of intellectual intuition, is theoretically possible only through endless approximation. (*Essays and Letters*, 62)

Though there are some differences between Hölderlin's terminology in this earlier letter to Schiller and his later letter to Niethammer, in both cases Hölderlin is essentially identifying 'intellectual intuition' with 'aesthetic intuition'. And his claim is that while the unity of the Absolute cannot be adequately grasped through purely theoretical or practical judgement, it can be grasped aesthetically.

In the preface written for the penultimate version of his novel *Hyperion* (1795), Hölderlin elaborates his conception of the Absolute and its relation to the beautiful. He also introduces a historical and dialectical conception of the Absolute, according to which modern humanity has divided itself from a former unity of being:

> The blessed unity, Being, in the sole sense of the word, is lost for us, and we had to lose it, if we were to strive for and achieve it. We tear ourselves free from the peaceful *hen kai pan* of the world, in order to establish it through ourselves.[10]

Once in the past, we were one with the unity of being, but now nature and spirit are at odds with one another and in the novel this is reflected in Hyperion's frequently divided states of mind and his oscillating moods between communion with nature and affirmation of the self.[11] In line with his letter to Schiller, Hölderlin goes on to elaborate that in our knowing and acting we can only infinitely approximate this unity of being (*FHA* X, 264). However, in contrast to both the theoretical and the practical, Hölderlin regards the beautiful as a revelation of the Absolute:

> We would have no intimation of that infinite peace, of that Being, in the sole sense of the word, we would not strive at all to unite ourselves with nature ... if, nevertheless, this infinite unification, this Being, in the sole sense of the word were not present. It is present – as Beauty; to speak with Hyperion, a new kingdom awaits us, where the Beautiful is Queen. – (*FHA* X, 264)

In other words, the Absolute is manifest in the experience of the beautiful, which at the same time reveals the unifying ideal of all knowledge and action. What Hölderlin in 'Being Judgement Possibility' calls 'intellectual intuition' is realisable within the realm of the beautiful.

Within the novel, this significance of the beautiful is attributed both to art and to ecstatic experiences of the divine beauty of nature. The protagonist, Hyperion, is initiated into divine beauty through his love of Diotima, the beautiful soul. Hölderlin thus conjoins love and beauty in the manner of Plato's *Symposium* but distinctively links this metaphysical conception of beauty to nature and the Absolute. After a long passage in which Hyperion vividly recounts an elevated experience of the divine harmony of nature, Hyperion states: '[D]o you know its name? The name of that which is one and all? Its name is beauty' (*Hyperion*, 41). Here Hölderlin has transgressed the boundaries of both Kant's and Schiller's aesthetics and is articulating what he would have elaborated systematically had he written his 'New Aesthetic Letters'. Beauty is neither simply the harmonious unity of otherwise opposing human tendencies as it is in Schiller nor is it merely a subjective experience of reflecting judgement as it is in Kant. Rather, it is a revelation of the ultimate unity of existence or the Absolute. The Absolute is known through the aesthetic intuition of the beautiful.

What is distinctive of the beautiful – both in the form of natural beauty and in the form of art – is a special relationship between the one and the many, the whole and the parts. Hölderlin emphasises that the

Absolute is the 'one and all', and similarly describes the beautiful (drawing on Heraclitus) in *Hyperion* as 'the one differentiated in itself' (*Hyperion*, 67). The Absolute as revealed in the beautiful is thus not a oneness that precedes differentiation but rather differentiation that is disclosed in its participation in the one. Like Schiller, but with a metaphysical significance that goes beyond Schiller, Hölderlin can thus affirm the beautiful as the reconciliation of oppositions without annihilating difference. Just as in the 'play drive' (Schiller) reason and sensibility are both engaged but in such a way that the conflict between them disappears, so for Hölderlin the beautiful manifests a deeper harmony between the self and nature, without reducing one term to the other.

Elsewhere, like a number of his contemporaries, Hölderlin characterises the alliance of nature and art in organicist terms.[12] A complex organism consists in both a great differentiation of the parts and a deep interdependence of the part and the whole (for example, the heart of a mammal is a highly differentiated organ and if the heart is not functioning the whole organism cannot function) such that part and whole are constitutive of one another. The same kind of integral relation of part and whole is revealed in the work of art (to alter a phrase in a Bach cantata is to alter or destroy the sense of the whole), which can thus be described, to use Goethe's expression, as the 'spiritual organic'.[13] The harmony, or better symphony, of part and whole (whether in nature or art) is manifest in the experience of the beautiful.

With the above reflections in mind we can resolve the aporia that seemed to be implied by 'Being Judgement Possibility'. Whereas rational judgement presupposes a unity of the Absolute but is unable to know this unity itself (it involves a correlation of A [subject] and B [object], which presupposes X [the Absolute], but does not experience A and B as one in X), in aesthetic intuition the participation of subject and object in the higher unity of the Absolute is no longer a mere presupposition but actually made manifest.

At this moment I would like to revise Hegel's account of the historical emergence of absolute idealism by way of aesthetics. According to Hegel, Schiller had shown through aesthetic beauty how what otherwise appears as opposed can be thought as a unity. In the aesthetic there is a 'unity of universal and particular, freedom and necessity, spirit and nature'.[14] However, it is Schelling who, in the *System of Transcendental Idealism* (1800), makes the Absolute as idea into 'the principle of knowledge and existence ... Thereby philosophy has attained, with Schelling, its absolute standpoint; ... it was now that the *concept* of art, and the place of art in philosophy was discovered.'[15] While there are some differences between Hölderlin's and Schelling's aesthetics, Hölderlin had made the crucial philosophical steps as early as 1795–6. The capstone of Schelling's *System* is his account of the work of art as that which reveals the ultimate unity of subject and object, spirit and nature, the conscious and the unconscious that elsewhere appear divided.[16] Schelling's conception of 'intellectual intuition' is also significantly indebted to Hölderlin; Schelling defines 'aesthetic intuition' as 'intellectual intuition' made objective.[17] A notable difference is that for Schelling it is only art that reveals the ultimate unity of nature and mind, whereas for Hölderlin both natural beauty and the beauty of art reveal the Absolute. (The contrast is, of course, even greater with the mature Hegel's aesthetics, where natural beauty is no longer a key concern because, unlike art, it is not a self-conscious creation of spirit.)

As we have seen, Hölderlin argues that without the supplement of an aesthetic sense, philosophy could not grasp the ultimate unity of existence. How, then, does Hölderlin envisage the proper relation between art and philosophy? We can begin to answer this question by turning to Hölderlin's imaginative presentation of ancient Athenian culture in *Hyperion*, in which he also suggests a future ideal wherein the oppositions of modernity would be resolved. When, in *Hyperion*, Hölderlin speaks of a unity from which modern humanity has become separated he is primarily thinking of ancient Greek culture as one in which nature, humanity and the divine were united with one another.

Hyperion conveys the ancient Athenians as beautiful souls in whom there was a balanced harmony between the sensible and the supersensible, nature and spirit.[18] He explains that the first child of divine beauty was art, meaning, of course, the art and poetry of Greek mythology. At this time, 'man and his gods were one' (*Hyperion*, 65). The second daughter of beauty was religion, which Hyperion defines as 'love of Beauty' (*Hyperion*, 65). Hyperion then explains that 'without poetry' the Athenians 'would never have been a philosophical people' (*Hyperion*, 66). The beautiful, 'the one differentiated in itself', was necessary for the emergence of philosophy, because it is only through acquaintance with the infinite whole – given in beauty – that philosophy can proceed to analyse and divide the whole into its parts (*Hyperion*, 66–7). At the same time, the emergence of philosophy entails a separation from the whole of poetry or mythology, and with this in mind we can add a further historical dimension to Hölderlin's critique of Fichte in 'Being Judgement Possibility'. The standpoint of the rational consciousness of the philosopher comes about through a separation from the prior unity of being that is granted in mythology. The rift that thus emerges between subject and object, mind and nature, cannot be healed by philosophy. For these reasons, Hyperion not only regards poetry as the origin of philosophy in ancient Greece, but also proclaims poetry as that which will resolve the oppositions of philosophy in the future.[19] By implication, when Hyperion speaks of poetry as the end of philosophy he is again thinking of poetry in a mythological sense, of 'man and his gods'.

At this point it is instructive to turn to another key text in the development of German idealism, namely the so-called 'Oldest System-Programme of German Idealism' (circa 1796–7), which boldly sets forth many of the same ideas that can be detected in *Hyperion*. While scholars continue to debate the original authorship of the manuscript preserved in Hegel's handwriting (the main contenders remaining Hölderlin, Schelling or Hegel), commentators generally regard its conception of beauty as deriving from Hölderlin.[20] In recent years, Eckart Förster has made a strong case for Hölderlin as its author and suggested that it outlines nothing less than Hölderlin's programme for his 'New Aesthetic Letters'.[21] The text clearly expresses ideas about the anthropological and political significance of the aesthetic that are indebted to Schiller, but with a metaphysical and epistemological conception of beauty that is more Hölderlinian than Schillerian.

In the 'Oldest System-Programme' we find Hölderlin's elevated conception of beauty that accords with *Hyperion*:

> [T]he idea that unites them all, the idea of *beauty*, taking the word in a higher Platonic sense. I am now convinced that the highest act of reason, that in which reason contains all ideas, is an aesthetic act, and that *truth and goodness* are only united [*verschwistert*] *in beauty*. (*Essays and Letters*, 341–2)

Beauty in the Platonic sense of a metaphysical idea and not in a subjective Kantian or Schillerian sense is what will unite all other ideas, the good and the true, the practical and the theoretical. As in *Hyperion*, Hölderlin (for the present purposes I am assuming that he is the author[22]) claims that poetry will become 'the educator of humanity' as it had been in the beginning and will unite and supersede 'all other arts and sciences' (*Essays and Letters*, 342). Poetry was the origin of science and philosophy in ancient Greece and it is in poetry that they will be reunited. Hölderlin then specifies that, just as mythology was the origin of philosophy, this reunification in poetry will be achieved in the form a new mythology. Thus Hölderlin's programme for an aesthetic education of humankind culminates in a programme for a new mythology. Hölderlin writes:

> I will speak here of an idea which, as far as I know, has never entered anyone's head before – we must have a new mythology, but this mythology must stand in the service of ideas, it must be a mythology of *reason*. (*Essays and Letters*, 342)

Two questions must be asked of this new mythology. Firstly, what more precisely is the role of this new mythology? Secondly, in what respects does it both serve and surpass philosophy? It is fairly easy to provide part of the answer to the first question: Hölderlin tells us that the new mythology will make the people rational and philosophy sensuous and thereby unite the people and the philosophers.[23] This can be seen as an expansion on Schiller's idea that the aesthetic forms a common ground between rationally disposed and sensuously disposed people.[24] But what Schiller applies to the aesthetic more generally Hölderlin applies to a (new) mythology more specifically. In addition, the 'Oldest System-Programme' takes the political programme of aesthetic education even further than the republican ideals advocated by Schiller's *Aesthetic Letters* and Hölderlin's *Hyperion*,[25] while being continuous with their implications, in that its author claims that the state 'must *stop*' (cease to exist) because it undermines freedom by subsuming the individual like a cog in a machine.[26]

The idea of a mythology that serves reason and unites the people and the philosophers might at first sound like Hölderlin is representing a variant of a view that is familiar to us from the mature Hegel's philosophy in which art and mythology present in an inferior sensuous form what the philosopher grasps in the self-transparency of conceptual thought. For Hegel, art thereby makes the Absolute to some degree accessible to all the people who are not able to grasp it philosophically. However, as has already been made evident, Hölderlin regards mythology as surpassing the capacities of philosophy alone (the philosopher too needs the new mythology).

While in certain respects the idea of a mythology of reason resonates with the values of the Enlightenment in its critique of superstition and its avowal of rationality (but without the antagonism between reason and myth, and a superior estimation of the former, which is characteristic of Enlightenment thought),[27] Hölderlin is also deeply interested in the religious dimension of myth.

In the essay 'Fragment of Philosophical Letters', Hölderlin emphasises that the central factor in any myth is 'the God of the myth' (*Essays and Letters*, 239).[28] For Hölderlin, the mythical figure of a god represents a higher, divine unity of a particular context or sphere of life. We all exist in different contexts of life, and the religious dimension is neither a transcendence that is distant from these contexts, nor is it reducible to subject and object or self and world insofar as they are conceived as separate from each other. Hölderlin's conception of this religious dimension could be described as an 'immanent transcendence' in that it transcends the subjective and objective spheres while at the same time uniting or embracing them.

The divine unity of a context of life can neither be captured in purely physical, empirical or historical terms, nor can it be grasped in purely universal, rational or moral terms. The religious dimension of life is a concrete, specific unity of subjectivity and objectivity, infinity and finitude, eternity and history, which, Hölderlin argues, can only be represented in the form of myth. Hölderlin regards myth as conjoining what otherwise remains opposed (the empirical and the rational, etc.) and thus he calls myth the 'intellectual-historical' (*Essays and Letters*, 238).

In that we all live in limited contexts, each person can, in a certain respect, have her own god – understood as the felt higher unity of her context. Moreover, Hölderlin indicates that the images of gods in a particular culture will in part reflect that culture (*Essays and Letters*, 234–5). Nevertheless, there are more limited spheres of life – and myths that correspond to them – and more encompassing ones. In 'Fragment of Philosophical Letters' Hölderlin thus speaks of the importance and possibility of uniting various myths into a single mythology, which at the same time can serve to unite diverse people:

> In addition, one could speak here about the unification of several people into one religion, where everyone honours his own god and all honour a common one in poetic representations, where everyone celebrates his own higher life and all celebrate a common higher life, the celebration of life, in a mythical way.[29]

While Hölderlin places a great emphasis on unity in his writings, this is not a unity that sacrifices diversity, opposition and difference. Already in the second book of *Hyperion* he writes, 'Like lovers' quarrels are the dissonances of the world. Reconciliation is there, even in the midst of strife' (*Hyperion*, 133). And as I have indicated, the beauty or harmony of nature (and of art) in Hölderlin should be understood polyphonically. With the further development of Hölderlin's poetry and thought this tendency to affirm unity in difference (and even what appears as extreme opposition) increases.[30] With regard to the question of mythology this emphasis on difference is manifest in Hölderlin's express polytheism. In the 'Oldest System-Programme', Hölderlin claims that we need 'monotheism of reason' and 'polytheism of the imagination'.[31] A 'monotheism of reason' is apparent in Hölderlin's emphasis on the unity of the Absolute in his philosophical reflections. A 'polytheism of the imagination' is evident in his poetic works. Hölderlin's mythopoetic polytheism could be described as polyphonic harmony raised to the level of the archetypal (or universal) imagination.

As we have seen, the ultimate unity can only be grasped aesthetically and mythically. Nevertheless, there is an analogy between the plurality of gods integrated in a mythology and the system of ideas that is articulated in philosophy. It is along these lines that we can understand how there could be a 'mythology of reason'. This mythology would at once serve the ideas of philosophy and yet surpass philosophy in its capacity to integrate the many and the one, the finite and the infinite, the historical and the eternal, nature and spirit. This aspect of Hölderlin's position shows deep affinities with Schelling's arguments in *The Philosophy of Art* that the gods of (Greek) mythology and the ideas of philosophy 'are one and the same'.[32] The gods of mythology are, according to Schelling, at once individual beings (in a metaphysical sense) and universals or archetypes.[33] The mythological world as a whole is analogous to a system of ideas, but with a more thoroughgoing organic interpenetration and mutual determination of part and whole; this organic unity is manifest in the relationship between the particular sphere of each god and the totality of gods.[34]

The 'Oldest System-Programme' ends with the enthusiastic declaration that a new mythology must be created. Hölderlin writes: 'A higher spirit, sent from heaven, must found this new religion amongst us, it will be the last, the greatest task of humanity' (*Essays and Letters*, 342, translation modified). It is my view that Hölderlin is here expressing his own deepest aspiration and sense of divine mission as a poet. Hölderlin had promised Niethammer that his 'New Aesthetic Letters' would proceed 'from philosophy to poetry and religion'.[35] The religious dimension of Hölderlin's aesthetic programme is evident in the significance that he grants to mythology.

One of the most striking characteristics of Hölderlin's poetry is its polytheistic syncretism. The highest expression of Hölderlin's philosophical aesthetics is thus his dedication towards writing a new, poetic mythology, which is reflected in his increasing commitment to poetry rather than philosophy. While Hölderlin's revival and transformation of Graeco-Roman mythology is the most pervasive mythical tradition in his poetry, he also frequently draws on and fuses Graeco-Roman mythology with Germanic and Christian myths. The significance of Hölderlin's mythopoetic syncretism clearly resonates with one of the central aims that Schelling envisages for the new mythology in his *Philosophy of Art*. By simultaneously synthesising the historical and spiritual dimensions of Christianity with the nature gods of Graeco-Roman mythology, Hölderlin unifies what appears as successive and divided in the process of history (Christianity emerges later and in antithesis to paganism) and facilitates a higher reconciliation of nature and spirit.[36]

Here I will limit my examples of Hölderlin's syncretic mythology to a few well-known poems, starting with the elegy 'Bread and Wine' ('Brod und Wein', circa 1800) and the hymn 'Celebration of Peace' ('Friedensfeier', circa 1802). There are two reasons for these choices. Firstly, both of these poems explicitly thematise and expand on Hölderlin's conception of world-history that is sketched in earlier works, including *Hyperion*. In the imaginative form of a poetic mythology these poems convey the history of humanity's relationship to and alienation from the Absolute. Secondly, what is presented as the promise of a reunification of nature, humanity and the divine in 'Bread and Wine' is figured as a mythical event of actual reconciliation in 'Celebration of Peace'. In short, these poems embody and extend Hölderlin's philosophical aesthetic programme to write a new mythology.

'Bread and Wine' characterises modernity, in contrast to ancient Greece, as a time in which the gods are absent from human culture and nature. What Hölderlin elsewhere expresses in philosophical terms as a separation from the Absolute is figured here as an absence of the gods. The setting of the poem is night-time, which is also the figurative darkness of divine absence, with the hope of a return of the day, the return of the gods. What Hölderlin expresses in philosophical terms as a desire for reunification with the Absolute appears in the elegy as the desired return of the gods. In the seventh strophe, Hölderlin famously asks what purpose poets might serve in this time of divine absence and intimates an answer. The poets are compared to the priests of the wine-god Dionysus, 'who roamed from land to land in holy night' (*FHA* VI, 251). Although they wander in the night of the gods' absence, it is a 'holy night' because in remembrance of the departed gods they are preparing the way for their return. In the language of the 'Oldest System-Programme', the poets are preparing to receive the inspiration that will facilitate the dawning of the new mythology.

The deep syncretism of Hölderlin's poetry is evident in strophes eight and nine. The theme of divine absence is conveyed in the image of the Father God having turned away from humans, who mourn this loss. Christ, simply referred to as a 'quiet Genius', is presented as though the last of a lineage of Greek gods, one who brought heavenly consolation and 'announced the day's end' (*FHA* VI, 251). But the 'heavenly choir' left the gifts of bread and wine as a sign of their former presence and the promise of their return. These gifts are at once the bread and wine of the Eucharist and fused with the nature gods of Greek mythology. Hölderlin thus conjoins these sacraments with a Pagan re-enchantment of nature as the manifestation of godly presences. Bread is described as a fruit of the Earth that is blessed by light, and wine is, of course, the drink of Dionysus, who has already been invoked as the god of the poets. Christ who is the son of God the Father, and Dionysus who is the son of Father Zeus are fused into one. In the final (ninth) strophe this fusion is carried further in the characterisation of the 'Syrian' (Christ) as the 'Torchbearer' (*Fakelschwinger*), a clear allusion to the torch-bearing Dionysus, who comes in the interim between the departure and the return of the gods (*FHA* VI, 252).[37]

Even if Jochen Schmidt is right that there is a shift in Hölderlin's thought from 'Bread and Wine' to 'Celebration of Peace' – from a more cyclical to a more progressive philosophy of history – the deep continuities between the elegy and the hymn should not be overlooked.[38]

While 'Celebration of Peace' was occasioned by a particular historical moment of peace, the Treaty of Lunéville (1801) and the Treaty of Amiens (1802),[39] the hymn assumes world-historical and eschatological dimensions. The setting of the poem is 'evening', and Hölderlin plays on the words for Orient and Occident, 'Morgenland' and 'Abendland', with their connotations of the dawn of history in the East and the evening of history in the West. However, the evening of history in 'Celebration of Peace' is not the evening that turns into the night of 'Bread and Wine', the night of divine absence or of the 'death of God', to invoke Nietzsche. Rather, the evening in 'Celebration of Peace' figures the eschatological end and apotheosis of history in a new golden age in which humanity and the gods are reconciled.

The poem opens with natural descriptions and the presentation of a banquet, with intimations that the natural landscape is the banquet hall of the gods. This echoes the passages in 'Bread and Wine' (strophe four) where the landscape of Greece is described as 'the house of the heavenly ones' and a 'festive hall' (*FHA* VI, 249). At the evening hour the gods have gathered from afar for a banquet in celebration of peace. Among the heavenly guests, the speaker believes that he has seen the 'prince of the feast' or 'festivity' [*Fest*] (*FHA* VIII, 642), a godly apparition of peace, who, in my reading (though he may at the same time allude to other figures), is the figure of Christ.[40] The 'prince of the feast' is thus the 'prince of peace', though Hölderlin does not directly employ this well-known epithet for Christ. Later in the poem Hölderlin writes:

> [T]o the All-Living from whom
> Many joys and songs have sprung
> There's one who is a son, and quietly powerful is he,
> And now we recognise him.
>
> (*Poems and Fragments*, 459)

The 'All-living' is an epithet for the Father who, in many respects, can be regarded as a mythical figuration of the Absolute. Whereas 'Bread and Wine' speaks of the Father God having turned away from humanity, 'Celebration of Peace' affirms that 'now we know' him, and therefore also 'the spirit of the world has inclined to humans' (*FHA* VIII, 643). A sense of the end and culmination of history is conveyed in the image of 'The quiet God of time', who now 'steps out of his workshop', the workshop of history (*Poems and Fragments*, 461, translation modified).

The 'prince of the feast' is the 'most beloved' around whom all the heavenly ones are assembled (*FHA* VIII, 644). It is important to recall that in the elegy 'Bread and Wine' Christ announces that night (divine absence) will follow his departure, but in the gifts of bread and wine humanity is given the promise of a return of the gods. In 'Celebration of Peace' the actual fulfilment of this promise is represented in the mythological vision of a return of the gods gathered around Christ at the banquet at 'the evening of time' (*FHA* VIII, 644). 'Celebration of Peace' mythologically figures a reconciliation of the gods, humanity and nature at the end of history. In its eschatological affirmation the poem also embodies a fulfilment of the hope of the final sentence of the 'Oldest System-Programme' concerning the new mythology: 'A higher spirit, sent from heaven, must found this new religion amongst us, it will be the last, the greatest task of humanity' (*Essays and Letters*, 342, translation modified).

'Celebration of Peace' represents a high-water mark in Hölderlin's poetic figuration of a symphony of the gods. Whether Hölderlin believed for a moment that the end of history was actually imminent remains a question (the poem concludes with a more reserved tone). What is beyond doubt, however, is that the return of the gods that is figured only as a promise and potentiality in 'Bread and Wine' is presented as a visionary actuality *to the poet* in 'Celebration of Peace'. Furthermore, irrespective of the imminence or remoteness of the new golden age as a historical (or post-historical) actuality, this mythological vision conveys a utopian ideal of harmony and peace between individuals and of reconciliation between humanity, nature and the divine.

As one to whom the gods (at times) manifest themselves and in light of his view of our age as one in which the gods are absent, Hölderlin's ultimate formulation of his aesthetic programme lies in his poetically articulated mission of mediating a return of the gods and, through this return, facilitating a new golden age. Even if for a moment Hölderlin really thought that a new golden age was imminent, like Schelling he acknowledges that the emergence of a new mythology and golden age depends on more than the work of any single individual.[41] A defining characteristic of any mythology is its implication of a unity of the collective, a participation of individuals in the shared spirit of an age. While Heidegger seriously embraced Hölderlin's poetry as a new mythology (though he did not explicitly refer to it as such) in the highly fraught political context of national-socialist Germany, this was a problematic appropriation. To the extent that Heidegger's reading of Hölderlin is entangled in the historical context of an authoritarian state, it betrays the democratic roots (and even 'anarchic' roots – if Hölderlin authored the 'Oldest System-Programme') of Hölderlin's mythopoetics in Schiller's aesthetics. The new mythology cannot be imposed on citizens in a top-down fashion; it can only emerge through the free collaboration of individuals. Hölderlin can, I think, best be regarded along the same lines as Schelling regarded Goethe, namely as one of the modern poets, who, within his individual sphere and time, worked in the direction of a new mythology.[42]

Hölderlin and Schelling's call for a new mythology challenges Hegel's later argument that only philosophy can resolve the oppositions of modernity. However, whereas Hegel regarded his philosophy as successful in resolving the apparent contradictions of modernity, Hölderlin and Schelling envisage the new mythology as a not yet realised ideal. This ideal, with its emphasis on the need for a reconciliation between humanity and nature, assumes a new pertinence in our current time of ecological crisis and what has come to be regarded by some as a new geological age of the 'Anthropocene' in which humans are directly responsible for transformations (destruction) to the earth on a global scale (including climate change and a sixth mass extinction).[43] Firstly, like a number of his contemporaries, Hölderlin affirms a deeper community between the natural and the spiritual, which strongly contrasts with Cartesian dualism and the latter's complicity in our willingness to destroy the environment.[44] Secondly, Hölderlin identifies a moment of alienation from nature as constitutive of the very structure of modern rationality, which can only be remedied with the aid of the aesthetic and, more specifically, the mythopoetic imagination.

As a further illustration of the workings of Hölderlin's mythopoetic imagination, I would like to turn away from his poetic depictions of world history and utopian vision of a symphony of gods, and closely consider the way in which a single poetic passage can serve to transfigure the reader's vision of nature. The elegy 'Homecoming' ('Heimkunft', circa 1801) is filled with rich descriptions of the beauty and sublimity of landscapes, which from the beginning seem joyfully to presage a favourable journey home. The poem opens with a pre-dawn depiction of the Alps. The second strophe conveys the break of day. Even if the poem were modified such that all references to gods and angels were omitted, the reader would still be granted a rich sense of nature's sublimity. In these respects the reader is already drawn towards the divine. (It should be kept in mind that already in the literary depictions of nature in *Hyperion*, the experience of natural beauty is presented in a way that moves far beyond the merely pleasant or the picturesque and is, rather, conveyed as a form of divinely or spiritually inspired harmony, as involving enthusiasm or *Begeisterung*.[45]) The first two lines of the second strophe describe the radiance of the dawn on the mountain summits as follows: 'The silver heights above, meanwhile, peacefully gleam, / Full of roses already, up there, is the shining snow'

[*Ruhig glänzen indeß die silbernen Höhen darüber, / Voll mit Rosen ist schon droben der leuchtende Schnee*] (*FHA* VI, 311). A peaceful atmosphere is conveyed in the gleaming of the silver mountain heights above an Alpine village that is described at the end of the previous strophe. This atmosphere of calm bears comparison to Goethe's use of the substantive form of the adverb 'Ruhig' in 'Over all the summits / is peace' [*Über allen Gipfeln / ist Ruh*], although Goethe evokes the peace of twilight whereas Hölderlin is describing the quiet of dawn.[46] This peaceful atmosphere lends a contemplative mood to the description. The speaker and the reader are drawn into a space of aesthetic contemplation. While there is a foregrounded mood of calm, the scene is not one of pure passivity. The verb 'glänzen' and the participle 'leuchtend' convey an active radiance, a sign in ancient and modern literature of a divine presence or epiphany, and the characteristic temporal marker 'indeß' ('meanwhile') underscores the dawning day as a temporal happening. In addition, we know that the poet is in movement, on a return journey to his *Heimat*. The setting of this strophe is one that is recognisably both beautiful and sublime; we are poetically witnessing the beauty of a sunrise on sublime mountain peaks. The second line describes the pink glow of dawn on the shining snow with the metaphor 'full of roses'. The metaphor of 'roses' serves to give an intense sense of the rose-like hue, as though, more than a mere colour or effect of light, it is animate and an embodiment of the feeling that we associate with the flower. 'Voll' conveys a sense of plenitude. We also hear behind the metaphor 'full of roses' the Homeric figure of 'rosy-fingered dawn' and all that antiquity signifies in Hölderlin. These two lines are followed by an intensification in the experience of the beautiful: 'And yet higher, above the light, there dwells the pure / Blessed God, whom the play of holy rays makes glad' [*Und noch höher hinauf wohnt über dem Lichte der reine / Seelige Gott vom Spiel heiliger Stralen erfreut*] (*FHA* VI, 311). Yet higher, in the sky-heaven, dwells the god, which Hölderlin later (in the fifth strophe) identifies with the 'Father'. The god is clearly not only sensed as though spatially above the dawn glow on the mountain peaks, he is also in a spiritual and experiential sense higher than the sensible appearance of the dawn (while, nevertheless, being continuous with visible nature). At this point it is as though the natural phenomena have become transparent to the presence of the 'blessed god' who takes joys in the 'sacred rays', whose 'sacredness' clearly derives from their own participation in divinity. The 'sacred' or 'holy rays' and the appearance of the sky are as though features of the Father, in which the poet – and via the poem, the reader – recognises the face of the invisible god. Hölderlin thus renders natural phenomena as a transparency through which the god is beheld, synthesises nature and spirit, the sensible and the supersensible.[47]

Conclusion

In the present essay I have reconstructed a trajectory from Hölderlin's philosophical aesthetics to his programme for a new mythology, to his poetry as the highest embodiment of his mythopoetic aspiration. In the course of doing so, I have also indicated Hölderlin's crucial and distinctive place in the emergence of the philosophical standpoint of absolute idealism.

Some interpreters of Hölderlin contend that he regarded the Absolute as a unity from which human consciousness emerged but that must remain forever ineffable and unknowable. In contrast, I have argued that Hölderlin's mature conception of history,[48] as it is expressed in his poetic and literary works, shares – despite important differences – Hegel's view that the end is a higher state and synthesis than the unity of the beginning. To put it a little crudely using terms for musical texture, the monophony of the beginning divides into a polyphonic dissonance that is reconciled in the polyphonic harmony of humanity, nature and the gods. In contrast to Hegel who ultimately concluded that philosophy was the most adequate form by which to reconcile the oppositions of modernity, Hölderlin thought that poetry in the form of *mythopoiesis* could mediate the highest reconciliation.

The philosophical and aesthetic programme that Hölderlin first articulates in his plan to write 'New Aesthetic Letters' finds its richest and most complex embodiment in the symphony of humanity, nature and the gods that is conveyed in his mature poetry, a symphony that is at the same time a utopian and eschatological ideal for a harmonious society of free individuals that is reconciled with nature. While at times Hölderlin seems to imply that a new golden age may have been imminent as a genuine historical (or post-historical) possibility, this is unlikely to meet with much understanding in our present time, which for various historical reasons has become more sceptical of grand narratives. Nevertheless, in our contemporary situation of ecological crisis Hölderlin's affirmation of an ultimate unity of nature and mind, his critique of a one-sided rationalism and its implications in our alienation from nature, and his affirmation of the aesthetic and mythopoetic imagination as a way of reconciling humanity and nature are even more relevant than they were circa 1800. Hölderlin's poetry can, moreover, continue to inspire us in the vital work of imagining and realising a more harmonious (and less destructive) relationship between humanity and nature.

Hölderlin's poetic word for the symphony of humanity, nature and the gods is simply 'Gesang' or 'song'. The gist of much of this essay is captured in well-known lines from 'Celebration of Peace', though my aforementioned reservations about the imminence of the new golden age should be kept in mind. It is instructive to note that this passage in earlier versions of the poem included lines that connect the 'conversation' or 'Gespräch' that 'we are' to the naming of the gods or the 'heavenly ones' ('der Himmlischen') (*FHA* VII, 155).

> Viel hat von Morgen an,
> Seit ein Gespräch wir sind und hören von einander,
> Erfahren der Mensch; bald sind [wir] aber Gesang.
>
> (*FHA* VIII, 643)

> Much from the morning on,
> Since we have been a conversation and heard from one another,
> Has humanity learned; but soon [we] will be song.

Notes

1. See, for example, Dieter Henrich, *The Course of Remembrance and Other Essays on Hölderlin*; Christoph Jamme, *'Ein ungelehrtes Buch': Die philosophische Gemeinschaft zwischen Hölderlin und Hegel in Frankfurt, 1797–1800*; Frederick Beiser, *German Idealism: The Struggle Against Subjectivism, 1781–1801*, pp. 375–406.
2. While there are significant connections in the concurrent developments of Hölderlin's and Hegel's thought (see note 1), it is Hegel's mature system (beginning with *The Phenomenology of Spirit* [1807]) that has had the greatest influence on subsequent philosophy. It is for this reason that in this essay I have focused on contrasting Hölderlin's thought circa 1795–1802 with Hegel's mature philosophy.
3. G. W. F. Hegel, *Aesthetics: Lectures on Fine Art*, vol. 1, p. 62.
4. Hegel, *Aesthetics*, p. 63.
5. See note 2.
6. Friedrich Schiller, *Über die ästhetische Erziehung des Menschen in einer Reihe von Briefen*. For a good philosophical reconstruction of Schiller's *Aesthetic Letters*, see Frederick Beiser, *Schiller as Philosopher: A Re-examination*, pp. 119–68.
7. See Violetta L. Waibel, 'Wechselbestimmung: Zum Verhältnis von Hölderlin, Schiller und Fichte in Jena'.
8. Dieter Henrich, 'Hölderlin on Judgment and Being: A Study in the History of the Origins of German Idealism', in *The Course of Remembrance*, pp. 71–89.
9. Beiser, *German Idealism*, pp. 375–406.
10. *FHA* X, pp. 263–4. All translations of Hölderlin's work in this essay are my own unless otherwise noted.
11. Cf. Dieter Henrich, 'Hegel and Hölderlin', in *The Course of Remembrance*, p. 124. Cf. Richard Eldridge, *The Persistence of Romanticism*, pp. 85–101.
12. See, for example, the letter to Schelling from July 1799, in *Essays and Letters*, p. 153. See also Violetta L. Waibel, 'Kant – Fichte – Schelling', in *Hölderlin-Handbuch: Leben – Werk – Wirkung*, 94–106.
13. Johann Wolfgang Goethe, 'Einleitung in die Propyläen', in *Sämtliche Werke nach Epochen seines Schaffens*, vol. 6.2, p. 13.
14. Hegel, *Aesthetics*, p. 62.
15. Hegel, *Aesthetics*, p. 63.
16. Schelling, *System of Transcendental Idealism*, pp. 219–36.

17. Schelling, *System of Transcendental Idealism*, p. 229.
18. See *Hyperion*, 64–8.
19. See *Hyperion*, 66.
20. See, for example, the collection of essays in response to Otto Pöggeler's influential argument that Hegel is the original author. Christoph Jamme and Helmut Schneider (eds), *Mythologie der Vernunft: Hegels 'ältestes Systemprogramm des deutschen Idealismus'*.
21. Eckart Förster, '"To Lend Wings to Physics Once Again": Hölderlin and the "Oldest System-Programme of German Idealism"'; Eckart Förster, 'A New Program for the Aesthetic Education of Mankind?'.
22. Even if Hölderlin were not the author, key ideas in the 'Oldest System-Programme' can be discerned in Hölderlin's other works. The 'Oldest System-Programme' is instructive in that it sets forth these ideas with a striking boldness and concision.
23. See *Essays and Letters*, p. 342.
24. For further background on the emergence of the idea of a 'new mythology' and Hölderlin, see Manfred Frank, *Der kommmende Gott: Vorlesungen über die neue Mythologie*, pp. 123–87, pp. 245–84; Bärbel Frischmann, 'Hölderlin und die Frühromantik', pp. 113–14; Christoph Jamme, *Einführung in die Philosophie des Mythos*.
25. Hyperion's characterisation of Greek democracy in his speech about ancient Athens echoes Schiller's aesthetic politics in the *Aesthetic Letters*. See *Hyperion*, pp. 63–8.
26. See *Essays and Letters*, p. 341.
27. Frank, *Der kommende Gott*, pp. 189–90; Christoph Jamme, *Mythos als Aufklärung*, pp. 167–83.
28. There has been debate as to whether the 'Fragment of Philosophical Letters' – alternatively known as 'On Religion' – might be a fragment of Hölderlin's 'New Aesthetic Letters'. Irrespective of the correct answer to this question, its perspective on myth is deeply relevant to Hölderlin's aesthetic philosophy and poetry. For an illuminating discussion of the likely date of this text (estimates range from 1796 to 1800), see Charlie Louth, '"jene zarten Verhältnisse": Überlegungen zu Hölderlins Aufsatzbruchstück *Über Religion/Fragment Philosophischer Briefe*'.
29. *Essays and Letters*, 239. Hölderlin does not give any examples to illustrate how more limited religions and myths can be united in more encompassing ones. However, the emergence of the Olympian pantheon out of earlier local mythologies might provide a fitting example, in that this brought about a more universal mythology that united a wider community of people in ancient Greece.
30. See Jamme, 'Ein ungelehrtes Buch', pp. 317–48.
31. On the likelihood that Hölderlin derived these expressions concerning monotheism and polytheism from his encounters with Goethe, see Förster, '"To Lend Wings to Physics Once Again"', p. 192.
32. Schelling, *The Philosophy of Art*, p. 42. Schelling's lectures on the philosophy of art were first given in the Winter semester of 1799–1800. They were repeated and revised in subsequent years. The cited translation is derived from his 1804–5 lectures.
33. Schelling, *Philosophy of Art*, p. 35, p. 42. For example, what in a rational culture is described as the unity and changeability of nature, in mythology is embodied in the real individual Proteus (p. 44).
34. Schelling, *Philosophy of Art*, pp. 41–4.
35. See note 28.
36. Schelling, *Philosophy of Art*, pp. 75–7. Jochen Schmidt makes similar points about the significance of the syncretic mythology articulated in Hölderlin's poems 'Friedensfeier', 'Der Einzige' and 'Patmos'. Jochen Schmidt, *Hölderlins geschichtsphilosophische Hymnen*, pp. 106–15.
37. On Hölderlin's fusion of Dionysus and Christ and its historical precedents, see Frank, *Der kommende Gott*, pp. 245–342.
38. Schmidt, *Hölderlins geschichtsphilosophische Hymnen*, p. 8.
39. See *FHA* VIII, p. 583. These treaties marked the end of the War of the Second

Coalition against revolutionary France. Hölderlin's poem was not discovered until 1954.
40. Interpretations of the figure of the 'prince of the feast' diverge widely in the scholarship, including Napoleon, the Father god, Christ and a personification of peace itself. Bart Philipsen makes the significant point that the ambiguity of this figure and the diversity of possible allusions are in keeping with Hölderlin's syncretic conception of the divine (this ambiguity is, for example, similar to the fusion of Christ and Dionysus in 'Bread and Wine'). Bart Philipsen, 'Gesänge (Stuttgart, Homburg)', p. 368. See also Mark Ogden, *The Problem of Christ in the Work of Friedrich Hölderlin*, pp. 155–70.
41. Schelling, *Philosophy of Art*, pp. 51–3. This comes to expression in a number of ways in Hölderlin's work: for example, in the repeated sense of discord between the poet's utopian vision and the reality of the age as a whole (expressed, for example, in *Hyperion* and 'Bread and Wine'), the ultimate place of the god (rather than a human individual) as the binding force of a mythology as articulated in 'Fragment of Philosophical Letters', and the elegiac sense that the people are not yet ready for the new mythology in elegies including 'Bread and Wine' and 'Homecoming'.
42. Schelling, *Philosophy of Art*, p. 74. In that Hölderlin actively sought to work in this direction on the basis of ideas very closely related to Schelling's own, to some extent he is an even better representative of Schelling's views than Goethe.
43. On the relevance of Schelling's idea of a 'new mythology' to contemporary ecological concerns, see Bruce Matthews, 'The New Mythology: Romanticism between Religion and Humanism'.
44. The view that Cartesian dualism is emblematic of the modern western dissonance between mind and nature and complicit in our destructive relationship to the environment has been argued by many scholars in the environmental humanities. In that, for Descartes, nature is a machine and only humans have a soul (characterised by the capacity to think), Cartesian dualism supports both human exceptionalism and the exploitation of nature (no more than an inanimate mechanism). Many environmentalist scholars argue that an ecological ethics requires that we recognise agency and animation in other-than-human nature and a greater continuity between humanity and the environment. Hölderlin's thought and poetry, like that of a number of his contemporaries in the Romantic era, can aid us in this task. For one illuminating discussion of Cartesianism and environmentalism, see Val Plumwood, *Feminism and the Mastery of Nature*, pp. 104–40. On the ecological significance of Hölderlin's re-sacralisation of nature in relation to other writers of the Romantic era, see Kate Rigby, *Topographies of the Sacred*, pp. 177–91.
45. See, for example, *Hyperion*, pp. 39–41.
46. Goethe, 'Wandrers Nachtlied', in *Sämtliche Werke*, vol. 5.2, p. 53, my translation.
47. On the ecological significance of Hölderlin's re-sacralisation of nature, see Rigby, *Topographies of the Sacred*, pp. 177–91.
48. This higher reconciliation is also already implied at the end of *Hyperion* in that Hyperion's previous strife in life makes possible a more intimate reconciliation with nature. *Hyperion*, pp. 131–3.

Bibliography

Beiser, Frederick, *German Idealism: The Struggle against Subjectivism, 1781–1801* (Cambridge, MA: Harvard University Press, 2008), pp. 375–406.
Beiser, Frederick, *Schiller as Philosopher: A Re-examination* (Oxford: Oxford University Press, 2005).
Eldridge, Richard, *The Persistence of Romanticism: Essays in Philosophy and Literature* (Cambridge: Cambridge University Press, 2001).

Förster, Eckart, '"To Lend Wings to Physics Once Again": Hölderlin and the "Oldest System-Programme of German Idealism"', *European Journal of Philosophy*, 3: 2 (1995), pp. 174–98.
Förster, Eckart, 'A New Program for the Aesthetic Education of Mankind?', in *A New History of German Literature*, ed. David Wellbery and Judith Ryan (Cambridge, MA: Harvard University Press, 2004), pp. 470–5.
Frank, Manfred, *Der kommmende Gott: Vorlesungen über die neue Mythologie*, vol. 1 (Frankfurt am Main: Suhrkamp, 1982).
Frischmann, Bärbel, 'Hölderlin und die Frühromantik', in *Hölderlin-Handbuch: Leben – Werk – Wirkung*, ed. Johann Kreuzer (Stuttgart: J. B. Metzler, 2002), pp. 107–16.
Goethe, Johann Wolfgang, *Sämtliche Werke nach Epochen seines Schaffens: Münchner Ausgabe*, ed. Karl Richter et al., 20 vols (Munich: Carl Hanser Verlag, 1985–98).
Hegel, G. W. F., *Aesthetics: Lectures on Fine Art*, vol. 1, trans. T. M. Knox (Oxford: Oxford University Press, 1975).
Henrich, Dieter, *The Course of Remembrance and Other Essays on Hölderlin*, ed. Eckart Förster (Stanford: Stanford University Press, 1997).
Jamme, Christoph, *'Ein ungelehrtes Buch': Die philosophische Gemeinschaft zwischen Hölderlin und Hegel in Frankfurt, 1797–1800* (Hamburg: Felix Meiner, 1983).
Jamme, Christoph, *Einführung in die Philosophie des Mythos: Neuzeit und Gegenwart* (Darmstadt: Wissenschaftliche Buchgesellschaft, 1991).
Jamme, Christoph, *Mythos als Aufklärung: Dichten und Denken um 1800* (Munich: Wilhelm Fink Verlag, 2013).
Jamme, Christoph and Schneider, Helmut (eds), *Mythologie der Vernunft: Hegels 'ältestes Systemprogrann des deutchen Idealismus'* (Frankfurt am Main: Surkamp, 1984).
Louth, Charlie, ' "jene zarten Verhältnisse": Überlegungen zu Hölderlins Aufsatzbruchstück *Über Religion/Fragment Philosophischer Briefe*', *Hölderlin-Jahrbuch*, 39 (2014–15), pp. 124–38.
Matthews, Bruce, 'The New Mythology: Romanticism between Religion and Humanism', in *The Relevance of Romanticism: Essays on German Romantic Philosophy*, ed. Dalia Nassar (New York: Oxford University Press, 2014), pp. 202–18.
Ogden, Mark, *The Problem of Christ in the Work of Friedrich Hölderlin* (London: Modern Humanities Research Association, 1991).
Philipsen, Bart, 'Gesänge (Stuttgart, Homburg)', in *Hölderlin-Handbuch: Leben – Werk – Wirkung*, ed. Johann Kreuzer (Stuttgart: J. B. Metzler, 2002), pp. 347–78.
Plumwood, Val, *Feminism and the Mastery of Nature* (London: Routledge, 1993).
Rigby, Kate, *Topographies of the Sacred: The Poetics of Place in European Romanticism* (Charlottesville: University of Virginia Press, 2004).
Schelling, F. W. J., *System of Transcendental Idealism (1800)*, trans. Peter Heath (Charlottesville: University Press of Virginia, 1978).
Schelling, F. W. J., *The Philosophy of Art*, trans. Douglas W. Stott (Minneapolis: University of Minnesota Press, 1989).
Schiller, Friedrich, *Über die ästhetische Erziehung des Menschen in einer Reihe von Briefen*, in *Schillers Werke: Nationalausgabe*, vol. 20 (Weimar: Hermann Böhlaus Nachfolger Verlag, 1962), pp. 309–412.
Schmidt, Jochen, *Hölderlins geschichtsphilosophische Hymnen 'Friedensfeier' – 'Der Einzige' – 'Patmos'* (Darmstadt: Wissenschaftliche Buchgesellschaft, 1990).
Waibel, Violetta L., 'Wechselbestimmung: Zum Verhältnis von Hölderlin, Schiller und Fichte in Jena', *Fichte-Studien*, 12 (1997), pp. 43–69.
Waibel, Violetta L., 'Kant – Fichte – Schelling', in *Hölderlin-Handbuch: Leben – Werk – Wirkung*, ed. Johann Kreuzer (Stuttgart: J. B. Metzler, 2002), pp. 90–106.

Chapter 9

The Transition Between the Possible and the Real: Nature as Contingency in Hölderlin's 'The declining fatherland...'

Anja Lemke

Hölderlin's essay fragment 'The declining fatherland...' represents a transitional text in several respects. On the one hand, it concludes the grand project of a modern tragedy that Hölderlin had pursued through three versions of *The Death of Empedocles*. On the other, the historical-philosophical reflections undertaken in the fragment provide the theoretical point of reference for the hymns and the late Sophocles translations.[1] The text reflects the tragedy project and lays the poetological and historical-theoretical foundations for the hymns. Thus it corresponds in Hölderlin's work to that which he discusses: to the transitional. At the centre of this transition – such, at least, is the thesis pursued here – stands a transformed view of the relationship between humanity and nature that Hölderlin had first gained step-by-step in his work on the *Empedocles* project and which becomes a historical-philosophical model in the essay fragment. This model allows the fragment to conceive of revolutionary upheavals from the modern paradigm of reality and possibility in the sense of contingency rather than from the schema of tragic entanglement. In this paradigm, nature can no longer be thought of as the All in All [*das All-Eine*] that, as the other to the finiteness and mortality of human life, constitutes life's source. In place of the still predominant 'regressive utopia of the immediacy of nature'[2] at the beginning of the *Empedocles* complex, in which it is a matter of restoring the original intimacy with nature, there arises an attempt to find forms of representation for dealing with the loss of such intimacy.

This development can already be traced through the different versions of *The Death of Empedocles* and in the essay 'The declining fatherland...', Hölderlin draws the balance from the attempt to write a modern tragedy as the tragedy of such a loss. In doing so he simultaneously accentuates the relationship between humanity and nature once again, since the

'All of Nature' as the foundation of human existence no longer appears to humanity as the other of temporality and history but instead clearly emerges as part of history.[3] Hölderlin arrives at the view that humans are first able to experience the totality of being as the 'world of all worlds' (*Essays and Letters*, 271) in historical upheaval as the transition between possibility and reality in which – and herein lies the modern moment of Hölderlin's conception – this upheaval is experienced as the violent intrusion of contingency. It is the task of poetry to put this modern experience of contingency into words by showing how the formation of meaning takes place as a precarious processing of actualised possibility through the establishment of differences. Poetry makes cuts; it introduces moments of difference. It gives rhythm to the violent and threatening contingency that befalls a person and marks moments of sense within it. In what follows, this thesis will be unfolded by briefly outlining the stations of the *Empedocles* project in order to analyse, in a second step, the essay fragment more closely.

The *Empedocles* project

The first draft of the *Empedocles* drama, the so-called Frankfurt Plan, originates in 1797 parallel to the work on *Hyperion* and there are, in fact, crucial connections between the original concept of tragedy and the key questions of the novel. It even seems that with his plunge into Mount Etna, Empedocles seeks to realise the ideal that Hyperion pursued, though never achieved: 'To be one with all that lives, to return in blessed self-forgetfulness into the All of Nature' (*Hyperion*, 3). It is thus no coincidence that Hyperion recalls the death by immolation of Empedocles:

> Yesterday I went to the summit of Aetna. There I remembered the great Sicilian, who, weary of counting the hours, knowing the soul of the World, in his bold joy of life there flung himself down into the glorious flames. (*Hyperion*, 126)

The longing for death is marked as the attempt of the self to leave the sphere of the finite and to merge with the infinite flow of nature. The Frankfurt Plan, which initially portrays Empedocles as a single figure in the conflict between individuality and totality, also follows this same longing for reunification with nature understood as that which is universal and unending. Unable to recognise the absolute in the human-finite sphere, Empedocles is

> a sworn enemy of all one-sided existence and thus restless, dissatisfied, suffering even in truly pleasant conditions simply because they are particular

conditions and are truly fulfilling only when they are felt to participate in a great harmony with all living things; because he cannot live, feel love in these conditions with the depth of a god's omnipresent heart; because as soon as his heart and mind attend to the concrete particular, he is bound by the law of succession. (*Hyperion*, xl)

The suffering of Empedocles is a suffering due to the limitations of the finite-human sphere, which bind the individual to the law of temporality. Although the infinite flow of nature allows the human sphere to emerge from it, and although this flow marks the beginning and end of the course of life, it also makes unification with unending nature impossible during life. Only death warrants the return to the 'All of Nature'; it allows a renewed fusion with the universal and makes it possible to leave the law of succession behind.

In the course of the three versions of the tragedy, Hölderlin gradually gives up this strict separation of two spheres and shifts the relationship between nature and humanity to the temporal-historical plane. This essentially takes place in the drama project through the role of the citizens of Agrigentum and the question associated with them of a revolutionary political reversal introduced by Empedocles and initiated by his death. To the extent that the question of the all-important fusion with the All in All is tied to the concrete political dimension of revolutionary upheaval, representation itself becomes a problem for Hölderlin, and he now needs a solution to the question of the communication of this fusion in signs in order to tie it to the historical occurrence. Yet every effort to solidify this union in signs would necessarily force the claim to universality associated with the All of Nature back to the narrowness of the finite-human sphere and would reduce the All in All to an individual, particular moment. Thus 'The Ground of the *Empedocles*' justifies sacrifice on the grounds that 'the extremes really and visibly' had physically united in the offering, which

> resolved the problem of fate, which can, however, never resolve visibly and individually, because otherwise the universal would be lost in the individual, and (what is still worse than all the great movements of fate, and is the only thing that is impossible) the life of a world would die out in a single detail. (*Essays and Letters*, 265)

It is therefore less the glaring contradiction, much emphasised in the research, between the desire for death-by-fusion, on the one hand, and the characterisation of this desire as hubris, on the other, that determines the difficulties of the dramatic composition in the three versions[4] as it is much more the question of an adequate form of representation for the unifying and disunifying event. Hölderlin must prevent the universality of the All of Nature from particularising and fixating itself in the individual, but at the same time he must keep it within the realm of what can be communicated and imparted. Hölderlin's solution is, famously, the death of the individual as the establishing figure for the community, the tragic figure of cathartic purification that shows the, at first seemingly successful, unifying event to be a moment of 'the greatest strife' in which both sides mutually drive each other to their extremes. This figure

> by its death reconciles and unites the warring extremes out of which it emerged more beautifully than in its own life, in that the union is now not a single individual and is therefore not too intimate, in that the divine no longer appears physically, in that the happy deceit of the union ceases in precisely that degree, in which it was too individual and unique . . . and . . . emerges . . . more clearly. (*Essays and Letters*, 262–3)

The fact that, in *Empedocles*, neither the moment of the unification of man and nature at the beginning of the drama nor death ever find their way onto the stage already indicates what can never be shown here in detail, namely that the eighteenth-century emblematic model of theatre as a form of representation cannot be made consistent with the renunciation of every form of fixation and individualisation of the event that Hölderlin so emphatically demanded. Still, the hope that death, as the establishing sacrifice, might found the new community in the sense that community forms itself around the remembrance of this death demonstrates the problem of confusing the messenger with the message and slipping into idolatry.[5]

In the analysis that follows, it is important that two figures intersect in *The Death of Empedocles*, which Hölderlin also attempts to convey in conjunction with the hymns. One is the vertical figure of the encounter between humanity and the gods, between culture and the power of nature that in ever new attempts occurs as unification in the greatest strife, as the tragic encounter of fusion and separation. Hölderlin concisely summarised this genuinely tragic event in the third part of the 'Notes on the *Oedipus*':

> The representation of the tragic depends primarily on this: that the fearful enormity of God and man uniting, and the power of nature becoming boundlessly one with man's innermost being in rage, thereby comprehends itself, that the infinite unification purifies itself through infinite separation. (*Essays and Letters*, 323)

At the same time and closely linked to it, the relationship between humanity and the gods, between culture and the power of nature also always presents itself to Hölderlin as a historical relationship. This already appears in *The Death of Empedocles* in the sense that it is essentially a matter of revolutionary upheaval bound together with a unification event, and not least a matter of how such revolutionary reversal can again become a liveable form of community for people. This horizontal model, which essentially represents a grappling with the question of temporality and historicity, increasingly moves into the foreground. The violent appearance of nature with which human beings see themselves confronted becomes itself a temporal phenomenon. This can also be seen in the late theory of tragedy in the context of the Sophocles translations where Hölderlin expressly says that God is 'nothing else than time' (*Essays and Letters*, 324) and the 'tearing spirit of time' (*Essays and Letters*, 326) appears there as a categorical reversal, as it also does in the hymns. For example, in 'The Rhine' there is the figure of the nuptials of humanity and the gods that is connected through the course of the river to a moment of temporal extension. How this focus on temporal extension, the relationship of humanity and nature can, for Hölderlin, be accentuated differently is the central theme of 'The declining fatherland . . .'

'The declining fatherland . . .'

The decisive change in Hölderlin's poetic and historical-philosophical conception that takes place in the fragment 'The declining fatherland . . .' is the solution to the complex problem of the encounter between humanity and nature as it pertains to the tragic hero.[6] With this text, Hölderlin leaves behind the stage of tragedy because he takes leave of the concept of the tragic individual. Consequently, he begins to consider the means by which humans can experience the divine All of Nature, the foundation of all being, as an event in the course of history itself. In so doing, he retains the guiding question of the *Empedocles* project, as he is still concerned with how the particular world of human beings relates to the All of Nature and how this All of Nature can be restrained and made experienceable as the ground of all existence in all its destructive power without annihilating the human being but also without missing, incorporating and prematurely assimilating that which is aorgic. Nature is presented as the 'world of all worlds', as Hölderlin calls it in 'The declining fatherland . . .', but it is now no longer a concrete form as was the case with the tragic hero. It is instead presented as a process, a formation in the transformation of history itself. The starting position of two spheres that had already become problematic in the *Empedocles* project is thereby definitively abandoned. Nature appears in the course of history – more strongly still, nature is the essential engine of this course. 'For', according to the formulation at the beginning of the fragment,

> the world of all worlds, the all in all, which always *is*, only *manifests* itself in all time – or in the decline or in the moment, or, more genetically, in

the becoming of the moment, and in the beginning of time and the world. (*Essays and Letters*, 271)

The infinite, the All in All or All-Encompassing Nature comes to be represented now only in the course of time and, indeed, in precisely those places where this course loses its continuity through historical upheavals, transitions and revolutionary cataclysms. For Hölderlin, there not only begins a new historical phase in these moments of upheaval, but also – and here he permits the natural-philosophical considerations from the *Empedocles* project to carry over into the paradigm of possibility and reality – there appears the fullness of the possible itself. Transition is the dissolution of an existing particularity and the formation of a new particularity, but in the movement of this formation, there appears the ground of its own possibility. What the human being otherwise at most senses – that the reality of life is just one possibility among many possibilities – can be experienced in this moment of transition:

> In living existence, one kind of relation and *kind of substance* predominates; although all others can be discerned in it, in the transition the possibility of all relations predominates, but the particular one is to be extracted, to be drawn from it, so that through it as infinity the finite effect emerges. (*Essays and Letters*, 271)

That reality must be 'extracted' from the fullness of the possible, and as such actively produced, is what draws the transition close to the artistic process, and it is no coincidence that Hölderlin ties the notion of the representation of the 'world of all worlds' to language in the moment of transition when he writes that the transition and beginning are 'like the language expression sign representation of a living, but particular whole' (*Essays and Letters*, 271). Yet it is crucial that the human being does not initially experience this process of dissolution actively as a process of formation, but rather as the intrusion of contingency. What is first encountered is

> the first, raw pain of the dissolution, which in its depth is *still too* unknown to the sufferer and observer . . .; there, the newly emergent, the idealic is undefined, more an object of fear, whereas by contrast the dissolution as such, *seems* existent, more real [*reales Nichts*], and the real or that which is dissolving is contained in necessity in the state between being and non-being. (*Essays and Letters*, 272)

Here it becomes clear that revolutionary upheavals, when they are as elementary as Hölderlin understands them as the expression of the world of all worlds, are not manufactured and controlled by human beings; rather, they first and foremost befall them. 'Before historical subjects can "make history", history befalls them, and this event is, according to Hölderlin, first and foremost experienced as suffering from an epochal upheaval', writes Helmut Hühn in his central study *Mnemosyne: Zeit und Erinnerung in Hölderlins Denken* [*Mnemosyne: Time and Memory in Hölderlin's Thought*].[7] It is exactly this transitional moment in which Hölderlin now locates the power of nature as a moment of the senseless, the aorgic. He finds the power of nature in the paradoxical figure of a history that is not yet a history because it appears as pure 'nothing'. History happens to people, and this happening is existentially threatening should it be discerned as the intrusion of a seemingly 'real nothing' in which the human being no longer has a single point of orientation and purchase. Hölderlin talks about the indefinite New encountering the human being as an 'object of fear', though in this case, one could also speak instead with Heidegger about anxiety because it is the fact that there are no clearly defined objects that the human being fears. Rather, the human being fears, as *Being and Time* puts it, the 'naked "that" in the nothingness of the world',[8] that lets Dasein experience its own existence in its complete, uncanny openness. The moment of transition actually represents the 'possibility of all relations' (*Essays and Letters*, 271), as Hölderlin puts it, but what is experienced first is that all concrete relations break off, that the structure of meaning that frames human existence dissolves, that the network of references – the 'particular reciprocal relationship' (*Essays and Letters*, 271) of nature and humanity – that keeps the relevant circumstances stable ruptures. With this conception, Hölderlin is far removed in his thinking from a view of nature as the infinite other to the finite sphere of humanity. Rather, he confronts nature as an experience of this finiteness insofar as it appears as a 'real nothing' (*Essays and Letters*, 274).

What Hölderlin describes here shows how much he was concerned in 1800 not only with pursuing the speculative ideas of German Idealism in his poetological considerations, but also with connecting them to contemporary historical-philosophical debates. Similarly to Schlegel – who, along with Fichte and Goethe's *Wilhelm Meister*, famously counted the French Revolution as one of the three central tendencies of the age[9] – Hölderlin's question about the role of poetry in modernity, the question of 'who wants poets at all in lean years',[10] revolves most decidedly around the problem of coping with a fundamental changeover from providence to contingency. The poetological considerations of a 'categorical reversal' (*Essays and Letters*, 324) as a 'reversal of every mode of understanding and form' (*Essays and Letters*, 331) that already define the *Empedocles* project and are further developed in the late theory of tragedy are not least an attempt to find an adequate poetic answer to the incisive caesura of a new understanding of time. In this sense, Hölderlin's departure from the tragic *Empedocles* project is connected to the genre discussion that takes place around 1800. Goethe, for example, pursued this discussion in his correspondence with Schiller and thematised it in *Wilhelm Meister*, while the Romantics – first and foremost Friedrich Schlegel – made it the point of departure for their own theory of the novel. In brief, the novel becomes a genre of modernity for Goethe as well as for the Romantics in spite of all internal differences equally because, unlike tragedy's concern with the representation of the necessity of tragic guilt, it is capable of making contingency observable.[11] What happens to the modern hero in the novel can no longer be embedded in a tragic context but instead remains coincidental until that hero, for his part, momentarily endows it with significance. This specific handling of contingency that, sometime around 1800, singles the novel out as the genre that is able to render an answer to the increasing complexity of the living environment in a functionally differentiated society by proposing and playing through experimental spaces of possibility remains to this day the basic argument for the characteristics of the genre.[12]

Hölderlin notably does not follow the attempt to write a modern tragedy with a novel; instead, the novel *Hyperion* was a precursor for his tragedy project. His genre-theoretical reflections – which are, in addition to the accumulated notes entitled 'On the Different Modes of Poetic Composition', mainly recorded in the complex doctrine of the 'alternation of tones' in the long treatise 'When the poet is once in command of the spirit . . .' – do not rely on the novel as the Romantic model of the inclusion of all genres, but rather on the mutual complementarity of genres in which the development flows for him from the novel through drama to the hymns without giving up the interconnectedness of the genres in the process. There are multiple reasons for this, and they would require an intensive genre-poetical investigation.[13] In the current context, it seems important to me to recall that while the novel gives up the hero's ties to fate, it is – particularly in the eighteenth century – geared toward the schema of the course of life of the individual subject. And it is precisely this focus on the individual that had already become problematic for Hölderlin in his attempt at a modern tragedy because the central experience of modernity for him, in which the power of nature in the form of contingency and the experience of the infinite meet, cannot be adequately represented. Likewise, Hölderlin's passage through the various genres can be understood as an attempt to find an adequate linguistic expression for a new understanding of reality. To speak with Hans Blumenberg, it takes

> reality as the result of an actualization, a progressive certainty which can never reach a total, final consistency, as it always looks forward to a future that might contain elements which could shatter previous consistency and so render previous 'realities' unreal.[14]

It is this new understanding of time, of an open future, for which the aesthetics of the time must seek an answer, and Hölderlin's merging of historical philosophy and poetics in 'The declining fatherland . . .' offers a conceptual model for this that outlines a relationship between possibility and reality. This model points toward a philosophy of temporality like that which was first worked out by Edmund Husserl and then expanded upon by Hans Blumenberg and Niklas Luhmann in the twentieth century on behalf of phenomenological anthropology and systems theory.[15]

In the fragment, Hölderlin differentiates between the real dissolution, which the catastrophic experience with nothingness described above triggers, and the idealic dissolution that he also calls 'idealic memory' (*Essays and Letters*, 272). It offers a 'look back along the path, which had to be travelled, from the beginning of the dissolution up to the point where out of the new life, a memory of the dissolved, and, out of that, as explanation and union of the gap and the contrast which sets in between the new and the past, the memory of the dissolution can follow' (*Essays and Letters*, 272–3).

The idealic dissolution is a 'reproductive act' through which 'life passes through all its points' (*Essays and Letters*, 273) but without once again establishing one of these points as an enduring new conception in the process. Rather, it is incumbent upon this idealic dissolution to rehearse dissolution and restoration so that every life connection is represented as the process of such interplay. This reproductive act, which indeed runs through the real dissolution once again, thus repeating it, is also simultaneously a creative act because it actually produces the connection in the first place. For Hölderlin, it is the 'free imitation of art' (*Essays and Letters*, 272). It falls to this to bring forth a representation of the 'state between being and not-being' in which 'the possible everywhere becomes real, and the real becomes ideal' (*Essays and Letters*, 272). But this is not simply an act of retrospective sense-making through which poetry retroactively inserts historical catastrophes into historical chains of causation. Rather, it is a matter of making processuality experienceable as the movement of possibility and reality as a not-to-be-immobilised process of designing and revoking meaning, as continuous formation without ever coalescing into a fixed form. It is the task of poetry once again to run through the real dissolution point for point in order to allow the foundation of the possible to appear in this way from the real first confrontation with the 'world of all worlds' (*Essays and Letters*, 271) as 'nothing' (*Essays and Letters*, 274). In this retrospective transition, poetry does not engender stable reality. Rather, it results in a verbal outlining of the possible: the nothing that encounters the power of nature is creatively transferred to the realm of the possible and marked as the difference between reality and possibility.

This idealic dissolution is fearless. The beginning- and end-point has already been set, found, secured, for that reason this dissolution is also more secure, more unimpedable, bolder, and it manifests itself as that which it actually is, as a reproductive act, by which life passes through all its points, and in order to attain the whole sum, it does not linger over any one, and dissolves itself at each, in order to recreate itself in the next. (*Essays and Letters*, 273)

But that also means that poetry does not already deliver a proposal for a 'new fatherland' in which 'nature and man . . . stand [anew] in a particular reciprocal relationship' (*Essays and Letters*, 271). Rather, it falls to poetry to make the 'world of all worlds' that initially presents itself to humans as a 'real nothing' experienceable as the fullness of the possible (*Essays and Letters*, 274). This is what the comparison of the representation of the 'world of all worlds' with language means when at the beginning of the fragment it says, 'For the world of all worlds . . . only *manifests* itself in all time – or in the decline or in the moment . . . and this decline and beginning is like the language expression sign representation of a living, but particular whole' (*Essays and Letters*, 271).

Language, as Johann Kreuzer has pointed out, means here 'less a finished structure than an occurrence'.[16] Language connotes an act of language determination. It aims less at concrete naming than at a movement, an event, in which what stands between the forms of reality, each of the particular worlds, the fatherland as a particular reciprocal relationship between nature and humanity, attains representation. This is what takes place in the idealic dissolution.

This retrospective, creative passage contains two central and interconnected moments in Hölderlin's poetics. First, poetry is marked as the process by which we humans are able to observe the creation of meaning as the creation of difference between possibility and reality, whereby Hölderlin makes clear that this creation of meaning is not to be conceived as a simple linear model in which new possibilities are actualised and that which was formerly possible disappears as something past. Simultaneously – and this is the second decisive moment – Hölderlin conceives of a complex model of poetic remembering, in place of a linear temporality, that allows poetry to deliver possibility anew within something past in the sense that the formerly real is precisely not modernised again through renewed representation.

To the extent that Hölderlin is no longer concerned with showing how possibility is converted into reality, but rather how the possible preserves its side in this process because actuality can constitute itself momentarily only against the backdrop of a horizon of possibilities, he frees the modalities of possibility and reality from the primacy of the *actus* over the potency prevailing in the history of philosophy of his time and approaches an understanding of possibility that shows it to be an indispensable moment in the temporally determined process of constructing meaning. In this sense, Hölderlin's historical philosophical model achieves an understanding of temporality that conceives of the present merely as the effect of an open future and an ever-changing past. He anticipates a conception of meaning that is, as Luhmann puts it, a 'unity of actualization and potentialization, reactualization and repotentialization as a self-propelling ... process'.[17] What Luhmann understands here as meaning in a systems-theoretical sense is thought of by Hölderlin as a philosophy of history in which reality and possibility are linked exactly as Luhmann describes the unity of actualisation and potentialisation. For 'the *possible*, which steps into *reality*, as *reality dissolves*' ('*Essays and Letters*, 272) does not simply take the place of this former reality but instead remains in a complex relation to that which is dissolved through the 'memory of that which is dissolved' (*Essays and Letters*, 272), and for Hölderlin it falls to language to establish this connection as a moment of the constitution of meaning without solidifying it. It is much more a matter of allowing it to appear in its fleetingness and processuality within the dynamic of poetic language.

Poetry's task, according to Hölderlin, is to create meaning through the establishment of differences in the idealic dissolution by once again delineating and linguistically setting all points of the violent and categorical reversal that has befallen humanity. For Hölderlin, it is tied to a poetics of memory – and herein lies what is peculiar about this poetic – that is marked as a letting go of that which is to be remembered, as a renunciation of memory in the Hegelian sense of representation as internalisation. Idealic dissolution remembers by dismissing what is past and, precisely by doing so, opening a space that enables one to experience the transition itself, the in-between between being and not-being, between that which is no longer and that which is not yet as the 'possible everywhere' (*Essays and Letters*, 272). This is Hölderlin's contribution to the debate surrounding memory, remembrance and recollection through which he so thoroughly distances himself from Hegel's model of memory. For Hölderlin's conception of remembrance does not re-present that which is past in the sense of a subjective movement of memory that attempts to make the past present once again. Instead, it comprehends remembrance as an act of loss. Bearing that which is past in mind means letting it go in its irretrievability as a past reality, but it is precisely through the recognition of loss that the previously real shows itself also to be part of the possible; it transforms itself into unfulfilled possibility – remaining as a virtual aspect of that which is newly to-be-actualised in conjunction with this – without being represented in memory. This will be the great theme of the hymns that consistently tie that which Hölderlin develops in 'The declining fatherland

. . .' to the chiastic historical model of antiquity and modernity formulated in the Böhlendorff letter and makes it the point of departure along with the eschewal of mimesis in order to generate new possibilities from the modern experience of contingency through this avoidance. 'The declining fatherland . . .' provides the historical-philosophical foundations for this.

Translated by Chris Long

Notes

1. The text that begins with the words 'The declining fatherland . . .' was first known by the title 'Das Werden im Vergehen' ['Becoming in Decline'], which did not come from Hölderlin. The Frankfurt Edition identifies the text with its first words and dates it hypothetically to the turn of the century 1799/1800, thus in the period of his work on *The Death of Empedocles*. The essay fragment begins on page 147 of the Stuttgart Folio on which the plan for the continuation of the third version of *Empedocles* is also located and runs in the right-hand column through the next ten recto pages. The deliberations above follow the argumentation of the Frankfurt Edition that the writing down of the text is dated after the 'Plan for Continuing the Empedocles' but nonetheless relates directly to the *Empedocles* project in a thematical sense. See also *FHA* XIV, 135–78.
2. Theresia Birkenhauer, 'Natur', p. 209. With this characterisation of nature as the timelessly conceived ground of being with which Empedocles seeks to unite himself anew through death on Mount Etna, Birkenhauer references older ways of reading the drama complex from which she clearly distances herself by not regarding the various versions of the death of Empedocles as fragments but rather as one composition in which the 'symbol' of suicide is not already pre-established but is instead first tested through its dramatic development. See also Birkenhauer, 'Natur', pp. 207–25 and comprehensively in Birkenhauer, *Legende und Dichtung*. The argumentation followed here, however, attempts to underscore the moment of development and does not assume that Hölderlin's understanding of nature in the *Empedocles* is thoroughly characterised by a striving for reunification with the All-One symbolised in a death wish. It regards such a motivation, however, as a point of departure from which the various drafts of the tragedy do not fail but are instead modified in the different versions. For an inquiry into a shift in Hölderlin's view of nature in the direction of historicity, see Christoph Jamme, *Ein ungelehrtes Buch*, pp. 326–7.
3. Such an accentuation around the moment of historicity is also underscored by Johann Kreuzer. See Johann Kreuzer, 'Zeit, Sprache und Erinnerung: Die Zeitlogik der Dichtung', in *Hölderlin Handbuch. Leben –Werk – Wirkung*, ed. Johann Kreuzer (Stuttgart/Weimar: Metzler, 2002), pp. 147–61. On the connection between poetry and temporality, see also Johann Kreuzer, *Erinnerung. Zum Zusammenhang von Hölderlins theoretischen Fragmenten 'Das untergehende Vaterland . . .' und 'Wenn der Dichter einmal des Geistes mächtig ist . . .'* (Königstein: Hain, 1985).
4. The problem of the adequate justification for death, which oscillates in the tragedy between the desire for death, a sin offering and punishment for the hubris of desiring to merge with the All-One, has continuously engaged the research on *Empedocles*. See, for example, Jürgen Söring, *Die Dialektik der Rechtfertigung: Überlegungen zu Hölderlins Empedokles-Projekt*, Ernst Mögel, *Natur als Revolution*, pp. 7–13, and Christoph Jamme, *Ein ungelehrtes Buch*, pp. 310–14.
5. See Anja Lemke, 'Die Tragödie der Repräsentation' pp. 68–87. On the problem of the representation of the unification event, see also Rüdiger Campe, 'Erscheinen und Verschwinden', pp. 53–71 as well as Sibylle Peters and Martin J. Schäfer, 'Selbstopfer und Repräsentation', pp. 282–5.

6. That the fragment no longer ties its historical-philosophical deliberations to the figure of the individual was first pointed out by Söring. See Söring, *Die Dialektik der Rechtfertigung*. In this sense, see also Helmut Hühn in his excellent study *Mnemosyne: Zeit und Erinnerung in Hölderlins Denken* to which this essay owes crucial suggestions.
7. Hühn, *Mnemosyne*, p. 137. Translated by Chris Long.
8. Martin Heidegger, *Being and Time*, p. 266.
9. 'Die Französische Revolution, Fichtes Wissenschaftslehre, und Goethes Meister sind die größten Tendenzen des Zeitalters'. Friedrich Schlegel, 'Athenäum-Fragment 216', in *Friedrich Schlegel – Kritische Ausgabe seiner Werke*, vol. 2, p. 198.
10. The complete line reads: 'I don't know, and who wants poets at all in lean years?', *Poems and Fragments*, 270.
11. In Chapter 7, Book 5 of *Wilhelm Meister's Apprenticeship*, where the advantages and disadvantages of drama and the novel are discussed, one finds the statement

> that in the novel some degree of scope may be allowed to Chance . . . on the other hand, that Fate, which, by means of outward unconnected circumstances, carries forward men, without their own concurrence, to an unforeseen catastrophe, can have place only in the drama; that Chance may produce pathetic situations, but never tragic ones; Fate, on the other hand, ought always to be terrible; and is in the highest sense tragic, when it brings into a ruinous concatenation the guilty man, and the guiltless that was unconcerned with him. (Goethe, *Wilhelm Meister's Apprenticeship*, p. 361)

12. For example, Lukács's *Theory of the Novel* never tires of stressing the loss of the closedness of the transcendental world of the Greeks as the crucial difference between epic and the novel: 'The circle within which the Greeks led their metaphysical life was smaller than ours . . . the circle whose closed nature was the transcendental essence of their life has, for us, been broken.' Lukács, *The Theory of the Novel*, p. 33. Or see Blumenberg, for whom (and in connection with Luhmann) the possibility of the novel at all hinges on its ability to represent a world as a possible world in 'The Concept of Reality and the Possibility of the Novel', pp. 29–48.
13. On the doctrine of the alternation of tones, see Lawrence Ryan, *Hölderlins Lehre vom Wechsel der Töne*. For a good overview, see Holger Schmidt, 'Wechsel der Töne', pp. 118–27.
14. Blumenberg, 'The Concept of Reality', p. 33.
15. The interdependencies of Husserl, Blumenberg and Luhmann are manifold. Here, for Blumenberg, it only relates to his habilitation *Die ontologische Distanz* as well as the recently published volume from his posthumous papers, *Phänomenologische Schriften 1981–1988*. On Luhmann's engagement with Husserl, see Niklas Luhmann, *Die neuzeitliche Wissenschaft und die Phänomenologie*. On the relationship of Blumenberg to Luhmann, see among others Rüdiger Campe, 'Blumenberg, Luhmann, and Contingency', pp. 81–99.
16. Kreuzer, 'Zeit, Sprache und Erinnerung', p. 151. Translated by Chris Long. On the connection between poetry and temporality, see also Johann Kreuzer, *Erinnerung*.
17. Niklas Luhmann, *Soziale Systeme*. Translated by Chris Long.

Bibliography

Birkenhauer, Theresia, 'Natur in Hölderlins Trauerspiel Der Tod des Empedokles', in Thomas Roberg (ed.) *Friedrich Hölderlin: Neue Wege der Forschung* (Darmstadt: Wissenschaftliche Buchgesellschaft, 2003), pp. 253–73.

Birkenhauer, Theresia, *Legende und Dichtung: Der Tod des Philosophen und Hölderlins Empedokles* (Berlin: Vorwerk 8, 1996).
Blumenberg, Hans, 'The Concept of Reality and the Possibility of the Novel', in Richard E. Amacher and Victor Lange (eds), *New Perspectives in German Literary Criticism* (Princeton: Princeton University Press, 1979), pp. 29–48.
Blumenberg, Hans, *Die ontologische Distanz: Eine Untersuchung über die Krisis der Phänomenologie Husserls* (Kiel: unpublished *Habilitation*, 1950).
Blumenberg, Hans, *Phänomenologische Schriften 1981–1988*, ed. Nicola Zambon (Berlin: Suhrkamp, 2018).
Campe, Rüdiger, 'Blumenberg, Luhmann, and Contingency', in *Telos*, 158 (Spring 2012), pp. 81–99.
Campe, Rüdiger, 'Erscheinen und Verschwinden. Metaphysik der Bühne in Hölderlins "Empedokles"', in Bettine Menke and Christoph Menke (eds), *Tragödie – Trauerspiel – Spektakel* (Berlin: Theater der Zeit, 2007), pp. 53–71.
Goethe, Johann Wolfgang, *Wilhelm Meister's Apprenticeship and Travels I*, trans. Thomas Carlyle, in *The Works of Thomas Carlyle*, ed. Henry Duff Traill (Cambridge: Cambridge University Press, 2010), vol. 23.
Heidegger, Martin, *Being and Time*, trans. Joan Stambaugh, rev. Dennis J. Schmidt (Albany: State University of New York Press, 2010).
Hühn, Helmut, *Mnemosyne: Zeit und Erinnerung in Hölderlins Denken* (Stuttgart/Weimar: Metzler, 1997).
Jamme, Christoph, *Ein ungelehrtes Buch. Die philosophische Gemeinschaft zwischen Hölderlin und Hegel in Frankfurt 1797–1800* (Bonn: Bouvier, 1983).
Kreuzer, Johann, 'Zeit, Sprache und Erinnerung: Die Zeitlogik der Dichtung', in Johann Kreuzer (ed.), *Hölderlin Handbuch. Leben –Werk – Wirkung*, (Stuttgart/Weimar: Metzler, 2002), pp. 147–61.
Kreuzer, Johann, *Erinnerung. Zum Zusammenhang von Hölderlins theoretischen Fragmenten 'Das untergehende Vaterland . . .' und 'Wenn der Dichter einmal des Geistes mächtig ist . . .'* (Königstein: Hain, 1985).
Lemke, Anja, 'Die Tragödie der Repräsentation. Politik und Theater in Hölderlins "Empedokles-Projekt"', in *Hölderlin-Jahrbuch*, 37 (2011), pp. 68–87.
Luhmann, Niklas, *Die neuzeitliche Wissenschaft und die Phänomenologie* (Vienna: Picus, 1996).
Luhmann, Niklas, *Soziale Systeme: Grundriß einer allgemeinen Theorie* (Frankfurt am Main: Suhrkamp, 1987).
Lukács, Georg, *The Theory of the Novel: A Historico-Philosophical Essay on the Forms of Great Epic Literature* (Cambridge, MA: MIT Press, 1977).
Mögel, Ernst, *Natur als Revolution: Hölderlins Empedokles-Tragödie* (Stuttgart/Weimar: Metzler, 1995).
Peters, Sibylle and Schäfer, Martin J., 'Selbstopfer und Repräsentation', in *Hölderlin-Jahrbuch*, 30 (1996–9), pp. 282–5.
Ryan, Lawrence, *Hölderlins Lehre vom Wechsel der Töne* (Stuttgart: Kohlhammer, 1960).
Schlegel, Friedrich, 'Athenäum-Fragment 216', in Hans Eichner (ed.), *Friedrich Schlegel – Kritische Ausgabe seiner Werke* (Munich/Paderborn/Vienna: Ferdinand Schöningh, 1967), vol. 2, pp. 198–9.
Schmidt, Holger, 'Wechsel der Töne', in Johann Kreuzer (ed.), *Hölderlin Handbuch. Leben –Werk – Wirkung* (Stuttgart/Weimar: Metzler, 2002), pp. 118–27.
Söring, Jürgen, *Die Dialektik der Rechtfertigung* (Frankfurt am Main: Athenäum, 1973).

Chapter 10

'My whole being fell silent, and read': Peter Handke's Hölderlin and Heidegger Reception

Jacob Haubenreich

In 1979 the Austrian writer Peter Handke published the groundbreaking novel *Slow Homecoming* and in 1980 he was working on *The Lesson of Mont Sainte Victoire* (hereafter *The Lesson*). These texts are usually said to mark a paradigm shift in Handke's career: a crisis of writing led to a so-called 'classical turn' or 'turn to nature', a reorientation from the experimental avant-garde poetics of his earlier work toward a mode of narration informed by German Romanticism and Classicism.[1] Based on Handke's own travels in North America, *Slow Homecoming* depicts the experiences of the geologist Valentin Sorger who, through observing and sketching the forms of the earth's surface in Alaska, becomes awakened to the beauty of nature – an obviously Romantic trope – and undergoes a kind of transformation from scientist into artist.[2]

After returning to Europe, Handke visited an exhibition of Paul Cézanne's late work and subsequently undertook two journeys to Aix-en-Provence to travel the *route Cézanne*, which became the basis of *The Lesson*. Cézanne's method of *réalisation*, of transforming nature into paint, served as a model for Handke's own emerging project of observing and representing. Handke's turn to nature was indeed tied to a material practice. Beginning in the mid-1970s, Handke undertook a project of daily note-taking, filling notebooks with descriptions and drawings of nature and various ephemera alongside formulations of passages that would appear in print.[3] Handke's note-taking constituted a crucial component in the writerly project for which Handke has become known – a project associated with slowness, re-mythification and the re-sacralisation of reality in the hyper-technologised, media-saturated present.[4]

But Handke was also a prolific reader.[5] In a 1979 interview, he commented on his experience of rereading great writers:

> Years back in school I was fascinated by Homer, by Pindar, by Heraclitus, and I have re-read everything which I, and perhaps many others, read too early, this time more slowly. Goethe. But there is one who I only now totally comprehend and who for me writes a holy scripture in a complete objective sense, and that is Hölderlin. I had not understood him in this way before. But now I can read his work as far better writing, as moral, high-standing, holy scripture, where one is not forced to believe but, because sentences stand like mountain ranges, can simply believe, or at least see an ideal.[6]

Indeed, as Handke writes in the first sentence of *The Lesson*, 'On my return to Europe, I needed my daily ration of written matter and read and reread a good deal', and he narrates re-reading Hölderlin's *Hyperion* directly after his first trip to Aix: 'I reread Hölderlin's *Hyperion*, finally understood every sentence, and was able to look on its words as images.'[7]

Handke's notebooks of the late 1970s and early 1980s, however, reveal an even more intensive engagement with Hölderlin's writing than is generally recognised, because this engagement is often only obliquely detectable in his published work.[8] This essay explores how Handke took up and transformed key Hölderlinian figures and concepts and what it meant to do so in the late twentieth century. In response to the increased acceleration of life and the alienation of humans from nature, Handke turned to natural beauty and poetry as critical correctives. He announced in his Kafka Prize speech in 1979 that, 'striving after forms for my truth, I am looking for beauty ... for the classical, the universal, which, following the practical teaching of the great painters, only achieves form through constant observation and contemplation of nature'.[9] Although this re-orientation was often criticised as a withdrawal from the political scene, it might alternatively be considered – when viewed in relation to its Romantic genealogy – as deeply in tune with the development of contemporary environmental consciousness.

I suggest that Handke's project of writing can be viewed as a kind of *new* 'new mythology'. Likely co-authored by Hölderlin, 'The Oldest Programme for a System of German Idealism' calls for a 'new mythology' to counteract the mechanisation of humanity in the modern state. At the centre of this 'new mythology' is the power of poetry.

> Poesy regains a higher dignity, and in the end becomes again what it was in the beginning: *the educator of humanity*; for there will be no more philosophy, no history, Poesy alone will survive all other arts and sciences. (*Essays and Letters*, 342)

This is an essay, in large part, about *teachers*.[10] In poetry, Hölderlin saw the potential for a revival of art, indeed of culture more broadly conceived, as well as for the restoration of humans' relationship to nature and to the divine. A similar conception of poetry, directly influenced by Hölderlin (and others), would serve as a wellspring for Handke's own creative activity at a critical moment in his career. This essay pieces together Handke's Hölderlin reception in four parts. The first examines Handke's attunement to nature and everyday experience, a process in which *Hyperion* played a central role. Handke engaged with key concepts from Hölderlin not only through direct engagement with his texts, but also, as the second section shows, in his reading of Heidegger, for whom Hölderlin also proved critical. Parts three and four examine Hölderlin's influence on Handke's interrogation of form and the representation of nature; the nature of poetry and the poet's task; and the significance of the material act of writing in Handke's emerging poetic programme.

'My whole being falls silent and listens'

One phrase reverberates powerfully throughout Handke's work of this period: 'my whole being falls silent and listens' [*Mein ganzes Wesen verstummt und lauscht*] (*Hyperion*, 3; *FHA* XI, 585). This phrase from Hölderlin's *Hyperion* is taken up by Handke routinely and transformed, becoming a pivot that unifies several critical thematics of his work: receptive attention to and transcription of his surroundings (including nature), a new mode of seeing, and the activity of reading and gleaning from works and the world. Ultimately, what might seem a purely passive stance vis-à-vis the external world is rendered, in Handke's work, an active mode of engagement with works, authors and surrounding world.

Following his return from Greece, Hyperion narrates an experience of oneness with nature: 'My whole being falls silent and listens . . . [L]ost in the wide blue, I look up into the ether and down into the sacred sea, and I feel as if a kindred spirit were opening its arms to me, as if the pain of solitude were dissolved in the life of the Divinity' (*Hyperion*, 3). Handke notes this passage in his notebook on 24 August 1980 while walking in the Slovenian Karst: ' "My whole being falls silent and listens" (that is possible here, and that's it too; rustling of the pencil in the stillness / Pliskovica)' [*'Mein ganzes Wesen verstummt und lauscht' (das ist hier möglich, und das ist es auch Rauschen des Bleistifts in der Stille / Pliskovica)*].[11] Handke pulled from the same letter of *Hyperion* on 14 March 1979 after arriving in Berlin: 'Hölderlin (nature): "I feel as if a kindred spirit were opening its arms to me, as if the pain of solitude were dissolved in the life of the Divinity" (airplane today in the twilight above desolate Berlin)' [*Hölderlin (Natur): 'Mir ist, als öffnet ein verwandter Geist mir die Arme, als löste der Schmerz der Einsamkeit sich auf ins Leben der Gottheit' (Flugzeug heute in der Dämmerung über dem öden Berlin)*].[12] Like Hyperion, gazing up into the heavens and down into the sacred sea, so too does Handke occupy a liminal zone, not on a cliff but in an airplane, gazing up into the sky and down onto the city spread out like a dull sea before him.

The formulation of *verstummen und lauschen* captures something quintessential about Handke's evolving project of slowness and attentiveness that reverberates throughout numerous texts of this period. In *Across* (1983), this mode of listening is even evoked in the surname of the protagonist Andreas Loser, which Handke explicitly connects to 'the dialect verb *losen*, meaning 'listen' or 'hark'.[13]

The notion of *lauschen* as employed by Handke, however, does not merely concern the sense of hearing. Rather, it encapsulates a physical and metaphysical receptivity, the transformation of one's entire being into a sensory organ wholly attuned to nature. In *Across*, Loser yearns for a mode of perception that extends beyond the five senses, a 'kind of seeing' encapsulated in the Greek word *leukein*.[14] Something similar is also imagined in Sorger's technique of 'comprehensive vision' that 'transformed the whole of him into a body which became a radically extroverted organ of all the senses'.[15] Indeed, in *History of the Pencil*, while describing memory, Handke yet again invokes the broader sensorium in relation to this phrase reminiscent of Hyperion:

> 'Memory', for me, is not the scent of a pastry or the salon of the duchess, but rather the drops of rain in the dust of the field path at dawn: it is the moment when 'my whole being' still, thirty years later, 'falls silent and listens'; the great eye and ear of the world.[16]

Handke's expanded conception of Hölderlin's *verstummen und lauschen* comes to play a role in his broader project and in the 'lessons' he would learn from other creators, notably Cézanne. In *History of the Pencil*, he directly correlates 'lauschen' with Cézannean seeing: 'On Hyperion's recurring statement before nature: "My entire being falls silent and listens": the being that falls silent in fact has to do with "listening", not with "looking". And seeing colors (better yet: seeing light) corresponds here to "listening".'[17]

In *Repetition* (1986), the *Hyperion*-indebted formulation is also evoked in Filip Kobal's description of the 'blind window' (another visual inflection of the phrase), in which Handke conceptually relates or even equates, through an alliterative replacement of words, *lauschen* with a mode of reading, *lesen*:

> The blind window ... owed its effect to the absence of something ordinarily present: to its opacity. Thanks to its extreme vagueness, it reflected my

gaze; and the muddle of languages, the confusion of voices within me fell silent: my whole being fell silent, and read [*Mein ganzes Wesen verstummte und las*].[18]

In connecting *lauschen* and *lesen*, Handke evokes the Romantic notion of the Book of Nature. This was a potent concept in this period: throughout *The Lesson*, Handke equated natural forms with writing, even coming to understand Cézanne's paintings as a kind of picture writing, a transformation of nature's language into pictorial form.

Handke's connection of *lesen* to *lauschen* reframes a potentially passive receptivity (listening) as an active process of registering and creating. The German *lesen* is rooted etymologically in the notion of *auflesen*, gathering, implying a conception of reading as an active process of collecting and coordinating associations between a given range of texts (broadly defined, encompassing art, nature, even reality itself) that the reader assembles. This was never far from Handke's mind; indeed he carefully cultivated a practice of relentless note-taking: of walking, reading and recording, and of observing and gathering into his notebooks. While *verstummen und lauschen* was clearly a critical concept in his texts, it was one that he entwined with a different type of attunement and communion with nature, of *lesen* as *auflesen*.[19] Hölderlin's conception of receptivity becomes the basis of Handke's poetics of production.

'. . . poetically man dwells . . .'

Before turning to Handke's broader reception of Hölderlin's writing beyond *Hyperion*, it is necessary to take stock of how Handke's engagement with Hölderlin was mediated in part by Heidegger. If Hölderlin was critical in framing the processes and attitudes central to Handke's emergent poetological project, the author's notion of poetics and the ethics of poetry owes much to his engagement with Heidegger. These two writers functioned synergistically in Handke's reconceptualisation not only of writing, but also of what writing might do for an increasingly beleaguered humanity.

On 25 September 1978 in Alaska, Handke read Heidegger's 'Building Dwelling Thinking', recording numerous quotes in his notebooks. In a letter to Alfred Kolleritsch, Handke cast his reverence for Heidegger's essay in the same terms he would use to describe Hölderlin's poetry, namely as gospel: 'Dear Fredy, I am thankful to you for mentioning the essay by Heidegger about dwelling when we were en route; I have read it here almost like a gospel [*Evangelium*].'[20] References to the essay also

appear in notebooks of 1979, when Handke read Heidegger's essay '...
Poetically Man Dwells ...'.

In 'Building Dwelling Thinking', Heidegger describes dwelling as a fundamental feature of being, and building as 'letting-dwell'. Humans build, in the sense of 'making' or 'constructing', not only structures in which to dwell, but many kinds of things. Dwelling, moreover, involves 'staying with things', both natural and man-made. Heidegger associates both concepts, building and dwelling, with caring for and protecting, sparing and preserving.[21]

But what exactly does dwelling preserve? Heidegger introduces the notion of the fourfold, an originary oneness of earth, sky, mortals and divinities. In '... Poetically Man Dwells ...' he describes the 'facing' of these elements toward each other, the span between them, as the 'dimension'. Dwelling, Heidegger writes, involves going through [*durchgehen*] and persisting through [*durchstehen*] the dimension. Things, in turn, are locations [*Orte*] that grant space to the fourfold; through protecting and caring for things, humans spare and preserve the fourfold. Through such activity, humans dwell, in turn, 'in the fourfold among things'.[22]

Handke took extensive notes on 'Building Dwelling Thinking' in his notebooks, quoting passages that address all of the salient concepts of the essay as outlined above.[23] These concepts echo throughout Handke's works of the following years. *Slow Homecoming*, for example, contains numerous descriptions of earth and sky, the two physical components of the fourfold. In one passage, Handke describes Sorger as 'alive to the pitch-black night sky above and behind him and to the deep-black earth beside and below him ... For a moment he had felt the strength to propel his whole self into the bright horizon and there dissolve forever into the undifferentiated unity of sky and earth.'[24] Handke's description of Sorger's act of projecting himself into the horizon, the space in which they meet, specifically recalls Heidegger's notion of humans traversing the span of the fourfold. One notebook note even describes Sorger explicitly as a Heidegger-devotee: 'After a while S. suddenly believed him; he (H.) was the first in a long time whose language he believed' [*Nach einiger Zeit glaubte S. ihm plötzlich; er (H.) war der erste seit langem, dessen Sprache er glaubte*].[25] Even Sorger's name, which means 'worrier', but also one who cares for or tends, encapsulates Heidegger's conception of being in terms of caring. Indeed, in *Being and Time*, Heidegger develops the idea of care, *Sorge*, as Dasein's unique mode of being-in-the-world: 'Dasein, *ontologically* understood, is care. Because being-in-the-world belongs essentially to Da-sein, its being toward the world is essentially taking care.'[26]

Heidegger's notions of building, dwelling and the fourfold were developed in part through his reading of Hölderlin. In '... Poetically Man

Dwells . . .', Heidegger describes poetry as the originary act of building: 'Poetry first causes dwelling to be dwelling. Poetry is what really lets us dwell. But through what do we attain to a dwelling place? Through building. Poetic creation, which lets us dwell, is a kind of building.'[27] Whereas in 'Building Dwelling Thinking', Heidegger describes human dwelling as a 'persisting through' and 'going through' the fourfold, he defines dwelling in '. . . Poetically Man Dwells . . .' in terms of measuring.

> The upward glance passes aloft toward the sky, and yet it remains below on the earth. The upward glance spans the between of sky and earth. This between is measured out for the dwelling of man. We now call the span thus meted out the dimension . . . To write poetry is measure-taking, understood in the strict sense of the word, by which man first receives the measure for the breadth of his being.[28]

Handke reads '. . . Poetically Man Dwells . . .' after returning from North America but before making his first trip to Aix, and records several notes about the text. The first reads: 'The measure consists in the way in which the god who remains unknown, is revealed as such by the sky (On Hölderlin)' [*Das Maß besteht in der Weise, wie der unbekannt bleibende Gott als dieser durch den Himmel offenbar ist (Über Hölderlin)*].[29] Handke returns to this thought three pages later when he writes: 'For sure: writing poetry as taking measure between earth and sky; but how to not go insane or otherwise perish in the process? (today I would have almost burst)' [*Sicher: Dichten als das Maßnehmen zwischen Erde und Himmel; wie aber dabei selbst nicht wahnsinnig werden oder anders zugrunde gehen? (Heute wäre ich fast geplatzt)*].[30] Although Handke's direct references to '. . . Poetically Man Dwells . . .' are few, it is heard in Handke's elevation of poetry, writing and artistic production more generally as means of caring and preserving, indeed of living in the world. An act of building, poetry, for Heidegger, is letting-dwell, yet humans do not dwell poetically by default. 'For dwelling can be unpoetic only because it is in essence poetic', he writes, and characterises a 'plight of dwelling' [*Wohnungsnot*] in our 'precarious age' [*bedenklichen Zeit*].[31] Dwelling, in turn, must be learned: Handke directly cites Heidegger's statement that 'The real dwelling plight lies in this, that mortals ever search anew for the nature of dwelling, that they *must ever learn to dwell*'.[32] To do so, they must 'take the poetic seriously'.[33]

Handke's poetic reorientation, in turn, might be understood as a process of learning to dwell through the processes of observing and writing. And if poetry plays a crucial role in helping teach humans to dwell, this implies, in turn, that poets take on a key role in nurturing humankind's existence.

'Poets in a destitute time'

Handke's turn to nature involved a 'search for forms' through which to transmit this experience into writing.[34] This section presents many quotes from Hölderlin from the pages of Handke's notebooks. Accounting for these passages allows us to see the centrality – not necessarily graspable in Handke's published work – of Hölderlin's investigations of form and the representation of nature in shaping Handke's writerly programme and his evolving sense (stemming in part from Heidegger) of writing and the writer's task.

On 28 July 1979 Handke quoted, in his notebook, a letter from Hölderlin to Christian Ludwig Neuffer on form and the representation of beauty:

> '. . . die seinem <u>sanften Geist</u> diese <u>strenge</u> Form aufnötigen . . .'
> '. . . weil das Schöne, so wie es sich in der Wirklichkeit darstellt, von den Umständen, unter denen es hervorgeht, notwendig eine Form annimmt, die ihm nicht natürlich ist, und die nur dadurch zur natürlichen Form wird, daß man eben die Umstände, die ihm notwendig diese Form gaben, hinzunimmt'. (an N.)
> 29.7 'Unter dem Apfelbaum' (Schönheit des in den Adern durchscheinenden Blattes)
> die unschuldigen Farben der Kindheit
> Sprache zu haben, das ist schon die Hoffnung

> '. . . which force his <u>gentle spirit</u> to adopt this <u>stern</u> form . . .'
> '. . . and beauty, when it appears in reality, necessarily assumes a form from the circumstances in which it emerges which is not natural to it and which only becomes its natural form when it is taken together with the very conditions which of necessity gave it the form it has'. (to N.)
> 29.7 'under the apple tree' (beauty of the leaf shining through in the veins)
> the innocent colours of childhood
> to have language, that is already the hope[35]

Hölderlin here suggests that the appearance of beauty in reality is itself already a representation of the ideal of beauty; in turn, the poetic representation of natural beauty requires a 'natural' form that corresponds to it. Handke's first note of 29 July transforms Hölderlin's theory into a visual experience by offering a visual metaphor directly after the transcription of Hölderlin's words. Lying on the earth looking upward, Handke sees the sun shining through the translucent leaves of an apple tree that renders their veins visible: beauty literally shines through the forms of nature. Handke reflects on the 'innocent' colours of a child's fresh view of the world and expresses desire for an adequate language in which to represent this experience.

Two weeks later, a momentary glimpse of nature's beauty prompts a comparison of Hölderlin's nature descriptions to Goethe's:

> Der Herbst an den nackten hellgelben Platanenstämmen (die Sprache der Jahreszeiten sprechen wollen, als höchste, umfassende Sprache) [du Roule] G.'s Naturbeschreibungen: zu merken, wie <u>frisch</u> die 'Landschaft' damals noch war – wie die einfachsten Worte genügten, das bloße Benennen und 'Ansagen' (kein <u>Beschwören</u> wie bei H.)

> Autumn on the bare, light yellow sycamore trunks (wanting to speak the language of the season, as highest, encompassing language) [du Roule] G.'s nature descriptions: noticing, how <u>fresh</u> the 'landscape' still was then – how the simplest words sufficed, the mere naming and 'announcing' (no <u>incantation</u> as with H.)[36]

Handke's longing to speak the 'language of the seasons' reflects Hölderlin's desire for a natural poetic form guided by nature's own representation of beauty through form. Whereas Goethe uses the simplest words to merely name and announce nature, according to Handke, Hölderlin relies on a language of incantation [*Beschwören*]. Two pages prior, Handke compares the two writers on other grounds, namely by emphasising Hölderlin's ability to lift or elevate the reader: 'Nurturing myself (toward the eternal) toward lasting language; Goethe's poems address only those currently receptive to being cheered, while Hölderlin's poetry can also uplift those who are unhappy (Selest)' [*Mich selber (zur ewigen) zur dauernden Sprache erziehen; Goethes Gedichte sprechen nur zu dem aktuell glücksbereiten Menschen, während Hölderlins Poesie auch den gerade Unglücklichen erheben kann (Selest)*].[37]

Handke's commentary on the uplifting dimensions of Hölderlin's poetry reflects a broader interrogation of the poet's task. On 22 July 1979 in Berlin, he records several lines from the poem 'An die Parzen' ('To the Fates'):

> Ruhe käme in mein Schreiben, wenn ich, bedächtig, die Teileinheiten (Einteilungen) des Lebens herausfände (so scheint mir alles, was ich geschrieben habe, zu hektisch; es läuft zu schnell ab)
> 'Doch ist mir einst das Heilige, das am / Herzen mir liegt, das Gedicht gelungen, // Willkommen dann, O Stille der Schattenwelt!' (An die Parzen)

> Peace would come into my writing, if I were to discover deliberately the individual elements (divisions) of life (everything that I have written seems to me too hectic, it goes off too quickly)
> 'But when what's holy, dear to me, the / Poem's accomplished, my art perfected, / Then welcome, silence, welcome cold world of shades!' ('To the Fates')[38]

Handke's desire for peace in his writing echoes the lines he transcribes from 'To the Fates', which express the poet's longing to achieve a successful poem before he can depart from the earth.

The welcoming of death in 'To the Fates' recalls Hölderlin's evocation of the 'beautiful death' [*schönen Tod*] in the final stanza of the second version of 'Dichtermut' ('The Poet's Courage'). On 28 July, Handke cites from this poem as well as 'Wie wenn am Feiertage . . .' ('As on a holiday . . .'), both of which examine the perilous task of the poet:

> 'Sind dem dir nicht verwandt alle Lebendigen, / Nährt die Parze dem nicht selber im Dienste dich? / Drum so wandle nur wehrlos / Fort durchs Leben, und fürchte nichts!' (Dichtermut) [1801]
>
> . . .
>
> 'Doch uns gebührt es, unter Gottes Gewittern, / Ihr Dichter! mit entblößtem Haupte zu stehen./ Des Vaters Strahl, ihn selbst, mit eigner Hand/Zu fassen und dem Volk ins Lied / Gehüllt die himmlische Gabe zu reichen'.
>
> 'Is not all that's alive close and akin to you, / Does the Fate not herself keep you to serve her ends? / Well, then, travel defenseless / On through life, and fear nothing there!' ('The Poet's Courage') [1801]
>
> . . .
>
> 'Yet, fellow poets, us it behooves to stand / Bareheaded beneath God's thunder-storms, / To grasp the Father's ray, no less, with our own hand / And, wrapping in song the heavenly gift, / To offer it to the people.'[39]

In the first strophe of 'The Poet's Courage', the poet stands unprotected and defenseless, but is emboldened to move through life without fear. 'As on a holiday . . .' offers a similar image of the poet standing 'bareheaded', drinking 'heavenly fire', grasping 'the Father's ray, no less, with our own hand' (*Poems and Fragments*, 397). The poet-cum-priest offers the 'heavenly gift' to mortals 'wrapped' in the form of song [*der Gesang*] such that they can receive it without it destroying them (*Poems and Fragments*, 397).

The poet, as mediator between mortals ('sons of Earth', 'peoples') and divinities ('gods'), traverses the distance between earth and sky: 'More full of meaning and more audible to us, / Drift on [*hinwandeln*] between Heaven and Earth and amid the peoples' (*Poems and Fragments*, 397; *FHA* VIII, 558). The poet's task is thus one of movement, of journey. In 'The Poet's Courage', Hölderlin similarly describes the poet's existence in terms of travelling ('wandle'), an obvious connection to Handke's own processes of hiking, travelling, traversing and recording his observations in his notebooks, the basis of his writerly project (*Poems and Fragments*, 205; *FHA* V, 697).

Wandeln, however, signifies not only walking or going, but also converting and transforming, and *die Wandlung* is the term for the transubstantiation during the Catholic mass. 'As on a holiday . . .' casts the poet as a priest-like figure, and the poetic act as a kind of transubstantiation, a comparison most explicitly framed in 'Bread and Wine' (*Poems and Fragments*, 263–73). Such transformative potential features prominently in Handke's work; transubstantiation is described or noted explicitly in *Slow Homecoming*, *Across*, *Repetition* and *The Lesson*. Handke compares Cézanne's *Rochers près des grottes au-dessus de Château-Noir*, which he describes as 'the picture of pictures', to the communion chalice, and thus Cézanne's process of *réalisation* to the ceremony of transubstantiation.[40] The notion of transubstantiation and the role of the author as a kind of priest thus connects, for Handke, Hölderlin to Cézanne, the writer's pivotal influence during this period, and undergirds Handke's project of re-sacralisation or re-mythification.

Recalling Heidegger's definition of poetry in terms of building and letting-dwell, of preserving and protecting, Handke describes Cézanne's *réalisation* as a 'transformation and sheltering of things endangered'.[41] In our 'precarious age', Heidegger writes, humans do not know how to dwell, and in 'What Are Poets For?', he takes up a key line from Hölderlin's 'Bread and Wine', declaring that '"poets in a destitute time" must especially poetise the nature of poetry' [*Darum müssen 'Dichter in dürftiger Zeit' das Wesen der Dichtung eigens dichten*].[42] In characterising his destitute era, Hyperion similarly laments that humans have become 'demoralised and corrupted' and that 'our priests no longer have any influence' (*Hyperion*, 15). Handke was invested in these pages, quoting the following lines of the same *Hyperion* letter: 'The incurable corruption of my century became so apparent to me from so many things that I tell you and do not tell you' [*Die Unheilbarkeit des Jahrhunderts war mir aus so manchem, was ich erzähle und nicht erzähle, sichtbar geworden*].[43]

Handke's interest in these passages stemmed from his increasing dissatisfaction with modernity, one that made Hölderlin's own laments potent. 'The Oldest Programme' also addresses the deplorable condition of humanity, diagnosing the mechanisation of human life in the modern state: 'We must therefore also go beyond the State. – For every State has to treat free human beings like mechanical cogs; and it should not do that; thus it must *stop*' (*Essays and Letters*, 341). Handke echoes this characterisation in his Kafka Prize speech, asserting that those who deny the existence of nature [*es gebe doch keine Natur*] have become machines: 'Those who say this, voluntarily caught in their dwelling and driving machines, having become machines themselves, perhaps only eschew the open' [*Die das sagen, scheuen, freiwillig gefangen in ihren Wohn- und Fahrmaschinen, selber Maschinen geworden, vielleicht nur das Freie*].[44]

For Hölderlin and Handke, the hope for salvation lies in writing and writers who will act as teachers: 'in the end', as 'The Oldest Programme' reminds us, 'Poesy . . . in the end becomes what it was in the beginning – *the educator of humanity*' (*Essays and Letters*, 342). Diotima declares to Hyperion that, through his development as a poet, he will become a 'teacher of our people' [*Erzieher unsers Volks*] (*Hyperion*, 73; *FHA* XI, 691). Handke describes Kafka in similar terms as 'our great teacher' and 'teacher of mankind', and Cézanne as '*the* teacher of mankind in the here and now'.[45] Writers can thus be thought of as teachers who, in Heideggerian terms, teach mortals how to dwell poetically, which, as demonstrated earlier, means to dwell with an eye toward the heavens and the gods as a necessary counterpoint to humans.

Handke comes to conceive of this salvation in slightly different terms, however. In the finale of *Repetition*, which evokes the Hölderlinian-Heideggerian notion of poets traversing the divide between mortals and divinities, Handke casts *storytelling* as that which holds sacred, redemptive, restorative power:

> Storytelling, there is nothing more worldly than you, nothing more just, my holy of holies. Storytelling, patron saint of long-range combat, my lady. Storytelling, most spacious of all vehicles, heavenly chariot . . . Storytelling, music of sympathy, forgive us, forgive and dedicate us . . . Story, repeat, that is, renew.[46]

This shift comes with, I argue, a fundamental reorientation of writing towards the material. If the poet's task consists of mediating the divine, transforming the beauty of nature into song, and thereby teaching humans how to dwell poetically, for Handke, this is not merely an abstract metaphysical reflection. Rather, as his notebook pages remind us, it is one of physical, material practice.

'To grasp . . . with our own hand'

It is fitting that Hölderlin was among the 'teachers' who played a role in Handke's turn to nature, for Hyperion's own communion with nature is (like Handke's) awakened through his experience with multiple companions and guides: Alabanda, Diotima, and above all Adamas. Handke was attuned to these connections, copying into his notebook Hyperion's comparison of Adamas to a plant:

> As a man stands before a plant whose peace soothes his struggling spirit, and simple content returns to his soul – so he stood before me.
> And I – was I not the echo of his quiet inspiration? did not the melodies of his being repeat themselves in me? What I saw, I became; and what I saw was divine. (*Hyperion*, 8)

Hyperion becomes an echo chamber in which the melodies of Adamas's being reverberate. Through his vision, Hyperion both encounters and becomes the divine.

A fellow traveller, Adamas guides Hyperion in his development as a poet, introducing him to the classical ruins of the Greek world:

> [A]nd there I sat, playing sadly beside him, scraping the moss from a demigod's pedestal, digging a marble hero's shoulder out of the rubble, cutting the brambles and heather from the half-buried architraves, while my Adamas sketched the landscape ... I move through the past like a gleaner [*Ährenleser*] over the stubblefield when the landowner has harvested; he gathers up every straw [*da liest man jeden Strohhalm auf*]. (*Hyperion*, 9; FHA XI, 593)

Guided by Adamas, Hyperion becomes an active participant in a process of restoration, specifically a gleaner, a gatherer of fragments of the past.

The conception of poetic activity through metaphors of manual activity – here restoring a whole from ruins – continues in Hyperion's wanderings with Alabanda, during which he compares the task of the poet to the shovelling of rotting leaves in order to prepare ground for new growth. Handke transcribes only a piece of this scene, when Alabanda remarks, '... and high words, when they do not echo in high hearts, are like a dying leaf rustling down onto dung' [... *und hohe Worte, wenn sie nicht in hoher Herzen widertönen, sind wie ein sterbend Blatt, das in den Kot herunterrauscht*].[47] Alabanda goes on to ask, 'What are you going to do?', to which Hyperion responds, 'I will take a shovel and throw the dung into a pit' (*Hyperion*, 20). Clearing the muck, Hyperion creates fertile ground for new growth, the regeneration of humankind, 'the world's second age' (*Hyperion*, 51).

If the activities of working the earth or gleaning from fields serve as common metaphors for writing, these metaphors become material realities both in descriptions within Handke's texts and in his own writerly practice. In *Repetition*, Handke writes:

> Time and again, as I climbed to the top of the vineyard ... I felt the need to bend down, to reach [*greifen*] into the earth, to collect [*sammeln*], to take something with me [*etwas mitzunehmen*]. Keep it, keep it, keep it! Bits of coal were encrusted in the slate. I dug them out and today, a quarter of a century later, I am drawing quavering black strokes [*Striche*] on my white writing paper with them.[48]

Kobal appears as a gatherer or gleaner of physical material from the earth, but the material he gathers, here charcoal, becomes a writing implement, the very material of writing. This is a recursive process, the charcoal used to depict its own scene of gathering.

For Handke, writing is *essentially* material. His search for forms included the cultivation of material practices of wandering, gathering, recording and writing. On the very notebook page on which he cited Hölderlin's letter to Christian Ludwig Neuffer concerning the need for 'natural' form in representing nature poetically, he turns from this metaphysical conception of form to the very implements of writing laid out before him:

> Abend am Schreibtisch: Im Vordergrund steht der gelbe Bleistift, vor dem Hintergrundmasse der schwarzen Schreibmaschine
> Jeden schönen Gegenstand in der Hand drehen, auch den entferntesten (wie ein Glas Wein)
>
> Evening at my writing desk: the yellow pencil stands in the foreground, in front of the background mass of the black typewriter
> Turning every beautiful object in my hand, even the most distant (like a glass of wine)[49]

Here again, representation takes on a material presence. Whereas Handke's quotation of Hölderlin is written in pen, he turns to the graphite of pencil to describe that very same implement on the table before him.

Sorger's experiences in *Slow Homecoming* reflect the importance of the physical practices, specifically wandering and manual transcription, for Handke's poetological project of slowness. Handke writes that Sorger 'preferred drawing to photography, because it was only through drawing that he came to understand the landscape in all its forms'.[50] It is only though the *slow* practice of sketching, demanding close looking and careful tracing in comparison to the instantaneity of photography, that he can know a place.

Handke's practice of daily note-taking might be characterised as slow and voracious at once. He wrote constantly, while travelling by train, sitting on park benches or in cafes and hiking, and used writing utensils (pencils, pens and markers) of numerous colours to inscribe notebooks of different formats and qualities of paper, bound in different materials (linen, leather, vinyl, paper). Formulations of passages that would later appear in print pepper less formed reflections and quotidian scribblings. Though many writers maintain draft books or diaries, what makes Handke's notebooks so unique is that they are part of a clearly defined, sustained artistic project that Handke has pursued continuously for over four decades. Since the beginning, Handke has filled hundreds of notebooks, tens of thousands of pages, with written notes, drawings and ephemera, and he continues to this day.

Handke also learned fundamental 'lessons' from Cézanne about moving slowly, attentively and repeatedly through the same places and carefully observing and recording what he observed. Yet Cézanne's process was important not only for its repetition, but also for its physical and material modes of representation, which Handke saw as the basis of Cézanne's *réalisation*. In describing the 'pictures of pictures', Handke writes:

> Then, taught by the praxis of the canvas itself, I realized that in that historical moment the things, the pines and rocks, on a plain surface but . . . in colors and forms bound to the actual spot ('above the Château Noir'), had joined hands to form a coherent picture writing unique in the history of mankind.
> Thing-image-script in one: that is the miracle . . . Cézanne's rocks and trees . . . were woven into incantations by the painter's dramatic brushstroke [*von dem dramatischen Strich (und dem Gestrichel) der Malerhand*] . . . They were *things*, they were *images*, they were *script*; they were brushstrokes – and all these were in harmony.[51]

It is again notable that Handke's teachers come to lay atop one another. Indeed Handke describes Cezanne's forms with the same term – 'incantation' [*Beschwörung*] – that he used to compare Hölderlin's nature descriptions to Goethe's. Handke sees Cézanne's painted forms not only as images but also as a kind of text or 'picture writing'; in his description of re-reading *Hyperion* after travelling to Aix, Handke similarly describes seeing Hölderlin's words as images: 'I reread Hölderlin's *Hyperion*, finally understood every sentence, and was able to look on its words as images.'[52]

Like Cézanne, whose project entailed not only moving through nature and looking at it carefully, but also a distinctive physical mode of composition, Handke cultivated a practice and poetics of slowness that went far beyond his long walks and note-taking, extending into his broader processes of textual composition. In this period, Handke would begin generating his first typewritten text drafts by rereading, gathering and rewriting notes from his notebooks; these first drafts were then retyped and carefully edited multiple times.[53] And, beginning in the late 1980s, Handke shifted to constructing his prose texts *entirely* by pencil, the slowest medium of textual production in comparison to the typewriter or computer. As Handke writes in *History of the Pencil*, 'What corresponds to me as a tool [*was entspricht mir als Werkzeug*]? Not the camera, also not the typewriter (and not the fountain pen or the paintbrush). But what corresponds to me as a tool? The pencil.'[54]

If Hölderlin, Heidegger and Cézanne were among Handke's teachers, who like Adamas guided him to 'fall silent and listen', Handke, like Hyperion, takes on the role of 'teacher of our people', of a 'poet in a destitute time'. Handke's writing reorients readers to the wondrousness of nature and everyday phenomena, and does so via his particular material practice. The process of compiling and coordinating so many textual passages, recollections and observations from his notebooks produces incredibly complicated, detailed, sometimes even disjointed prose. Composed out of these material pieces, Handke's intricate, vivid descriptions decelerate the modern reader's habituated pace of reading. His texts are slow reads by design. Through the experience of reading – *verstummen und lesen* – readers are encouraged to slow down and observe more carefully their own world, and thus reconnect with nature and become attuned to its beauty.

Notes

1. Höller, *ungewöhnliche Klassik*, p. 9; Huber, *Versuch*, p. 111.
2. Bülow, 'Raum', p. 120.
3. On Handke's project of notetaking, see Bülow, 'Tage'; Pektor, 'Wartet'.
4. For a thorough discussion of this project, see, for example, Carstensen, *Romanisches*.
5. See Carstensen, *tägliche*; Pektor, *Peter*, pp. 80–5.
6. Schlueter, 'Interview', p. 60.
7. Handke, 'The Lesson', pp. 141, 186.
8. To date there is little scholarship that focuses on Handke's Hölderlin reception. For exceptions, see Deibl, 'Und'; Haubenreich, 'Poetry'. Handke's engagement with Hölderlin also extends beyond the timespan I consider. See Deibl, 'Und', p. 161.
9. Handke, 'Rede', p. 74. All unnoted translations are by the author.
10. On Handke's young daughter as a kind of teacher during this period, see Haubenreich, 'Notebooks'.
11. Handke, *Notizbuch 022*, p. 83.
12. Handke, *Notizbuch 019*, p. 59; *Hyperion*, 3.
13. Handke, *Across*, p. 15.
14. Ibid. p. 15.
15. Handke, *Slow*, p. 53.
16. Handke, *Die Geschichte*, p. 96.
17. Ibid. p. 234.
18. Handke, *Repetition*, p. 99; Handke, *Die Wiederholung*, p. 136.
19. On *Lesen*, *Auflesen* and *Ährenlesen* in relation to Handke's Hölderlin reception, see Haubenreich, 'Poetry'.
20. Bülow, 'Raum', p. 120.
21. Heidegger, *Poetry*, p. 156, 145, 149.
22. Ibid. p. 148–9, 154, 218; Heidegger, *Gesamtausgabe* VII, pp. 154, 159.
23. A full transcription is provided in Bülow, 'Raum', pp. 120–2.
24. Handke, *Slow*, pp. 15–16.
25. Bülow, 'Raum', p. 121.
26. Heidegger, *Being*, p. 53.
27. Heidegger, *Poetry*, p. 213.
28. Ibid. pp. 218–19.
29. Handke, *Notizbuch 020*, p. 86; Heidegger, *Poetry*, p. 220.
30. Handke, *Notizbuch 020*, p. 89.
31. Heidegger, *Poetry*, pp. 224, 158–9; Heidegger, *Gesamtausgabe* VII, pp. 153, 163.
32. Bülow, 'Raum', p. 122; Heidegger, *Poetry*, p. 159.
33. Heidegger, *Poetry*, p. 226.
34. Handke, *Slow*, p. 3.
35. Handke, *Notizbuch 021*, p. 46; *Essays and Letters*, p. 110; *FHA* XIX, p. 332.
36. Handke, *Notizbuch 021*, p. 69.
37. Ibid. p. 67.
38. Ibid. p. 37; *Poems and Fragments*, 15 (modified by author).

39. Handke, *Notizbuch 021*, p. 45; *Poems and Fragments*, 205, 397–9.
40. Handke, 'The Lesson', p. 181.
41. Ibid. p. 181.
42. Heidegger, *Poetry*, p. 159, 92 (modified by author); Heidegger, *Gesamtausgabe* VII, p. 272.
43. Handke, *Notizbuch 019*, p. 59; *Hyperion*, 16.
44. Handke, 'Rede', p. 74.
45. Handke, 'Rede', p. 4; Handke, 'The Lesson', p. 176.
46. Handke, *Repetition*, pp. 245–56.
47. Handke, *Notizbuch 019*, p. 59; *Hyperion*, 20.
48. Handke, *Repetition*, pp. 235–6 (modified by author); Handke, *Die Wiederholung*, p. 319–20.
49. Handke, *Notizbuch 021*, p. 89.
50. Handke, *Slow*, pp. 28–9.
51. Handke, 'The Lesson', p. 178 (modified by author); Handke, *Die Lehre*, pp.78–9.
52. Handke, 'The Lesson', p. 186.
53. Pektor, *Peter*, p. 212.
54. Handke, *Die Geschichte*, p. 63.

Bibliography

Bülow, Ulrich von, 'Die Tage, die Bücher, die Stifte: Peter Handkes Journale', in Klaus Kastberger (ed.), *Peter Handke: Freiheit des Schreibens – Ordnung der Schrift* (Vienna: Zsolnay, 2009), pp. 237–66.

Bülow, Ulrich von, 'Raum Zeit Sprache: Peter Handke liest Martin Heidegger', in Anna Kinder (ed.), *Peter Handke: Stationen, Orte, Positionen*, (Berlin and Boston: de Gruyter, 2014), pp. 111–40.

Carstensen, Thorsten, *Romanisches Erzählen: Peter Handke und die epische Tradition* (Göttingen: Wallstein, 2013).

Carstensen, Thorsten (ed.), *Die tägliche Schrift: Peter Handke als Leser* (Bielefeld: Transcript, 2019).

Deibl, Jakob, 'Und: Erzählen und Verwandeln bei Peter Handke: Hölderlin-Metamorphosen in der "Wiederholung"', in Jan-Heiner Tück and Andreas Bieringer (eds), *'Verwandeln allein durch Erzählen': Peter Handke im Spannungsfeld von Theologie und Literaturwissenschaft* (Freiburg: Herder, 2014), pp. 155–73.

Handke, Peter, 'Rede zur Verleihung des Franz-Kafka-Preises', in Peter Handke, *Meine Ortstafeln: Meine Zeittafeln: 1967–2007* (Frankfurt am Main: Suhrkamp, 2007), pp. 73–5.

Handke, Peter, 'The Lesson of Mont Sainte Victoire', in Peter Handke, *Slow Homecoming*, tr. Ralph Manheim (New York: New York Review Books, 2009).

Handke, Peter, *Across*, tr. Ralph Manheim (New York: Collier, 1985).

Handke, Peter, *Die Geschichte des Bleistifts* (Salzburg: Residenz, 1982).

Handke, Peter, *Die Lehre der Sainte-Victoire* (Frankfurt am Main: Suhrkamp, 1980).

Handke, Peter, *Die Wiederholung* (Frankfurt am Main: Suhrkamp, 1986).

Handke, Peter, *Notizbuch 019*. February–April 1979. Deutsches Literaturarchiv, Marbach, HS.2007.0010.00019.

Handke, Peter, *Notizbuch 020*. April–July 1979. Deutsches Literaturarchiv, Marbach, HS.2007.0010.00020.

Handke, Peter, *Notizbuch 021*. July–November 1979. Deutsches Literaturarchiv, Marbach, HS.2007.0010.00021.

Handke, Peter, *Notizbuch 022*. November 1979–October 1980. Deutsches Literaturarchiv, Marbach, HS.2007.0010.00022.

Handke, Peter, *Repetition*, trans. Ralph Manheim (New York: Farrar, Straus & Giroux, 1988).
Handke, Peter, *Slow Homecoming*, trans. Ralph Manheim (New York: New York Review Books, 2009).
Haubenreich, Jacob, 'Notebooks and Children's Drawings, or The Inter-Authorship of Peter Handke's *Kindergeschichte*', *Seminar. A Journal of Germanic Studies*, 54: 1 (2018), pp. 66–103.
Haubenreich, Jacob, 'Poetry, Painting, Patchwork: Peter Handke's Intermedial Writing of *Die Lehre der Sainte-Victoire*', *German Quarterly*, 92: 2 (2019), pp. 187–210.
Heidegger, Martin, *Being and Time*, trans. John Stambaugh (Albany: State University of New York Press, 1996).
Heidegger, Martin, *Gesamtausgabe*, 102 vols (Frankfurt am Main: Klostermann, 1975–).
Heidegger, Martin, *Poetry, Language, Thought*, trans. Albert Hofstadter (New York: HarperCollins, 2001).
Höller, Hans, *Eine ungewöhnliche Klassik nach 1945: Das Werk Peter Handkes* (Frankfurt am Main: Suhrkamp, 2013).
Huber, Alexander, *Versuch einer Ankunft: Peter Handkes Ästhetik der Differenz* (Würzburg: Königshausen & Neumann, 2005).
Locke, Richard, 'Down and Out in Paris', *New York Times*, 22 July 1984, www.nytimes.com/1984/07/22/books/down-and-out-in-paris.html?pagewanted=all (last accessed 3 January 2019).
Pektor, Katharina, '"Wartet nur – ich bin jemand, der sich organisiert", Peter Handkes Projekt des Notierens', in Marcel Atze and Volker Kaukoreit (eds), '*Gedanken reisen, Einfälle kommen an': Die Welt der Notiz* (Vienna: Praesens, 2016), pp. 300–23.
Pektor, Katharina (ed.), *Peter Handke: Dauerausstellung Stift Griffen* (Salzburg and Vienna: Jung & Jung, 2018).
Schlueter, June, 'An Interview with Peter Handke', *Studies in 20th Century Literature*, 4: 1 (1979), pp. 63–73.

Part IV
The Place of Poetry

Chapter 11

Nature, Nurse, *Khôra*: Notes on the Poetics of Hölderlin's Ode 'Man'

Csaba Szabó

The ode 'Man' [*Der Mensch*] is not one of Hölderlin's most frequently discussed poems. Hölderlin sent it to Schiller in June 1798 along with a few other poems, but Schiller decided not to publish it. Of the poems that Hölderlin wrote in the late 1790s, 'Man' remains largely unnoticed. The interpretation that I will offer here aims to show, among other things, not only that the poem anticipates the late Hölderlin's natural philosophy, but also that the inherent tension of the ode as an experiment in language prepares the way for the poetics of the late phase.

The first preliminary version of the poem exists in the form of a draft written around 1797 that bears the title 'The Birthday of Man' [*Der Geburtstag des Menschen*]. This draft was created around the same time as the draft of another dramatic ode *Empedokles* about the Greek philosopher who threw himself into the volcano of Mount Etna. As a result of the historical proximity of these two drafts, Empedocles' death appears close to the birth (or birthday) of man, a birth that the poem presents in a cosmogonic context since it accompanies the birth of the habitable Earth, the self-generation of Earth as the place of life. And while Empedocles jumps into the volcanic crater of Mount Etna, the poem about the birth of man opens with the sudden rise and emergence of an island out of the ocean – that is, with a volcanic activity emerging from the ground that nevertheless remains ungrounded and unfounded.

A sudden eruption – the special insular place ('the loveliest island') that is being prepared for the birth of man is the product of volcanism. This is how the long and fragile sentence that initiates the discourse of the poem unfurls itself with interruptions like deposits of words.[1]

The opening of the draft speaks about the mountain peaks. The peak of a volcanic mountain is a special place that might shatter and explode again just as suddenly as it came into being. The peak, the place, trembles, reduces itself to rubble and spills over – and so it is born again.[2] This way of presenting the question of the *place* as the place of trembling and shaking should call our attention to a possible wide-reaching intertextual reference to Plato's *Timaeus*. For *khôra*, which is the name of the place of space in the *Timaeus* and functions there as a 'third type' of thing or a 'third genus' [*triton genos*] in addition to being and becoming, is shaken and, in turn, shakes everything that it receives.[3] This is what we read in a passage of the *Timaeus* where *khôra* is called the 'wetnurse of becoming':

> There are being, space, and becoming, three distinct things that existed before the heavens came to be. Now as the *wetnurse* of becoming turns *watery and fiery* and receives the character of earth and air, and as it acquires all the properties that come with these characters, it takes on a variety of visible aspects, but because it is filled with powers that are *neither similar nor evenly balanced*, no part of it is in balance. It *sways irregularly in every direction* as it is *shaken* by those things, and being set in motion it in turns shakes them.[4]

In addition to the shaking of *khôra*, however, it is above all the characterisation of the receiving place as the 'wetnurse of becoming' that suggests that Hölderlin's ode makes reference to the *Timaeus*. Furthermore, it is not only the re-emergence in the poem of the Platonic images and motifs dealing with *khôra* that indicates that Hölderlin's poem critically engages the *Timaeus* as a precursor of the speech attempted in it, but also the poem's cosmogonic-cosmological content as well as its concurrent problematisation of myth as a form of discourse and its problematisation of the relationship between myth and logos. I will highlight these connections at the relevant places in the following discussion.[5]

The beginning of the poem remains a fragment of a charming mythical cosmogony that leads us up to the appearance of the human being:

> Kaum sproßten aus den Wassern, o Erde, dir
>   Der jungen Berge Gipfel und dufteten
>   Lustathmend, immergrüner Haine
>   Voll, in des Oceans grauer Wildniß
>
> Die ersten holden Inseln; und freudig sah
>   Des Sonnengottes Auge die Neulinge
>   Die Pflanzen, seiner ewgen Jugend
>   Lächelnde Kinder, aus dir geboren.
>
> Da auf der Inseln schönster, wo immerhin
>   Den Hain in zarter Ruhe die Luft umfloß,
>   Lag unter Trauben einst, nach lauer
>   Nacht, in der dämmernden Morgenstunde

Geboren, Mutter Erde! dein schönstes Kind; –
    Und auf zum Vater Helios sieht bekannt
        Der Knab', und wacht und wählt die süßen
            Beere versuchend, die heil'ge Rebe

Zur Amme sich; und bald ist er groß; ihn scheun
    Die Thiere, denn ein anderer ist, wie sie
        Der Mensch; nicht dir und nicht dem Vater
            Gleicht er, denn kühn ist in ihm und einzig

Des Vaters hohe Seele mit deiner Lust,
    O Erd'! und deiner Trauer von je vereint;
        Der Göttermutter, der Natur, der
            Allesumfassenden möcht' er gleichen!

(*FHA* V, 448–9)

When scarcely from the waters, O Earth, for you
    Young mountain peaks had sprouted and, breathing joy,
        The first delightful islands, full of
            Evergreen copses, gave out their fragrance

Amid the sea's grey desert; and glad of them
    The Sun-God's eye looked down at the newly raised,
        The plants, the smiling children of his
            Weariless youth, and of you, their mother –

Then on the loveliest island where delicate
    And calm the air flowed ceaselessly round the copse,
        One morning, born in early half-light
            After a temperate night, and bedded

Beneath the clustered grapes, lay your loveliest child; –
    And up to Father Helios now, the boy
        Turns eyes that know him, wakes and, tasting
            Berries for sweetness, as nurse he chooses

The holy vine; and soon is grown up. He's shunned
    By animals, for different from them is Man.
        Not you, his mother, nor his father
            Does he resemble, for in him, boldly

Uniquely blended, live both his father's soul
    And, Earth, your joy, your sadness, inveterate;
        He longs to be like her, like Nature,
            Mother of gods and the all-embracing!

(*Poems and Fragments*, 61)

Everything comes into being almost at the same time: immediately after the emergence of the peaks of the island mountains from the sea, they were covered with rich 'evergreen copses' [*immergrüner Haine*] and barely after this emergence took place, man lay there as the teleological peak of this becoming. We will have to return to the question of the temporality of this becoming.

What is the place of the birth of man? And what is it like? Where is the human being found and how is he exposed there? Since man appears to be abandoned on a volcanic crater, we should remember that *krater* is the ancient Greek name for a mixing bowl that also appears in the *Timaeus* as the Demiurge's mixing bowl used at the creation of the human being (and, thus, indirectly it is also another image for *khôra*).[6] How can we think the insular, volcanic place of the exposure of man who was born this way? These questions emerge from the beginning of the poem, since it is not so much the day of man's birth but its place that is under discussion in the text, whose second half explicitly circumscribes the singular placelessness of the human being.

The structure of the ode could initially be outlined in the following way: the twelve stanzas of the poem form two equal halves. Strictly speaking, and in spite of the period at the end of the second stanza, a single sentence runs, in leaps, until the exact middle of the poem as it leads us from the birth of the birthplace of man to his grown-up, completed, fully upright existence. While the mythical narrative of the first half presents the image of happiness in a naive tone, the second half describes in a rather serious manner the foolish acts of man, who now seems to be anything but a happy creature. It is, then, all the more surprising and apparently unfounded (and, in its groundlessness, thus resembling the opening scene of the poem) when, in the last stanza, a rhetorical question emerges. The final six stanzas of the poem read:

> Ach! darum treibt ihn, Erde! vom Herzen dir
>   Sein Übermuth, und deine Geschenke sind
>   Umsonst und deine zarten Bande;
>   Sucht er ein Besseres doch, der Wilde!
>
> Von seines Ufers duftender Wiese muß
>   Ins blüthenlose Wasser hinaus der Mensch,
>   Und glänzt auch, wie die Sternenacht, von
>   Goldenen Früchten sein Hain, doch gräbt er
>
> Sich Höhlen in den Bergen und späht im Schacht
>   Von seines Vaters heiterem Lichte fern,
>   Dem Sonnengott auch ungetreu, der
>   Knechte nicht liebt und der Sorge spottet.
>
> Denn freier athmen Vögel des Walds, wenn schon
>   Des Menschen Brust sich herrlicher hebt, und der
>   Die dunkle Zukunft sieht, er muß auch
>   Sehen den Tod und allein ihn fürchten.
>
> Und Waffen wider alle, die athmen, trägt
>   In ewigbangem Stolze der Mensch; im Zwist
>   Verzehrt er sich und seines Friedens
>   Blume, die zärtliche, blüht nicht lange.

> Ist er von allen Lebensgenossen nicht
>   Der seeligste? Doch tiefer und reißender
>   Ergreift das Schiksaal, allausgleichend,
>   Auch die entzündbare Brust dem Starken.
>
> (FHA V, 449)

> O that is why his arrogance drives him far
>   From your safe-keeping, Earth, and in vain are all
>   Your gifts and all your gentle fetters –
>   Little to him who wants more, the wild one!
>
> Beyond his fragrant river-side meadows, out
>   Into the flowerless waters is Man impelled
>   And though with golden fruit his orchard
>   Gleams like the star-jewelled night, yet caves for
>
> Himself he digs in mountains and scans the shaft,
>   Remote from his great father's untroubled light,
>   Disloyal also to the Sun-God,
>   Scorner of cares never fond of drudges,
>
> For woodland birds more freely draw breath, and though
>   Man's breast more grandly, proudly expands, his gaze
>   Can penetrate the future's darkness
>   Death he sees too and alone must fear it.
>
> And arms against all creatures that live and stir
>   In pride for ever anxious he bears; consumes
>   Himself in discord; and not long the
>   Delicate bloom of his peace contents him.
>
> Is man not blessed, not blissful compared to all
>   His fellow creatures? Yet with a tighter hold,
>   More deeply Fate, all levelling, grips the
>   Strong one's inflammable heart to wrench it.
>
> (Poems and Fragments, 63)

'Is Man not blessed, not blissful compared to all / His fellow creatures?' [*Ist er von allen Lebensgenossen nicht / Der seeligste?*]. The silent answer that corresponds to the rhetorical question – which, in order to counterbalance the superlative blessedness of mankind, is given in a sentence about the 'all-levelling' [*allausgleichend*] Fate that takes hold of man and tears him apart – remains strangely uneven. Although Fate is described here as 'all-levelling', the promised equilibrium remains questionable, since it not so much 'equals out' but rather ruins the highest state of bliss – and because it is presented to us in the form of an indefinite comparison: 'with a tighter hold, / More deeply' [*tiefer und reissender*]. But it is not specified here in comparison to what the comparative forms should be understood. Thus, contrary to the poem's rhetoric here, the two sentences, as two halves of the last stanza do not form an even balance as they break up and simply interrupt the speech of the poem. 'Fate' (*Schicksaal*) remains here a concept that functions more like a placeholder within a frame which, nevertheless, intervenes in an open place, namely in man's 'inflammable heart' [*entzündbare Brust*]. But this grasping intervention that reaches into the 'inflammable heart' leads us back to the beginning of the poem since, as a place, the 'inflammable heart' recalls the opening volcanic activity, the birth of the birthplace of man.[7]

The last stanza not only repeats the division of the poem into two halves but its imbalance also raises questions that seem to shake the whole poem like subterranean shocks. The poem does not answer the question of the human being as its title seems to promise, but rather allows questions to emerge in that it itself quite unexpectedly poses an arrogant and faltering question whose status wavers between being a genuine question and a rhetorical question: 'Is Man not blessed, not blissful compared to all / His fellow creatures?' [*Ist er von allen Lebensgenossen nicht / Der seeligste?*]. The structurally implied absence of an answer to the rhetorical question draws attention to the absence of language in man as he is presented in the poem and itself leads to the question: Who poses this one question? Who is speaking in this speech, in this poem? Is this even a poem? Is it a blessed, that is a happy and felicitous speech? A successful, effective poem? Is it possible to determine a criterion for its success based on the poem itself? Or is it at best half-successful because, although it is about the human being, it fails to consider man as a speaking living organism? Is this a failure? In any case, or at least so it seems on second glance, the question of human language does not belong to the subject matter of the poem – even if the discussion of the desire to resemble nature, which can be thought only as a linguistically constituted wish, implies that the human being is a speaking, living creature.

'He longs to be like her, like Nature, / Mother of gods and the all-embracing! / O . . .' [*der Natur, der / Allesumfassenden möcht' er gleichen! / Ach!*] – this is how an 'Ach!' erupts in the middle of the poem like a caesura. The 'Ach!' is a special moment of speech. It can belong both to the order of representation as well as to that of the represented. It can be read as a first act, as an interruptive beginning of a linguistic attempt to resemble nature. But this 'Ach!' can also belong to the order of representation, since it can be the expression of the painful astonishment of the speaker over man's arrogant desire to be like nature. The same way that the 'Ach!' staggers on the border between language and the absence of language, the order of representation and the order of the represented meet in it in the form of a caesura. As an interrupting interjection, the 'Ach!' in the middle of the speech articulates the speaker's participation in what his speech represents.[8] Either way, the 'Ach!' participates in the becoming of man.[9] But, in that case, the speech of the poem does not merely belong to this becoming, since it construes itself as the place where this becoming begins differently and begins to become something other. But how? Is it possible to read the poem as a later continuation of the initial breaking and outbreak of the 'Ach!' As a becoming-other of that beginning – as another interjection that begins differently? Is it the beginning of another language that interrupts the desire to resemble nature since it tries to correspond to it in a way that is other than speechless?

'Ach!': an incipient, disruptive attempt at language as the caesura of the poem 'Man' – and of man himself who, then, becomes unfaithful to all and speechless. The 'Ach!' divides the language of the poem into two halves, since two different forms of discourse determine the two parts of the poem: in the first part, the ostentatious fictionality of the mythical representation with a cosmogonic beginning; in the second half, a serious discourse that works with anthropological knowledge and philosophical concepts. We need to point out briefly here that in the eighteenth century the fictionality of all cosmologies was a frequently discussed topic and the relationship between myth and logos was a central question of Plato's philosophy.[10] In his essay on the *khôra* of the *Timaeus*, Jacques Derrida provided a new interpretation of this question but he did so by citing Hegel, who opposed myth and philosophical logos as unserious and serious forms of discourse respectively.[11] Furthermore, the question of the relationship between myth and logos and a third form of discourse that corresponds to the third genus of *khôra* once again points to the fact that in the background of Hölderlin's poem we might suspect an intensive engagement with Plato's *Timaeus*.[12]

Thus the simple, self-evident question that emerges here is the following: how does this poem as a form of human speech relate to the essence of the human being that it itself addresses as one of its subject matters? And how does it relate to the fact that the human being depicted in its second half appears not to be co-constituted by language? To what extent and in what way does the poem interpret itself as human speech? According to the poem, what would the specificity or the essence of human speech be?

The most pressing question, however, that takes precedence over all the others is this: which human being does the poem talk about? Man is determined by his origins. The birth of man occurs in the movement of and as the peak of a cosmogony and remains a sprouting, vegetable emergence. We should also note here that the poem that represents this cosmogonic becoming stages itself at its beginning as a similar sprouting and a shooting forth, as a volcanically erupting deposit of words Thus, the poem seems to suggest that it came into being in the same way as the beings depicted in it. The sprouting is not so much a sudden breaking forth from the ground as the groundless breaking up of the ground itself.[13]

The groundlessness of becoming is repeated and is continued in the first gestures of the newly born, suddenly present human being: this is the boy's first experiment – 'tasting / berries for sweetness'. In this first trial, he does not simply choose something as nourishment but chooses the vine for a specific purpose, namely as his nurse. The vine becomes the nurse of the abandoned boy. Since what is at stake here is evidently the place where the vine is chosen to be the nurse, and indeed the nurse of a becoming, it is again obvious – especially in the context of a playful cosmological sketch – that we should read the discussion of the nurse (of becoming) as a quote from Plato's *Timaeus*, where *khôra* is called among other things 'the wet-nurse of becoming'.[14] As a receptacle, *khôra* must remain shapeless herself in order to be able to receive the shapes that are themselves in the process of becoming. But *khôra* is not like any of the forms that it receives.[15]

What happens in the choice of the vine as the nurse of becoming is no less difficult to think than Plato's *khôra*. After all, man himself seems to resemble *khôra* in that he resembles no one at all, as the fifth stanza puts it, but also because he is shaken by all that he receives and, therefore, moves without rest, as the second half of the poem explains. So, in the end, for the surprisingly *khôra*-like constitution of man, the 'inflammable heart' stands as a place that receives what is different and unlike anything else and is, therefore, shaken in order to find balance and equilibrium, just like *khôra* in Plato.[16] The trembling question that seeks to grasp the essence of man must break forth from his breast: 'Is Man not blessed, not blissful compared to all / His fellow creatures?' [*Ist er von allen Lebensgenossen nicht / Der seeligste?*]. As is the case with Hölderlin's superlatives in general, this one ('der seeligste', which means the most blessed and the most blissful) is not simply the highest degree of a straight escalation but an expression of a peculiar movement that is neither fixed nor immobilised by its articulation. As the most blessed being, man is so only when he becomes aware of the misfortune of his own blessedness. The expression 'most blessed' is emblematic for this superlative movement that transcends itself, since the word 'blessed' always already carries with it a superlative meaning. Among other things, it means 'partaking of eternal salvation', 'highly fortunate', and 'overjoyed'.[17] Thus the expression 'the most blessed' is a superlative of the superlative that brings to language what is unbearable in the inner opposition of the superlative movement. The blessed one who raises himself to the level of the most blessed asserts his own bliss and at the same time denies it. For, if he is to be more blessed than the blessed, he is not yet or no longer blessed. 'Is Man not blessed, not blissful compared to all / His fellow creatures?' But there lies something in the middle of the rhetorical question whereby this arrogant question, instead of being an unsurpassable expression of the highest bliss, turns into an expression of misfortune: the middle of the question calls man one of all his 'fellow creatures'. What the rare compound word *Lebensgenosse* ['life-companion'] says in this sentence is nothing other than that the superlative tendency of the 'most blessed' must bring about its own failure. For, if bliss consists of being one among all the 'fellow creatures', then man's self-elevation to the level of the 'most blessed' must imply the renunciation of the communion with all 'fellow creatures' which, therefore, leads to the destruction of his happiness. The preceding stanza discusses precisely the unfaithful character of man with regard to all of his fellow-creatures: 'And arms against all creatures that live and stir / [. . .] he bears'. If, then, the rhetorical question that speaks of all his fellow creatures suddenly emerges without a ground (like a breathing weapon turned against itself), as a question it brings to language not so much man's contradictory character that leads to his characterlessness but rather its grounding reason: that man is not like himself. As an 'all-levelling' [*allausgleichend*] force, Fate is the equaliser of all by virtue of the misfortune that it metes out and the 'context of guilt' [*Schuldzusammenhang*] that it introduces – in the Greek sense, as Benjamin understood it following Hölderlin.[18] (The poem remains both guilty and indebted, in keeping with dual meaning of *Schuld*, inasmuch as it owes itself the idea of Fate since it does not represent man as a speaking living being. The speech of the poem, inasmuch as it seeks to totalise itself, logically concludes with the thought of Fate and thus, so to speak, closes off the order of the represented in misfortune.) Thus, by seeking to provide man with a balance and self-identity exclusively through an inflamed heart, guilt and misfortune, Fate once again exposes man's instability and lack of self-equality. Fate targets what is innocent in man: the inflammable heart – that is, his inner exposure as a constitutive openness. The inflammable heart, this weakness of the 'strong' that determines and opens up man to an inwardly exposed place (as a place of an ungraspable susceptibility to be grasped), resembles the place that at the beginning of the poem volcanically prepares the place for the birth of man. But this place is equal to itself only in that it breaks up and bursts apart, that is in that it does not remain the same: the 'inflammable heart' and, thus, man are just like this place.

But if we want to further examine the way the poem explores the essence of man as its subject matter, we must note that it is not only the theme of the poem that suggests here that we should also take into consideration Kant's essay on the 'Conjectures on the Beginning of Human History'.[19] Between Kant's essay and Hölderlin's poem there are – in spite of all the apparent conceptual differences – special textual correspondences which, however, need to be examined more closely in order to reveal the differences between Hölderlin's ideas in this poem and Kant's philosophy of history and nature. Kant's essay presents itself as a philosophical interpretation of the third chapter of Genesis, the story of the first human couple in the Garden of Eden and the story of the Fall. Kant interprets the eating of the fruit of the tree in the garden as a consequence of the 'first stirring of reason' [*ersten Regung der Vernunft*] that 'sought to extend the knowledge of foodstuffs beyond the bounds of instinct'.[20] On several occasions, he calls the eating of the fruit a 'first experiment' [*erster Versuch*] that goes against instinct, which for Kant is '[the] voice of God'.[21] In eating the fruit, man conducts his 'first experiment in free choice'[22] despite the objection of the voice of nature. A few lines earlier, however, Kant did explain that while Nature 'did not recommend' this first experiment, it also 'did not contradict it'.[23]

Strangely enough, Kant expresses himself in a contradictory manner about the possible contradiction in the relationship between nature and man in the very beginning, at the time of his first experiment. In any case, this first trial leads to something contrary to nature, because with the help of the 'imagination' reason is capable of 'inventing' desires that go against 'the natural impulse'.[24] Thus 'a whole host of superfluous or even unnatural inclinations' appear in man, and Kant calls this 'luxuriousness' [*Üppigkeit*].[25] In short, in this interpretation the eating of the forbidden fruit appears as the event in which man 'abandon[ed] his natural impulses' and became unfaithful to nature.[26] The result of this first experiment, however, is that man 'became conscious of his reason as a faculty' that can move beyond the limits set by nature. Although the first attempt 'probably did not turn out as expected', it was 'nevertheless enough to open man's eyes' as 'he discovered in himself an ability to choose his own life'.[27] Thus, the performance of the first act of free choice is at the same time the discovery of free choice as a free choice.

But what motivates man to contradict nature and to become unfaithful to it? Nothing other than the comparison of the food preferred by instinct 'with anything which a sense other than that to which his instinct was tied [. . .] represented as similar in character'.[28] The similarity of possible nourishments was the invitation for the first attempt to choose not what was given by nature for man but something similar to it. After the fact, from the perspective of possible harm, this free choice reveals itself to be an experiment in defiance, which man has made 'despite' nature's objection.[29] The experience of freedom is, therefore, immediately followed by 'anxiety and fear'. In other words, 'His defiance becomes fear' [*Sein Trotz wird Angst*] – as it is stated in a preliminary version of Hölderlin's poem (*FHA* IV, 71). In addition, the 'luxuriousness' [*Üppigkeit*] of man, which is mentioned by Kant only as a late consequence of the first experiment, also appears in the first draft of Hölderlin's poem, where he calls the barely born human being (who lies there almost like a fallen fruit) the 'most luxurious fruit' [*üppigste Frucht*] (*FHA* IV, 55). Furthermore, in the completed version of the poem, on the day of his birth the boy tastes a quite luxurious fruit himself, the sweet berries.

At this exact moment, Hölderlin's poem seems to quote Kant's words about the first experiment in 'free choice': 'tasting / Berries for sweetness, as nurse he chooses // The holy vine' [*wählt die süßen / Beere versuchend, die heil'ge Rebe // Zur Amme sich*]. What counts here, however, is not merely the interplay of the experiment in tasting (*Versuch*) and the choice. The scene actually reads like a childish Greek rewriting of the story of the fall from Genesis: the first man on an island as beautiful as paradise tastes a fruit and this act 'influenced his way of life decisively'.[30] But neither in Kant nor in Hölderlin does this first experiment appear as a fall into sin. Both are concerned with the presumed beginnings of human history. In both, a first experiment in tasting initiates man's actual becoming as an ambiguous process of development, 'from the guardianship of nature to the state of freedom', as Kant puts it.[31]

For Kant, the first experiment is a free act – which means that it is free from natural instinct. This experiment manifests itself as a choice only in the process of its performance. It does not take what nature would suggest but – contrary to nature – something similar that is still an unknown other taken in another way: it is tried and tasted. As such, it is taken only partially and, therefore, remains open to the possibility of taking something other or to try it in another way. What remains decisive here is that the eruption into the open of free choice occurs only in the execution of the first experiment initiated by the comparison, and that the tasted 'state of freedom' as freedom from nature opens up free choice, that is the 'abyss' of the freedom for an 'infinite range' of possible choices.[32] The first attempt to taste something similar as nourishment turns into a free choice and, at the same time, necessarily into the choice of free choice itself.

In spite of its differences from the Kantian conception of natural teleology, Hölderlin's account also shows a mutating duplication of choice in man's decisive first experiment. Hölderlin's poem presents this experiment as the actual becoming-human of man, and stages it in such a way that it involves a choice. The boy 'tasting / Berries for sweetness, as nurse he chooses // The holy vine'. This image, which is as dense as it is decisive, could be understood in the following way: the boy tears the berries from the vine, which now appears as a giving hand or a presenting arm. But by grabbing the vine this way, the boy entwines himself like the vine as he coils up on it 'and soon is grown up'. The boy grabs the vine with his hand or with his hands, or (also) with his mouth, as if he were following with this gesture, as Kant says, the example of animals that feed themselves this way. And as he grabs the vine, he so to speak bends the space that receives him. But in this gripping and bending of the vine, space itself comes into motion: under the moving leaves of the grasped vine, the light of the sky and the air twinkle differently, moving more quickly and more movingly. Through the vine, the perspective of wide, cosmic relationships opens up.[33]

The boy in the process of his becoming does not choose (only) the sweet berries but (also) the vine, that is not only the food that he tastes but also what gives and grants this food to him. The choice of the vine as the nurse here does not amount to a defiant denial of nature. The basis of the choice is that the receptacle itself (the vine) is also received by what it receives (the boy), and this mutual reception is experienced as something 'sweet'. The choice corresponds to the giving, granting place that, in an act of hospitality, blesses the boy with sweet berries. This blessing is the felicity or extreme joy of correspondence. The tasting of the berries and the simultaneous choice of the vine as nurse is, at the same time, a self-encounter by the being in the process of becoming human that opens itself to a sprouting, springing becoming. What emerges in this process is an approximation of the sprouting vegetable origins of the cosmos.[34]

Thus, unlike for Kant, for Hölderlin the choice is not the extended knowledge of nourishment and, at the same time, the self-nourishment of emerging reason, but a determination, an act of nomination as nurse, an act of positing. That which in the order of representation is a violent positing of a metaphor (the vine as the wetnurse of man) corresponds in the order of the represented to a violent name. The boy nibbling on the berries also takes what receives him and his first experiment – he takes the vine as a place by choosing it to be the nurse. This taking alone corresponds to the reception, and the naming of the nurse springs from the taking, and thus language emerges as a place that corresponds to space as the nurse of becoming.

Does the decisive act of this scene, in the simultaneity of the tasting and the choice, give poetic expression to the secret of the birth of language as an onomatopoetic origin?[35] Eating and speaking seem to blend into each other here since the choice of the vine as the nurse is accompanied in the same moment by the act of naming, whereby the word 'nurse' (*Amme*) might appear to be a first babble.

The scene, however, seems to speak less about the origins of language than about the origin of the impulse to imitate that Walter Benjamin called the 'mimetic faculty'. The boy, still something like a nursing child, is not yet the man 'fully developed' as he is in Kant.[36] But after choosing the vine as the nurse, he will soon grow up. And the suddenly grown-up man is, then, portrayed as someone who has to wrestle with his mimetic faculty since he does not resemble his father, nor his mother, nor the animals; he is other than all the others; and so, as a being that is unlike the others, he is driven by the desire to be like all-embracing nature:

> [. . .] and soon is grown up. He's shunned
>   By animals, for different from them is Man.
>   Not you, his mother, nor his father
>   Does he resemble, for in him, boldly
>
> Uniquely blended, live both his father's soul
>   And, Earth, your joy, your sadness, inveterate;
>   He longs to be like her, like Nature,
>   Mother of gods and the all-embracing!

Man's impulse for imitation, his mimetic faculty, seems to be grounded in his being un-like the others, which is the unequal nature of man. To be like all-embracing nature – is that not an impossible wish? Or can this wish be fulfilled somehow? But how? And why does the impulse for imitation spring forth as such an arrogant desire? Or would resembling nature be less the highest fulfilment of the instinct for imitation than its overcoming or transformation – and, thus, the transformation of humanity? The riddle of all these questions seems to be poetically condensed in the nurse scene.

The poem states the reason why man is neither like his parents nor like others: because the essence of the parents is 'boldly' and 'uniquely' united in him. The instinct for imitation or the mimetic faculty of man, therefore, springs forth from this bold and uniquely unifying mixture of human essence that renders all its elements unlike each other. At the same time, to the extent that man does not resemble his cosmic parents, he needs a nurse. On the one hand, the choice of the vine as the nurse seems to be the first consequence of man's unlike nature. On the other hand, the choice of the nurse must already be determined by an instinct for imitation, by the mimetic faculty.

So, what is the relationship between man's need for a nurse and his mimetic faculty? Both testify to the same tendency, the same 'compulsion' of human existence to 'become similar and behave mimetically', as Benjamin put it in his essay 'On the Mimetic Faculty'.[37] If, following Benjamin, we understand the mimetic faculty as an original 'life-determining force', then it is conceivable that a need for a nurse always resonates within imitation – and, indeed, as a need for a nurse of becoming, of development, in which man learns to behave, originally on a cosmic scale.[38] It is, thus, conceivable that what man imitates becomes in a way the wetnurse of his becoming. And vice versa: man always has a mimetic relationship with what he chooses to be his nurse. So, the question emerges: when man chooses the vine as his nurse, in what kind of a mimetic relationship does he stand in relation to the vine? How does his mimetic faculty develop and train itself in relationship to the vine as nurse? And if this is man's first mimetic relationship, how and why does he desire to be like nature? Why does he wish to imitate the all-embracing? The first mimetic relationship with the vine as nurse must be closely connected with this wish.

By the same token, we should also ask how and why the bliss of choosing the vine for a nurse turns into a misfortune that unfolds in the *explicit* infidelity to the parents? The second half of the poem presents in a specific light man's clearly unsuccessful attempt to fulfil his desire to be like nature: man strives for an omnipresence that controls everything. This attempt could be called a misunderstanding of the wish or an aberration of the mimetic faculty, since in its poetic presentation nothing is more conspicuous than the fact that man remains speechless.[39] Since the attempt to resemble nature is evidently based on a specific understanding of space and language, the attempt is portrayed as an errant wandering about in space ('Into the flowerless water is Man impelled' and he 'digs in mountains') during which man carries 'arms against all creatures' instead of naming and addressing them. If the desire to resemble all-embracing nature is in fact the inheritance of man, then so is the possibility of misunderstanding this desire, the possibility that man might not be able to understand his own desire and, therefore, himself. This is why a preliminary version of the poem says that 'Man is incomprehensible (for himself)' [*es ist unbegreiflich (ist sich) der Mensch*] (*FHA* IV, 59).

The fact that the poem, then, nevertheless does speak in wonder of the bliss of man suggests – not least as a question – that man might be able to conform differently to his mimetic desire to be like nature. To formulate the matter as a thesis, we could propose the following: in contrast to the speechlessness of man depicted in the second half of the poem, this other way of responding to the desire would be nothing other than the speech of this poem as an experiment in language. This thesis, however, says that the poem manages to be like all-embracing nature. The question of how the poem manages to do this leads to another thesis that formulates the following assumption: in contrast to any conception of art as the imitation of nature, poetic speech can be experienced as something resembling nature when both are thought of as *khôra* according to Plato's definition in the *Timaeus* – as a receptacle or the nurse of becoming.

At this point, we must return to the question: in what kind of a mimetic relationship does man in his becoming stand with regard to the vine? For, the choice of the vine as the nurse [*Amme*] remains baffling. It is possible that from the infant's point of view there might be a sensible similarity between the berries and the maternal breast (as well as between the breast, *mamma*, and a volcanic mountain), and we might even see a similarity between the hanging grape of the wine and the udder of mammals.⁴⁰ But there is something else at work here that is more significant than the correspondence of these primary shapes, something that is also suggested by the paratextual appearance of the word *Euter* ('udder') as an anagram of *Treue* ('faithfulness'), that is by the linguistic constitution of events in the same place. This is even more evident in the case of the relationship between the tasted and the chosen: *Beere* ('berry') and *Rebe* ('vine') are anagrams of each other, and they are both anagrams of *Erbe* ('heritage') – the legacy that remains incomprehensible here and, as such, remain only its place as the place of the word, as a kind of crater: a mixing bowl for its elements.

Although there is no sensible similarity between man and the grapevine, it is conceivable that there is a nonsensuous similarity between them. At the moment when the boy tastes the sweet berry as he grabs the vine, he perceives his nonsensuous resemblance to the vine and, thus, behaves in a mimetic manner in relation to it. But what could this nonsensuous resemblance be? The easiest way to formulate an answer to this question might be to recall the cosmogonic context that the first stanzas invoke right up to this point. Both the human being and the vine are represented as children of earth and sky, who were created in barely different places and can be considered cosmogonically to be almost simultaneous: the one was created barely earlier than the other. But they are neither directly related nor sensuously similar to each other. They are similar to each other only in a nonsensuous way: in the cosmological constellation of their respective births.

This 'barely' [*kaum*], the first word of this poetic discourse, is the word for the difference within the same of the cosmological context, that is the word for what the mimetic relationship to something that is similar in a nonsensuous manner makes possible and, in fact, what brings about the compulsion to become similar and to behave in a mimetic manner in relation to what is similar in this nonsensuous way. The word *kaum*, the poem's opening word of origin, which, according to its etymology, bears witness to the emergence of language as lamenting and calling, stands in its place as an emblem of the genesis of language: the consonants *k* and *m*, an unvoiced velar plosive and a voiced bilabial (produced at the two boundaries of the oral cavity, the mouth-place of phonetic articulation), between which an *au*, an extended diphthong, arises. Then the second word, *sproßten* ('sprouted'), appears as another, different emblem for the emergence of 'words, like flowers'.⁴¹ Thus these first words do not only emblematise in their primary positions the origins of language, since they also signify language as the place and, with Benjamin's word, as the 'archive of nonsensuous similarity'.⁴² What counts here, therefore, is not the possible onomatopoetic character of the words 'barely' and 'sprouting', nor the fact that language and the word can be called 'places' in a metaphorical sense, but the nonsensuous resemblance of language and the word to the *khôra*, the place as the nurse of becoming. This first mimesis of language itself, the fact that it imitates something nonsensuous, namely the *khôra* – only this allows it to become a place, an archive of nonsensuous similarities. Thus language is the nurse of its own becoming.

But the boy's mimetic activity, which allows him to become similar to the vine in a nonsensuous way, appears in what happens immediately after the choice is made: 'and soon [he] is grown up'. This change underscores another aspect of the imitated nonsensuous resemblance. He is soon grown up not only because the berries of the vine provide him sufficient sustenance, but because he imitates a plant and, to be more precise, imitates in the plant its cosmic mode of becoming. The vine is a sprout – it sprouts, it suddenly shoots forth and grows, as it reaches into space and provides a place. This 'soon' repeats in a mimetic fashion the 'barely' of the cosmic genesis: 'scarcely [*kaum*] from the waters [...] young mountain peaks had sprouted', and soon, almost at the same time, the plants and the human being appeared. The sprout of the vine has been barely chosen as the nurse, and soon, almost simultaneously, the human being is grown up. Hölderlin's poetic description of this suddenness as the temporality of cosmic creation is closely related to Benjamin's understanding of the rapidity of reading as a condition of possibility or, more precisely, as the participation of the mind in the temporal movement 'through which, like a flash, similarity appears'.[43] Benjamin defines this rapidity as the critical moment in which nonsensuous similarity can be perceived. The critical instant of perception, even in the speed of reading, corresponds to the temporality of the cosmogonic 'barely'.[44] In this case, however, man would imitate not simply something sensibly perceptible produced by nature but nature's mode of production itself. To the extent that language can be the mimesis of *khôra* as the nurse of becoming, in the act of reading the human being can imitate nature and the origin of the cosmos itself.

The instant of becoming human through the mimetic choice of the vine is indeed the origin of the desire to be like nature but not its fulfilment, for, as Benjamin puts it, the moment 'flits past'.[45] How is it possible to take part of such an instant? In other words, how would another, linguistic fulfilment of the desire to be like nature possible – a fulfilment that would not be part of the deadly, breathless tendency toward totalisation that bears 'arms against all creatures that breathe'? Such a participation as another actualisation of the mimetic faculty remains possible if there is a nurse of becoming who grants a place for this becoming-similar (that every becoming is) by receiving different and unequal things – like Plato's *khôra*, which itself must remain formless. This place is language itself that, as a place of cosmogonic mixing, grants the possibility of another becoming-similar.

For Kant, the human being's first experiment constitutes the 'first stirring of reason' that perceives sensuous similarities. In Hölderlin's poem, the boy's gesture as man's first experiment is the first stirring of the mimetic faculty. And, as such, it is an act of reading. It is a reading, a first gathering of the grapes in the sense of a *Weinlese* (the harvest of grapes) whereby the two layers of reading – the *Lese* or the gathering (of the berries) and the selection or choice (of the vine) – blend into each other.[46] The rapidity with which the two layers of reading mix with each other creates a mobile, barely perceptible place: the human being whose becoming is tied to a specific place (*Auslese der süßen Beere* as the selection of sweet berries and a cultivation of the vine) but, at the same time, remains an errant, self-extracting and self-transplanting being (*Lese der Rebe selbst* as a tearing out, a picking, or grafting of the vine itself in the form of a transplantation and creation of colonies). This 'bold' and 'unique' mixture unfolds in Hölderlin's later poetry.

Translated by Roland Végső

Notes

1. See also, Celan, *Die Gedichte*, p. 180.
2. Heidegger recalls the original meaning of the word *Ort* (place) in the following passage: 'Originally the word "site" suggests a place in which everything comes together, is concentrated' [*Ursprünglich bedeutet der Name «Ort» die Spitze des Speers. In ihr läuft alles zusammen*]. Heidegger, 'Language in the Poem', p. 159. Although the currently available English translation makes this reference impossible to perceive, Heidegger speaks of the 'place' here as a 'peak' in the sense of the 'point of a spear'.
3. Plato, *Timaeus*, p. 41 (52a). See also, Derrida, '*Khôra*', p. 89.
4. Plato, *Timaeus*, p. 42 (52e–53a), emphasis added.
5. The significance of *Timaeus* for Hölderlin's poetry and thinking has already been recognised by a number of critics: Nägele, *Text, Geschichte und Subjektivität in Hölderlins Dichtung*, p. 230; Franz, 'Platons frommer Garten'; St. Lampenscherf, '"Heiliger Plato, vergieb . . ."'; Kocziszky, *Mythenfiguren in Hölderlins Spätwerk*, pp. 103–4; Bennholdt-Thomsen and Guzzoni, *Analecta Hölderliana*, p. 96; Bennholdt-Thomsen and Guzzoni: *Marginalien zu Hölderlins Werk*, p. 124; Luhnen, 'Hölderlins hymnisches Fragment "An die Madonna" als mythopoetisches Experiment', p. 268. However, as far as I can tell, beyond these isolated mentions, the intensity of these connections and the implications of these intertextual references have remained mostly unexplored. I will not attempt to carry out this task here, and I will restrict myself to some preparatory observations.
6. Plato, *Timaeus*, p. 29 (41d).
7. This 'heart' (or, more literally, 'breast') evokes the image of explosive volcanic activity not only because it is 'inflammable'. According to the *Deutsches Wörterbuch*, the word *Brust* can be etymologically related to the word *bersten* in terms that evoke a plantlike becoming: '[. . .] dasz diesem uralten wort unsere wurzel bresten, ahd. prëstan, goth. also bristan, dem nl. borst bersten unterliegt [. . .] brust ist die keimende,

vordringende, schwellende, knospende, wachsende, sich wölbende [...]'. See, Jacob and Wilhelm Grimm, *Deutsches Wörterbuch*, Vol. 2, col. 443. And somewhat later, we read: '*brottone, brouton* stimmen aber zum ahd. *priozan*, unserm *sprieszen* und dem altn. *briota*, goth. vermutlich *briutan, brechen*, woher *sich bristen, bersten, brust, briost*, wahrscheinlich auch *pectus* leiteten' (col. 447). The word *bersten* also appears in Hölderlin's poem 'Vulcan' – although there it does not refer to the deeds of the 'spirit of fire' but to those of Boreas who, in his own volcanic ways, 'pours out his black cloud-bundles' until 'down come great rocks from the bursting hillside [*berstenden Hügel*]' (*FHA* IV, 257).
 8. For a discussion of the 'Ach'-sound from the perspective of the philosophy of language and poetology as it appears in the proximity of *Ächzen* (moaning) in a central place of the Hyperion fragment and the fifth stanza of 'Patmos', see de Roche, *Friedrich Hölderlin: Patmos*, pp. 57–67. For the question of 'participation' in Hölderlin's works, see Schestag, 'Das Höchste', pp. 42–8.
 9. Furthermore, the 'Ach' also participates in the becoming of this poem as well. See *FHA* IV, 68 and 71.
10. See also, Fetscher, 'Korrespondenzen der Sonne'.
11. See Derrida, '*Khôra*', pp. 100–2.
12. The passage of *Timaeus* that introduces *khôra* as a 'third genus' and forms the basis of Derrida's questions about a third type of discourse goes as follows: 'And the third type is space, which exists always and cannot be destroyed. It provides a fixed site for all things that come to be. It is itself apprehended by a kind of bastard reasoning that does not involve sense perception, and it is hardly even an object of conviction' (52a–b).
13. For a discussion of sprouting in Hölderlin's poetry in its linguistic and vegetable contexts, see Schestag, 'Worte, wie Blumen', pp. 269–79.
14. Plato, *Timaeus*, p. 42 (52e–53a).
15. Plato, *Timaeus*, pp. 39–40 (50b–c, 51a).
16. See especially the descriptions of the breast in *Timaeus*, p. 63 (69d–70c).
17. *Deutsches Wörterbuch*, vol. 16, col. 521, 525. But it can also mean 'drunk' (col. 526).
18. Benjamin, 'Fate and Character', p. 204.
19. See Kant, 'Conjectures', pp. 221–34.
20. Ibid. p. 223.
21. Ibid. p. 223.
22. Ibid. p. 224.
23. Ibid. p. 223.
24. Ibid. p. 223.
25. Ibid. p. 223.
26. Ibid. p. 223.
27. Ibid. p. 224.
28. Ibid. p. 223.
29. Ibid. p. 224.
30. Ibid. p. 223. The childish nature of this poetic revision recalls once again the passages of *Timaeus* where the latter describes a dialogue between Solon and Egyptian priests. Here one of the old priests says 'Ah, Solon, Solon, you Greeks are ever children' (22b) and then proceeds to call Solon's speech a 'nursery tale' (23b). As is well-known, Hölderlin's *Fragment von Hyperion* refers to these passages of *Timaeus* (*FHA* X, 54). We should also remember Hölderlin's words from 'Colombo': 'Greek, childlike in shape [*griechisch, kindlich gestalte*]' (*Poems and Fragments*, 599; *FHA* VIII, 924).
31. Ibid. p. 226.
32. Ibid. p. 224.
33. See also the ending of *Fragment von Hyperion* in *FHA* X, 74.
34. An approximation of the plant? It would be hard to come up with a more audacious image that represents the human being as an originally cultural being. Already on the first day, the human being takes wine (or, at least, the sweet berries, the grapes) instead

of milk. The later Pindar commentary, 'The Life-Giving', describes the centaurs' decision to discard milk and, instead, to drink honey-sweet wine as the beginning of culture and, thereby, also the beginning of an errant wandering. In other places, in addition to the errant vine [*irrende Rebe*], Hölderlin also writes about the transplanted god of wine: 'da lachet verpflanzet, der Gott' (*FHA* Homburger Foliohelft, 33). Every plant is already transplanted: the word 'plant' itself says that planting is in essence transplanting. The question of transplanting, however, problematises the place that is taken up by what is transplanted. In Hölderlin's poem, as an abandoned child, man appears as a plant that was transplanted at his very origins. From the very beginning, man is a 'nursling' [*Ammenkind*] (*FHA* Homburger Foliohelft, 95). But the vine – the human child's nurse – is itself transplanted. Hölderlin's poetry presents the vine as an 'errant vine' ('An den Aether') and as a 'shapeless vine' in 'The German's Song' (*Poems and Fragments*, 105). The vine can become a nurse, the receptacle, because it is shapeless and unformed. And it can become the 'errant vine' because it itself has no other receiving place than its own. Lastly, the connections between the images of errant wandering and of the vine refer to the migrations of a cultivated plant that creates places without ever having its own place.
35. In a short footnote of his above-quoted writing, Kant also touches upon the onomatopoetic theory of the origins of language. See Kant, 'Conjectures', p. 222.
36. Kant, 'Conjectures', p. 222.
37. Benjamin, 'On the Mimetic Faculty', p. 720.
38. Ibid. p. 721.
39. It not a mere coincidence that a different version of the poem calls the 'arrogance' of man 'nameless' (*FHA* IV, 71).
40. See *Tinian*: 'der Wölfin Euter' (*FHA* VIII, 772).
41. Hölderlin, 'Bread and Wine' (*Poems and Fragments*, 268). For a discussion of this passage from 'Bread and Wine', see Schestag, 'Worte, wie Blumen', pp. 269–79.
42. Benjamin, 'On the Mimetic Faculty', p. 722.
43. Ibid. p. 722.
44. See also Hölderlin's description of the instant: *wiegt Aeonen unsers Pflanzenlebens auf* (*FHA* X, 52).
45. Benjamin, 'On the Mimetic Faculty', p. 722.
46. Ibid. p. 722.

Bibliography

Benjamin, Walter, 'Fate and Character', trans. Rodney Livingstone, in Marcus Bullock and Michael W. Jennings (ed.), *Selected Writings, Volume 1: 1913–1926* (Cambridge, MA: Harvard University Press, 1996), pp. 201–6.
Benjamin, Walter, 'On the Mimetic Faculty', trans. Edmund Jephcott, in Michael W. Jennings, Howard Eiland and Gary Smith (eds), *Selected Writings, Volume 2: 1931–1934* (Cambridge, MA: Harvard University Press, 1999), pp. 720–2.
Bennholdt-Thomsen, Anke and Guzzoni, Alfredo, *Analecta Hölderliana: zur Hermetik des Spätwerks* (Würzburg: Königshausen & Neumann, 1999).
Bennholdt-Thomsen, Anke and Guzzoni, Alfredo, *Marginalien zu Hölderlins Werk* (Würzburg: Königshausen & Neumann, 2010).
Celan, Paul, *Die Gedichte*, ed. Barbara Wiedemann (Frankfurt am Main: Suhrkamp, 2003).
Derrida, Jacques, '*Khôra*', trans. Ian McLeod, in Thomas Dutoit (ed.), *On the Name* (Stanford: Stanford University Press, 1993), pp. 89–127.
Fetscher, Justus, 'Korrespondenzen der Sonne: Kosmologische Strukturen in Hölderlins Hyperion', *Athenäum: Jahrbuch für Romantik*, 10 (2000), pp. 77–107.

Franz, Michael, '"Platons frommer Garten": Hölderlins Platonlektüre von Tübingen bis Jena', *Hölderlin-Jahrbuch* (1992–93), pp. 111–27.
Grimm, Jacob and Wilhelm, *Deutsches Wörterbuch* (Leipzig: 1854–1971).
Heidegger, Martin, 'Language in the Poem: A Discussion on Georg Trakl's Poetic Work', in *On the Way to Language*, trans. Peter D. Hertz (New York: Harper & Row, 1971), pp. 159–98.
Kant, Immanuel, 'Conjectures on the Beginning of Human History', in *Political Writings*, trans. H. B. Nisbet (Cambridge: Cambridge University Press, 1991), pp. 221–34.
Kocziszky, Éva, *Mythenfiguren in Hölderlins Spätwerk* (Würzburg: Königshausen & Neumann, 1997).
Lampenscherf, Stephan, '"Heiliger Plato, vergieb . . .": Hölderlins "Hyperion" oder Die neue Platonische Mythologie', in *Hölderlin-Jahrbuch* (1992–3), pp. 128–51.
Luhnen, Michael, 'Hölderlins hymnisches Fragment "An die Madonna" als mythopoetisches Experiment', in *Hölderlin-Jahrbuch* (2000–1), pp. 263–72.
Nägele, Rainer, *Text, Geschichte und Subjektivität in Hölderlins Dichtung: 'unessbarer Schrift gleich'* (Stuttgart: Metzler, 1985).
Plato, *Timaeus*, trans. Donald J. Zeyl (Indianapolis, IN: Hackett, 2000).
Roche, Charles de, *Friedrich Hölderlin: Patmos. Das scheidende Erscheinen des Gedichts* (Munich: Fink, 1999).
Schestag, Thomas, 'Das Höchste', in Thomas Schestag, *Parerga* (Munich: Boer, 1991), pp. 15–50.
Schestag, Thomas, 'Worte, wie Blumen', in Francis Ponge, *L'Opinion changé quant aux fleurs. Änderung der Ansicht über Blumen*, trans. Thomas Schestag (Basel: Urs Engeler, 2005), pp. 269–79.

Chapter 12

Not Rhythm

Jan Mieszkowski

In an 1840 text loosely based on old letters and memories of conversations that had taken place decades earlier, Bettina von Arnim relates that according to his friend Isaac von Sinclair, Hölderlin once said: 'Alles sei Rhythmus'.[1] While we are all familiar with the rhythms of gossip, here we are invited to indulge in some gossip about rhythm. The subjunctive mood of the verb underscores the second- or third-hand quality of this instance of reported speech. Citing the comment in German, one cannot help but reproduce a sense of the non-committal – the proposition is someone else's opinion and sharing it in this way by no means amounts to taking a position on its truth or falsity. By comparison, Hölderlin's statement sounds more definitive, if potentially enigmatic, when translated into English: 'Everything is rhythm'.

Uncertainty about the accuracy of von Arnim's report has not dampened scholars' enthusiasm for discussing it. In the process, it is often forgotten that 'everything is rhythm' is not a stand-alone aphorism, but rather a three-word snippet from a 113-word sentence that treats a daunting array of topics, including God, truth and the fate of humankind. The clauses that immediately follow 'alles sei Rhythmus' inform us, still in the mood of indirect speech, that Hölderlin also stated that 'the entire destiny of humanity is [*sei*] a heavenly rhythm, just as every artwork is [*sei*] a singular rhythm'.[2] From this perspective, the notion that von Arnim is recounting verbatim an oral report about what a third party once said starts to border on the implausible, it being unlikely that such a lengthy string of claims could be shared and then re-shared accurately. The air of the fanciful surrounding the purported quotation is further heightened by the fact that the syntax of von Arnim's sprawling sentence bears more than a passing resemblance to the rhythm of many of Hölderlin's own prose texts, suggesting that she may be offering a kind of stylistic tribute to, even a parody of, his writing.

A rhythm is a recognisable pattern of sound or literal or metaphorical movement. Efforts to clarify its nuances further often backfire, as a series of interdependent terms impose themselves, including pace, tempo, accent and of course meter, from which rhythm is invariably distinguished despite the fact that nearly all definitions of meter rely on some notion of rhythm. In such discussions, one not infrequently suspects that decisions have already been made about the nature of the ideas putatively under analysis, as when it is maintained that rhythm is the organisation of intensity or duration in ordered patterns, that is, that rhythm is ordered order. The ultimate claim to mastery over sameness and difference, rhythm is also a testament to its impossibility. If rhythm is all about what can be measured, calculated or predicted, it retains an indelible trace of the intuitive, the imponderable or the obscure. Either one can hear it or one can't; either one has it or one doesn't; and as Friedrich Schlegel said of irony, for someone who has no rhythm, it will forever remain a mystery.

By the turn of the nineteenth century, the word *Rhythmus* had become a mainstay of German letters. Friedrich Klopstock uses it in describing the metrical organisation of Greek, Latin and Hebrew texts, and it appears regularly in the writings of J. W. von Goethe, Friedrich Schiller and August Wilhelm Schlegel, where it refers not just to the dynamics of individual verses, but to patterns on virtually any scale or level of abstraction. While one may well have the sense that Hölderlin routinely discusses rhythm in his theoretical writings, the noun *Rhythmus* is markedly absent from most of his better-known texts on aesthetics and poetics. It never appears, for instance, in his longest essay, 'Wenn der Dichter einmal des Geistes mächtig ist . . .' [*When the poet has finally mastered the spirit . . .*], in which the study of *Streben* (striving), *Wechsel* (alternation) and *harmonische Entgegensetzung* (harmonious contraposition) unfolds without any mention of *Rhythmus* whatsoever.[3] The term does play a role in Hölderlin's commentaries on Sophocles' *Oedipus* and *Antigone*, in which he characterises the caesura as a 'counter-' or 'anti-rhythmic interruption' [*eine gegenrhythmische Unterbrechung*].[4] In both plays, the key break turns out to be a speech by the blind prophet Tiresias, the precise location of which ensures that none of the rhythmic forces at work in the drama predominates at the expense of the others. Here, rhythm manifests itself as something irreducibly multiple. There is always more than one rhythm with which to reckon, and when considered in isolation, any individual pattern is apt to reveal itself to be too strong, too weak or too irregular to coexist harmoniously with its brethren.

It is not clear what is involved in intervening in, much less derailing, such dynamics. If a rhythmic interruption (*rhythmische Unterbrechung*) is necessarily at risk of becoming part of the pattern it seeks to disrupt, a *gegen*-rhythmic interruption presumably resists such assimilation. Of course, as a prefix or a preposition, *gegen* is anything but unequivocal. Depending on the context, it can designate tendencies into, toward or against, describing a counterpart (*Gegenpart*) as much as an opponent (*Gegner*). One also speaks of exchanging one thing 'for' or 'against' – *gegen* – another. The upshot is that translating Hölderlin's *gegenrhythmische Unterbrechung* into English is necessarily a consequential interpretation in its own right. A *counter*-rhythmic interruption would be less a nullification of the rhythmic than the impetus for the emergence of a new series of alternations in which the initial pattern would become one moment in a broader rhythm of rhythms. In contrast, a truly *anti*-rhythmic interruption would not be a negation of rhythm, but rather a permanent threat to it that would neither lie entirely outside of the pattern on which it puts pressure nor paralyse it completely, since in either case the interruption would forfeit its status as an interruption.[5] Instead of a pause or break occurring at a particular moment in a play or line of verse, such a caesura would be a syncopation that makes its influence felt at every moment in a text, a ghostly stutter that is not part of the dominant beat or tempo yet somehow not utterly foreign to it.

What happens when we try to identify the hegemony of rhythm, or the inexorable insistence of the *gegen*-rhythmic, in Hölderlin's poems? The trajectory of his artistic production is often characterised as a shift from traditional to less traditional syntactic and metrical patterns that culminates in the late hymns (*Gesänge*). Here, in Theodor W. Adorno's well-known argument, the paratactic grammar unsettles the dominion of the subject-predicate schema to the point that its syntheses no longer organise the content of the discourse. For Adorno, the result is not an overcoming of rhythm, much less the advent of disorder. 'Dispensing with predicative assertion', he maintains, 'causes the rhythm to approach musical development.'[6]

Others have described the waning authority of logical forms in Hölderlin as an intensification of confusion – 'the dictatorship of rhythm at the cost of intellectual orderliness', as the Austrian novelist Stefan Zweig puts it.[7] Zweig parallels the changes in Hölderlin's texts with his psychological decline: 'The rhythm became freer proportionally with the severance of the logical ties in his mind until in the end the poet could no longer control the flow, and therefore, a living corpse, he was swept away by the current of his song.'[8] As Zweig acknowledges, his remarks invoke the content and imagery of the description von Arnim provided of a visit with Hölderlin early in his so-called period of madness: 'When I look at and listen to

[him], it seems to me as if a divine being must have overwhelmed him in a flood – a flood of language in which his intelligence is drowned.'[9] From this perspective, 'everything is rhythm' is less an acknowledgement of overarching order or design than a nod to the existence of uncontrollable forces.

The problem with paralleling Hölderlin's mental decline with an onslaught of rhythmic forces that gradually overcomes the logical ordering of his writings is that many of the poems he produced even decades after he had been deemed mentally incapacitated were composed of rhymed quatrains and treated traditional topics in unremarkable ways. If the mad poet was drowning in language, as Zweig and von Arnim suggest, the resulting texts were often metrically and thematically banal. At the same time, in drawing on an association of verbal power, rhythm and rushing waters, Zweig and von Arnim are entirely faithful to the aesthetic tradition in which Hölderlin worked. The 'rushing' or 'streaming' word celebrated in 'Bread and Wine' is one moment in a long chain of figures extending back to Horace's famous pronouncement that the style of Hölderlin's beloved Pindar was like 'a river running down a mountain, / which the rains have swelled beyond its known banks'.[10]

More important than any catalogue of emblems and motifs is the fact that the discourse on rhythm has always been concerned with the relationship between language and fluid mechanics. The Greek *rhuthmos*, the forerunner of the modern word found in English (*rhythm*), German (*Rhythmus*) and the Romance languages (*rythme, ritmo*), was derived from the Greek verb *rheo*, 'to flow'. Traditionally, lexicographers maintained that the idea of rhythm was 'inspired' or 'borrowed from' the movement of the waves in the sea, and to this day, many dictionaries still present this as fact. In a brief but often-cited essay, Émile Benveniste savages this story, beginning with a sarcastic summary: 'What could be more simple and satisfying? Man has learned the principles of things from nature, and the movement of the waves has given rise in his mind to the idea of rhythm, and that primordial discovery is inscribed in the term itself.'[11] Benveniste argues that the Greek *rheo*, the basis of the standard etymology, was never used to describe the sea, since 'what flows . . . is the river or stream, and a current of water does not have "rhythm"'.[12] This last remark may strike us as odd, since 'the rhythm of the river' is a commonplace notion that routinely appears in poems and songs as well as in everyday conversation. Benveniste's point, however, is that in its most ancient uses, the Greek *rhuthmos* meant not what we today understand by 'rhythm', but something closer to 'form', although not the form of *skhèma*, *morphè* or *eidos* – that is, not a defining shape, arrangement or appearance. To the contrary, *rhuthmos* referred to the contingent condition of something changeable or fluid that at any moment manifests itself in a singular, possibly never-to-be-repeated state, be this a puddle, an item of clothing or the particular mood in which one finds oneself.[13] If 'everything is *rhuthmos*', then everything is transient, fleeting and forever on the verge of adopting a new likeness.[14]

In addition to correcting the etymological record, Benveniste's argument encourages us to stop discussing poetic rhythm in terms of vague metaphors of movement – the 'flow' of the language – and to focus instead on the possibility that the crucial formal or semantic patterns of a text may be defined by their status as contingent rather than necessary, by their impermanence rather than their fixity. The language of rhythm would thus be a discourse of alternatives and accidents, and most importantly a discourse whose signifying or representational capacities are sustained by volatility rather than stability.

An Alcaic ode with precise metrical integrity, Hölderlin's 'Voice of the People' (1799–1800) offers an instructive example of how these dynamics inform his verse. From a formal perspective, the poem lies very much on the side of order; evidently the 'dictatorship of rhythm' is still being kept at bay. Thematically speaking, things are more complex. From its opening lines, the poem is all about the kind of relationship the poet can have with the voice or voices, real or imaginary, that he hears or claims to have knowledge of – voices which, beginning with his own, may turn out to be as uncontrollable as rushing waters:

Stimme des Volks.

Du seiest Gottes Stimme, so glaubt' ich sonst
 In heil'ger Jugend; ja, und ich sag' es noch!
  Um unsre Weisheit unbekümmert
   Rauschen die Ströme doch auch, und dennoch,

Wer liebt sie nicht?

(*FHA* V, 593)

Voice of the People.

You are the voice of God, so I believed formerly
 In holy youth; yes, and I say it again!
  No less indifferent to our wisdom
   Likewise the rivers rush on, and nonetheless,

Who does not love them?

(*Poems and Fragments*, 183, translation modified)

The text opens with an elaborate self-reflexive gesture. The first-person speaker identifies the voice of the people with the voice of God by apostrophising the poem's title. In this way, the text presents itself as a careful arrangement of verbal elements on a page as much as a monologue we just happen to overhear – that is, it calls attention to itself as a written medium, a work with a formal heading, in the very process of representing a first-person lyric voice that is loudly celebrating its own status as a source of speech.

As the voice of the poet attempts to affirm its self-identity based on its capacity to cite its own youthful outbursts, the tension between the text's representation of speech and its self-presentation as a written document increases. As with 'alles sei Rhythmus', the grammar indicates that we are dealing with a report about what someone else said ('du *seiest* Gottes Stimme'). In the act of quoting himself, the poet betrays his distance from his own statement even as the force of his remark purportedly stems from the fact that he is repeating a past claim in the here and now of the verse ('and I say it again!'). What actually appears in the poem, moreover, is not the youthful proclamation itself, but the pronoun 'it'. At the very moment that the power of an utterance is to be confirmed by its re-articulation, grammatical convention and metrical constraints see the decisive declaration replaced by a generic shifter. Further complicating matters, the identification of the voice of the people with the voice of God is underwritten by a saying of uncertain provenance, *vox populi, vox dei*, which is never cited but lurks as a paratextual reference with which the reader is presumed to be familiar. Even with the plethora of voices packed into the opening lines, it may be that what is not said or cited speaks as loudly as what is.

The next three lines of the poem offer a different argument for its foundational identification. The implication is that just as hearing the voice of the people is enough to love or exalt it despite the fact that it does not show much concern for us, so everyone loves the rivers despite the fact that they do not have much use for us and our pithy wisdoms – beginning, presumably, with our views on the relationship between the voice of the people and the voice of God. As the poem continues, the poet's concern with the rivers takes centre stage, and he presents them not simply as physical entities, but as historical forces, currents of foreknowledge and anticipation as well as of loss. Testifying to both the passing and possible return of the past as well as to the arrival and likely disappearance of the future, the rivers bespeak the contingency of *rhuthmos*. Accordingly, the first thing we are told about them is that they are unconcerned with us, our adoration of them notwithstanding, since they never adopt a position that could become the basis for a stable relationship with them. Similarly, the poet's ability to speak about the rivers and to incorporate them into various analogies does not confirm that they are his rivers. Indeed, neither the people nor God may have any concern for this poem about them, its opening apostrophes falling on deaf ears. In the end, the poet may not know how to give voice to a language that is of interest to anyone but himself, assuming that he, too, is not indifferent to what he is saying.

By repeatedly associating different entities or forces and then immediately challenging the meaningfulness of such connections, Hölderlin's poem suggests that its alignments of moving water and language may reveal the inherent volatility – if not outright instability – of analogy as such. The first five stanzas of the text see rushing currents juxtaposed with both mortal and divine powers, but these correspondences never become fixed semantic figures. The fluid remains irrepressibly fluid without thereby becoming something predictable on which one can rely. Particularly striking is the way in which the relationship between self-determination and external compulsion is contorted. In the same lines in which the river is described as plunging down the mountain from cliff to cliff at the mercy of gravity, it is said to be actively seeking repose, driven by 'the wonderful yearning for the abyss' (*FHA* V, 593; my translation). That this yearning is one facet of a larger dynamic of self-actualisation through self-destruction is made clear in the poem's final stanzas, as the tone becomes identifiably epic, and we hear the tale of Xanthus, an ancient city where the populace, besieged by foes, set themselves on fire rather than permit themselves to be enslaved. Incredibly, the denizens of this city made the decision twice, first when beset by Persian invaders, then five hundred years later when besieged by the Greeks. The very fact that such an ostensibly singular event could be repeated suggests the influence of historical or divine forces beyond the two groups' control, meaning that even these acts of mass suicide do not constitute unambiguously autonomous behaviour, the difference between self-willed and externally directed agency having become hopelessly blurred.

While 'Voice of the People' respects a precise metrical schema, we need only dip beneath the surface of its syntactic and sonorous rhythms to encounter other patterns whose organising principles are less clear, repetitions of syllables or individual letters (**noch**, **doch**, **dennoch**; **Götter**, **ergreift**, **gern**) that pop up for a line or two and then recede (*FHA* V, 593). The poem's name for the possibility that its formal parameters may be haunted by one or more *gegen*-rhythms can be found in its fourth line: *Rauschen*. The German word refers to a range of markedly different sounds, from the deafening thunder of a violent river to the barely audible rustling of leaves in the trees. Often translated into English with words that approach onomatopoeia – 'whirring', 'whooshing', 'swooshing' – *Rauschen* lies at the border between sense and non-sense. Although in all likelihood it has no message to share, one cannot quite escape the feeling that if one were but to cock one's ear and listen more carefully, one might discern some meaning in it.

In a poem called 'Voice of the People', this peculiar auditory phenomenon poses a clear threat. The text stakes its authority on its ability to make sense of what it hears, be this its own voice, the voices of others, or sounds in nature that may be likened to such voices. 'Who does not love the rushing waters?' asks the poet, but when *Rauschen* is involved, this cannot simply be a rhetorical question. Perhaps the poet himself dare not love the waters insofar as they are a persistent reminder that his voice, like the voice of the people or the voice of God, may never amount to more than white noise (*weißes Rauschen*).

In an essay on *Rauschen* in Joseph von Eichendorff, Adorno cites a line by the poet Rudolf Borchardt: 'I have nothing but *Rauschen*.'[15] Here and in several other texts, Adorno invokes this quotation to describe a poetic self that is characterised by the way in which language murmurs through it. While this may seem to be the opposite of von Arnim and Zweig's account of Hölderlin bowled over by a flood of language, Adorno cautions that Borchardt has a profound sense of the disintegrative potential of language. Whether as roaring noise or low, indistinct sound, *Rauschen* always conveys a sense of the precariousness of articulation. If 'everything is rhythm', to declare 'I have nothing but *Rauschen*' may be to say, 'I have nothing but *rhuthmos*', which is to acknowledge the way in which repetitions of syllables, letters or stresses ambiguously manifest themselves as either patterns *or* random scatterings, formal features *or* accidents. The language of *rhuthmos* is constantly on the way to and yet in retreat from a systematic arrangement of its elements, perpetually stumbling into and out of contingency without any of these shifts ever becoming a paradigmatic event around which to orient the discourse.

'Es rauschen die Wasser am Fels / Und Wetter im Wald' [*The waters roar on the rock / And thunderstorms in the wood*] (*FHA* VIII, 761; *Poems and Fragments*, 429). In this line near the close of Hölderlin's late hymn 'Germania', the *W* at the start of *Wasser* rushes (*rauscht*) through the statement about rushing *Wasser*. In contrast to 'Voice of the People', this 1803 poem is not organised by traditional metrical conventions, and rather than presenting its own vocalising capacities as the basis for claims about others' voices, it opens by declaring what it *cannot* do with its voice:

> Nicht sie, die Seeligen, die erschienen sind,
> Die Götterbilder in dem alten Lande,
> Sie darf ich ja nicht rufen mehr, wenn aber
> Ihr heimatlichen Wasser! jezt mit euch
> Des Herzens Liebe klagt, was will es anders
> Das Heiligtrauernde? Denn voll Erwartung liegt
> Das Land, und als in heißen Tagen
> Herabgesenkt, umschattet heut

> Ihr Sehnenden! uns ahnungsvoll ein Himmel.
> Voll von Verheißungen und scheint
> Mir drohend auch, doch will ich bei ihm bleiben,
> Und rükwärts soll die Seele mir nicht fliehn
> Zu euch, Vergangene! die zu lieb mir sind.
> Denn euer schönes Angesicht zu sehn,
> Als wärs, wie sonst, ich fürcht' es, tödtlich ists
> Und kaum erlaubt, Gestorbene zu weken.
>
> Entflohene Götter! auch ihr, ihr gegenwärtigen, damals
> Wahrhaftiger, ihr hattet eure Zeiten.
> Nichts läugnen will ich hier und nichts erbitten.
>
> (*FHA* VIII, 729)

> Not them, the blessed, who once appeared,
> Those images of gods in the ancient land,
> Them I am indeed no longer permitted to call, but if
> You waters of my homeland, now with you
> The love of my heart laments, what else does it want, in
> Its hallowed sadness? For full of expectation lies
> The country, and as though it had been lowered
> In sultry dogdays, on us a heaven today,
> You yearning rivers, casts prophetic shade.
> With promises it is fraught, and to me
> Seems threatening too, yet I will stay with it,
> And backward now my soul shall not escape
> To you, the vanished, who are too dear to me.
> To look upon your beautiful brows, as though
> They were unchanged, I am afraid, for deadly
> And scarcely permitted it is to awaken the dead.
>
> Gods who are fled! And you also, you present, back then,
> More real, you had your time, your ages!
> Nothing do I want to deny here and nothing request.
>
> (*Poems and Fragments*, 423, translation modified)

Like many of Hölderlin's poems, 'Germania' does not begin by referring to ideas or phenomena in the world that exist independently of its language. Instead, the text presents itself as a linguistic event, a collection of speech acts and comments about those acts that take place at a historically precarious juncture between a past in which 'those images of gods in the ancient land' once appeared and an uncertain future of premonitions, expectations and promises. This does not occur via an apostrophe to any particular force or authority or as an invitation to an addressee to enter into conversation or debate. To the contrary, the poet opens by averring that he is not permitted to hail 'the blessed'. That the text's primary concern is with a prohibition against speech is foregrounded by the fact that its first word is *nicht* – that is, it starts with a shout-out to the negative operator, as if it were being addressed in its own right, independently of its function in the clause that follows. Further adding to the inaugural word's isolation from the rest of the stanza, neither the grammar of the sentence that *nicht* introduces nor its function are clarified until *nicht* is repeated: 'Nicht sie die Seeligen' / 'Sie darf ich ja nicht rufen mehr'. Rather than constituting a double negation, the second *nicht* merely restates – and may thereby weaken – the first, raising doubts about whether either instance of the word actually has the power to invert the proposition in which it appears.

Given this uncertainty about how well negative operators function in this poem, it is striking that the second instance of *nicht* follows the word *ja*, which in other contexts simply means *yes*. In this case, *ja* is an intensifier, an adverbial 'para-yes' on the order of 'indeed' or 'surely', but in the face of the – now repeated – *nicht*, *ja* cannot help but say both *yes* and *no*. Having opened with *nicht*, the poem struggles to confirm that it can ever get beyond it, as if its first word were fated to have the last word on whatever follows. Driving this point home, one of the manuscript versions of the text reads:

Nicht ,
    sie, die Seeligen, die erschienen sind,
Die Götterbilder in dem alten Lande,
Sie darf ich ja nicht rufen mehr . . .

(*FHA* VIII, 729)

Separated from the sentence of which it is ostensibly a part by a space, a comma, and a line break, the word *nicht* is a kind of rogue element that has to be brought back into the fold. If 'Voice of the People' starts by apostrophising its own title, this poem opens by seeking to confirm that even if it can no longer call the gods, it can call on *nicht*. This is not the same thing as directing itself toward a particular affirmation or negation, either of which would necessarily refer to something already represented in language, an existing position that could be endorsed or rejected. To the contrary, to hail *nicht* is to apostrophise a word that is not derivative of any act of signification or representation, even as all such acts unfold in its shadow. Any proposition is open to the possibility of being modified by *nicht* and, crucially, this has nothing to do with the proposition's form or content. Whether or not *nicht* is literally present, it cannot be the case that *nicht* could not impose itself. If it is not always there, it is always at least not-there.

Variously termed a 'logical operator', 'function word' or 'negative particle', *nicht* may seem to behave more like a mathematical symbol ($-$ or $\neq$) than a word. Semantically situated at the point where the differential signification of semiosis meets the turns of rhetoric, it is a constant reminder that any term's identity is predicated on its status as not not-itself. Pre- or para-positional, the word *nicht* can become part of the articulation of a position, but the operation it effects can never be reduced to a positive content, a *yes* or a *no*. In this way, *nicht* threatens all verbal formations with their own contingency. It is an irrepressible rhythm of potential change – irrepressible because it informs anything said or written irrespective of whether or not its appearance remains a mere possibility. Any statement, positive or negative, must actively seek to confirm that it is not about to be undone by the advent of a new *nicht*, and even when one's remarks have come to a close, there is no way to guarantee that they will not subsequently be overturned by the expostulation that in American slang serves to refute everything that has come before it: 'Not!'

By beginning with this curiously isolated *nicht* and then gradually effecting its integration into a syntactic formation in which it is merely an adverb modifying a verb, 'Germania' stages the transformation of a *not* into a *no*, turning a differential gesture into one position among others. One drawback of dwelling on the vicissitudes of the text's first word is that we may overlook just how unusual the human–divine relationship characterised in the first stanza is, since there is virtually no analogue in the western tradition for a deity or deities on whom one is not permitted to call, no matter how doomed to failure the entreaty may be. Indeed, in many situations the appropriateness of a prayer is inversely proportional to one's right to offer it. At the same time, this potentially arresting fact is almost immediately rendered irrelevant, because at the start of the second stanza, the poet does directly address the deities ('Gods who are fled! And you also, you present, back then, / More real, you had your time, your ages!'), then immediately qualifies the apostrophe: 'Nothing do I want to deny here and nothing request'. The poet who has averred that he is not permitted to call on the gods now does precisely this, but only in order to say that he has no reason for doing so, as if he were violating the proscription against hailing them for the sake of mere chatter, with no pretension to broadcasting a coherent message or beginning a substantive exchange. As improbable as it may be to envision gods whom one may not address, it is no less incredible to think of addressing them idly, without any goal, as if an utterance directed toward a deity could ever truly be devoid of aim or intent.

One might argue that in his opening declaration that he is not permitted to call upon the gods, the poet already in effect does speak to them, an instance of apophasis or paralipsis that may even reveal that the gods only exist in virtue of not-being-addressable, as the objects of a speech act that is never supposed to take place. In his first lecture course on Hölderlin's poetry, Martin Heidegger discusses 'Germania' at length and comes to this very conclusion. Insisting that what is at stake in this poem 'is not at all the superficial historical comparison between a previous state of the ancient world ... and some subsequent, contemporary state', he argues that the language of the text effects an active mourning of the gods and that this is what it means for there to be gods with whom we may have a relationship: 'truly taking seriously the gods that have fled, as having fled, is in itself precisely a remaining with the gods, with their divinity as a divinity that is no longer fulfilled'.[16]

In a critique of this interpretation, Andrzej Warminski argues that Heidegger domesticates the opening negation of Hölderlin's poem such that 'Not them, the blessed' comes to mean 'Precisely them, the blessed'.[17] Warminski focuses on Heidegger's claim that the disruptive power of the text's first word culminates in the rhetorical question of the fifth line. 'The "Not" with which [the poem] begins', Heidegger writes, 'is fundamentally not at all a denial that stands alone, nor the kind that pertains to renunciation, but finds its full and authentic significance in the phrase "what else does it want", speaking of the holy mourning heart.'[18] According to Heidegger, the inaugural 'not' turns out not to have meant 'not' – it is *not* in name alone – but the rhetorical question *does* resolve into something negative, 'nothing else'. Warminski suggests that nothing in the first stanza prevents us from reading the putatively rhetorical question literally. Given the ambivalence that surrounds every negative gesture in the text, it may not be a matter of what else the heart wants, but of what else the text, or the word *not* itself, wants.

If Warminski persuasively demonstrates that it is ultimately undecidable whether the first stanza's question is literal or rhetorical, Heidegger's corpus has no shortage of reflections on the nature of negation and on the word 'not' in particular, making it somewhat implausible that he has simply missed the provocation of the opening of Hölderlin's text.[19] In fact, Heidegger's reading of 'Germania' compulsively circles back to its opening line, each time declaring that with dozens of new pages of interpretation behind us, we are now finally in a position to contend with this first word that is not not-a-word, although it threatens to make all words say or be something that they are not. With the opening 'not', writes Heidegger, we are 'torn away suddenly and abruptly', even as the text has yet to give us a language to lose. Heidegger describes the resulting linguistic turbulence as a *Wirbel* (a whirl or vortex) and declares the core mood of the poem to be a primordial *Bewegtheit* – an agitation, choppiness or e-motionality that precedes any affirmative or negative position that might be represented in language.

Tempestuous though it may be, Heidegger stresses that 'this being torn back and forth' that will define our encounter with the poem is 'a rhythm'.[20] Giving full expression to Benveniste's *rhuthmos*, each word, phrase or clause of Hölderlin's text emerges in full awareness of its own precarious contingency. Rather than situating verbal elements in a pattern, the not-rhythm of 'Germania' tears them out of their context before they are in one, as if a stray *nicht* were always on hand to reverse whatever has just been articulated. Instead of an opposition between the *rhythmisch* and the *gegenrhythmisch* – which is fated to align itself with order, if only as an oscillation between order and disorder – we confront a series of skirmishes of *gegen* gegen *gegen*, a rhythm of op-positions that never lay claim to constituting an instance of *yes* or *no*.

Famous for what is often trivialised as a penchant for neologisms, Heidegger never tires of reminding us that genuine philosophical inquiry demands a constant refashioning of our relationship to a lexicon whose coherence and stability we tend to take for granted. This is less a matter of generating jargon than of allowing complexities to come to the fore that are normally masked by our assumptions about language usage, with the result that Heidegger often seems to be writing in an idiom all his own. In reading 'Germania', however, he takes a different stance and insists that we cannot invest in a particular word – *Dasein*, *Vorhandenheit*, *Versprechen* – and strive to bring its latent nuances to light. Arguing that in this poem the absent gods 'come to presence precisely in the absence of that which has been', Heidegger maintains that the text requires us to distinguish between 'that which has been [*das Gewesene*]', which will be sustained in being mourned, and 'that which is [merely] past [*das Vergangene*]'.[21] If this appears to be one of his signature gestures, a subtle refining of our conceptual terminology intended to advance our study of the topic, Heidegger immediately adds that 'to name the difference in meaning between having-been and past [*Gewesenheit und Vergangenheit*]', it is irrelevant which word we use for which concept, because 'however essential language can be in its telling, our immediate word usage is just as often contingent [*zufällig*] and arbitrary [*willkürlich*]'.[22] Far from simply disavowing the precision of these particular labels, Heidegger questions whether our vocabulary, however exact, can ever be a reliable analytic resource. Even more troubling, he offers no way of deciding when we should insist on certain formulations and when we should not commit to them at all. Although poetry is often taken to be a discourse in which diction is paramount, Hölderlin's uniquely unsettled verses force us to acknowledge the potential contingency of both their words and our own. No matter how carefully they are chosen, any terms mobilised to characterise the 'movements' of the language of 'Germania' will ultimately reveal themselves to be of provisional value at best.

From this perspective, 'everything is rhythm' and 'I have nothing but *Rauschen*' are two ways of acknowledging that to speak or write is never to be fully in control of the relationship between necessity and contingency. We do justice to the rhythms – or not-rhythms – of 'Voice of the People' and 'Germania' by treating their most calculated formulations, and our own, as potentially provisional stand-ins for a language that may never arrive. This is why the discourse on rhythm is fated to be an open-ended discussion of rumours and gossip ('von Arnim said that Sinclair said that Hölderlin said . . .'). Like Hölderlin's poet who insists that he addresses the gods for no reason whatsoever, we may find that we learn the most about rhythm when we chatter about it, giving free rein to a conversation that is simultaneously on the verge of acquiring a highly organised structure and devolving into white noise.

Notes

1. Arnim, *Die Günderode*, p. 547.
2. Ibid. p. 547, my translation.
3. See 'Wenn der Dichter einmal des Geistes mächtig ist . . .', *FHA* XIV, 179–323.
4. *FHA* XVI, 250 (*Anmerkungen zum Oedipus*), 411 (*Anmerkungen zur Antigonä*).
5. On the anti-rhythmic in Hölderlin, see Philippe Lacoue-Labarthe's 'The Caesura of the Speculative', *Typography*, pp. 208–47, as well as Jacques Derrida's concluding remarks on the caesura in his introduction to Lacoue-Labarthe's book: 'This interruption does not have the dialectical cadence of a relation between rhythm and non-rhythm, the continuous and the discontinuous, etc. It interrupts alternation, "the constraint of *opposition* in general", dialectic and the speculative, even the double bind when it retains an oppositional form' (Derrida, 'Introduction', p. 42).
6. Adorno, 'Parataxis', p. 132.
7. Zweig, *Hölderlin*, p. 126.
8. Ibid. p. 126.
9. Cited in Zweig, *Hölderlin*, p. 135.
10. *FHA* VI, 259; Horace, *The Odes of Horace*, p. 145.
11. Benveniste, 'The Notion of "Rhythm" in its Linguistic Expression', p. 281.
12. Ibid. p. 282. 'It is . . . we who are making metaphors today', continues Benveniste, 'when we speak of the rhythm of the waves' (Ibid. p. 287).
13. Benveniste writes that the Greek *rhuthmos* originally described ' "dispositions" or "configurations" without fixity or natural necessity and arising from an arrangement which is always subject to change' ('The Notion of "Rhythm"', p. 286). The sense of the term 'rhythm' with which we are familiar today was canonised by Plato, who describes the measured flow or arrangement of slow and rapid movements in dance over time, turning the spatial *rhuthmos* into something temporal that characterises the ordered process of a step, song or speech – anything that presupposes a continuous activity broken by meter into alternating intervals. In 'The Echo of the Subject', Lacoue-Labarthe quotes Benveniste on *rhuthmos* – 'it is "improvised, momentaneous, modifiable" form' – and comments: 'Thinking of Kant, one might say that [*rhuthmos*] is the form or figure as broached necessarily by time, or that time (that is to say, probably, repetition in its difference) conditions its possibility' (*Typography*, p. 201). Earlier in this essay, Lacoue-Labarthe has explained that he is attempting to read Hölderlin's 'everything is rhythm' with Stéphane Mallarmé's 'every soul is a rhythmic knot', as if the only way – or at

least the best way – to approach the topic of rhythm were by gathering provocative one-liners about it (ibid. p. 140).
14. In a text on the poetry of Stefan George, Martin Heidegger maintains that the key to the conceptualisation of rhythm is to break the identity of rhythm and movement. He follows Benveniste in arguing that the Greek *rhuthmos* originally meant not *Fluss* ['current or flow'] or *Fliesen* ['streaming, flowing'], but *Fügung*, which in modern German is a 'coincidence' ('a stroke of good luck'), although Heidegger plays on the older sense of fitting things together, hence a 'coordination, articulation or jointure'. As *Fügung*, he writes, rhythm concerns the establishment of repose: 'Rhythm, *rhuthmos*, does not mean flux and flowing, but rather structure [*Fügung*]. Rhythm is what is at rest, what structures [*fügt*] the movement [*Be-wegung*] of dance and song, and thus lets it rest within itself. Rhythm bestows rest' (Heidegger, *On the Way*, p. 149). For a somewhat different discussion of the relationship between rhythm and structure, see Agamben, *The Man Without Content*, pp. 94–103.
15. Adorno, 'In Memory', p. 69.
16. Heidegger, *Hölderlin's Hymns*, pp. 87–8.
17. See Warminski, *Readings in Interpretation*, pp. 64–71.
18. Heidegger, *Hölderlin's Hymns*, p. 87.
19. In his 1946 'Letter on Humanism', Heidegger extends arguments he has made in *Being and Time* and *What Is Metaphysics?* and maintains that ' "not" in no way arises from the no-saying [*Nein-sagen*] of negation' (Heidegger, *Basic Writings*, p. 237). On negation and 'not' in Heidegger, see Hamacher, 'The Relation', pp. 29–69.
20. Heidegger, *Hölderlin's Hymns*, p. 44, p. 99.
21. Ibid. p. 98.
22. Ibid. p. 98.

Bibliography

Adorno, Theodor W., 'In Memory of Eichendorff', in R. Tiedemann (ed.), *Notes to Literature*, trans. Shierry Weber Nicholsen (New York: Columbia University Press, 1992), vol. 2, pp. 55–79.
Adorno, Theodor W., 'Parataxis: On Hölderlin's Late Poetry', in R. Tiedemann (ed.), *Notes to Literature*, trans. Shierry Weber Nicholsen (New York: Columbia University Press, 1992), vol. 2, pp. 109–49.
Agamben, Giorgio, *The Man Without Content*, trans. G. Albert (Stanford: Stanford University Press, 1999).
Arnim, Bettina von, *Clemens Brentano's Frühlingskranz, Die Günderode*, in B. v. Arnim, *Werke und Briefe in vier Bänden*, ed. W. Schmitz and S. v. Steinsdorff, 4 vols (Frankfurt am Main: Deutscher Klassiker Verlag, 1986), vol. 1.
Benveniste, Émile, 'The Notion of "Rhythm" in its Linguistic Expression', *Problems in General Linguistics*, trans. M. E. Meek (Miami: University of Miami Press, 1971), pp. 281–8.
Derrida, Jacques, 'Introduction: Desistance', in P. Lacoue-Labarthe, *Typography: Mimesis, Philosophy, Politics*, ed. C. Fynsk (Cambridge, MA: Harvard University Press, 1989), pp. 1–42.
Hamacher, Werner, 'The Relation', trans. R. Végsö, *The New Centennial Review*, 8: 3 (2009), pp. 29–69.
Heidegger, Martin, *Basic Writings*, ed. D. F. Krell (New York: Harper & Row, 1977).
Heidegger, Martin, *Hölderlin's Hymns 'Germania' and 'Der Rhein'*, trans. W. McNeill and J. Ireland (Bloomington: Indiana University Press, 2014).
Heidegger, Martin, *On the Way to Language*, trans. Peter D. Hertz (New York: Harper & Row, 1982).

Horace, *The Odes of Horace*, trans. J. H. Kaimowitz (Baltimore: Johns Hopkins University Press, 2008).
Lacoue-Labarthe, Philippe, *Typography: Mimesis, Philosophy, Politics*, ed. C. Fynsk (Cambridge, MA: Harvard University Press, 1989).
Warminski, Andrzej, *Readings in Interpretation: Hölderlin, Hegel, Heidegger* (Minneapolis: University of Minnesota Press, 1987).
Zweig, Stefan, *Hölderlin, Kleist, and Nietzsche: The Struggle with the Daemon*, trans. E. and C. Paul (London: Pushkin Press, 2012).

Chapter 13

allowed, disallowed[1]

Thomas Schestag

Peculiar opening: 'every human being', notes Franz Kafka in a blue notebook in the summer of 1916,

> is peculiar, and by virtue of his peculiarity, called to flourish, but he must have found a taste for his own peculiarity. So far as my experience went, both in school and at home the aim was to blur all trace of peculiarity. This made the work of education easier, but also made life easier for the child, although, it is true, he first had to go through the pain caused him by discipline.[2]

The taste for peculiarity here is bound to trying – or tasting – the pain of breaking the obsessive resistance, built up by education at home and at school, that blocks the way towards the awareness of one's own peculiarity. The easy or unburdened life of the child has passed through the cost of pain. He passes through the pain to overcome the resistance built up by education against the child's taste for getting in touch with his peculiarity. The alleviated life of the child is the life enriched by tasting and testing the pain as a foretaste of the child's taste for his peculiarity. Every human being 'must', emphasises Kafka, in order to find his or her peculiarity also find a taste (*Geschmack*) for peculiarity: he or she must 'have come' to this taste (auf den Geschmack *gekommen sein*). But the child's taste or liking, of his own free will, for his own peculiarity, pushes back against the teleological coercion – an order (or law) – that he 'has to' find this taste. As if the decree – an ordinance (*Erlaß*) – to 'have to' find a 'taste' for one's peculiarity were the condition for leaving the language of ordinance, for leaving the area of commands and prohibitions traced out by it, like leaving off listening to a speaking that enforces obedience; in short, to see the decree-character (*Erlaß*character) of language dispensed with (*erlassen*); to break with legally binding speech, or more precisely: to pass through the cracks (*Risse*) in the outline (*Aufriß*) of legally binding speech. As if the child, in order to find a taste for his peculiarity, depended on having to go through the pain of 'having to' (*Müssen*) that is embodied by parents and teachers, a field of commands and prohibitions, thus to have to go through 'having to'. 'That was my peculiarity', writes Kafka, 'that I resisted the prohibition of reading further in a book at night, the command that I had to go to sleep, and decided to continue reading even without permission'.[3] My peculiarity was encapsulated in the unique *liaison* between permission and reading (and pleasure). It lay in the resolution – or more precisely, the *decision* – to yield to the uncontrollable pleasure for reading by allowing myself, without having been allowed to do so, to read further. What is peculiar about permission, it seems, is that it can be neither commanded nor prohibited. 'The prohibition against reading', claims Kafka, 'may only be an example, but a decisive one, as this prohibition had a deep impact.'[4] The deep impact of this prohibition – its unintentionally opaque reach and bottomless penetration – lies (less concealed than openly) in the fact that the prohibition against reading, in order to enter into force and to be able to produce an effect, must be read under any circumstance, yet must not be read under any circumstance: 'read that you should not read'! 'Read' (this): 'Don't read'! This reading, 'the uncontrollable pleasure for reading', is directed against the cracked, conflicted and double-edged prohibition of reading, and then passes through that prohibition, through the language of judgement and condemnation *in a peculiar way* (for that was my peculiarity). This reading splits the act of condemnation (*Aburteilen*) into distinct and separable parts, splitting *Ab-* and *-ur-* from *-teilen*, thus getting in touch, in the no-man's land of loose liaisons between pleasure and reading, between prescriptive law and prohibitive law, with the taste for a permission (*Erlauben*) which fails to turn into a *law* of permission, or *dictation*.

What are poets allowed to say? What do they allow themselves? And who (if such a question is allowed right at the outset) allows allowing? Do poets who, by virtue of writing, are called *poets* (*Dichter*) write under the *dictate* of a poetic law whose application and adherence to fulfilment or transgression in each poem emerges as an interpretation of the law? Or does the poem *dictate* (being called *Gedicht* for precisely that reason), almost in reverse, the law to which it corresponds in the first place? Do poems originate from laws or laws from poems? Assuming that poems dictate the law to which they correspond, is such a dictate an indication of a 'freedom according to the law of freedom', as Kant surmises in terms of 'art', or does 'nature' – the voice of nature – provide the rules of language from which the poem originates and to which it corresponds? But who commands, allows or prohibits such distinctions that claim a strict separation between 'nature' and 'art', 'necessity' and 'freedom', 'injustice' and 'justice'? Kant describes that which provokes such distinctions in the part of the introduction to *The Metaphysics of Morals* that addresses the difficulty of a division of a metaphysics of morals as 'the act of free choice in general' (*der Akt der freien Willkür überhaupt*). Thus, strictly speaking, a 'law of freedom' (*Freiheitsgesetz*) would not mean a law *of* freedom (*Gesetz der Freiheit*), but a law *out of* freedom (*Gesetz aus Freiheit*), in other words *freedom from the law* (*Freiheit vom Gesetz*): lawlessness (*Gesetzlosigkeit*). That authority that commands and prohibits would itself neither be commanded nor prohibited. Do poems arise lawlessly, but allow, in retrospect – without demanding or prohibiting it – to abstract a law of their emergence from the linguistic formation that is present *as* a poem? To decipher a 'system' in the poem? The difficulty of the division (*Einteilung*) of a system is that all legislation (that prescribes an action) requires a law of lawgiving (*Gesetzgebungsgesetz*) that orders the law-to-be-enacted to prescribe an action. It remains open, however, from what reason (*Grund*) or what reason*lessness* (*Grundlosigkeit*) the law of lawgiving arises. A crack (*Sprung*) runs through its origin (*Ursprung*). It is this crack that Kant has in mind when he writes:

> The deduction of the division of a system, i.e., a proof that it is both complete and continuous – that is, that a transition from the concept divided to the members of the division takes place without a leap (*divisio per saltum*) in the entire series of subdivisions – is one of the most difficult conditions which the architect of a system has to fulfil.[5]

The division takes place in an *un*guided, *un*disclosed manner, *at odds* (*uneins*) with itself. The parts that rise from the division of a system, such as 'nature' and 'art', remain – in each of their parts, in each syllable, each letter – *separable*: subject of that *tmesis* that they rise from without *having risen* (*entsprungen zu sein*). In the word 'system' we have nothing but an anagram of *tmesis* before us.[6] The construction of a 'system' is haunted by the 'critique' that is supposed to lay its foundation (*Grundstein*), the critique from which the system is supposed to rise. No part of a system – not even the word 'system' – sets in motion or guides its division. No part seamlessly forms a part of that ladder that the system should form as a scale of continuity in regard to its arrangement of levels (lines or verses): the system, at each level and in each word – *escalates*.

What, then, allows the construction of a poem from parts to become a (poetic) system? What in a poem allows the suspension of its perception as a lawgiving law in regard to systematic cohesion? Is it 'poetic licence'?

What does a poem allow (itself)? In terms of poetic licence, Théodore de Banville has nothing to spare but a half sentence in the chapter 'Licenses poétiques' of his *Petit traité de poésie française* (Paris 1871): 'Il n'y en a pas' ('There is none'). And Banville (who already in his own name bans from the city a kind of poetry that takes or, in other words, allows itself liberties: *Banville*) comments on his *apodictum* against poetic licence, a prohibition clothed in a series of statements, as follows:

> Le premier qui imagina d'accoupler ce substantif *licence* et cet adjectif *poétique* a créé et lancé dans la circulation une bêtise grosse comme une montagne, et qui, par malheur, ne s'est pas bornée à accoucher d'un seul rat! Comment et pourquoi y aurait-il des *licences* en poésie? Quoi! sous prétexte qu'on écris en vers, c'est-à-dire dans la langue rhythmée et ordonnée par excellence, on aurait le droit d'être désordonné et de violer les lois de la grammaire ou celles du bon sens!

> The first one to whom it occurred to couple the substantive *license* with the adjective *poetic* has committed a foolishness and put it in circulation. This foolishness is as big as a mountain and, unfortunately, has born more than a rat. How and why should there be *license* in poetry? What! Under the pretext of writing verse – the ordered and rhythmic speech *par excellence* – one would have the right to create disorder and to violate the laws of grammar and common sense![7]

The language (of healthy common sense) is subject to (grammatical) laws; the law of poetry, however, transcends this subservience: it follows the law of metrics. The law (or set of laws) of poetry is *grammato-metric*. According to Banville, nothing that shatters this order is allowed to poets. He prohibits (not only to himself) any question about the formation (and disfigurability) of grammatical and metrical laws, any question about the origin (or lack of origin) of 'poetic licence'.

Between poetry as law and the lawless poem, between commanded and prohibited poetic avenues of approach, between the division of all laws in general, and above all into *commands* and *prohibitions* (as in Kant's section of *Groundwork to the Metaphysics of Morals* that deals with the *Introduction to the Metaphysics of Morals*) – *between* poem and law – there appears, as well as in the outline of each of these divided domains, the question of *allowing*. Rather inconspicuously in the first phrase of Jacob Grimm's essay, *Von der Poesie im Recht* (1815, *Zeitschrift für geschichtliche Rechtswissenschaft*): 'For once it should be allowed to grasp the [language of the] law (*Recht*) from the viewpoint of poetry and to create living evidence of one in the other.' But in the next sentence, Jacob Grimm turns the permission for such an attempt into a command: 'It is our German ancestry that now asks for and demands such an attempt.'[8] It is no longer allowed, but rather commanded, 'to grasp the law' (*Recht*) 'from the viewpoint of poetry', whereby poetry is again grasped from the viewpoint of law, and allowance – suspended. The question of allowance comes up in the previously mentioned passage regarding the preconceptions (the preconceptual version of preconceptions) from the *Introduction to the Metaphysics of Morals*. There, Kant elaborates as follows:

> The categorical imperative, as expressing an obligation in respect to certain actions, is a morally practical law. But because obligation involves not merely practical necessity expressed in a law as such, but also actual necessitation, the categorical imperative is a law either of command or prohibition, according as the doing or not doing of an action is represented as a duty. An action which is neither commanded nor forbidden is merely allowed, because there is no law restricting freedom, nor any duty in respect of it. Such an action is said to be morally indifferent (indifferens, adiaphoron, res merae facultatis). One may ask whether there are such morally indifferent actions; and if there are, whether in addition to the preceptive and prohibitive law (lex praeceptiva et prohibitiva, lex mandati et vetiti), there is also required a permissive law (lex permissiva), in order that one may be free in such relations to act, or to forbear from acting, at his pleasure? If it were so, the moral right in question would not, in all cases, refer to actions that are indifferent in themselves (adiaphora); for no special law would be required to establish such a right, considered according to moral laws.[9]

As a law, the categorical imperative is either a prescriptive or a prohibitive law. Asking the question of the relation between the allowed action that is neither commanded nor prohibited and the law as such, Kant raises the issue of the overextension of the law, of the demolition of its categorical nature: a no man's land within the outline (*Aufriß*) of the question of laws, an area of territorial breakdowns within the outline of those territorial claims. Earlier in the text, Kant had introduced, or inserted, the 'preconception' of 'allowed' action as follows:

> Every action is *allowed* (licitum) which is not contrary to obligation; and this freedom not being limited by an opposing imperative, constitutes a moral right as a warrant or title of action (facultas moralis). From this it is at once evident what actions are *disallowed* or illicit (illicita).[10]

An action that is neither binding nor non-binding is called 'allowed'. Allowed actions are 'authorised' actions, but a crack runs through both the joint (*Fuge*) and the authorisation (*Befugnis*), because, on the one hand, the allowed action as authorised action, almost an obligation, joins unjoined parts. Thus it may be rightly (*mit Fug und Recht*) called authorised (*befugt*). On the other hand, however, 'by joining together' (hence on the one hand and on the other hand play into 'one another'), the *allowed* action lays bare a crack in the joint, a crack in the connection that the connected parts cover up. The allowed action takes place between the binding and the non-binding, neither *entirely* binding nor *entirely* non-binding, but in the joint: it lays bare cracks (*Risse*) in the outline (*Aufriß*) of the word *joint* (*Fuge*). Now, using Kant's *pre*conceptual form (or joint) of the preconception *allowed* in reference to language, what does the doing of an allowed action, happening *close to* language (*sprachnah*), as a para-linguistic doing – *poiein* – do to the words of a language in which – at first sight – a poem is written? What is, in other words, *allowed* to be *said* (allowed not only to poets)? And who is authorised (*befugt*) to speak? No law (of linguistic action) is able to anticipate the answer (which is neither commanded nor forbidden) to such questions. In the passage in which the pre-concept *allowed* is not grasped in a binding manner but characterised merely negatively as 'not contrary to obligation', it is not understandable what 'allowed' means, and even less does it go without saying what 'disallowed' could mean. The meaning of what is 'allowed' escapes conceptual, and thus linguistically determined, terminological obligation. What is 'allowed' is what suspends the categorical imperative with all of its duty-bound actions out of privation, necessity and compelled action. Allowed actions are neither ethical nor unethical, neither good nor evil (one may call them 'innocent'). They are called 'ethically neutral': indifferent. One may ask what it means (or could mean) to say: 'One may ask'. As if this phrase (which may be referred to as neither commanded nor forbidden) secretly came up accompanied by the tacit question of whether such a question is allowed, whether one can also omit to ask or refrain from asking that which *can* be asked, and what, precisely at this point between asking a question and refraining from asking it, it means that one *may* ask – 'fragen *kann*', writes Kant, 'whether there are such actions.' One may ask, if 'allowed' actions do exist at all. One may ask (at this point): is *what one may ask* neither commanded nor forbidden but rather *allowed*? Does to ask such questions remain indifferent towards *posited* questions, raised in view of answers? Can what *can* be asked also be left unasked? Is, as Kant hints at this point toward a question that one may ask, 'a law of *permission*' required 'regarding whether anyone is free to do something or to *refrain from it at will*'? 'To do or to refrain from it': what is allowed is what I can, at will (*nach Belieben*), not only do – a doing that also encompasses the Greek *poiein* – but also refrain from, or not do. Can I, in turn, *do* this *not*- or *none*-doing? Or – *refrain from doing (lassen)*? In what is called allowance a peculiar (*eigentümliches*), and peculiarly non-binding, decree as well as a desisting from doing and not-doing alike (or refraining from, if not leaving – abandoned) are at play, a desisting *in extremis* from allowance (itself). Something like, if it is allowed to say so, a disallowing (*Entlaubnis*). Kant allows for a question – 'One may ask' – but it remains open *who* is asking here, and whether the question is truly posed or plays at the threshold of a quotation: If there are allowed actions – though (and I quote) 'one may ask' if such questions do exist at all – must there also exist a law of *permission* (*Erlaubnisgesetz*)? A *lex permissiva*, according to Kant, would only then *have to be called for* (*geboten*) if the allowed action were not ethically indifferent – thus not allowed, but rather disallowed. In regard to what is called 'allowed', there must not only *not* be a law of *permission*, but no *law* at all, for allowed actions may act or not act at all: *allowed* actions do suspend the question whether to act or not to act. Allowed *linguistic* acts suspend the decision on the character of a *linguistic* doing or not doing in general, but in particular, they suspend the decision on the character of a *poetic* doing or not doing. *Why poets* (one may ask) as long as poetry remains limited to *doing*, to *poiein*? What would a poetising be that in *doing* deciphers – or in other words, *allows for* – a refraining from or not-doing? Would such a poetry, tentatively called 'allowed' poetry, that is neither commanded nor prohibited and that neither commands nor prohibits, in other words not *dichtet* – that is, dictate – and without being strictly speaking *counter*-poetic (for it allows one to perceive in poetic doing a not- or un-doing); would such a poetry, not subordinated to any poetic *law*, and neither embodying nor breaking such law; neither dissolving nor fulfilling the law; would *permitted* poetry be, similar to the innocent character of allowed actions that are called ethically indifferent, not simply innocent, but – for it would allow *linguistic indifference* to come to the fore – *most* innocent, as Hölderlin puts it in a letter to his mother in January 1799, '[Dichtung] diß unschuldigste aller Geschäffte' (*FHA* XIX, 350): [poetry] this most innocent of all businesses? 'One may ask': are allowed actions – actions that neither merely *do* nor merely *refrain from doing* – still actions? Are allowed actions that neither do nor do *not*, nor *un*do, but rather do *as if* they did (suspending the decision whether they actually do or truly and effectively abstain from doing) thus refrain *as if* they refrained (suspending the decision whether they actually omit or omit omission)? One may ask, I say, and by saying so I probably do also say that I, without raising the question *indeed*, allow for such a question (without asking for permission): are *allowed* actions not only ethically – and legally – but also linguistically and, in particular, *poetically* indifferent? *Poetic indifference* would consist in this – or lay bare – that a strict separation between *doing* and *leaving* (undone) (*zwischen Tun und Lassen*), only came loosely (but without simply resisting obligation) and inconspicuously (as if omitted) into appearance: in touch with language.

An introductory note that Hölderlin added, *après coup*, to a first draft of 'Der Rhein' (summer 1802), captures 'the law of this poem':

Das Gesez dieses Gesanges ist, daß die zwei ersten Parthien der Form <nach> durch Progreß u. Regreß entgegengesezt, aber dem Stoff nach gleich, die 2

folgenden der Form nach gleich dem Stoff nach entgegengesezt sind die
lezte aber mit durchgängiger Metapher alles ausgleicht. (*FHA* VIII, 603)

The law of this poem is that the first two parts are formally opposed as progression and regression, but are alike in subject matter; the two succeeding parts are formally alike but are opposed as regards subject matter; the last part, however, balances everything out with a continuous metaphor.[11]

According to the 'law' outlined above, the poem, composed of fifteen stanzas, is divided into five triads of stanzas, sections (*Parthien*) or parts. According to the overarching distinction between 'form' and 'subject matter', the first two triads are formally opposed as progression and regression, but are alike in terms of subject matter. In reverse, the two succeeding ones are opposed (again as progression and regression) in terms of subject matter, but formally alike. The third triad, though, balances everything out with 'a continuous metaphor'. 'The law of this poem is', writes Hölderlin: this almost apodictic opening (that seems to subordinate the poem under a poetic law), however, leaves open whether the law to which 'this poem' corresponds or conforms *dictates* (more or less categorically) the course of this poem, or, almost in reverse, whether the law as law of this *one*, of no *other* poem, only originates from the poem 'Der Rhein', but cannot be abstracted (*bereinigt*) from the poem from which it originates – a poem that describes nothing but the originating of the Rhine, nothing but the originating of the poem 'Der Rhein' – cannot be freed from (*überhoben*) the poem, and can thus no longer be described as having originated (*entsprungen*) from the poem. 'The law of this poem is', or seems to be, this: neither does the poem originate from the law, nor the law from the poem. (Rather, they both share a leap – *Sprung*). It is as if one could ask at this point: is the poem allowed to originate (*entspringen*) from the law; is the law allowed to originate from the poem? The law of this poem concerns a balancing relationship between positing (*Setzung*) and counter-positing (*Entgegensetzung*), or less distinct, between *positing* and *-positing* (*Setzung, -setzung*), between law and counter-law (*Gesetz und Entgegengesetz*), or more indistinguishably, between *law* and *-law* (*Gesetz und -gesetz*): a balancing relationship in the outline (*im Aufriß*) of the positing of law. Is, one may ask, such a balancing out a third, a law of balance, or (more cautiously speaking) a balancing *gesture* (*Geste*), between the law of progression and the law of regression; in other words, between a commanding and prohibiting, between an anticipatory and withholding, between a prescriptive and prohibiting law, is there one more law? Is there, between *lex praeceptiva* and *lex prohibitiva*, a *lex permissiva* at work? Or does there intervene, in-between the two, a gesture – uncalled for, allowed – that remains indifferent with respect to the law (and that lays bare a peculiar indifference in the law's relation to itself, in the nature of dominion)? In the poem 'Der Rhein', the word 'allowed' surfaces in a place that does not conform to the 'law of this poem' but without contradicting it either. According to its law, subdivided into five sections of three stanzas each, the poem remains indifferent with respect to other cuts through the partition of the poem – open between law and poem. The same applies to the middle of the poem which itself – almost in reverse – remains indifferent with respect to the 'law of this poem'. Precisely in the middle of the poem, in the second stanza of the third triad, exactly in the middle of this middle, in the midst of the eighth (*achten*) stanza of the poem, which *disregards* (*nicht achtet*) the law of this poem – as if, according to both the law and the poem, one had to *outlaw* (*ächten*) it, because of its un*real* (un*echt*) character. This occurs exactly in the middle of the middle of the poem 'Der Rhein', a middle that neither conforms to the law of progression nor to the law of regression, neither to a law of subject matter nor to a formal law, but whose relationship to the law of the poem, 'of this' poem (which poetises the originating of both the law and the poem), can at best be seen as indifference with respect to both laws as well as to the 'law of this poem'. This is precisely where indifference to the poem and to the law is being addressed, where both the poem and the law seem to be put at risk, because no counterpart (*Gegenüber*), neither a counter-poem (*Gegengesang*) nor a counter-law (*Gegengesetz*), is mentioned, exactly in that place where the two halves of the poem that are not being mentioned in the note about the law, because the 'law of this poem' follows other divisions, seem to pause. As if balanced, for a while. Therefore, where the 'mystery of things of pure origin'[12] (*Rätsel des Reinentsprungenen*) may come up (an enigma of which it is previously said that 'Auch / Der Gesang kaum darf es enthüllen' ['Even song / May hardly reveal it']) (*FHA* VIII, 629) precisely where law and poem originate (or have their origin) and where the 'law of this poem' seems to be unstitched (*aufgetrennt*) – it is precisely there where the word 'erlaubt' comes to the surface:

> Denn weil
> Die Seeligsten nichts fühlen von selbst,
> Muß wohl, wenn solches zu sagen
> Erlaubt ist, in der Götter Nahmen
> Theilnehmend fühlen ein Andrer,
> Den brauchen sie.
>
> (*FHA* VIII, 631)

> For since
> The serenest beings feel nothing on their own accord,
> There must be, if to say so
> Is allowed, another who, taking part,

Feels in the gods' names, it
Is him they need.

Because they are immortal, the serenest beings or gods are without feeling. Their perfection lacks imperfection: the gods lack a sense of failing that, here, is condensed to *feeling*. In the poem, gods and human beings, immortals and mortals are being contrasted as extremes or, to use a word from the eighth stanza, as 'unequal' (*Ungleiches*). The hubris of the mortals consists in 'striving' (*trachten*) – this is how the last line of the seventh stanza transitions to the eighth – to 'equal the gods'. Yet, in terms of *feeling*, the eighth stanza, in the middle of the entire poem – neither law nor poem – does not only brush (*streifen*) the counter-word of 'insensitivity' (*Fühllosigkeit*), but articulates in order to balance out the missing feeling of those who do not feel and the feeling to fall short of being without feeling, the 'theilnehmende Fühlen' (participating feeling) of another with the phrase 'wenn solches zu sagen / Erlaubt ist, in der Götter Nahmen' ('if to say so / Is allowed . . . in the gods' names'). It is in the name (*Nahme*) that infallibility (of those who do not feel) and fallibility (of those who feel) get in touch (*nehmen Fühlung*) with one another. This getting in touch is called 'theilnehmend' ('taking part'). What both share is a flaw (*Fehl*), a failing (*Fehlen*) or fallibility (*Fehlbarkeit*): those who are infallible lack the ability to fail; those who are feeling lack the ability not to feel. This *part*aking feeling as a *getting in touch* in which the feeling (that I feel: being alive) plays into feeling (that I do not feel: not being alive) and appears to be interposed between *permission* and *command*. The middle of the poem – 'Der Rhein' – (its innermost, outermost seam: an unploughed strip (*Rain*) disfigures the command 'must' (*muß*), by adding 'perhaps' (*wohl*), thus turning it into a 'must perhaps' (*muß wohl*), a parody of the categorical imperative. The enforcement of the imperative depends on a permission: 'if to say so / Is allowed'. However, the permission 'to say so' does not, in the end, depend on a 'decree' (*Erlaß*) because the assumption of an entity that grants or concedes a permission – 'if to say so / Is allowed' – is outdone (*überholt*), left behind (*übervorteilt*) by that which remains to be said. It appears to be suspended, and that which remains (allowed) to be said is peculiarly exempted (*eigentümlich erlassen*), abandoned (*verlassen*) or omitted (*unterlassen*), even free of permission (*der Erlaubnis ledig*), and is addressed (again, 'if to say so / Is allowed') in a disallowed way: *entlaubt*. That there is 'another who feels / In the Gods' names'. The *part*icipating feeling, or *getting* in touch (Fühlung*nahme*), takes part in a way that in the taking part one can not only decipher participation in a whole that is composed of parts or 'sections' (be it law, hymn or poem), but also – in a more interfering or more par*taking* way – the disintegration of each of the parts or sections out of which the whole appears to be arranged (*gefügt*). *Taking* (*Nehmen*) does not only mean receiving (*Entgegennehmen*) as acceptance of a gift – here, *of a* given *word* – but (almost contrary to that assumption about *taking*): cutting into (*Einschneiden*), unstitching (*Auftrennen*), splitting (*Spalten*). Participation cuts participation off (*die Teilnahme fällt der Teilnahme ins Wort*) and specifies each *entire* word that originates from participation or a series of participations, as the failing or missing (*Fehl*) of another, but in a way that both participations, held together, yield neither as undivided halves nor as halves of an entire word. They also do not display a word segmented into *its own*, that is into its *constituent* parts. The phrase 'in the gods' names' (*in der Götter Nahmen*), an echo of the overused turn of phrase 'in God's name', (quietly) defies the fate that seems to have been decreed from inside this turn of phrase: as if something had been *allowed* to be said *in the name* (of the law, of the poem, of God); for the more *part*icipating feeling (or *taking* part) does not only intervene 'in the gods' names', thus not in God's name or in the name of God, in a random (also linguistic) event, but also – turning against them (*gegenwendig*) – cuts in 'the gods' names' (*in der Götter Nahmen*), that is into names of gods (*Götternahmen*), unstitches the names, but hardly articulating in words, may they be given or broken, nor in any (given, broken) language the instability (*Unbestand*) of words – initiated by the incisive taking of names. The more *part*icipating feeling takes the groundlessness of words and language (*Sprache*) to the fallow (*Brache*). It leaves them (almost abandoned), to put it with a Kantian expression used by Hölderlin, to the 'free use' (*freier Gebrauch*) which deciphers a *break* (*Bruch*) in *custom* (*Brauch*) – one of the translations of the Greek *nómos*. Yet, the break is fissured with breaks: books (*Bücher*), beeches (*Buchen*), letters: *Buch-staben*. What is at play, at free play 'in the gods' names', almost to be felt, almost without feeling, neither completely sensible, nor completely anaesthetic, are the names, *partial* names (*Teil*nahmen), due to those more *part*icipating feelings. At play in Rhine (*Rhein*) are things of *pure* origin (*Rein*entsprungenes), and other takes: otherwise: *anderes – anders*. Neither unallowed nor forbidden, neither allowed nor called for.

At one point towards the end of his early investigation 'Two Poems by Friedrich Hölderlin: "Dichtermut"– "Blödigkeit"', Walter Benjamin comes up with an astounding phrase:

> Only now shall Hölderlin's phrase 'sacredly sober' be uttered, now that its understanding has been determined. Others have noted that these words exhibit the tendency of his later creations. They arise from the inner certainty with which these stand in their own intellectual life, in which sobriety is neither unallowed nor forbidden, it is allowed, called for (*erlaubt, geboten*

ist), because this life is in itself sacred, standing beyond all exaltation in the sublime.[13]

What remains open in this passage is whether the creations (*Schöpfungen*) originate from the words of the 'sacredly sober' (that Benjamin cites from one among Hölderlin's later creations, the poem 'Hälfte des Lebens'), or whether these originate from those, or whether both contain or hold each other back. And who (or what) originates from whom (or what). The 'inner certainty', with which these words or poems stand 'in their own intellectual life', is permeated by cracks. In this life, 'sobriety' is 'now allowed, called for . . . because it . . . stands outside of all exaltation in the sublime'. The turn of phrase 'erlaubt, geboten', placed in the middle of this sentence, stands displaced. No word, merely a comma, relates *allowed, commanded* to one another. The gap leaves open whether the word 'commanded' originates from the word 'allowed', leaving it behind, or whether the word 'allowed' already contains the word 'commanded' and is taken into it, or whether these two words' relation is coloured by indifference, whether they confirm, correct or contradict each other. And whether permission or command calls for or *dispenses from* (*erläßt*) the phrase 'allowed, commanded' at this point or not. This phrase intensifies an inhibition, and it quotes an inhibition. It echoes Kant's hesitation at one point in the *Introduction to the Metaphysics of Morals*, to pass on from what is called 'merely being allowed' – 'to do . . . something at will or not do it' – to the assumption of a law or command of permission. Does it take *courage*, at this point in Benjamin's investigation, to summon up the phrase 'allowed, commanded'? Is it sign of 'timidity' (*Blödigkeit*) or of shyness to free what is called 'allowed' from the shadow of what is called 'commanded'? That, in this passage, being-allowed moves on to the commanded, may have its reason in a presupposition that underlies Benjamin's examination: that only the poem 'Blödigkeit', developed out of the poem 'Dichtermut', which Benjamin calls 'first draft', fulfils the poetic law: 'that the poetic law has not yet fulfilled itself in this Hölderlinian world'.[14] It is the presupposition of a *poetic law* remaining unfulfilled in one poem, but coming to fulfilment in another, that underlies and urges Benjamin's investigation to let what is called 'allowed', separated only by a comma from what is called 'commanded', originate from a *lex permissiva* or to take it back into a prescriptive law.

Years later, the hesitation before the word 'allowed' resurfaces in another essay: 'On the Critique of Violence'. In connection with the attempt of a 'sweeping critique' of the legal or executive, and thus lawfully sanctioned use of violence as such (a violence that would also be at work in the application of *poetic laws*), Benjamin rejects two famous maxims. The first is a citation from Goethe's *Torquato Tasso*: 'Allowed is what pleases' ('Erlaubt ist, was gefällt'). Such a maxim, according to Benjamin,

> merely excludes reflection on the moral and historical spheres, and thereby on any meaning in action, and beyond this on any meaning in reality itself, which cannot be constituted if 'action' is removed from its sphere.[15]

This critique of the phrase 'Allowed is what pleases' follows Kant in the assessment that *allowed* action would be 'ethically-indifferent' and finds itself tangled up in the turn of phrase 'One may ask':

> One may ask whether there are such . . . actions; and if there are, whether in addition to the preceptive and prohibitive law . . . there is also required a permissive law (lex permissiva), in order that one may be free in such relations to act, or to forbear from acting, at his pleasure?[16]

Allowed *doing* would be one that, in the origin of the will to *act*, plays into some *un*-doing, a doing that is *amiss, omitted* and *refrained from*. Back before the sweeping critique of legal violence as such, the maxim 'Allowed is what pleases' articulates a critique of *action* which, in its intention to act, and thus, in an eminent sense also to act *linguistically*, deciphers a deliberate refraining from (*aus freien Stücken*). In speaking – an inability (to speak) that pleases. The phrase 'Allowed is what pleases' jeopardises nothing less than the belief in the reality of humankind. It is perhaps no coincidence that Torquato Tasso (the poet), attributes, from memory or from back-before memory (*Vorerinnerung*) – in which a deliberate speaking seems to be at play – of the gone by golden age, the speaking of this phrase to animals addressing humans:

> That golden age . . .
> Where every bird in unrestricted air
> And every beast that rambled hill and valley,
> Said to our kind: Allowed is what pleases.[17]

The other maxim, in which Benjamin registers his doubt, is the *Categorical Imperative*:

> More important is the fact that even the appeal, so frequently attempted, to the categorical imperative, with its doubtless incontestable minimum program – act in such a way that at all times you use humanity both in your person and in the person of all others as an end, and never merely as a means – is in itself inadequate for such a critique.[18]

A note to this passage clarifies that Benjamin takes offence at the wording, as limited as it may be, to make use of humanity as 'means'. The 'rather' (*Vielmehr*, literally: much more) of the doubt points to a *too little*, namely to the phrase 'never merely as a means'. The wording 'never merely' says 'too little': it already says *too much*. Only *less*, namely to consider humanity never altogether – not only never *merely* – as a means, would have been *more*. Benjamin's doubt of the *famous wording* inscribes the question of what *may be allowed*, under the presupposition that there are human beings, into the framework of ethical action and non-action without getting in touch with a speech that neither serves as ends nor as means, that may neither be called 'language as such' nor 'language of man' (and perhaps not even 'language'), but proceeds (*verfährt*) without purpose or means. A speech in which – almost like in the muting (*Stillstellung*) of *too little* and *too much* that Benjamin briefly touches upon in his note – the turning indifferent (*Vergleichgültigung*) of speech serving means and ends comes to the fore.

The next to last stanza of the poem 'Andenken' commemorates the friends' dwelling – exposed – on the sea, 'einsam, jahrlang, unter / Dem entlaubten Mast' (*FHA* VIII, 805) ('alone, year after year / under the leafless mast'). The rigid 'mast' is the 'mast' (*Mastbaum*) of which the word *tree* has been cut off; it is missing twigs, thick branches (*Zweige, dichte*). Yet, as if to make up for what is missing from the defoliated trunk (*am entlaubten Stamm*), the particle *-ast* (limb of a tree) of the word *Mast* (a truncated anagram of *Stam-* : trunk) allows to remember the missing branches, leaves and limbs. In the last line of the poem – 'Was bleibet aber, stiften die Dichter' ('What remains, however, is brought about by the poets') (*FHA* VIII, 805) – it is less the moveable *pen* (*Stift*), absent from the page (or leaf), or the *poets* who do not bring about (*stiften*) a genealogical tree (*Stammbaum*), but the defoliated leaf (*entlaubte Blatt*), treeless (*baumlos*), that remains. One cannot rely on the traces it leaves. To the eyes that fix the gaze on both the leaf and the letters to find hold, seeking to see, the leaf remains – precisely for *that* reason, *non*-reason (*Ungrund*), exempted: *loose* (*erlassen*: *-los*).

A letter to Milena from the middle of August 1920 revisits, this time differently, the loose entanglement of *reading, pleasure, permission* and *prohibition* that Kafka had traced out, years earlier, in the note about a taste for the unsublatable peculiarity in each human being. This time it is about the peculiar reading of an enigmatic scene of branching gestures: the narration of the moment of the fall from paradise, between Adam and Eve at the foot of a leafy tree (full of fruit). Kafka's comment on what Milena had written in a previous letter about 'people who share their mornings and evenings and those who don't'[19] paves the way to the reading of this scene. This, too is a *scene*, or more precisely, the comparative contemplation of a position

(*Lage*), a laying together of two people at night, who either lay together due to a marital contract or deliberately (*aus freien Stücken*) share a lair, and who, by doing so, may break that contractual marital bond (*Band*), that (old or new) covenant (*Bund*) under certain conditions. Writes Kafka:

> Precisely the latter situation is the more favourable. They have done something bad, possibly or certainly, and the filth of this scene derives essentially from their being strangers (*Fremdsein*) – as you correctly say – and it is physical filth just like the filth in an apartment that has never been occupied and is suddenly, savagely torn open. This is bad but nothing decisively has happened, no decision to affect both Heaven and Earth, it really is just 'playing with a ball', as you call it.[20]

The word 'bad' (*schlimm*) frames the ends of the scene of the two lying together at night awake (*nachtwach*). It is a cover word. For as a synonym of the word 'bad' (*schlecht*) it traces (*reißt an*) the entanglement of the sexes (*Geschlechter*) into each other, sexes that tear each other open and enter into one another like into apartments that were never previously occupied. It is, without finding one's way into habits, into the occupation of a dwelling, without finding one's way into *dwelling with one another* (*Beiwohnen*), a foreign dwelling, unfamiliar to dwelling, a dwelling without a dwelling (barely familiar with the 'without' (*-ohne*) in dwelling (*Wohnen*), between evening and morning, unfamiliar with dwelling in one's own sex, unfamiliar with the entanglement – cracked open, fissured – of the sexes. They tear apart – wild, foreign to each other – the foreign night, that they openly (but not decisively) share between 'pleasure' (*Lust*) and 'reading' (*Lesen*) because they have, both strangers, *picked* each other *up* (*aufgelesen*): between *permission* and *prohibition*. With 'dirt' (*Schmutz*), a word that Kafka seems to cite from Milena's letter, the word 'pain' (*Schmerz*) from his earlier comment about pleasure and taste for peculiarity in each human being openly comes into play (almost as an echo) between *defence*lessness (*Schutz*losigkeit) and *shame*lessness (*Scham*losigkeit). Kafka, comparing and picking up or intercepting Milena's words about 'playing with a ball', moves on to the reading of that other scene:

> It is as if Eve had indeed picked the apple (sometimes I think I understand the Fall like no one else), but just to show it to Adam – because she liked it. It was the biting that was decisive; of course playing with the apple also wasn't allowed, but neither was it prohibited.[21]

Kafka compares Eve's tearing the apple off the tree (of knowledge) with the game in which the foreign lovers, out of love for foreignness, in each other, find a taste or a liking for the peculiarity of the unfamiliar that they *share*: to caress (*kosen*) and to taste (*kosten*) the *peculiar, divisible* foreignness of gender – untranslatable into habit – being condensed here into a torn off fruit (an apple): *to tear open*. (Or break). This caressing, tearing open, and this sharing of the foreignness of sex at night is like tearing the apple off the tree away from the trunk, from branches and leaves, both a defoliating (*Entlauben*) and showing, the showing being an offer to get in touch because, as Kafka writes, she liked him. She has found a taste for him. For the tearing off and for the showing of the fruit. No leaf, no *fig* leaf was between them. *He*, however, remains suspended in these lines between 'Adam' and 'apple'. The *showing* (*Zeigen*) of the fruit is a *branched* (*verzweigtes*) showing. Pleasure of reading in the branched sign (*verzweigtes Zeichen*). Pleasure of reading as tearing off, open and apart. The (radical) liking of a defoliated, branched showing of the foreign fruit plays on the threshold to the decision that Kafka condenses into the *biting into* (*Hineinbeißen*): on the threshold to the yet to be made judgement (of taste) that results in the knowledge about the apple in a way that the taste for the apple (the savouring and tasting of the apple), as well as the liking (of the branched showing), are *supposed to* fall out of the judgement: merely post-positioned (*nachgestellt*) as a means on the way to gain of knowledge, to assimilation and appropriation (including separation and segregation), towards dwelling in the foreign gender (*Geschlecht*) that is alienated (*ent*fremdet) from the foreign and that, outcast from the foreign (*Fremde*), distastefully transitions to the ordinary, into habit. The liking – still of the biting into the fruit – plays on the threshold of the judgement yet to be pronounced, the pronounced judgement. While playing was not allowed, it was not prohibited either. It plays, like children's (verbal) hopscotch, between (German) *war* (was) and *zwar* (though). While the *playing-with-it* (still including the biting-into-it, the decision-making, and the judging) was not allowed, it was not prohibited either. It was a showing that offered itself (*entbietendes Zeigen*). It was defoliated, disallowed (*entlaubt*): shameless, innocent, undecided liking (liking of the undecided) that does not stop cutting even into the judgement once pronounced, turning the *pronounced* (*gefallene*) into the *pleasing* (*gefallenden*). The pronounced judgement does *not ex*clude the liking of cuts through that which has been pronounced, and it does not exclude the unsublatable pleasure of an oddly tearing and fissured way of reading of that which has been pronounced. It does *not ex*clude it. In other words: does *not in*clude it.

Translated by Annette Budzinski and Jonathan Luftig

Notes

1. The original title of this essay is *erlaubt, entlaubt*. In German, 'entlaubt' means 'defoliated'. The context of this essay, though, allows for an additional reading: 'opposite of *permitted*', 'disallowed'.

2. Kafka, *Wedding Preparations in the Country*, pp. 221–2, translation modified.
3. Kafka, *Nachgelassene Schriften und Fragmente II*, p. 8. If not otherwise indicated, cited sources are translated by Annette Budzinski and Jonathan Luftig.
4. Ibid. p. 9.
5. Kant, *Practical Philosophy*, p. 383.
6. The rhetorical term *tmesis* refers to the splitting of a word through the insertion of another word.
7. Banville, *Petit traité de poésie française*, pp. 63–4, trans. Thomas Schestag.
8. Jacob Grimm, *Kleinere Schriften*, pp. 152–91.'Es ist wol auch einmal erlaubt, das recht unter dem gesichtspunkt der poesie zu fassen und aus der einen in das andere lebendiges zeugnis geltend zu machen. einen solchen versuch fordert und verlangt jetzo zumal unser deutsches alterthum [. . .]'. English translation by Thomas Schestag.
9. Kant, *Werke in zehn Bänden*, vol. VII, pp. 21–2. The English translation is from Kant, *Introduction to the Metaphysics of Morals*, p. 31, translation modified.
10. Ibid. p. 30.
11. Hölderlin, *Hyperion and Selected Poems*, 259.
12. Hölderlin, *Poems and Fragments*, 433.
13. Benjamin, *Selected Writings I*, p. 35, translation modified.
14. Ibid. p. 24.
15. Benjamin, *Reflections*, p. 284.
16. Kant, *Introduction to the Metaphysics of Morals*, p. 24.
17. Goethe, *Verse, Plays and Epic*, p. 80, translation modified.
18. Benjamin, *Reflections*, pp. 284–5.
19. Kafka, *Letters to Milena*, p. 160.
20. Ibid. p. 160.
21. Kafka, *Letters to Milena*, p. 161. In the original, the phrase 'weil er ihr gefallen hat' ('because she liked it/him') may refer to both Adam and the apple.

Bibliography

Banville, Théodore de, *Petit traité de poésie française* (Paris: G. Charpentier, Éditeur, 1883).
Benjamin, Walter, *Reflections*, in Peter Demetz (ed.), *Essays, Aphorisms, and Biographical Writings*, trans. Edmund Jephcott (New York: Schocken, 1986).
Benjamin, Walter, *Selected Writings I: 1913–1926*, ed. Marcus Bullock and Michael W. Jennings (Cambridge, MA: Harvard University Press, 2004).
Goethe, Johann Wolfgang von, *The Collected Works, Vol. 8: Verse Plays and Epic*, ed. Cyrus Hamlin and Frank Ryder, trans. Michael Hamburger, Hunter Hannum and David Luke (Princeton: Princeton University Press, 1995).
Grimm, Jakob, *Kleinere Schriften* (Berlin: Ferd. Dümmlers Verlagsbuchhandlung, 1882), vol. 6, pp. 152–91.
Kafka, Franz, *Letters to Milena*, trans. Philip Boehm (New York: Schocken, 1990).
Kafka, Franz, *Nachgelassene Schriften und Fragmente*, ed. Jost Schillemeit (Frankfurt: Fischer, 2002), vol. 2.
Kafka, Franz, *Wedding Preparations in the Country* (London: Penguin Classics, 1978).
Kant, Immanuel, *Introduction to the Metaphysic of Morals*, trans. William Hastie (Edinburgh: Clark, 1887).
Kant, Immanuel, *Practical Philosophy*, trans. Mary J. Gregor (Cambridge: Cambridge University Press, 1996).
Kant, Immanuel, *Werke in zehn Bänden*, ed. Wilhelm Weischedel (Darmstadt: Wissenschaftliche Buchgesellschaft, 1975), vol. 7 (*Schriften zur Ethik und Religionsphilosophie*, Zweiter Teil).

Notes on Contributors

Annette Budzinski teaches German at Towson University in Maryland. Her research focuses on practices, theories and literary representations of *Bildung* since 1750, including German readings and translations of Dante. She has presented work on Dante, Herder, Schlegel and Tieck and has translated philosophical essays and literary criticism.

Márton Dornbach is Visiting Assistant Professor at the Johns Hopkins University and works on German literature and philosophy from the Enlightenment to the present. His publications include *Receptive Spirit: German Idealism and the Dynamics of Cultural Transmission* (Fordham, 2016) as well as articles on Schopenhauer, Wagner and Austro-Hungarian political legacies. His current research projects cover Benjamin's and Adorno's strategies of literary interpretation and address the role of theoretical imagination and anthropomorphism in *Naturphilosophie* from Schelling to Jonas.

Bruno C. Duarte received his PhD in Philosophy at the Université Marc Bloch in Strasbourg under the direction of Philippe Lacoue-Labarthe with a thesis on Hölderlin and Sophocles. He has been a postdoctoral fellow at the Free University Berlin, a visiting scholar at Brown University and a Fulbright visiting scholar at the Johns Hopkins University.

Luke Fischer is a philosopher and poet in Sydney. His books include *The Poet as Phenomenologist: Rilke and the New Poems* (Bloomsbury, 2015), the poetry collection *A Personal History of Vision* (UWAP, 2017) and the co-edited volume *Rilke's Sonnets to Orpheus: Philosophical and Critical Perspectives* (Oxford University Press, 2019). He is an honorary associate of the University of Sydney.

NOTES ON CONTRIBUTORS | 253

Achim Geisenhanslüke is Professor of Comparative Literature at the Goethe University Frankfurt. He has published numerous books on literary theory and aesthetics as well as European literature from the seventeenth century to the present, including most recently: *Die Sprache der Liebe: Figurationen der Übertragung von Platon zu Lacan* (Fink, 2016), *Trauer-Spiele: Walter Benjamin und das europäische Barocktheater* (Fink, 2016), *Wolfsmänner: Zur Geschichte einer schwierigen Figur* (transcript, 2018) and *Die Sprache der Infamie I–III* (Fink, 2014–19).

Jennifer Anna Gosetti-Ferencei is Professor and Kurrelmeyer Chair in German and an affiliate Professor in Philosophy at the Johns Hopkins University. She is author of *The Life of Imagination: Revealing and Making the World* (Columbia, 2018), *Exotic Spaces in German Modernism* (Oxford, 2011), *The Ecstatic Quotidian: Phenomenological Sightings in Modern Art and Literature* (Pennsylvania State, 2007), *Heidegger, Hölderlin, and the Subject of Poetic Language* (Fordham, 2004) and a book of poems, *After the Palace Burns*, which won the Paris Review Prize.

Jacob Haubenreich is Assistant Professor of German at Southern Illinois University, Carbondale. His work draws on a range of philological and posthermeneutic approaches to examine the material and visual dimensions of texts as essential components of literature. His research has been supported by the Fulbright Program, the German Literature Archive (Marbach), the Austrian Academy of Sciences and the Rare Book School. He is currently completing a book manuscript tentatively entitled 'Rends in the Page: Rilke, Handke, Bernhard and the Materiality of Textual Production'.

Anja Lemke is Professor of German Literature at the University of Cologne and Co-Director of the Käte Hamburger Centre 'Morphomata'. She is author of *Konstellation ohne Sterne: Zur geschichtlichen Zäsur bei Martin Heidegger und Paul Celan* (Fink, 2002) and *Gedächtnisräume des Selbst: Walter Benjamins 'Berliner Kindheit um Neunzehnhundert'* (Königshausen & Neumann, 2005) and was a member of the collective body that produced *Art works: Ästhetik im Postfordismus* (b-books, 2015). She co-edited with Christoph Jamme an essay volume devoted to Hölderlin, *'Es bleibet aber eine Spur / Doch eines Wortes' – Zur späten Hymnik und Tragödientheorie Friedrich Hölderlins* (Fink, 2004). Currently she is working on a book on contingency and possibility in the novel around 1800 that is part of research collaboration with Niklaus Largier on 'Figurations of Possibility from Late Medieval Religious Philosophy to Modern Thought and Literature'.

Chris Long is an independent scholar in Baltimore, Maryland.

Jonathan Luftig teaches at Morgan State University in Baltimore and has published essays on Kant, de Quincey, Shelley and Jean-Luc Nancy. He is currently working on a project on the political thought of Werner Hamacher as well as a study focused on de Quincey's reading of Kant.

Jan Mieszkowski is Professor of German and Comparative Literature at Reed College in Portland, Oregon. He is the author of *Labors of Imagination: Aesthetics and Political Economy from Kant to Althusser* (Fordham, 2006), *Watching War* (Stanford, 2012), and *Crises of the Sentence* (Chicago, 2019). Mieszkowski's recent articles explore a range of topics in romanticism, modernism and critical theory. He has also published and lectured widely on the spectacles of the permanent war economy.

Katrin Pahl is Associate Professor of German and Co-Director of the Program for the Study of Women, Gender, and Sexuality at the Johns Hopkins University. Her research is situated in the field of affect and emotion studies with an emphasis on gender and sexuality. Her publications include *Tropes of Transport: Hegel and Emotion* (Northwestern, 2012) and *Sex Changes with Kleist* (Northwestern, 2019).

Thomas Schestag is Professor of Literature in the Department of German Studies at Brown University. He has written extensively on European literature and thought from the eighteenth century to the present. His most recent publications include *Namenlose* (Matthes & Seitz, 2020) and, as an editor, Francis Ponge's *Le Soleil / Die Sonne* (Matthes & Seitz, 2020).

Csaba Szabó teaches German literature at the Eszterházy Károly University of Applied Sciences in Eger (Hungary). He received his PhD in Literary Studies at the Lajos Kossuth University Debrecen (Hungary) in 2003 with a thesis on Hölderlin entitled *'erlaubt, geboten' (Beiträge zu Hölderlins Zäsuren und Zitieren)*. He has written essays on Konrad Bayer, Walter Benjamin, Heidegger, Kafka, Mandelstam, Nietzsche and Simone Weil as well as articles on Hungarian poets such as Miklós Radnóti and Mihály Babits. He is the Hungarian translator of essays by Hölderlin, Friedrich Schlegel and Günter Figal as well as books by Heidegger, Benjamin, Kierkegaard and Hamacher.

Nathan Taylor received his PhD in German Studies from Cornell University in 2017 with a dissertation entitled *The Value-Form: Economies of Prose in Tieck, Keller, and Walser*. He is currently a postdoctoral fellow at the Goethe University Frankfurt and has written articles on Hans Blumenberg, modern theories of prose, media studies and the Frankfurt School.

Rochelle Tobias is Professor of German and Director of the Max Kade Center for Modern German Thought at the Johns Hopkins University. Her work has focused on modern European poetry and twentieth-century philosophy with an emphasis on phenomenology. She is the author of *The Discourse of Nature in the Poetry of Paul Celan* (Johns Hopkins, 2006) and co-editor with Philippe P. Haensler and Kristina Mendicino of the essay volume *Phenomenology to the Letter: Husserl and Literature* (de Gruyter, forthcoming).

Roland Végső is Susan J. Rosowski Associate Professor of English at the University of Nebraska-Lincoln, where he teaches literary and critical theory and twentieth-century literatures. His primary research interests are contemporary continental philosophy, modernism and translation theory. He is the author of *The Naked Communist: Cold War Modernism and the Politics of Popular Culture* (Fordham, 2013) and *Worldlessness after Heidegger: Phenomenology, Psychoanalysis, Deconstruction* (Edinburgh, forthcoming). In addition, he is also the translator of numerous philosophical essays and books, including Rodolphe Gasché's *Georges Bataille: Phenomenology and Phantasmatology* (Stanford, 2012) and Peter Szendy's *All Ears: The Aesthetics of Espionage* (Fordham, 2016).

Index

'Absolute', 143, 144, 145–8, 154, 155
absolute idealism, 143, 144, 148–9
Achilles, 51, 52–3, 54
Across (Handke), 181
Adorno, T. W., 221, 226
Aeneid (Virgil), 81, 82
aesthetic harmony, 145
aesthetic intuition, 146, 149
aesthetic state, 145
aesthetics, 30–1, 143–4
   On the Aesthetic Education of Humankind (Schiller), 144–5
   and intellectual intuition, 146
   'New Letters on the Aesthetic Education of Humankind' (Hölderlin), 145
   see also beauty
All in All [*das All-Eine*], 164, 166, 169
All of Nature, 165, 166, 168
'All-living', 155
allowance, 238–41, 243, 245, 246–7; *see also* permission
'An die Parzen' (Hölderlin), 186–7
'An Hölderlin' (Rilke), 40
'An unsre großen Dichter' (Hölderlin), 28
'Andenken' (Hölderlin), 248
animals, 34
Anmerkungen zur Antigonä (Hölderlin) *see* 'Notes on the *Antigone*' (Hölderlin)
Anthropocene, 1–2, 157
Antigone (Sophocles), 11, 77–8, 129; *see also* 'Notes on the *Antigone*' (Hölderlin)
anxiety, 170
Apollo, 53–4
argumentum ad absurdum, 5

Aristotle, 44–5, 46
Armin, Bettina von, 219, 221–2
art
   Greek v. Hesperian, 58, 80–1, 82, 111–12, 129
   and nature, 147–8
   and philosophy, 144, 149–50
   Rilke, 33
   Schelling, 2
   'Voice of the People' (Hölderlin), 104
'As on a holiday ... ' (Hölderlin), 12, 53, 75–6, 77, 187–8
Aufzeichnungen des Malte Laurids Brigge, Die (Rilke), 24

Banville, T. de, 238
beauty, 30–1, 185–6
   Death of Empedocles, The (Hölderlin), 48–9, 52
   'Homecoming' (Hölderlin), 157–8
   Hyperion (Hölderlin), 3, 147–8
   'Oldest Programme for a System of German Idealism, The', 150
   Peter Handke, 179
bees, 64–5
Being and Time (Heidegger), 61, 170, 183
'Being Judgement Possibility' (Hölderlin), 4, 31–2, 145–6, 147, 148
Beiser, F., 146
Belebende, Das (Pindar / Hölderlin) *see* 'Life-Giving, The' (Pindar / Hölderlin)
Benjamin, W.
   'On the Critique of Violence', 246–8

'On the Mimetic Faculty', 210, 211, 213, 214
'Two Poems by Friedrich Hölderlin', 245–6
Bennholdt-Thomsen, A., 60, 62, 63–4, 66
Benveniste, É., 222–3, 232n
'Birthday of Man, The' (Hölderlin), 199–200
Blumenberg, H., 171
Böhlendorff letter, 80–1, 82, 111, 118
Borchardt, Rudolf, 226
'Bread and Wine' ('Brod und Wein') (Hölderlin), 7, 29–30, 53, 153–4, 156, 222
'Brevity' (Hölderlin), 29
'Building Dwelling Thinking' (Heidegger), 182–3, 184

care, 51, 52, 54
Cartesian dualism, 157, 162n
categorical imperative, 239, 240, 244, 247–8
'Celebration of Peace' (Hölderlin), 155–7, 160
Cézanne, P., 178, 181, 182, 188, 189, 191–2
Chakrabarty, D., 2, 18n
choice, 208–10, 237
Cicero, 112
command, 235, 236, 237, 238–9, 244
comprehensive vision, 181
concept and image, 126–8, 132, 134–5
and nature, 128–9
condemnation, 236
'Conjectures on the Beginning of Human History' (Kant), 207–10
consciousness, 1, 4–5, 10, 11, 29
poetic, 32–9, 40
Corngold, S., 104
cosmology, 44–6, 49, 205
Cratylus (Plato), 90

'Da stieg ein Baum' (Rilke), 35
Danube, 79, 86
Death of Empedocles, The (Hölderlin), 54–5, 104, 165–8, 199
beauty, 48–9, 52
elements, 44–5, 46–7, 50–2
'declining fatherland ..., The' (Hölderlin), 8–9, 164–5, 168–75, 175n
deities *see* gods
Derrida, J., 205, 216n
'Dichterberuf' (Hölderlin), 30
'Dichtermut' (Hölderlin), 187

dictation, 236
discordant accord *see* harmonious opposition
Duineser Elegien (*Duino Elegies*) (Rilke), 33, 34, 37
Duvillard, B., 60
dwelling, 183, 184, 249

earth
 Death of Empedocles, The (Hölderlin), 45, 46, 50, 51
 'An Hölderlin' (Rilke), 40
 'The Ister' (Hölderlin), 89–90
 'The Life-Giving' (Pindar / Hölderlin), 87–9
 'Notes on the *Antigone*' (Hölderlin), 91
 Sonnette an Orpheus (Rilke), 35
ecological crisis, 1–2
ego, 4
egological point of view, 37
'Eichenbäume, Die' (Hölderlin), 26–9, 32, 35–6
Eins und Alles (Goethe), 3–4
elements, 44–6, 47, 50–1, 87–90
'Eleusis' (Hegel), 3
Empedoclean fire, 118
Empedocles, 25, 28, 32, 34, 120n
 cosmology, 44, 45–6, 49
 see also Death of Empedocles, The (Hölderlin); 'Ground of Empedocles, The' (Hölderlin)
Enlightenment, 67
ether, 46, 47–8
'everything is rhythm', 219, 232

fate, 203–4, 207
fear, 170
feeling, 244
Fichte, J. G., 2, 4, 31, 37
fire of heavens, 78–82, 83
First Outline (Schelling), 11–12
'For when the grape vine's sap' (Hölderlin), 70
form, 185, 186, 189–90, 222
'Fragment of Philosophical Letters' (Hölderlin), 151–2
Frankfurt Plan, 165
free choice, 208–10, 237
freedom, 237
French Revolution, 103, 113–16
Frey, Hans-Jost, 106–7
'Friedensfeier' (Hölderlin) *see* 'Celebration of Peace' (Hölderlin)

Geburtstag des Menschen, Der (Hölderlin), 199–200
Genesis, 208, 209, 248–50
genres, 76–7, 171
geological agents, 2, 18n
German idealism, 117, 150
'Germania' (Hölderlin), 226–32
Germany, 113–14, 116–17, 118
Geulen, E., 106, 107
gods, 7, 11
   'Bread and Wine' (Hölderlin), 154
   'Celebration of Peace' (Hölderlin), 155–6
   Death of Empedocles, The (Hölderlin), 45, 46
   'Fragment of Philosophical Letters' (Hölderlin), 151–2
   'Germania' (Hölderlin), 226–7, 229–30
   'Homecoming' (Hölderlin), 158
   'Notes on the Oedipus' (Hölderlin), 77
   The Philosophy of Art (Schelling), 153
   'The Rhine' (Hölderlin), 13–14, 98, 244, 245
   Titans, 59, 61–2
   'The Titans' (Hölderlin), 65–9
   'Voice of the People' (Hölderlin), 97–100
   'Wenn aber die Himmlischen' (Hölderlin), 14–15
Goethe, J. W. von, 3–4, 158, 171, 186, 220
Greek art, 58, 80–1, 82, 111–12, 129
Greek mythology, 24
Greek poetry, 58, 59, 69n
Grimm, J., 238, 251n
'Ground of Empedocles, The' (Hölderlin), 81

'Hälfte des Lebens' (Hölderlin), 38
Handke, P., 178–9
   form and nature, 185–6
   and Heidegger, 182–4
   nature and everyday experience, 180–2
   poetry, 186–9
   writing, 188–9, 190–1
harmonious opposition, 5, 12, 50, 52, 75
Hartmann, M., 118
Hegel, G. W. F., 3, 144, 151, 157
Heidegger, M., 37, 40, 156
   Being and Time, 61, 170, 183
   'Building Dwelling Thinking', 182–3, 184
   on 'Germania' (Hölderlin), 230–1
   'Hölderlin and the Essence of Poetry', 7

'… Poetically Man Dwells …', 183–4
   rhythm, 233n
   'What Are Poets For?', 188
   'Heimkunft' (Hölderlin), 157–8
Henrich, D., 146
Heraclitus, 90
Hercules, 84–6
Herodotus, 109, 110
Hesiod, 59, 65
Hesperian art, 58, 80–1, 111–12, 129
Hesperian poetry, 58, 59, 69n
history
   and art, 81
   human v. natural history, 2, 18n
   and nature, 5–10, 168–70
   and time, 58–60, 61
History of a Pencil (Handke), 181, 192
Hölderlin, F.
   differences between Rilke and, 23–4
   mental decline, 221–2
   relation to Rilke, 23, 40
'Hölderlin and the Essence of Poetry' (Heidegger), 7
'Homecoming' (Hölderlin), 157–8
Homer, 65
   Iliad, 53, 78
honey, 65
Horace, 112–13, 222
human beings
   and animals, 34
   as geological agents, 2, 18n
   and gods, 11, 14–15
   and nature, 25, 26–7, 28, 29, 33
human history, 2, 18n
Hyperion (Hölderlin)
   'Absolute', 146–8
   art and philosophy, 149–50
   beauty, 3, 147–8
   history, 103–4
   natural philosophy, 4
   nature, 25–6, 28, 29, 31, 33
   Peter Handke, 179, 180–2, 188, 189–90
   Titans, 62
   tragedy, 165, 171
   tragic sacrifice, 13
   unity in difference, 152

'I', 4–5, 11, 31–2
idealic dissolution, 172, 173, 174
idealic memory, 172
Iliad (Homer), 53, 78
image and concept, 126–8, 132, 134–5
   and nature, 128–9

imitation *see* mimetic faculty
immanent transcendence, 151
infidelity, 77–8
inner space ('Innenraum'), 38–9; *see also* *Weltinnenraum* ('world's inner space')
intellectual intuition, 146, 147, 149
interiority, 38; *see also Weltinnenraum* ('world's inner space')
intimacy, 47
inwardness, 37
Ion (Plato), 65
'Ister, The' (Hölderlin), 75, 91
    Danube, 86
    elements, 87, 89–90
    fire of heavens, 78–80, 81, 82, 83
    rivers and dwelling, 82–4, 85–6

Jacobi, F. H., 3
'Journey, The' (Hölderlin), 85–6

Kafka, F., 235, 236, 248–50
Kant, I., 30–1
    'Conjectures on the Beginning of Human History', 207–10
    The Metaphysics of Morals, 237, 239–41, 246
khôra, 200, 202, 205, 206, 212, 214, 216n
'Kürze, Die' (Hölderlin), 29

landscape painting, 33
language, 173, 174, 204–5, 212, 213–14, 240
    and rhythm, 222–3, 226
law *see* poetic law
legends, 106–7, 108
Leibniz, G. W., 30
Lessing, G. E., 3
Lesson of Mont Sainte Victoire, The (Handke), 178, 179, 182, 188
'Life-Giving, The' (Pindar / Hölderlin), 87–8, 90, 123–37, 217n
    concept and image, 126–8, 132, 134–5
    concept-image and nature, 128–9
    myth, 130
    time, 128, 131–2
    translation, 123–4, 125, 130, 134, 135–7
longing, 31
love, 44, 47, 49, 50, 51–2, 53, 54

'Man' [*Der Mensch*] (Hölderlin), 199–215
    and Benjamin's mimetic faculty, 210–15
    and Kant's 'Conjectures on the Beginning of Human History', 207–10
    language, 204–5, 212, 213–14
    'most blessed', 206–7
    preliminary version, 199–200
    reference to Plato's *Timaeus*, 200, 202, 205, 206, 212
    structure, 202, 204
Mayser, E., 115
melancholy, 69
memory, 174, 181
Metaphysics of Morals (Kant), 237, 239–41, 246
mimetic faculty, 210–15
'Mnemosyne' (Hölderlin), 13, 51, 53, 54, 58, 59
modernity, 63, 171, 188
myth, 130–1, 132, 151–2, 205
mythology, 24, 150–1, 152–3, 156–7
    'Bread and Wine' (Hölderlin), 153–4
    'Celebration of Peace' (Hölderlin), 155–6
    poetry, 179

Nägele, Rainer, 103
natural philosophy, 1, 2–5
nature
    and art, 147–8
    and concept-image, 128–9
    and history, 5–10, 168–70
    Rilkean nature and poetic consciousness, 32–9
    and tragedy, 10–15
    and tragic subjectivity, 25–32
'New Letters on the Aesthetic Education of Humankind' (Hölderlin), 145
New Poems (Rilke), 32
nicht, 227–9
'Notes on the *Antigone*' (Hölderlin)
    earth, 91
    Hesperian art, 129–30
    Hyperion, 26
    myth of Niobe, 61, 77, 78
    nature, 111
    rhythm, 220
    tragedy, 76, 77, 118
'Notes on the *Oedipus*' (Hölderlin), 10, 11, 77, 167, 220
novels, 171
'Nymph, The' (Hölderlin), 54; *see also* *Mnemosyne* (Hölderlin)

'Oak Trees, The' (Hölderlin) *see* 'Eichenbäume, Die' (Hölderlin)

Oedipus Rex (Sophocles), 10, 11, 77; see also 'Notes on the *Oedipus*' (Hölderlin)
'Oldest Programme for a System of German Idealism, The', 3, 13, 150–1, 152, 153, 156, 179, 188–9
On the Aesthetic Education of Humankind (Schiller), 144–5
'On the Critique of Violence' (Benjamin), 246–8
On the Fable of the Ancients (Hölderlin), 130–1
'On the Mimetic Faculty' (Benjamin), 211, 213, 214
'One and All' (Goethe), 3–4
Orpheus, 34–5

Pan, myth of, 110–11
peculiarity, 235–6
perception, 181
permission, 236, 238, 240–1, 244, 246; see also allowance
Petit traité de poésie française (Banville), 238
Phaidros (Plato), 48
philosophy
  and art, 144, 149–50
  and mythology, 151
Philosophy of Art, The (Schelling), 153
philosophy of nature, 1, 2–5
Pindar, 52, 53, 63, 65, 84–5, 86–8, 112–13, 222; see also 'Life-Giving, The' (Pindar / Hölderlin)
place, 200, 213–14
Plato, 46
  Cratylus, 90
  Ion, 65
  Phaidros, 48
  Timaeus, 200, 202, 205, 206, 212, 216n
play drive, 145, 148
Plutarch, 113, 114
poetic consciousness, 32–9, 40
poetic indifference, 241
poetic law, 236–7, 238
  'Der Rhein' (Hölderlin), 241–5
poetic licence, 237–9
poetic speech, 65
poetic tonality, 5
'… Poetically Man Dwells …' (Heidegger), 183–4
poeticisation, 35
poetics of memory, 174
poetological reflection, 63

poetology, 31, 49–50, 111–12
poetry, 1, 165, 172–3, 174, 190
  Greek v. Hesperian, 58, 59, 69n
  Handke, P., 186–9
  Heidegger, 184
  and mythology, 149–50, 179–80
poets, 28
  and bees, 64–5
'Poet's Courage, The' (Hölderlin), 187
poikilia, 65
polytheism, 152, 153–4
Praz, M., 113
prohibition, 236

rage, 51, 54
rationality, 30
reading, 236, 248, 249, 250
reason, 208
reflection, 25–6, 34, 63
religion, 151–2, 153; see also gods; polytheism
remembrance, 174
Repetition (Handke), 181–2, 189, 190
'Rhine, The' ('Der Rhein') (Hölderlin), 75, 86, 94–5
  gods, 13–14, 98, 244, 245
  nature and history, 5–7, 8, 10
  nature and humanity, 168
  poetic law, 241–5
rhythm, 219–32, 232–3n
  'Germania' (Hölderlin), 226–32
  'Voice of the People' (Hölderlin), 223–6
Rilke, R. M.
  differences between Hölderlin and, 23–4
  nature and poetic consciousness, 32–9
  relation to Hölderlin, 23, 40
'River of Rivers in Connecticut, The' (Stevens), 94
river poems, 75–6; see also 'Ister, The' (Hölderlin); 'Life-Giving, The' (Pindar / Hölderlin); 'Rhine, The' (Hölderlin); 'Voice of the People' (Hölderlin)
Romantics, 171
roots, 44, 45, 46, 49; see also elements

Schelling, F. W. J.
  consciousness, 4
  First Outline, 11–12
  mythology, 143, 144, 157
  nature, 1, 13
  The Philosophy of Art, 153

System of Transcendental Idealism, 2, 3, 148–9
Schiller, F., 144–5, 199, 220
Schlegel, A. W., 170, 171, 220
Schutjer, K., 4–5
self-determination, 225
'Seyn, Urtheil, Modalität' (Hölderlin) *see* 'Being Judgement Possibility' (Hölderlin)
Shaw, M., 46
Slow Homecoming (Handke), 178, 183, 191
Socrates, 48
Sonnette an Orpheus (*Sonnets to Orpheus*) (Rilke), 33, 34–6
speech, 204–5, 212
Stevens, Wallace, 94
'Stimme des Volkes' (Hölderlin) *see* 'Voice of the People' (Hölderlin)
storytelling, 189
strife, 44, 49, 50, 51, 54
subjective idealism, 31–2, 37
subjectivity, 130
  tragic, 25–32
subject-object divide, 143, 145–6, 149
System of Transcendental Idealism (Schelling), 2, 3, 148–9

Theogony (Hesiod), 59
'There rose a tree' (Rilke), 35
Theunissen, M., 63
Timaeus (Plato), 200, 202, 205, 206, 212, 216n
time, 59
  'The declining fatherland…' (Hölderlin), 172
  forms of, 63–4
  'The Life-Giving' (Pindar / Hölderlin), 128, 131–2
  rivers, 90–1
  'The Titans' (Hölderlin), 60–2, 66, 68
  tragedy, 168
Titans, 58–9, 62–4
'Titans, The' (Hölderlin), 60–2
  gods and mortals, 65–9
  poets and bees, 64–5

'To Aether' (Hölderlin), 47–8
'To the Fates' (Hölderlin), 186–7
tones, triad of, 49
tragedy, 10–15, 63, 76–7, 165, 168
tragic subjectivity, 25–32
transition, 164, 169, 170
translation, 123–4, 125, 130, 134, 135–7
transubstantiation, 187–8
triad of tones, 49
'Two Poems by Friedrich Hölderlin' (Benjamin), 245–6

unity of being *see* 'Absolute'

'Voice of the People' (Hölderlin), 95–118
  denunciation v. assimilation, 103–5
  eagle analogy, 98–100, 108
  French Revolution, 103, 113–16
  rhythm, 223–6
  river analogy, 95–8, 106
  Xanthos, 95, 100–3, 105, 106–10, 111, 112, 113, 115–18
Von der Poesie im Recht (Grimm), 238

Wanderung, Die (Hölderlin), 85–6
Warminski, A., 230
Weltinnenraum ('world's inner space'), 36–7, 38, 39
'Wenn aber die Himmlischen' (Hölderlin), 14
'Wenn nämlich der Rebe Saft' (Hölderlin), 70n
'What Are Poets For?' (Heidegger), 188
Wie wenn am Feiertage. (Hölderlin) *see* 'As on a holiday …' (Hölderlin)
Wissenschaftslehre (Fichte), 31
Wordsworth, W., 94, 97
'world of all worlds', 165, 168–9, 172, 173
writing, 188–9, 190–1

Xanthos, 95, 100–3, 105, 106–10, 111, 112, 113, 115–18, 225

Zeus, 61, 68, 84, 111, 129
Zweig, S., 221

EU representative:
Easy Access System Europe
Mustamäe tee 50, 10621 Tallinn, Estonia
Gpsr.requests@easproject.com

www.ingramcontent.com/pod-product-compliance
Lightning Source LLC
Chambersburg PA
CBHW070322240426
43671CB00013BA/2331